SIXTH EDITION

Math Principles

FOR FOOD SERVICE OCCUPATIONS

SIXTH EDITION

Math Principles

FOR FOOD SERVICE OCCUPATIONS

Anthony J. Strianese

Pamela P. Strianese

DELMAR
CENGAGE Learning™

Australia • Brazil • Japan • Korea • Mexico • Singapore • Spain • United Kingdom • United States

DELMAR
CENGAGE Learning

Math Principles for Food Service Occupations, 6th edition
Anthony J. Strianese and Pamela P. Strianese

Vice President, Career and Professional Editorial: Dave Garza

Director of Learning Solutions: Sandy Clark

Senior Acquisitions Editor: Jim Gish

Managing Editor: Larry Main

Product Manager: Anne Orgren

Editorial Assistant: Sarah Timm

Vice President, Career and Professional Marketing: Jennifer Baker

Marketing Director: Wendy Mapstone

Marketing Manager: Kristin McNary

Associate Marketing Manager: Jonathan Sheehan

Production Director: Wendy Troeger

Senior Content Project Manager: Kathryn B. Kucharek

Senior Art Director: Casey Kirchmayer

For product information and technology assistance, contact us at
Cengage Learning Customer & Sales Support, 1-800-354-9706
For permission to use material from this text or product,
submit all requests online at **www.cengage.com/permissions.**
Further permissions questions can be e-mailed to
permissionrequest@cengage.com

Library of Congress Control Number: 2010936397

ISBN-13: 978-1-4354-8882-3

ISBN-10: 1-4354-8882-2

Delmar
5 Maxwell Drive
Clifton Park, NY 12065-2919
USA

Cengage Learning is a leading provider of customized learning solutions with office locations around the globe, including Singapore, the United Kingdom, Australia, Mexico, Brazil, and Japan. Locate your local office at: **international.cengage.com/region**

Cengage Learning products are represented in Canada by Nelson Education, Ltd.

To learn more about Delmar, visit **www.cengage.com/delmar**
Purchase any of our products at your local college store or at our preferred online store **www.CengageBrain.com**

Printed in the United States of America
6 7 8 9 10 11 12 23 22 21 20 19

Contents

Early in my life I became involved in the restaurant business, not really by choice, but at a time when my family (which was in the commercial fishing industry) was suffering quite a bit. This was back in the 1950s, when the industry collapsed. At that time, I was looking forward to experiencing some time on a fishing boat, but I did not see my future in it. My mother and father always spoke to me about an education, as my brother pursued a teaching career and became a famous water polo coach. My sisters, too, were geared toward the education field, and therefore I thought it would be good for me to pursue this avenue. By going to school, I began to learn the principles of mathematics and the importance it bears on any career.

I guess I knew from an early age that I wanted to be in business for myself, and, in order to do this, I would have to know my numbers. Any kind of business is based on math, which everyone needs to understand. I took accounting in high school and college, which helped me when I began keeping the books for five restaurants while continuing my college education. It gave me a better understanding of the use of numbers and how they work together for a bottom line, or a profit. You learn at an early point when you are involved in the operation of restaurants, as I was then and still am now, how important the numbers are.

I went into business in 1968 with my partner and developed the Sardine Factory Restaurant on Cannery Row, and we knew that the numbers were not great. With only $950 in cash to start with, we found a dilapidated old building on the wrong side of the tracks in an area that had depreciated due to the commercial industry collapse. The canneries turned into old buildings and structures that were just sitting there, empty. We created a gem within that realm, and the Sardine Factory is a restaurant that was designed to represent the Cannery Row era. We have pictures in what we call the "Cannery Row Bar/Lounge" that depict the commercial fishing industry, reflective of my family background, and some of the produce industry, reflective of my partner's family. We knew we had to make the restaurant a success, and it has been since day one.

We took the initiative with some unique ideas, such as using local produce and seafood, which is common today but was not being done at the time, and we created an abalone soup that is still our signature soup today. The restaurant evolved from a small, 70-seat establishment to a five-room, 225-seat restaurant, which includes the elegant "Captain's Room," the beautiful glass-dome "Conservatory Room," and our unique "Downstairs Wine Cellar Room." The wine cellar has won the Grand Wine Spectator Award consecutively over many years. And the restaurant has won many top awards for its cuisine, service, and ambiance. We have sommeliers who serve the wine from our wine cellar, which holds close to 40,000 bottles of wine and 1,300 different types. Our seafood is brought in fresh to the restaurant, and we also serve some great USDA Prime steaks; we are known for both.

Many celebrities come to the restaurant, and we even had the *Lifestyles of the Rich and Famous* TV show tape a segment in the "Downstairs Wine Cellar Room." Famous actors and singers have dined here, including Bing Crosby, Phil Harris, and Paul Newman; and, of course, Clint Eastwood filmed the famous *Play Misty for Me* in our restaurant, and is still a good friend of ours to this day. Television personalities (such as Ray Romano), famous golfers (such as Tiger Woods), and many others like to come play golf and dine at great restaurants with great cuisine. In addition, we have hosted many politicians, such as governors, senators, assemblyman, and so forth from all over the United States, not to mention Leon Panetta—the former White House chief of staff and current director of the Central Intelligence Agency (CIA)—with whom I grew up.

I am proud to say that the restaurant has become world famous. We have been honored with the DiRoNA (Distinguished Restaurants of North America) Award and have received numerous other awards, such as the Mobile and the 4-diamond AAA, which have brought a tremendous amount of recognition to the restaurant. We are one of the few restaurants to receive these awards on the Monterey Peninsula, and we have set the pace for the local hospitality industry and have even brought national recognition to the area. We have been named one of the top 25 overall restaurants and one of the top 10 seafood restaurants in the country. With all the awards and recognitions, the restaurant continues to be a success because the numbers work. With food and labor costs, we are dealing in dollars and cents every day, and that is what this book is about: giving you an opportunity to understand the importance of math and how it relates to your business success throughout the years, from when you first start out until you retire. The restaurant and hospitality business relies on numbers to work, and that relates to any restaurants operating independently, in hotels, and in other establishments. As chefs/owners, anything related to our business is based on numbers that will give us the facts and statistics for budgets that we hope will provide us continued success. By reading this book, and following its understanding of the role of math and how it can prepare you for employment in business, or if you eventually own your own business, this is a must-read for you to be a success and reach the goals you have set forth in your career to achieve.

Executive Chef Bert Cutino, CEC, AAC, HBOT, HOF

Cofounder/COO, The Sardine Factory Restaurant

701 Wave Street, on the famous Cannery Row

Monterey, CA

Bert Cutino is a leader in the hospitality industry. He and his partner, Ted Balestreri, have been recognized as two of the "50 Power Players" in food service in the United States by Nation's Restaurant News. *In 1968, they co-founded The Sardine Factory restaurant in a nearly abandoned area known as Cannery Row. The restaurant was located in a building that once fed sardine workers. Cannery Row, with its approximately 30 restaurants, over 100 specialty shops, hotels, and visitor attractions, now draws 51 percent of the tourists that visit the Monterey Peninsula. The Sardine Factory was one of the innovators in serving California wines and implementing the premier wine program in the United States. From its 70-seat beginning, The Sardine Factory Restaurant has grown to five rooms and has more than tripled its seating capacity. The restaurant is one of the most successful, widely recognized, and highest grossing dining establishments in the United States. The Sardine Factory has been the recipient of virtually every major restaurant and wine award in the industry, including the prestigious DiRoNA, since 1993; with its 40,000 bottles of wine and close to 1,300 labels, the restaurant has earned the Grand Wine Spectator Award since 1982; the* Nation's Restaurant News *Hall of Fame Award (1981); and the* Restaurants & Institutions *Ivy Award (1980). In addition, The Sardine Factory was also honored as one of 50 restaurants in the United States to serve at President Ronald Reagan's inaugurations in 1981 and 1985. Chef Cutino has held several national offices in the hospitality industry. He has served as head of the American Academy of Chefs (AAC) and has won gold medals and has been awarded both the American Culinary Federation's (ACF) Chef of the Year Award and the Chef Professionalism Award. When asked about the success of the restaurant, he states that "success has been achieved through an unwavering commitment to quality. Every person on the staff, from waitpersons to kitchen staff, must be able to present him- or herself as a professional and strive for excellence!"*

Preface

Many students, when told they are required to take a math course, react with fear due to the poor math experiences they have had in the past. Once students realize how important and relevant math is in the food service industry, however, they become motivated to learn, understand, and use math correctly to accomplish their goals of becoming a chef, baker, manager, or any of the many other occupations in the food service industry. When we (the authors) were dining at Wolfgang Puck's American Grille at the Borgata Hotel Casino and Spa in Atlantic City, executive chef/associate partner Aram Mardigian spoke to us about the importance of math. He told us that when he was in culinary school, his main focus was to learn how to cook. In his first work experience, he continued to focus on cooking. As his career progressed, so did his understanding of the importance of using math to control costs and make a profit. Now he uses the knowledge and skills of math on a daily basis to make the restaurant profitable. The authors of this sixth edition have had great success in teaching their students math skills and applications.

In researching this book, the authors have received interesting and passionate responses about the role that math plays in food service careers from chefs, managers, and owners throughout the United States and Canada. In conversations with these individuals, one fact became clearer and clearer: the more successful an individual was in his or her career, the more passionate he or she was to get the message to students about the importance of learning and using math to become a success in business. One common theme was articulated repeatedly by chefs and managers interviewed by the authors: with the knowledge and the proper usage of math, a business will succeed and the individual will succeed. Like cooking or baking, math is a sequential process. The professionals the authors spoke with pointed out that an individual must first master the basic culinary skills before he or she can create a gourmet meal or spectacular dessert. The authors know that math is sequential in the same way. If students learn the basics (how to add and subtract), they can use math to convert recipes and calculate food and labor cost percentages. If they have not mastered the basics, math becomes frustrating for students because they cannot solve the problems and soon believe that they can't do math at all. It becomes a self-fulfilling prophecy. In contrast, if students know the basics, then math becomes a joy because with their knowledge of basic math skills, they have the ability to convert recipes and calculate food and labor cost percentages.

The sixth edition has been completely revised by the authors of the book. The authors have read and reread the fifth edition and have calculated every example and problem in the book. All examples have been checked for accuracy by ourselves and an independent technical reviewer. New problems have been added to challenge the students. Step-by-step instructions for problems and concepts have been included. Throughout the book, the authors have included a series of TIPS (To Insure Perfect Solutions) to assist the student in solving problems and understanding concepts of math. Each chapter has a Chef, President, Manager, or Owner Sez feature, which is a quote from a food service professional about the importance of math in his or her own particular operation.

The sixth edition has been revised to parallel and include all the required knowledge and competency standards mandated by the American Culinary Federation Accrediting Commission, which is administered by the American Culinary Federation Education Foundation. The authors have added new material that reviewers told them was needed and have eliminated information that reviewers told them was not needed in a math book. In addition, the chapters have been set up in a format that follows a logical flow, starting with the basics of math and ending with financial statements. The authors also added step-by-step calculator instructions through a series of table illustrations. The practice problems are labeled consecutively in the book as Practice Problems 1–1, 1–2, and so forth; the first number is the chapter, and the second number is the set of practice problems. This will make it easier for instructors and students to locate the practice problems. The authors have added more critical thinking problems to make the math more relevant for the student. Throughout the book, the practice problems have been developed to provide a written assessment of student mastery of the objectives.

The content of the text has been divided into five coordinated parts to demonstrate subject association and simplify learning.

Part I, **The Calculator,** is placed at the beginning of the book. The authors believe that the calculator is an essential tool for math computation, just as a knife is a tool for the culinary professional. Because calculator skills and the use of calculators are being taught in elementary education, this chapter is placed in the front of the book. If the instructor does not feel that the chapter on calculators should be introduced until after the fundamentals are mastered, he or she can insert it into the curriculum where appropriate.

Part II, **Review of Basic Math Fundamentals,** consists of three chapters intended to refresh and sharpen the student's math skills. The emphasis is on methods used to solve mathematical problems related to food service situations. This information should be thoroughly reviewed, with exercise problems worked and referred back to whenever necessary. As stated previously, the authors know that learning math is a sequential process. The student must have mastered the fundamentals and have an understanding of basic math concepts and computational skills before moving into more complicated problem solving.

Part III, **Math Essentials and Cost Controls in Food Preparation,** consists of five chapters that focus on the math essential to the preparation of both food and baked products. This part includes weights and measures, a revised section on using the metric system in the kitchen, portion control, converting and yielding recipes, as well as production and baking formulas. Chapter 9 covers costing in recipes, food, and labor.

Part IV, **Math Essentials in Food Service Recordkeeping,** consists of four chapters concentrating on the math necessary for keeping important records accurate and current. This part covers determining cost percentages and how to price a menu. It also includes inventory procedures, purchasing and receiving, and daily production reports. New information on how to calculate purchases as they affect food cost percentages has been added as well.

Part V, **Essentials of Managerial Math,** has added material. Chapter 14 concentrates on the math knowledge that is needed in front of house operations. Chapter 15 deals with payroll, taxes, and financial statements. A section in this chapter demonstrates how to figure out the break-even point for a business. The information in Chapter 15 includes the types of math procedures that are typically the responsibility of management.

Instructor Resources

The sixth edition of *Math Principles for Food Service Occupations* includes an instructor resources CD-ROM with the following features:

- A **Pretest** and **Posttest** for the purpose of evaluating the student's math skills prior to, and upon completion of, the course (this had been in the core text in previous editions). The pretest and posttest consist of math questions that assess the student's understanding of the concepts in the 15 chapters, which are needed to have a successful career in the food service industry.

- An **Instructor's Manual** with answers to the chapter review questions, as well as answers to the pretest and posttest.

- A **computerized testbank** in ExamView® featuring additional critical thinking and short-answer questions.

- Microsoft PowerPoint® lecture slides.

- Recipe charts and tables provided electronically for recipe-making purposes.

- Lesson plans.

- Suggested syllabi for different curriculum needs.

New to This Edition

Overall—Every chapter has been reviewed, and new math questions, as well as an increase in thought provoking questions, have been added to this edition. Practice problem reviews are labeled as a topic, and questions are numbered consecutively in each chapter. This has resulted in a total of over 2,000 questions (excluding the pretest and posttest questions). All problems have been checked by an independent technical reviewer. There are a total of more than 30 discussion questions. There is more consistency with rounding examples (in almost all cases, rounding is done to the hundredths place), and this consistency is reflected in the directions for the Practice Problem reviews. The authors continue to update how to solve problems, illustrating them in a step-by-step method. There are new methods using helpful mnemonic devices and acronyms to assist the student in how to remember procedures and formulas, such as "BLT," "NO," and the "Big Ounce." Additional emphasis has been placed upon food and beverage cost controls. And more female chefs and food service professionals are included in the Chef Sez and Manager Sez features of the book.

New topics added to this edition are controlling beverage costs; clarifying and explaining the difference between fluid ounces and avoirdupois ounces; metric sizes of bottles of alcoholic beverages; and yield testing and how to conduct these tests. In addition, charts and step-by-step explanations of how to control costs through examining purchases, both food and liquor, are included. New sections have been added that explain transfers and how they affect percentage costs, and how to balance checking account statements. A completely new art program of illustrations has been introduced.

Chapter 1: Using the Calculator—The chapter has been updated to include newer types of calculators that can be used to solve problems. A detailed figure has been added to illustrate the numerical value of digits using both whole numbers and decimal numbers. All examples of how to solve problems using the calculator have been revised using a step-by-step approach. The process and the reason for rounding in math has been explained and illustrated. A new Chef Sez feature has been added to the chapter.

Chapter 2: Numbers, Symbols of Operations, and the Mill—A more precise example of how to write checks is illustrated. The Manager Sez feature has been updated. The explanation of math periods has been made clearer.

Chapter 3: Addition, Subtraction, Multiplication, and Division—Many of the practice problems have been updated, and a new President Sez feature has been added.

Chapter 4: Fractions, Decimals, Ratios, and Percents—A section and illustration on how to read and understand the place values of decimal numbers has been added. Many problems have been updated.

Chapter 5: Weights and Measures—The term *avoirdupois ounces* is introduced and explained. The difference between avoirdupois ounces and fluid ounces is highlighted, especially referring to their proper use in weights and measures.

More illustrations are used to assist in learning the measurement of teaspoons and tablespoons and their relationships to each other, along with their relationships to an ounce. New figures have been added to illustrate the common equivalents between volume and count. Scoop sizes are shown as exact and are consistent throughout the text. A new female pastry chef is quoted in the Chef Sez feature. The exact equivalent between decimal numbers and ounces in a pound has been illustrated in a new figure.

Chapter 6: Using the Metric System of Measure—Sizes of bottles of alcoholic beverages have been introduced in their metric measurements, and the equivalent U.S. fluid ounce size have been stated. Problems have been added that require solutions using the metric system to determine the amount of glasses of wine that can be obtained using glasses that are measured in U.S. fluid ounces.

Chapter 7: Portion Control—New information has been added to this chapter, especially concerning butcher's yields. An entire section has been added on yield testing and how to conduct these tests. More information is included on convenience foods, and determining if or how much convenience foods the food service establishment should use is discussed. Determining cost per portion has been revised to make the math clearer. The term *fabrication* is introduced and used to determine yield testing. Drained weight is explained, and problems associated with drained weight tests are given.

Chapter 8: Converting Recipes, Yields, and Baking Formulas—A step-by-step illustration of using proportions is given. New questions concerning formulas that use proportions to solve problems have been added. A new acronym, NO, has been added to assist the student in remembering how to determine the working factor when converting recipes.

Chapter 9: Food, Recipe, and Labor Costing—A new term, *wraparound*, is introduced, and its value in costing out recipes is explained. The yield test is shown in a step-by-step procedure chart to show how to determine the actual cost for an Edible Portion (E.P.) portion of meat. Detailed food, recipe, and labor costing examples are given and explained with new problems to reinforce the mathematical concepts. The sections on labor costs have been updated to include tipping and bonuses.

Chapter 10: Determining Cost Percentages and Pricing the Menu—Charts have been reformulated to make the concepts in this chapter easier to understand. Questions concerning food cost percentages have been structured in a different manner to make it easier to arrive at the correct answers. A section explaining why rounding to the hundredths place is beneficial to the food service professional has been added. Using the sample menus from the Desmond Hotel, questions have been developed and examples given so that the menus are being used in the context of the chapter. Many more questions have been developed using the concepts taught in the Chef's Magic Circle.

Chapter 11: Inventory Procedures and Controlling Costs—This chapter has undergone a major revision. A new section on how to calculate purchases as they affect food cost percentages has been added. Two female hospitality professionals have given their reasons on why knowing how to use math has been crucial to the success of their two restaurants. A section has been added that teaches how to control costs by comparing purchases. This chapter has over 300 questions that will give the reader an additional amount of practice at the concept of inventory procedures and controlling costs.

Chapter 12: Purchasing and Receiving—This chapter has also been revised heavily. A new section has been added to explain the importance of transferring costs from one department to another. The chapter also illustrates and explains how to calculate the importance of costs as they are transferred from one department to another. There is more in-depth explanation of how to write purchase specifications and how to use them to manage food costs effectively. Emphasis is placed upon how to receive purchases properly. An entire section is devoted to convenience foods, and the process of determining if or how much convenience foods the food service establishment should use is explored.

Chapter 13: Daily Production Reports and Beverage Costs—Added to this chapter is an entire section on alcoholic beverages. An additional female chef has been profiled in Chef Sez. The section on alcoholic beverages explains how to control costs and areas to check in case theft of alcoholic beverages or theft of income from alcoholic beverages is suspected. The section on alcoholic beverages also discusses types of alcoholic beverages and various methods of how to control costs with the sale of spirits, wines, and beer. The chapter also explains how to determine beverage cost percentages, and additional problems have been added so the reader can practice. Charts and figures on how to recognize variances in alcoholic beverage purchases are shown. Higher-level, thought-provoking questions are included to allow readers to consider different scenarios of why beverage costs are not in line with established beverage cost percentage standards.

Chapter 14: Front of the House and Managerial Mathematical Options—The difference between tipping, service charge, gratuity, and administrative charge is explained. Legal opinions are cited concerning adding an automatic gratuity onto an à la carte check. In figuring out daily cash receipts, gift certificates have been included. The section on all-inclusive pricing and how to back out sales tax and gratuity has undergone a total revision from the previous edition; and an entire new section and questions have been added to train readers on how to balance their checking account statements.

Chapter 15: Personal Taxes, Payroll, and Financial Statements—The questions in this chapter have been updated, and a new Owner Sez feature has been added.

This book is a "keeper." This will be a valuable reference tool as you climb the career ladder. The material contained in this text will provide the student with sufficient math knowledge to demonstrate confidence and utilize skills that will lead to rapid job advancement in his or her career. Math, along with culinary skills and proper friendly service, is an essential part of the equation that makes a food service operation a success. Many talented chefs have succeeded in business, while others have failed. The authors emphasize that there is more to operating a successful food service operation than putting quality food before the guest.

Acknowledgments

When we decided to revise the sixth edition of *Math Principles for Food Service Occupations*, we knew that we would need help acquiring examples, information, and illustrations. We were fortunate that our travels have taken us to many locations where we could interview chefs, managers, and owners. Because of our many interests and participation at conventions and conferences, we have made important and meaningful contacts with influential leaders in the American Culinary Federation, New York State Hospitality and Tourism Association, New York State Restaurant Association, the Albany County Convention and Visitors Bureau, participants in the Sante Restaurant Symposiums, and graduates of the Hotel, Culinary Arts, and Tourism program at Schenectady County Community College (SCCC). Our experience in writing the four editions of *Dining Room and Banquet Management, The Food Service Industry Video Series,* and the fifth edition of *Math Principles for Food Service Occupations,* as well as writing two opinion pieces for *Nation's Restaurant News*, has afforded us many research opportunities.

When undertaking this sixth edition, we asked ourselves how we could improve this textbook from the fifth edition. We wanted to make this book stand out from other math books in the hospitality and culinary field. The material in this sixth edition meets all the required knowledge and competencies in the knowledge area for business and math skills required for accreditation by the American Culinary Federation Accrediting Commission. We knew we could bring a positive perspective about math to the student because of our six decades of teaching experience at the elementary and college levels. Also, we knew that we could call upon our hospitality experience throughout our various careers as cook, chef, bookkeeper, waitperson, food and beverage manager, butler, bartender, and banquet manager to reflect the importance of math in the food service industry to the student. But we wanted something more—we wanted to make the math meaningful. So, in each chapter, we added a feature that started off being called "Chef Sez." As we got more and more into writing the book and talking to professionals, we expanded this concept to include managers and owners in the food service profession. In these vignettes, leaders in this profession explain to the reader why math is important. In alphabetical order, we list the following contributors and their titles:

James V. Bigley, Vice President, HMB Consultants, Voorheesville, NY;

Joseph Carr, Fine Wine Producer, Joseph Carr Wines, Napa Valley, CA;

Bert P. Cutino, Certified Executive Chef, American Academy of Chefs, Chief Operating Officer, Cofounder, and Chef, The Sardine Factory Restaurant, Monterey, CA;

Nadsa de Monteiro, Executive Chef/Owner, The Elephant Walk Restaurant Group, Inc, Boston, MA;

Phelps Dieck, Chef/Owner, the Green Monkey and Brazo, Portsmouth, NH;

Gale Gand, Executive Pastry Chef/Partner of Restaurant TRU, and James Beard Foundation Outstanding Pastry Chef, Chicago, IL;

Robert Gioia, General Manager, Villa de Flora & Java Coast, Gaylord Palms Resort & Convention Center, Orlando, FL;

George R. Goldhoff, General Manager, Gold Strike Casino and Resort, Tunica, MS;

Peter Huebner, President and Owner of Canada Cutlery Inc., Pickering, Ontario, Canada;

Irene Maston, Certified Executive Chef, American Academy of Chefs, Chef/Owner, The Andrie Rose Inn, Ludlow, VT;

Noble Masi, Certified Master Baker, Retired Senior Chef Instructor, The Culinary Institute of America;

Thomas Rosenberger, Certified Executive Chef, Director, Food and Beverage Management Programs, Department of Resorts and Gambling, Community College of Southern Nevada, North Las Vegas, NV;

Fritz Sonnenschmidt, Certified Master Chef, Past Chairman of the American Academy of Chefs, Ambassador for the Culinary Institute of America, Hyde Park, NY, and author of the book *Charcuterie;*

Rick Sampson, President and Chief Executive Officer, New York State Restaurant Association, Albany, NY;

Derek Swartz, Director of Operations, ARAMARK Corporation, Citi Field, Queens, NY

Richard Wagner, former Executive Pastry Chef, Oahu Country Club, Honolulu, HI, and Chef/Instructor/Lecturer at the Kapiolani Community College at the Diamond Head Campus in Honolulu, Hawaii;

Deb Weeks, Owner, the Green Monkey and Brazo, Portsmouth, NH.

We were fortunate to have several individuals at Delmar Cengage Learning who assisted us with this project: Jim Gish, our Acquisitions Editor and the driving force to continue to expand the culinary and hospitality list at Delmar Cengage Learning; our two Product Managers, Nicole Calisi, who got this edition up and running, and Anne Orgren, who worked with us to complete the sixth edition of this textbook; Kathy Kucharek, our Content Project Manager who facilitated the production of this text; and Sarah Timm, Editorial Assistant.

Faculty and staff members at SCCC assisted us with their knowledge and feedback on specific topics in this edition. We thank Professor Paul Krebs, C.C.E., and Professor Susan Hatalsky C.C.E., C.E.C., for their assistance with the concepts and math that deal with baking; Kevin Brown and Associate Professor Kim Williams, who patiently checked out Part V, "Essentials of Managerial Math"; and Certified Executive Chef and Certified Hospitality Administrator Christopher Allen Tanner, who gave us information about the use of math in the culinary profession. We are thankful to the culinary arts students at SCCC, who gave us feedback on what they liked and what they thought should be added to this textbook.

Special thanks must be given to these individuals and organizations. We thank the American Culinary Federation (ACF) and their Education Foundation for developing their math standards for culinary professionals; and Candice Childers, the ACF Assistant Director of Accreditation; Peter Kimball, the ACF accreditation manager; and Michael Feierstein, the ACF accreditation administrative coordinator, who have offered Toby the opportunity to be part of the visiting teams to verify that both high schools and colleges are meeting the standards for accreditation. They also supplied us with the standards for accreditation. We owe a debt of gratitude to Nina Rodriguez, executive assistant to Bert Cutino, for communicating so quickly and efficiently with us in obtaining and updating the foreword for this edition. We give a special thanks for and acknowledgment of the superb workmanship of Don Gennett and Brenda Eckler of the White Studio in Albany, NY, for the photo of the two of us.

We also wish to thank three individuals who shared their knowledge and thoughts about math in this industry: Jacob Brach, C.C.C., Regional Culinary Manager for Rich Products in Buffalo, NY; Michael St. John, Executive Chef of the Desmond in Albany, NY; and Aram Mardigian, Executive Chef/Associate Partner of Wolfgang Puck's American Grille at the Borgata Hotel Casino and Spa in Atlantic City, NJ.

We also want to express our gratitude to Professor Emeritus Gary Brenenstuhul for sharing his expertise with his gallon, quart, and pints chart; to reviewers Kimberly Otis, of SCCC, and Steven Rascoe and the math faculty of Sullivan University, who allowed us to use the "Big Ounce" diagrams in the book.

Finally, Toby would like to thank his supervisor, Dr. David E. Brough, Ph.D., C.E.C., C.C.E., and his employer, SCCC in Schenectady, NY, for the support and encouragement given to our undertaking of this sixth edition.

If you would like to contact us with questions, comments, or suggestions or any other pertinent information, you may contact either Delmar Cengage Learning or us directly by e-mail at strianaj@sunysccc.edu.

Pamela P. Strianese   *Anthony (Toby) J. Strianese*

Anthony (Toby) J. Strianese is a professor in the Department of Hotel, Culinary Arts, and Tourism at Schenectady County Community College (SCCC). Toby has been an educator since 1974, specializing in teaching "Mathematics for the Culinary Profession," "Food and Beverage Control," "Dining Room Management," "Banquet Management," "Wines of the World," and "Hospitality Management" courses. From 1991 to 2009, he was the chairperson of the SCCC Department of Hotel, Culinary Arts and Tourism. During his tenure, SCCC's culinary arts program received the maximum accreditation (three times) from the American Culinary Federation Education Foundation Accrediting Commission (ACFEFAC). He is a recipient of the State University of New York Chancellor's Award for Excellence in Administrative Services. He has been employed in the hospitality profession as a banquet manager, food and beverage controller, and a caterer.

Toby is a Certified Culinary Educator with the American Culinary Federation. He has represented the Saint Augustine, Florida–based ACFEFAC, conducting evaluation site visits, and he has participated in additional evaluation site visits as a Culinary Educator. As a National Evaluator, he has conducted site visits in six states to verify that these institutions meet ACFEFAC standards for accreditation purposes.

As a member of the New York State Restaurant Association Educational Foundation (NYSRAEF), Toby is a part of the NYSRAEF consulting team that provides expertise and advice to owners and operators on how to improve their restaurants' operations. Since 2006, Toby has been the chief judge for the NYSRAEF's ProStart Management competition. He serves as the Treasurer/Secretary of the six-member NYSRAEF Board of Directors.

In addition to serving on the NYSRAEF board, Toby is on the Board of Directors of the New York State Hospitality & Tourism Association and has served on the Executive Board of the Albany County Convention and Visitors Bureau (ACCVB). He served as chairperson of the ACCVB for three years.

Toby instituted and has been the coordinator for the Walt Disney World College program at SCCC since 1983. He served a two-year term as a member of the original Disney College Program National Advisory Board.

Pamela Strianese has had a varied career in the food service industry. She has been a caterer, catering cook, service person, and bookkeeper in restaurant operations. In addition, she is a member of the NYSRAEF consulting team that provides expertise and advice to owners and operators on how to improve their restaurants' operations. She is certified in sanitation practices and has earned the ServSafe certificate from the National Restaurant Association.

Pam, along with her husband Toby, are the co-authors of *Dining Room and Banquet Management*, 4th Edition, published by Delmar Cengage Learning. Pam and Toby have conducted seminars at the NYSRA show at the Jacob Javits Center in New York, utilizing their expertise on training individuals to give great service at banquets and in the dining room. They also have given seminars on the importance of treating guests well to Metropolitan Club Managers Association members and at Howe Caverns, a tourist attraction in upstate New York. In addition, they have had opinion articles published in *Nation's Restaurant News* entitled "To Treat Guests Well, Avoid the Eight Deadly Sins of Service" and "Students Learn Valued Management Skills at ProStart Competition." They have also been judges for the March of Dimes Iron Chef competition.

Since 2007, Pam has been the co-chairperson and a judge at the NYSRAEF ProStart Management competition. She has a B.A. from the State University of New York at Fredonia and an M.S. in education from the State University of New York at Albany. She has been an educator for over thirty years. She has served on numerous committees for curriculum development during her career.

Reviewers

The authors and Delmar Cengage Learning would like to thank the following reviewers:

Technical Reviewer

Frank L. Burns Jr.

President, K & M Hospitality Group

Sixth Edition

Alexander O. Edionwe

The University of Texas—Pan American

Edinburg, TX

Lawrence A. Fischer

Saint Paul College

Mendota Heights, MN

Paul Hall

Sullivan University

Louisville, KY

James M. Hammond

Sullivan University

Louisville, KY

Kendell Hoyer

Le Cordon Bleu Las Vegas

Las Vegas, NV

Robert M. Koeller

The Chef's Academy

Indianapolis, IN

Lisa Little

Jones County Junior College

Ellisville, MS

Dean Louie

Maui Community College

Kahului, HI

Esther J. Miller

SUNY Cobleskill

Cobleskill, NY

Jay Miller

Laney College

Oakland, CA

Kimberly Otis

Schenectady County Community College

Schenectady, NY

Steven Rascoe

Sullivan University

Louisville, KY

Mary B. Zappone

Westmoreland County Community College

Youngwood, PA

Previous Editions

Doug Armstrong, Instructor
New Hampshire Community Technical College
Laconia, NH

Victor Bagan, Instructor
Hibbing Community College
Grand Rapids, MI

Joseph Crompton, Instructor
Heywood Career and Technology Center
Columbia, SC

Tom Dillard, Instructor
Seattle Central Community College
Seattle, WA

Ann Dooley, Assistant Professor
Baltimore International College
Baltimore, MD

Margie Gallo
Sullivan University
Louisville, KY

Robert Garlough, Professor
Grand Rapids Community College
Grand Rapids, MI

William Gibson, Instructor
Kauai Community College
Lihue, HI

Dan Golio, Instructor
Art Institute of New York City
New York, NY

Linda Jaster, Instructor
Texas State Technical College
Waco, TX

Ron Jones, Department Chair
McIntosh College
Dover, NH

Tom J. Jones, Instructor
Sullivan University
Lexington, KY

Joyce Martin, Instructor
East Central College
Union, MO

Mary Petersen, Executive Director
Foodservice Educators Network International
Annapolis, MD

David Rosenthal, Department Chair
Contra Costa Community College
San Pablo, CA

Barbara Van Fossen, Associate Professor
Jefferson Community College
Steubenville, OH

one

The Calculator

Chapter 1 Using the Calculator

Chapter 1 introduces the calculator as an important tool in food service occupations. This chapter will provide instruction on the use of the calculator, utilizing the operations of addition, subtraction, multiplication, and division. Problem solving will be illustrated by using chain calculations, the constant function, the percent key, the memory function, and the plus/minus key to convert a positive number to a negative number and vice versa.

Using the Calculator

Objectives

At the completion of this chapter, the student should be able to use the calculator to:

1. Find sums, differences, products, and quotients.
2. Solve problems by using chain calculations.
3. Multiply or divide repeatedly using the constant function.
4. Find sums and differences by using a percent.
5. Find products and quotients by using a percent.
6. Solve problems using the memory function.
7. Use the plus/minus key to convert a positive number to a negative number, and vice versa.

Key Words and Abbreviations

calculator	AC	CM or MC	constant function
C	M+	MRC	memory function
CE	RM or MR	chain calculations	plus/minus key

Rounding

The **calculator** is one of the most important tools used in food service occupations. It is portable, which means that an employee/owner can use it on the loading dock to check invoices, as well as in the kitchen to convert recipes. Calculators are easy to use and accurate.

There are so many different types of calculators on the market today that it becomes a major decision when a purchase must be made. To help reach a decision, it is best to read literature on the various kinds before finalizing your choice. In this age of electronics, there are many choices: solar-powered calculators, scientific calculators, full-featured solar-powered scientific calculators, solar mini-desktop calculators, and inexpensive handheld calculators, just to name a few. With the advances in technology, many cell phones now have a calculator function as well. The authors also advise students to purchase a simple calculator, one that is not capable of performing scientific or financial calculations. An example of a simple calculator is shown in Figure 1–1.

Figure 1–1
Handheld calculator.
© Cengage Learning 2012

Another important tool used in food service occupations is the computer. Many computers have built-in calculators, as do software programs such as Microsoft Excel.

Purchasing a Calculator

If the calculator you use is for normal functions, it would be an advantage to purchase a solar calculator with fair-sized solar panels that can be used in just about any light.

A good-sized keyboard is another plus, as it is easier to press buttons using a finger rather than the end of a pencil, which must be used on very small keyboards. The features required for most food service math functions can be found in most inexpensive handheld calculators. This is the kind of calculator used in this chapter to explain the necessary functions employed most often in the food service industry. The authors' intent is to help the student become more familiar with the main calculator functions and more comfortable using them. Not every calculator has the same features, and even the keyboards vary from one model to another. For this reason, you should always read and study your calculator instruction booklet.

To Insure Perfect Solutions
Make sure your solar-powered calculator has a backup battery.

Using a Calculator

The face of the small handheld calculator usually contains the keys listed in Figure 1–2. However, the operation key may have a different placement depending on the calculator. Also listed are the functions that these keys perform.

The instructions provided in this chapter will apply to most calculators. However, remember that some differences will exist between models. The calculator functions shown in Figure 1–2 are those that you will use during your food service career. The functions that would be of little use, such as the square root key, will not be discussed. The student should calculate all examples presented to acquire practice and a complete understanding of the functions explained.

To Insure Perfect Solutions
Calculators work differently. Read *all* directions that come with your calculator.

Figure 1–2
Calculator keys.
© Cengage Learning 2012

ON/OFF	Press to activate the power and turn the calculator on, or turn off the power by pressing it again. The *OFF* key usually clears the calculator, including the memory register. Not all solar calculators have an *ON/OFF* key.
C	When the power is on, press this key to clear the calculator of all functions except the memory function.
CE	Press to clear an incorrect keyboard entry that has not been entered into the function. It does not clear the memory function.
CA or AC	If it is included on the keyboard, this key clears the calculator of all functions, including the memory function.
0–9	Numeral entry keys.
.	Decimal point key. Used to enter a decimal point into a number.
=	Equal or result key.
+	Plus or addition key.
−	Minus or subtraction key.
×	Times or multiplication key.
÷	Division key.
%	Percentage key—moves the decimal point two places to the left in the result.
√	Computes the square root of the number in the display. Not used in food service calculations. Used in scientific calculations.
+/−	Change sign key. Does not appear on all calculators. Used to convert a positive number to a negative number, and vice versa.
M+	Memory plus key. Adds a display number to the memory.
M−	Memory minus key. Subtracts a number from the memory.
RM/MR	Recall Memory or Memory Recall key. Displays content in memory. Does not clear memory.
CM/MC	Clear Memory or Memory Clear key. Displays memory figures and clears the memory.
MRC	Memory recall and clear key. Recalls the memory and also clears the memory. When key is depressed once, memory is recalled. Depressed twice, memory is cleared.

To Insure Perfect Solutions

Always press the clear key *before* you start to enter any new calculation.

The first step in the use of any calculator is to make sure it is cleared and ready to receive calculations. This is done by depressing the *ON* key, meaning the power is "on" and the calculator is "clear." At this point, it is also wise to do a few simple problems to make sure the batteries and the calculator are functioning properly. The simple test problems may be addition and percent.

The following is an example of a simple test addition problem:

At a banquet, a cook has to prepare two separate entrees: one for 37 prime ribs, the other for 65 boneless chicken breasts. How many clean plates must the cook have to serve the meals? If the cook used a calculator, the cook would solve the problem as illustrated in Table 1–1.

Table 1–1
Solving an addition problem using a calculator (© Cengage Learning 2012)

Steps	Procedure	Display Window
1.	Press the clear key on your calculator.	0
2.	Press the keys [THREE] (3), [SEVEN] (7).	37
3.	Press the [PLUS] (+) key.	37
4.	Press the keys [SIX] (6), [FIVE] (5).	65
5.	Press the [EQUAL] (=) key.	102
6.	The answer [ONE HUNDRED AND TWO] (102) is shown in the display window.	102

The following is an example of a simple percentage multiplication problem.

Mr. Ortiz booked a banquet for 600 guests. Because of the great speaker booked, he calls and states that he anticipates an increase of guests by 30 percent. How many meals would the chef have to prepare for Mr. Ortiz's banquet?

Think of this as 30 percent more meals than the original 600. Therefore, the answer will be greater than 600 meals. See Table 1–2 for the solution.

Table 1–2
Solving a multiplication problem using a calculator (© Cengage Learning 2012)

Steps	Procedure	Display Window
1.	Press the [CLEAR] key on your calculator.	0
2.	Press the keys [SIX] (6), [ZERO] (0), [ZERO] (0).	600
3.	Press the [MULTIPLICATION] (×) key.	600
4.	Press the keys [DECIMAL] (.), [THREE] (3), [ZERO] (0).	0.30
5.	Press the [EQUAL] (=) key.	180
6.	The answer [ONE HUNDRED AND EIGHTY] (180) is shown in the display window.	180

This means that the chef would have to increase the number of meals by 180. Since the original number of meals was 600, the additional 180 meals would have to be added to the original number, as shown in Table 1–3.

Table 1–3
Solving an addition problem using a calculator (© Cengage Learning 2012)

Steps	Procedure	Display Window
1.	Press the [CLEAR] key on your calculator.	0
2.	Press the keys [SIX] (6), [ZERO] (0), [ZERO] (0). *This is the original number of meals to prepare.*	600
3.	Press the [PLUS] (+) key.	600
4.	Press the keys [ONE] (1), [EIGHT] (8), [ZERO] (0). *The additional 30 percent of meals.*	180
5.	Press the [EQUAL] (=) key.	780
6.	The answer [SEVEN HUNDRED EIGHTY] (780) is shown in the display window.	780

The Four Basic Methods of Operation

The four basic methods of operation—addition, subtraction, multiplication, and division—are carried out on the calculator in the order that you would do the problem manually, or say the problem verbally. For example, to add 8 and 6, you would enter 8 + 6 =. The answer, 14, would then appear in the display window. To subtract 6 from 14, you would enter 14 − 6 =. The answer, 8, would again appear in the display window.

Try the following practice exercises to see if you have mastered how to use a calculator for the four basic operations. Correct answers are given.

Addition practice exercises:

    a. 37 + 46 + 54 =   *(Answer:* 137)

    b. 48 + 52 + 78 =   *(Answer:* 178)

    c. 3,463 + 225 + 2,218 + 4,560 =   *(Answer:* 10,466)

    d. 32.5 + 519.43 + 2,226.06 + 18.03 =   *(Answer:* 2,796.02)

    e. 26,423 + 22.08 + 2,946 + 3,220 + 445.046 =   *(Answer:* 33,056.126)

Subtraction practice exercises:

    a. 33,682 − 18,620 =   *(Answer:* 15,062)

    b. 3,895.28 − 1,620.29 =   *(Answer:* 2,274.99)

    c. 48,920.56 − 32,826.69 =   *(Answer:* 16,093.87)

    d. 8,668.78 − 4,878.28 =   *(Answer:* 3,790.50)

    e. 956 − 482.739 =   *(Answer:* 473.261)

Multiplication practice exercises:

    a. 86 × 256 =   *(Answer:* 22,016)

    b. 1,620 × 62 × 18 =   *(Answer:* 1,807,920)

    c. 4,482 × 22 × 6.8 =   *(Answer:* 670,507.2)

    d. 46.5 × 7 × 12.2 × 18.4 =   *(Answer:* 73,068.24)

    e. 438.75 × 34.5 =   *(Answer:* 15,136.875)

Division practice exercises:

    a. 2,175 ÷ 15 =   *(Answer:* 145)

    b. 7,137 ÷ 156 =   *(Answer:* 45.75)

    c. 6,256.25 ÷ 175 =   *(Answer:* 35.75)

    d. 82.9 ÷ 4.5 =   *(Answer:* 18.422)

    e. 6.5 ÷ 0.25 =   *(Answer:* 26)

A Note About the Process of Rounding

Throughout this textbook, there are groupings of practice problems for the student to complete. In many of the review problems, the directions are to round the answer to the hundredths place (in numerical terms) or to the cent (in monetary terms). There are different purposes for rounding. One purpose is to simplify a very long answer. When using a calculator, the answer often will have many digits to the right of the decimal point. For example: 100 divided by 7 results in the answer 14.285714. To make the answer less cumbersome, the skill of rounding is useful.

Here is an illustration of the numerical value of the digits in the answer 14.285714:

1	4	.	2	8	5	7	1	4
Tens	Ones	Decimal Point	Tenths	Hundredths	Thousandths	Ten Thousandths	Hundred Thousandths	Million

The Process of Rounding

The authors realize that mathematically, rounding should take place using all digits in the answer. However, to be consistent throughout the book, the authors will round using the number in the thousandths place (the third number to the right of the decimal place). In monetary terms, this number is called the *mill*. There will be times when an answer will result in no rounding being necessary.

An example of this is 100 divided by 5, which results in an answer of 20.

Step 1: Divide 100 by 7.

The answer that appears on the screen of the calculator is 14.285714.

Step 2: Determine the third digit to the right of the decimal place in the answer (in the thousandths place). In the number 14.285714, it is the digit 5.

Step 3: If the digit in the third place (thousandths place) to the right of the decimal is 5 or higher, raise the digit in the second place (hundredths place) up 1 number. In the answer, the digit 5 in the thousandths place is 14.285714. In this example, because the number in the thousandths place is 5, the 8 (in the hundredths place) is *rounded up* to 9.

The answer to the problem, rounded up correctly, is 14.29.

However, if the digit in the third place (thousandths place) to the right of the decimal is less than 5, do not change the digit in the second place (hundredths place). For example, the answer of 100 divided by 9 equals 11.111111. The third digit 1, which is the digit in the thousandths place, is less than 5, so the answer would be 11.11. Mathematically, this is called *rounding down* (this means not to change the number in the rounding place).

Realistic Rounding in the Food Service Industry

In the chapters specifically devoted to problems of ordering food and costing, the authors will provide explanations for the necessity to round up. Here is an example to illustrate why common sense must be used, as opposed to proper mathematical theory. A chef was preparing a party for 32 guests, with cake for dessert. The recipe specifications and yield for the cake result in 10 pieces from one cake. The chef must determine how many cakes to bake to have enough pieces to serve the 32 guests at the party. The chef divides 32 by 10, resulting in 3.2 cakes. It is pretty difficult to bake "0.2" of a cake. Therefore, the chef must determine how many cakes to bake. If the chef used proper math theory, he would have to look at the 2 in the tenths place (one place to the right of the decimal). Because this number is less than 5, following the mathematical rule of rounding down, the chef would bake only three cakes. Mathematically, the chef was correct in rounding down. Realistically, however, it wouldn't make sense to round down to three cakes because that would mean that two guests would not be served any cake and they would have to go without cake (Horrors!!!). It makes sense to round up and bake four cakes.

Practice Problems 1–1   Addition, Subtraction, Multiplication, and Division Using the Calculator

Round answers to the hundredths place.

Addition

1. $47 + 59 + 318 =$ _____
2. $78 + 135 + 393 =$ _____
3. $278 + 409 + 720 =$ _____
4. $3{,}263 + 298 + 2{,}229 + 4{,}685 =$ _____
5. $24.6 + 618.42 + 2{,}430.07 + 19.07 =$ _____

Subtraction

6. $23{,}583 - 16{,}220 =$ _____
7. $6{,}795.26 - 2{,}613.25 =$ _____
8. $56{,}750.35 - 31{,}999.67 =$ _____
9. $8{,}765.25 - 5{,}109.36 =$ _____
10. $987 - 452.634 =$ _____

Multiplication

11. $78 \times 563 =$ _____
12. $1{,}586 \times 82 \times 16 =$ _____
13. $3{,}774 \times 31 \times 5.8 =$ _____
14. $46.8 \times 8 \times 13.3 \times 12.2 =$ _____
15. $579.33 \times 62.4 =$ _____

Division

16. $1{,}675 \div 15 =$ _____
17. $7{,}391 \div 158 =$ _____
18. $8{,}245.25 \div 182 =$ _____
19. $99.2 \div 0.25 =$ _____
20. $7.5 \div 26 =$ _____

To Insure Perfect Solutions

When performing chain calculations, write down the intermediate results. Calculators do not provide an entry history. By writing down intermediate results, it is easier to find mistakes.

Chain Calculations

Because the calculator is portable, a chef or cook may use it in many areas of the food service operation, such as to calculate invoices or inventory. Invoices or inventory often require the food service employee to solve problems using **chain calculations.** Chain calculations involve a series of numbers and a variety of math operations. Many chain calculations involve all four basic operations. However, because specific math rules and steps apply when doing all four basic mathematical operations, the authors will limit the discussion of chain calculations to simple addition and subtraction problems. Chain calculations using addition and subtraction are carried out on the calculator in the same order as a person would say the problem verbally. For example:

$$29 + 120 - 38 + 25 - 12 = 124$$

would be 29 plus 120 minus 38 plus 25 minus 12 equals 124.

Here is an example of how a chain calculation would be used in a restaurant setting. The prep cook has to figure out how many 10-ounce steaks are left on Thursday morning. She has to take into account how many she cut and how many the restaurant sold from Monday through Wednesday. On Monday, she cut 150 steaks. The restaurant sold 86 steaks. Tuesday, she cut 45 more steaks, and the restaurant sold 62 steaks. Wednesday, she cut 25 steaks, and the restaurant sold 70 steaks. How many steaks are left for Thursday?

To solve the problem, it should be stated verbally as "150 minus 86 plus 45 minus 62 plus 25 minus 70 equals how many steaks are left." Table 1–4 illustrates how this problem will be solved.

Table 1–4
A chain calculation on a calculator (© Cengage Learning 2012)

Steps	Procedure	Display Window
1.	Press the [CLEAR] key on your calculator.	0
2.	Press the keys [ONE] (1), [FIVE] (5), [ZERO] (0). Number of steaks cut on Monday.	150
3.	Press the [MINUS] key. Purpose: To subtract the number of steaks sold on Monday.	150
4.	Press the keys [EIGHT] (8), [SIX] (6). Number of steaks sold on Monday.	86
5.	Press the [PLUS] (+) key. Number of steaks left shown in the display window.	64
6.	Press the keys [FOUR] (4), [FIVE] (5). Number of steaks cut on Tuesday.	45
7.	Press the [MINUS] key. Number of steaks left shown in the display window.	109
8.	Press the keys [SIX] (6), [TWO] (2). Number of steaks sold on Tuesday.	62
9.	Press the [PLUS] (+) key. Number of steaks left shown in the display window.	47
10.	Press the keys [TWO] (2), [FIVE] (5). Number of steaks cut on Wednesday.	25
11.	Press the [MINUS] (−) key. Number of steaks left shown in the display window.	72
12.	Press the keys [SEVEN] (7), [ZERO] (0). Number of steaks sold on Wednesday.	70
13.	Press the [EQUAL] (=) key. Number of steaks left shown in the display window. Purpose: To find the number of steaks left on Thursday morning.	2
14.	Answer: Two steaks are left on Thursday morning.	2

Practice the following chain calculation exercises. Note that calculators do not have dollar ($) signs. Dollar signs have been added in problem d, and also in several of the practice problems of the chain calculation exercises.

a. $97 + 120 − 38 + 12\ 25 =$ (*Answer:* 166)
b. $1,440 − 1,200 + 45 − 2 + 6 =$ (*Answer:* 289)
c. $395 − 42 + 225 − 448 =$ (*Answer:* 130)
d. $\$53,785.25 − \$32,726.85 + \$2,253.75 =$ (*Answer:* $23,312.15)
e. $596 − 58 + 24,568 − 1,420.6 =$ (*Answer:* 23,685.4)

Practice Problems 1–2   Chain Calculations

Write the answer as it appears on your calculator; do not round.

21. $95 + 232 - 77 + 4 =$ _____

22. $1{,}260 - 1{,}051 + 290 - 2 + 3 =$ _____

23. $476 - 50 + 492 - 515 =$ _____

24. $\$42{,}685.50 - \$31{,}628.75 + \$0.05 =$ _____

25. $657 - 42 - 17{,}111 + 1{,}932.4 =$ _____

To Insure Perfect Solutions

Make certain that *YOUR* calculator has a constant function. Not all calculators do!

Constant Function

The **constant function** may be used to multiply or divide repeatedly by the same number. *The constant is entered first when multiplying and becomes the multiplier.* The multiplier remains in the calculator as a new multiplicand is entered. The [EQUAL] (=) key is depressed to get the result. For example, find the product for each of the following:

The sales tax on meals is 6.5 percent. Using 6.5 percent as the constant, the restaurant manager must figure out the amount of sales tax for these three banquets:

   a. $252.00
   b. $79.00
   c. $2,456.92

Remember that 6.5 percent must be changed to the decimal 0.065 (the decimal moves two places to the left when the % sign is removed) and entered first, followed by the × sign and then the multiplicand. Pressing the [EQUAL] (=) key will give each product. The constant and × sign are entered only once.

Table 1–5 illustrates how these three problems are solved using the constant. The answers are rounded to the nearest cent.

Table 1–5

Using a constant function on a calculator to multiply and add (© Cengage Learning 2012)

Steps	Operation	Display Window
1.	Press the [CLEAR] key on your calculator.	0
2.	Press the keys [DECIMAL] (.), [ZERO] (0), [SIX] (6), [FIVE] (5). *This is the percentage of sales tax that must be charged on the banquets.*	0.065
3.	Press the [MULTIPLICATION] key (×). *Purpose: To find the amount of the sales tax on banquet a.*	0.065
4.	Press the keys [TWO] (2), [FIVE] (5), [TWO] (2). *The amount of banquet a.*	252
5.	Press the [EQUAL] (=) key. *Purpose: To determine the dollar amount of the sales tax that is charged on banquet a. Banquet a must pay $16.38 in sales tax.*	16.38
6.	Press the keys [SEVEN] (7), [NINE] (9). *The amount of banquet b.*	79
7.	Press the [EQUAL] (=) key. *Purpose: To determine the dollar amount of the sales tax that is charged on banquet b. Banquet b must pay $5.135 in sales tax.*	5.135
8.	*The answer would be rounded off to the hundredths place, resulting in the answer of $5.14 sales tax for banquet b.*	
9.	Press the keys [TWO] (2), [FOUR] (4), [FIVE] (5), [SIX] (6), [DECIMAL] (.) [NINE] (9), [TWO] (2). *The amount of banquet c.*	2456.92
10.	Press the [EQUAL] (=) key. *Purpose: To determine the dollar amount of the sales tax that is charged on banquet c. Banquet c must pay $159.6998 in sales tax.*	159.6998
11.	*The answer would be rounded off to the hundredths place, resulting in the answer of $159.70 sales tax for banquet c.*	

As you can see, the constant and × sign are entered only one time. New multiplicands are entered without reentering the constant or × sign.

Practice Problems 1–3 Multiplying by a Constant

What is the amount of sales tax on the following amounts, if the 6.5 percent sales tax rate is used as the constant? Round answers to the hundredths place.

26. $545.00 = _____

27. $78.50 = _____

28. $3,982.65 = _____

29. $5,236.55 = _____

30. $7,219.39 = _____

Dividing by a Constant

In division, the constant is entered after the first dividend is entered. It becomes the divisor and remains in the calculator as each new dividend is entered. For example, find the quotient in the following problem:

A restaurant manager may use division to set the price of menu items once the raw food cost is known. The formula to set the menu price is raw food cost divided by the desired food cost percentage. Using 40 percent as the desired food cost, the restaurant manager sets the menu price for the three items using the previous formula. Therefore, 40 percent is the constant. Calculate the menu price for each of the three items here using 40 percent as the desired food cost. Table 1–6 shows the steps in each calculation.

If the raw food cost is:

a. 2.95
b. 3.27
c. 12.22

Table 1–6
An illustration of using a constant function on a calculator (© Cengage Learning 2012)

Steps	Operation	Display Window
1.	Press the [CLEAR] key on your calculator.	0
2.	Press the keys [TWO] (2), [DECIMAL] (.), [NINE] (9), [FIVE] (5). *This is the raw food cost for problem a.*	2.95
3.	Press the [DIVISION] (÷) key. *Purpose: To put in the amount of food cost percentage to determine the selling price of the menu item in problem a.*	2.95
4.	Press the keys [DECIMAL] (.), [FOUR] (4), [ZERO] (0). *40% is the desired food cost percent.*	0.40
5.	Press the [EQUAL] (=) key. *The answer will be the menu price of problem a.*	7.375
6.	The menu price is rounded off to the nearest cent, to $7.38.	
7.	Press the keys [THREE] (3), [DECIMAL] (.), [TWO] (2), [SEVEN] (7). *This is the raw food cost for problem b.*	3.27
8.	Press the [EQUAL] (=) key. *The answer will be the menu price of problem b.*	8.175
9.	The menu price is rounded off to the nearest cent to $8.18.	
10.	Press the keys [ONE] (1), [TWO] (2), [DECIMAL] (.), [TWO] (2), [TWO] (2). *This is the raw food cost for problem c.*	12.22
11.	Press the [EQUAL] (=) key. *The answer will be the menu price of problem c.*	30.55

Remember that 40 percent must first be changed to the decimal 0.40 (the decimal moves two places to the left when the % sign is removed) and entered after the first dividend. The procedure for entering would be the dividend followed by the [DIVISION] (÷) sign, which is entered only once, as is the constant, which is entered last. Pressing the [EQUAL] (=) key will give each quotient.

The restaurant manager uses the steps in Table 1–6 to determine the three menu prices.

Practice Problems 1-4   Dividing by a Constant

Using 35 percent as the desired food cost percentage, find the menu price based upon the raw food cost of the following questions.

Round answers to the hundredths place.

31. $3.34 = _____

32. $0.75 = _____

33. $9.16 = _____

34. $5.68 = _____

35. $1.29 = _____

Discussion Question 1-1

Are there any reasons why a food service professional should not rely on the answers obtained from using a calculator? Defend your answer thoroughly.

"Math's role in being an executive chef and general manager is crucial. In order to develop recipes, cost out food, order food, and schedule accordingly, you need a good understanding of mathematics."

Robert Gioia
General Manager, Villa de Flora and Java Coast
Gaylord Palms Resort & Convention Center
Orlando, Florida

Mr. Gioia is the general manager of the 350-seat Villa de Flora restaurant. This buffet-themed restaurant serves breakfast, lunch, and dinner seven days a week. It is set in the grand style of a Mediterranean villa. Rob oversees the six demonstration kitchens, which form a European-style market. The menu at Villa de Flora is inspired from cuisines from France, Italy, Greece, and Spain. The coffee shop, Java Coast, is open 24 hours a day, serving pastries, coffee, sandwiches, salads, and desserts. This restaurant serves over 500 guests per meal period. Mr. Gioia's career has advanced from being executive chef of Villa de Flora to general manager. In his capacity of general manager, he also is responsible for the Haagan-Dazs Ice Cream Shoppe, which is open 12 hours each day. All in all, Mr. Gioia is responsible for scheduling 60 employees at this resort, which has 1,406 guest rooms.

Multiplying, Dividing, Adding, and Subtracting by a Percentage

Many times in the food service business, a monetary discount is given for buying goods in bulk. This discount is expressed in the form of a percentage. For example, if a business buys five slicing machines, it may receive a 10 percent discount. To know the amount of the discount, the chef/owner must be able to multiply by a percentage. Chefs, banquet managers, cooks, and food service employees need to understand how to multiply using percentages because, many times, their bonus or gratuity depends on a percentage of the gross or net sales. As stated previously in the chapter, a chef/owner may divide by a desired food cost percentage to set a menu price once the raw cost is determined.

Multiplication and division by a percentage are functions that are performed just as you would express the problem orally. For example, you would say "580 dollars times 5.5 percent," so on the calculator, you enter 580×5.5 percent, and the correct answer appears in the display window as 31.9 (this is $31.90 in dollar terms). Or you can change 5.5 percent to the decimal 0.055 and proceed to find the solution by entering $580 \times 0.055 = 31.90$. The calculator will place the decimal point automatically, but the dollar sign must be added.

Multiplying by a Percentage

Table 1–7 demonstrates how to multiply by a percentage.

Problem: $896.25 \times 7.5\%$ or $0.075 =$

Table 1–7
How to multiply by a percentage using a calculator (© Cengage Learning 2012)

Steps	Operation	Display Window
1.	Press the [*CLEAR*] key on your calculator.	0
2.	Press the keys [*EIGHT*] (8), [*NINE*] (9), [*SIX*] (6), [*DECIMAL*] (.), [*TWO*] (2), [*FIVE*] (5).	896.25
3.	Press the [*MULTIPLICATION*] key (×).	896.25
4.	Press the keys [*DECIMAL*] (.), [*ZERO*] (0), [*SEVEN*] (7), [*FIVE*] (5). *Purpose: Change the percentage to a decimal.*	.075
5.	Press the [*EQUAL*] key. *The answer is shown on the display.*	67.21875
6.	The answer is rounded off to the nearest cent to $67.22.	

Exercises:

Try the following practice exercises to see if you have mastered multiplying by a percentage. Answers are rounded to the nearest cent.

a. $652.40 \times 6.7\%$ or $0.067 =$ (*Answer:* $43.71)

b. $2,900 \times 35\%$ or $0.35 =$ (*Answer:* $1,015.00)

c. $7,200.00 \times 15.6\%$ or $0.156 =$ (*Answer:* $1,123.20)

d. $958.20 \times 7.9\%$ or $0.079 =$ (*Answer:* $75.70)

Dividing by a Percentage

When dividing by a percentage, as stated before, the problem is entered just as you would express it orally. For example, you say "580 dollars divided by 5.5 percent," so you would enter 580 ÷ 0.055, and the correct answer would appear in the display window as 10545.454. Again, the calculator will place the decimal point automatically, but the dollar sign must be added.

A word of caution to readers: It is common to have the results of a problem seem strange or wrong because the resulting answer is larger than the original dividend. For example, a baker makes five pies for a restaurant. The restaurant manager will sell individual pieces of the pie as dessert. If the pies are cut into 10 slices, each slice represents 10 percent of one pie. What is the total number of slices that we will get from five pies? The problem, 5 ÷ 10 percent, will result in the answer of 50 pieces of pie. The number 50 is larger than the dividend of 5.

The problem reads: \$896.25 ÷ 75 percent or 0.75 =

The steps to solve the problem are shown in Table 1–8.

Table 1–8
How to divide with a percentage using a calculator (© Cengage Learning 2012)

Steps	Operation	Display Window
1.	Press the [CLEAR] key on your calculator.	0
2.	Press the keys [EIGHT] (8), [NINE] (9), [SIX] (6), [DECIMAL] (.), [TWO] (2), [FIVE] (5).	896.25
3.	Press the [DIVISION] (÷) key.	896.25
4.	Press the keys [DECIMAL] (.), [SEVEN] (7), [FIVE] (5). Purpose: Change the percentage to a decimal.	0.75
5.	Press the [EQUAL] key. The answer is shown on the display.	1195

Use the steps shown in Table 1–8 to solve the problem of how to divide with a percent, using a calculator.

Exercises:

Try the following practice exercises to see if you have mastered dividing by a percentage. Answers are rounded to the hundredths place.

a. \$652.40 ÷ 6.7 percent or 0.067 =   (*Answer:* \$9,737.31)
b. \$2,900.00 ÷ 35 percent or 0.35 =   (*Answer:* \$8,285.71)
c. \$7,200.00 ÷ 15.6 percent or 0.156 =   (*Answer:* \$46,153.85)
d. \$958.20 ÷ 7.9 percent or 0.079 =   (*Answer:* \$12,129.11)

Practice Problems 1–5   Multiplying and Dividing by a Percentage

Round answers to the hundredths place.

Multiplication

36. $872.20 \times 8.5\% =$ _____

37. $565.45 \times 7.5\% =$ _____

38. $3,700 \times 16.4\% =$ _____

39. $7,452.85 \times 6.8\% =$ _____

40. $928.95 \times 7.75\% =$ _____

Division

41. $425.60 \div 76\% =$ _____

42. $495.60 \div 7.4\% =$ _____

43. $2,890.00 \div 15.2\% =$ _____

44. $8,977.80 \div 6.4\% =$ _____

45. $956.26 \div 8.9\% =$ _____

Adding by a Percentage

When adding by a percentage, two steps are needed. First, you have to multiply to find the amount of money that you will add to the original price. Second, you have to add the amount of money that has been found to the original price. Table 1–9 illustrates the following problem.

Problem: The Showboat Restaurant purchased $593.51 worth of kitchen equipment. The sales tax was 5.5 percent. What was the total cost of the equipment?

Table 1–9
How to add with a percentage using a calculator (© Cengage Learning 2012)

Steps	Operation	Display Window
1.	Press the [CLEAR] key on your calculator.	0
2.	Press the keys [FIVE] (5), [NINE] (9), [THREE] (3), [DECIMAL] (.), [FIVE] (5), [ONE] (1). *This is the price of the kitchen equipment.*	593.51
3.	Press the [MULTIPLICATION] key (×).	593.51
4.	Press the keys [DECIMAL] (.), [ZERO] (0), [FIVE] (5), [FIVE] (5). *This is the sales tax percentage.*	0.055
5.	Press the [EQUAL] key. *The answer is shown on the display. This answer must be rounded to the hundreds place, which results in the answer of 32.64.*	32.64305
6.	Press the keys [FIVE] (5), [NINE] (9), [THREE] (3), [DECIMAL] (.), [FIVE] (5), [ONE] (1). *This is the price of the kitchen equipment.*	593.51
7.	Press the [PLUS] (+) key.	593.51
8.	Press the keys [THREE] (3), [TWO] (2), [DECIMAL] (.), [SIX] (6), [FOUR] (4). *This is the sales tax amount on the kitchen equipment.*	32.64
9.	Press the [EQUAL] key. *The answer is shown on the display.*	626.15

Subtracting by a Percent

Discounts are a normal part of doing business in the food service industry. Whenever a discount is given to a business, two steps must be calculated to solve the problem. First, the food service professional must multiply by a percentage to determine the amount of the discount. Second, he or she must subtract that amount from the original price. Table 1–10 shows how to subtract after finding the amount of a discount.

Problem: Kelly Hart purchased a new slicing machine for $2,560. She was given a 15 percent discount. What was the total cost?

Table 1–10
How to subtract with a percentage using a calculator (© Cengage Learning 2012)

Steps	Operation	Display Window
1.	Press the [CLEAR] key on your calculator.	0
2.	Press the keys [TWO] (2), [FIVE] (5), [SIX] (6), [ZERO] (0). *This is the price of the slicing machine.*	2560
3.	Press the [MULTIPLICATION] key (×).	2560
4.	Press the keys [DECIMAL] (.), [ONE] (1), [FIVE] (5). *This is the discount percentage.*	0.15
5.	Press the [EQUAL] key. *The answer is shown on the display.*	384
6.	Press the keys [TWO] (2), [FIVE] (5), [SIX] (6), [ZERO] (0). *This is the price of the slicing machine.*	2560
7.	Press the [MINUS] (−) key.	2560
8.	Press the keys [THREE] (3), [EIGHT] (8), [FOUR] (4). *This is the discount amount on the slicing machine.*	384
9.	Press the [EQUAL] key. *The answer is shown on the display.*	2176

Practice Problems 1–6 Adding and Subtracting by a Percentage

Figure out the total costs of the following problems. Round answers to the hundredths place.

46. $399.50 + 3.5% tax = _____

47. $4,892.15 + 16.8% gratuity = _____

48. $795.45 − 6.5% discount = _____

49. $4,192.14 − 11.6% discount = _____

50. $1,049.75 − 7.5% discount = _____

The Memory Function

The **memory function** is used to retain figures in the calculator. Even when the power is turned off, some calculators will retain figures. This function makes totaling an invoice or figuring other totals simpler when multiplying by a percentage. Because the keys of some calculators may vary slightly, it is wise to check a calculator's instruction booklet before using its memory function. For example:

Before starting, press the [**C**] and [*CM*] keys to clear the calculator and its memory. Figure 1–3 is a step-by-step outline of how to use the memory function to complete an invoice. Each step corresponds to a line of the Haines Foods, Inc., invoice, as shown in Figure 1–4.

Figure 1–3
Step-by-step outline for use of the memory function.
© Cengage Learning 2012

Step 1.	4 × 8.95 M+ ᴹ35.80
Step 2.	3 × 15.60 M+ ᴹ46.80
Step 3.	2 × 9.50 M+ ᴹ19.00
Step 4.	5 × 8.40 M+ ᴹ42.00
Step 5.	2 × 18.90 M+ ᴹ37.80
Step 6.	RM ᴹ181.40
Step 7.	× 10 % ᴹ18.14
Step 8.	M− ᴹ18.14 RM ᴹ163.26
Step 9.	15 ᴹ15. M+ ᴹ15.
Step 10.	RM ᴹ178.26

Figure 1–4
Invoice form.
© Cengage Learning 2012

Distributor:	Haines Foods, Inc.	Phone: 771-8800
		Date: April 20, 20—

Address: 70 Greenbrier Avenue
Ft. Mitchell, KY 41017

Distributors of Fine Food Products—Wholesale Only

No. of Pieces	Salesperson	Order No.	Invoice #
5	Joe Jones	2860	J 2479

Packed by: Sold To: Mr. John Doe
R.H. Street: 120 Elm Avenue
City/State: Covington, KY

Case	Pack	Size	Canned Foods	Price	Amount
4	6	#10 can	Sliced Apples	$8.95	35.80
3	6	#10 can	Pitted Cherries	15.60	46.80
2	12	#5 can	Apple Juice	9.50	19.00
5	24	1 lb.	Cornstarch	8.40	42.00
2	24	#2½ can	Asparagus	18.90	37.80
			Total Amount		181.40
			Less: Special Discount 10%		18.14
			Total Net Price		163.26
			Plus: Delivery Charge		15.00
			Total Invoice Price		178.26

Using the calculator, check the accuracy of the completed invoice of Webb Food Company, Inc. (Figure 1–5). Multiply the number of cases by the price to check the accuracy of the amount given on each line. When mistakes appear, make the necessary corrections. Also, check the total invoice price by adding all the figures in the amount column. You may do this exercise with or without the memory function. However, using the memory function for practice will increase your confidence in the future. To start checking the invoice using the memory function, the first line would be calculated as follows:

Problem: 6 cases of sliced apples at $20.87 for each case = 4 cases of sliced pineapple at $17.27 for each case =. Table 1–11 demonstrates the first two steps using the memory function.

Webb Food Company, Inc.
1225 South Street
Mechanicville, New York 12118
518.637.2592
webbfc@nycap.rr.com

Invoice Number 12223

Tancredi's Restaurant
Depot Square
Mechanicville, NY 12118

Case	Size	Product	Unit	Price	Amount
6	#10	Sliced apples	Case	20.87	125.22
4	#10	Sliced pineapple	Case	17.27	69.08
8	#10	Tomato puree	Case	13.85	110.80
7	#10	Green beans, cut	Case	11.58	81.06
3	#10	Tomatoes, whole peeled	Case	16.98	50.94
2	10 lbs.	Fettuccine, long	Lbs.	6.56	13.12
4	10 lbs.	Vermicelli, cut	Lbs.	4.20	20.80
2	13 oz.	Pickling spices	Oz.	4.18	8.36
3	6 oz.	Rubbed sage	Oz.	5.42	16.26
2	11 oz.	Thyme, ground	Oz.	5.89	64.79
5	46 oz.	Cranberry juice cocktail	Case	22.66	113.30
3	50 lbs.	Granulated sugar	Bag	16.70	50.10
		Total			723.83

Table 1–11

How to use the memory function using a calculator (© Cengage Learning 2012)

Steps	Operation	Display Window
1.	Press the [CLEAR] key on your calculator.	0
2.	Press the key [SIX] (6).	6
	This is the number of cases of sliced apples.	
3.	Press the [MULTIPLICATION] key (×).	6
4.	Press the keys [TWO] (2), [ZERO] (0), [DECIMAL] (.), [EIGHT] (8), [SEVEN] (7).	20.87
	This is the cost of one case of sliced apples.	
5.	Press the key [MEMORY+] (M+).	125.22M
	The answer for the apples is shown on the display.	
6.	Press the key [FOUR] (4).	4M
	This is the number of cases of sliced pineapple.	
7.	Press the [MULTIPLICATION] (×) key.	4M
8.	Press the keys [ONE] (1), [SEVEN] (7), [DECIMAL] (.), [TWO] (2) [SEVEN] (7).	17.27M
	This is the cost of one case of sliced pineapple.	
9.	Press the key [MEMORY+] (M+).	69.08M
	The answer for the pineapple is shown on the display.	
10.	Press the key [MEMORYR] (MR).	194.3M
	The answer is shown on the display.	
11.	Continue with the problem in Figure 1–5.	

Complete each line by following the procedure given in the previous example. To find the total invoice price, press the *RM* key (recall memory).

Discussion Question 1-2

Are any of the figures incorrect? What could have happened to cause the mistake(s)? What is the correct total? As the chef/owner, what steps would you take to correct the bill?

Practice Problems 1–7   Using the Memory Function

51. Complete the following invoice, using your calculator and its memory function. Round answers to the hundredths place.

Distributor:	Miller Foods, Inc.	Phone: 772-9654
		Date: April 22, 20—
Address:	2033 Elm Avenue	
	Norwood, OH 45212	

Distributors of Fine Food Products—Wholesale Only

No. of Pieces	Salesperson	Order No.	Invoice #
4	James Jones	2861	J 2480

Packed by:	Sold To:	Mr. Tim O'Connell
R.H.	Street:	916 Montague Street
	City/State:	Cincinnati, OH 45202

Case	Pack	Size	Canned Foods	Price	Amount
5	6	#10 can	Sliced Pears	$10.95	_____a.
3	6	#10 can	Sliced Peaches	12.85	_____b.
6	12	#5 can	Tomato Juice	9.50	_____c.
4	24	1 lb.	Cornstarch	8.40	_____d.
3	24	#2½ can	Asparagus	18.90	_____e.
			Total Amount		_____f.
			Less: Special Discount 12%		_____g.
			Total Net Price		_____h.
			Plus: Delivery Charge		$12.00
			Total Invoice Price		_____i.

Multiplying by a Percentage Using the Memory Function

Remember that percentage is a key function when developing a food service career. It is, as previously stated, the language of the food service industry. When discussing labor costs, food costs, and so forth, the figures are given as percentages. With this in mind, you can see the importance of understanding and developing confidence in using this function and dealing with percentages. For example:

The purchasing agent at Morrisey's Restaurant purchased five food items at $18.50 each and three food items at $12.60 each. If the sales tax on the total purchase was 6.5 percent, what was the total cost of the purchase? Table 1–12 demonstrates the steps in this calculation.

Table 1–12
How to use the memory function using a calculator (© Cengage Learning 2012)

Steps	Operation	Display Window
1.	Press the [CLEAR] key on your calculator.	0
2.	Press the key [FIVE] (5).	5
	This is the number of food items purchased.	
3.	Press the [MULTIPLICATION] key (×).	5
4.	Press the keys [ONE] (1), [EIGHT] (8), [DECIMAL] (.), [FIVE] (5), [ZERO] (0).	18.50
	This is the cost of one food item.	
5.	Press the key [MEMORY+] (M+).	92.5M
	The answer for the food items is shown on the display.	
6.	Press the key [THREE] (3).	3.M
	This is the number of food items purchased.	
7.	Press the [MULTIPLICATION] (×) key.	3.M
8.	Press the keys [ONE] (1), [TWO] (2), [DECIMAL] (.), [SIX] (6) [ZERO] (0).	12.60M
	This is the cost of one food item.	
9.	Press the key [MEMORY+] (M+).	37.8M
	The answer for the food items is shown on the display.	
10.	Press the [MEMORY RECALL] key (MR).	130.3M
	The answer for the food items purchased is shown on the display.	
11.	Press the [MULTIPLICATION] (×) key.	130.3M
12.	Press the keys [DECIMAL] (.), [ZERO] (0), [SIX] (6), [FIVE] (5).	0.065M
	This is the percentage of the sales tax.	
13.	Press the [EQUAL] key (=).	8.4695M
14.	Press the key [MEMORY+] (M+).	8.4695M
	This is the amount of sales tax that must be added to the original purchase.	
15.	Press the [MEMORY RECALL] key (MR).	138.7695M
	The answer for the sales tax plus the original purchase is shown on the display.	
16.	*The rounded-off answer of $138.77 is the total owed.*	

Practice Problems 1–8 Multiplying by Using the Memory Function

Round answers to the hundredths place.

52. Chenusa Jones purchased 10 items at $15.90 each. Sales tax was 6.5 percent. What was the total cost? _____

53. Bob Shirley purchased eight items at $6.25 each, and six items at $8.95 each. If the sales tax on the total purchase was 7.5 percent, what was the total cost?

_____

54. Bill Thompson made purchases costing $10.95, $54.76, $8.91, $8.98, and $0.19. If the sales tax was 7.75 percent of the total amount, what was the total cost?

_____

55. Hillary Meyers purchased 15 items at $16.20 each, and 4 items at $20.50 each. If the sales tax on the total purchase was 5.25 percent, what was the total cost?

_____

56. Sheryar Khan purchased items costing $99.90, $16.75, and $19.25. If the sales tax was 6.75 percent of the total amount, what was the total cost?

_____

Using the Plus/Minus Key

This change sign key is used to convert a positive number to a negative number and vice versa. The key is used only on certain occasions and would not be considered a popular key, like the 3 or 1 key. For example:

The Blue Bird Restaurant purchased some used equipment for $2,800.

The manager was given a special discount of 8 percent plus a sales tax of 6.5 percent. What was the total cost? Table 1–13 illustrates how to use the **plus/minus key.**

Table 1–13
How to use the *PLUS/MINUS* key using a calculator (© Cengage Learning 2012)

Steps	Operation	Display Window
1.	Press the [*CLEAR*] key on your calculator.	0
2.	Press the keys [*TWO*] (2), [*EIGHT*] (8), [*ZERO*] (0), [*ZERO*] (0). *Cost of equipment.*	2800
3.	Press the [*MULTIPLICATION*] (×) key.	2800
4.	Press the keys [*DECIMAL*] (.), [*ZERO*] (0), [*EIGHT*] (8). *Discount percentage.*	0.08
5.	Press the [*MINUS*] key (−). *Amount of discount.*	224.
6.	Press the keys [*TWO*] (2), [*EIGHT*] (8), [*ZERO*] (0), [*ZERO*] (0). *Cost of equipment.*	2800.
7.	Press the [*EQUAL*] (=) key. *Cost of equipment minus discount, showing a negative number.*	2576.−
8.	Press the [*PLUS/MINUS*] (+/−) key. *To convert the negative number to a positive number.*	2576.
9.	Press the [*MULTIPLICATION*] (×) key.	2576.
10.	Press the keys [*DECIMAL*] (.), [*ZERO*] (0), [*SIX*] (6), [*FIVE*] (5). *Sales tax percentage.*	0.065
11.	Press the [*EQUAL*] (=) key. *Sales tax cost.*	167.44
12.	Press the [*PLUS*] (+) key.	167.44
13.	Press the [*EQUAL*] (=) key. *Total cost of equipment with discount and sales tax.*	2743.44

In this calculation, the 2576 appears with a minus sign, which denotes a negative number. To add the 6.5 percent sales tax, that negative number must be converted to a positive number so that the sales tax amount can be added to the cost. This is accomplished by pressing the *PLUS/MINUS* key after the amount 2576− appears in the display window.

Practice Problems 1–9   Using the Plus/Minus Key

Round answers to the hundredths place.

57. The Chateau Restaurant purchased a dessert cart for $1,950. Because the cart was slightly damaged, the restaurant was given an 8.5 percent discount. A sales tax of 6.5 percent was added to the purchase price. What was the total cost? _____

58. The Sky Lark Restaurant purchased new china for $4,868.54. Because the china pattern was discontinued, the restaurant got a 9 percent discount on the price. A sales tax of 7.5 percent was added to the purchase price. What was the total cost? _____

59. A party was catered for 60 people. The bill came to $1,280. A senior citizen discount of 5.5 percent was given. A sales tax of 7 percent was added to the bill. What was the total bill? _____

60. A party for 90 people was served. The bill was $810. A discount of 4.5 percent was given because it was a school group. A sales tax of 7.5 percent was added to the bill. What was the total bill? _____

61. Four bakers' balance scales were purchased for $1,160. A 3 percent discount was given because the scales were purchased in quantity. A sales tax of 8 percent was added to the bill. What was the total bill? _____

Review of Basic Math Fundamentals

Part II contains a review of the basic math fundamentals used in most food service operations. Basic mathematical concepts are covered using whole numbers, fractions, decimals, and percentages. Common-sense guidelines in the use of the mill and rounding up when it comes to business situations are discussed. Competence in each area of this review section is essential for ensuring accuracy in working the math exercises presented in this text and for accurate recordkeeping when performing math functions in the food service industry.

two

Numbers, Symbols of Operations, and the Mill

Objectives

At the completion of this chapter, the student should be able to:

1. Read and write numbers.
2. Identify the symbols for the four basic operations of addition, subtraction, multiplication, and division.
3. Identify the mill and use it in solving problems.
4. Understand the reasoning for rounding up in a food service operation.

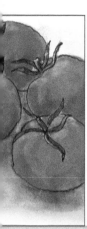

Key Words

whole numbers digits symbols of mill
unit period operations
numerals cent

The information presented in this chapter is intended to refresh your knowledge of basic mathematical terms and principles that you learned in your early school years but may not have put into practice often enough to retain. These terms and principles are important to all math functions. They will be used throughout the book, and they need to be fully understood for you to increase your math skills and function effectively in the workplace.

In the twenty-first century, the food service industry will continue to require employees to possess math skills. The industry is extremely competitive, and controlling costs (e.g., food, beverage, labor, etc.) is vital to the survival of any business venture.

Math skills start with the understanding of terms such as **whole numbers, units, numerals,** and **digits.**

You may feel that you fully understand all these terms, but studying this chapter may still help you become more comfortable with math.

Numerical Terms

Whole numbers are numbers such as 0, 1, 2, 3, 4, 5, 6, 7, 8, and 9, which are used to represent whole units rather than fractional units. A **unit** is a standard quantity or amount. Units, of course, are not limited to manufactured products. A unit may be a single quantity of like products, such as a case of apple juice. Units are often established by producers or manufacturers. The unit that they establish is usually a quantity that is convenient for both the consumer and producer. Some convenient and sensible units for individuals could include a quart or gallon of milk, a pound of butter, a pint or quart of strawberries, or a dozen oranges. In the food service industry, convenient and sensible units might include a #10 can of fruit or vegetables, a 100-pound bag of flour, or a 5-pound box of bacon. Convenient and sensible units also help a manufacturer or business keep track of inventories.

"What is your labor cost, your food cost, your beverage cost, your increase in covers over last month, your variable expenses, your overhead, your breakeven, your cost of capital, your revenue per square foot, your inventory turnover or your profitability? All of these are questions which you will need to know to operate an effective and profitable business. All of these questions can be answered by having the ability to understand and analyze numbers through mathematics. But many food service operators have difficulty interpreting these relationships; thus, they are only able to make decisions based on limited knowledge of the situation. A food service manager does not need to be an accountant to operate a profitable enterprise, but a food service manager does need to have a working knowledge of basic mathematics to make daily decisions on the health of their business."

George R. Goldhoff
General Manager
Gold Strike Casino Resort
Tunica, Mississippi

The 31-story Gold Strike Casino Resort has 1,133 guest rooms, Mr. Goldhoff is responsible for all hotel services, including all food and beverage operations. The food and beverage operations include convention space, lounges, bars, restaurants, a food court, a buffet, and room service. The convention space is ideal for generating food and beverage revenue. The Gold Strike can accommodate sit-down banquets for up to 650 guests. There is a prefunction space where receptions for up to 300 guests can be held. The convention space also includes four meeting rooms that can serve a total of 210 guests. Besides the convention space, the Gold Strike has a nightclub, a lounge, and a bar area for its guests. The Chicago Steakhouse is its fine-dining dinner restaurant, which has earned an Award of Excellence from the *Wine Spectator* magazine for its wine list. For more casual dining, the Atrium Café offers breakfast, lunch, dinner, and late-night menus. In addition, the food service operation includes three types of fast-food restaurants; Pizzeria Fresh, Burger City, and Gold's Deli, where patrons can get a quick "pick-me-up" and get back to the casino. The Gold Strike Buffet serves Italian, Asian, seafood, local regional, and American cuisines. The Buffet is famous for its Friday- and Saturday-night Steak & Lobster Buffet and its Saturday and Sunday Champagne Brunch.

Before becoming general manager of the Gold Strike Casino Resort, Mr. Goldhoff was Vice President of Food and Beverage at the 1,780-room Beau Rivage Resort & Casino in Biloxi, Mississippi. Mr. Goldhoff was responsible for designing all the food and beverage outlets when the luxury hotel had to be rebuilt after the devastation of Hurricane Katrina in 2005.

Mr. Goldhoff got his start in the hotel and casino business at the Bellagio hotel in Las Vegas, Nevada. As Executive Director of Food and Beverage, his position included the responsibilities of serving more than 17,000 people each day. His team accomplished this through the professional efforts of approximately 3,000 employees divided equally between the front and back of the house in 18 restaurants, 16 front bars, room service, 120,000 square feet of banquet space, and an employee dining room.

Numerals are used to represent or express numbers. For example, 8, 21, 450, II, and X are numerals because they express numbers. The individual numbers on a clock are numerals as well.

Digits are any of the numerals that combine to form numbers.

There are 10 digits, as shown in Figure 2–1, with names that you should be quite familiar with.

Figure 2–1
Digits.
© Cengage Learning 2012

0	1	2	3	4	5	6	7	8	9
zero	one	two	three	four	five	six	seven	eight	nine

Digits can be combined in various ways to produce different numbers. For example, 457 and 745 are both combinations of the digits 7, 5, and 4. The value of each digit depends on where it is placed in the combination of numbers. For example, the 4 in the number 457 is valued at 400. However, the 4 in the number 745 is valued at 40. Each place has a different name and therefore a different value, as shown in Figure 2–2.

Figure 2–2
Place value columns within each period.
© Cengage Learning 2012

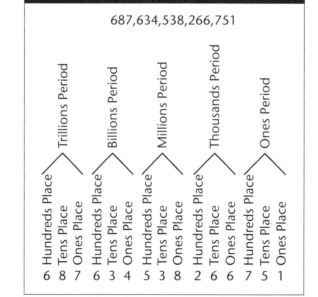

In large groups of numbers made up of four or more digits, the digits are placed into groups of three. Each of these groups is called a **period,** as shown in Figure 2–2. (This mathematical term "period" is not to be confused with the punctuation mark at the end of a sentence.) Periods are separated with commas in English-speaking countries. Readers should be aware, however, that in many non-English-speaking countries, spaces or periods (dots) are used to separate numeric periods, rather than commas. For example, an invoice from France for 1,500 toothpicks may be shown as 1 500 or even 1.500 instead of 1,500. And in the metric system

(discussed in more detail in Chapter 6), periods are separated by spaces rather than commas. The value of each digit is determined by its position in the place value columns. In Figure 2–2, the digit 5 is used twice. When it appears in the tens place of the ones period, the 5 represents 50. When it is used in the hundreds place of the millions period, it represents 500 million. As you can see, *place* is very important when numbers are grouped.

In the food service industry, the billions and trillions periods are very seldom or ever required. These periods are used by big business and by governments when discussing budgets and the national debt. Major restaurant chains and some popular restaurant establishments will present and use figures in the millions place, but that is usually the extent of profit or loss figures.

Commas are used to separate periods. They are used for financial records, such as profit and loss statements and balance sheets. Commas are also used when writing checks, both professionally and personally.

A chef/owner—or, for that matter, any person who pays bills—must know how to write a bank check. For most people, daily, monthly, and weekly checks are generally written in the hundreds of dollars. But there will be times when a person must write a check in the ten thousands and maybe even in the hundred thousands. Practice Problems 2–1 and 2–2 will allow the student to practice check-writing techniques using both numbers and words.

To Insure Perfect Solutions

When placing commas, start at the far right, or at the decimal point if there is one, and then count left three places and insert a comma.

Practice Problems 2–1   Placement of Commas

Rewrite the following numbers by adding commas in the correct place(s).

1. 5321 _____

2. 10495 _____

3. 396559318 _____

4. 26495 _____

5. 459987123 _____

6. 48973 _____

7. 420000000 _____

8. 41213728 _____

9. 86931100099 _____

10. 8725351280 _____

As stated before in this chapter, most food service professionals will have to write checks with smaller numbers, such as $195.23. This would be written as "one hundred ninety five and 23/100 dollars." When writing words on the write out line, always start as far to the left as possible. If not, unscrupulous merchants may add an extra number or word. Figure 2–3 illustrates the correct way to write a check, while Figure 2–4 illustrates the improper way to write a check.

Figure 2–3
Correctly written check.
© Cengage Learning 2012

Figure 2–4
Incorrectly written check (there is room to add thousands of dollars).
© Cengage Learning 2012

In the "Pay To The Order Of" row, imagine inserting a "9" before the figure $195.23, making it $9,195.23; and then putting the word "Ninety-" before the "one hundred ninety five," making the check read "Ninety-one hundred ninety five and 23/100." Obviously, this was not what you intended when you wrote this check; and it could cost you big.

Large numbers are also expressed with the names shown in Figure 2–5. The digit 0 in the ones column is needed to hold a place and to give the other digits their proper value. The digit 6 in the tens place would be 6, not 60, without the zero. The complete number shown in Figure 2–3 is read "eight billion nine-hundred twenty-five million four-hundred fifty-one thousand two-hundred sixty." Zeroes are not read. The number 149,000,000 is read "one hundred forty-nine million." The word "and" is not used in reading whole numbers.

8,925,451,260

Billions: 8
Hundred Millions: 9
Ten Millions: 2
Millions: 5
Hundred Thousands: 4
Ten Thousands: 5
Thousands: 1
Hundreds: 2
Tens: 6
Ones: 0

Figure 2–5
Place values.
© Cengage Learning 2012

Practice Problems 2-2   Writing Dollar Amounts in Words

Write out the words for the following dollar amounts. For example, $195.23 would be written as "one hundred ninety five and 23/100 dollars."

11. $2,856.19 _____

12. $20,495.25 _____

13. $49.95 _____

14. $492.49 _____

15. $63,666.18 _____

16. $63,682.63 _____

17. $892.75 _____

18. $8.88 _____

19. $88.88 _____

20. $105.16 _____

Symbols of Operations

There are four basic arithmetic operations: addition, subtraction, multiplication, and division. Math symbols are used to indicate which of these four operations is required in any given transaction or arithmetic problem. The importance of math symbols can be demonstrated by selecting two numerals and setting up problems using each of the four basic math symbols. The problems appear to be similar until the symbol is added.

(a)   10   (b)   10   (c)   10   (d) $10 \div 2 = 5$

    $\underline{+\ 2}$ $\underline{-\ 2}$ $\underline{\times\ 2}$ or $^{10}\!/_2 = 5$

    12   8   20   or $^{10}\!/_2 = 5$

As you can see, the math symbol used will yield different results and dictates the direction that the problem will take.

Example (a) is addition, (b) is subtraction, (c) is multiplication, and (d) is division. Figure 2–6 provides the names, meanings, and some examples of the symbols commonly used in the food service industry.

Figure 2–6
Mathematical symbols.
© Cengage Learning 2012

Symbol	Name	Meaning	Examples
+	plus sign	add to, or increase by	$8 + 99 = 107$ $2 + 19 = 21$ $361 + 12 = 373$
−	minus sign	subtract from, take away from, decrease by, or less	$17 − 9 = 8$ $23 − 5 = 18$ $49 − 9 = 40$
× or *	multiplication or times sign	multiply by, times, or the product of	$2 \times 12 = 24$ $9 \times 3 = 27$ $5 * 25 = 125$
÷ or /	division sign	divided by	$^4\!/_2 = 2$ $27 \div 9 = 3$ $100 \div 20 = 5$
___	fraction bar	separates numerator and denominator	$^6\!/_3 = 2$ $^{10}\!/_5 = 2$ $^{20}\!/_5 = 4$
.	decimal point	indicates the beginning of a decimal fraction	0.321 1.877 117.65
%	percent sign	parts per 100, by the hundredths	15% 12% 6%
=	equal sign	the same value as, or is equal to	$1 = 1$
$	dollar sign	the symbol placed before a number to indicate that it stands for a number of dollars	$12.00
@	at or per	used to indicate the price or weight of each unit when there is a quantity of a unit	5 dozen doughnuts @ $1.15/dozen 25 bags of potatoes @ 10 lbs./bag 100 ice cream cones @ $0.25 per cone

Practice Problems 2–3   Symbols of Operations

In the following problems or statements, the **symbol of operation** has been omitted. In each instance, determine the symbol that should be placed in the blank.

21. Meaning "by the hundredths." _____

22. Used to indicate the price of each unit. _____

23. Used to separate the numerator from the denominator when dealing with fractions. _____

24. Indicates the beginning of a decimal fraction. _____

25. A symbol placed before a monetary figure. _____

26. 24 _____ 15 = 360

27. 284 _____ 4 = 71

28. He purchased a dozen _____ $1.99 per dozen.

29. 28 × 2 _____ 56

30. A waitress is usually tipped 15 _____ of the total bill.

31. 1,540 _____ 5 = 308

32. 1,850 _____ 360 = 1,490

33. 2,075 _____ 190 = 2,265

34. The food cost for the month was 38 _____.

35. The restaurant purchased six cases of sliced apples _____ $12.50 per case.

The Mill

When dealing with monetary numbers, the term **cent** is used to represent the value of one hundredth part of a dollar. The third place to the right of the decimal is called a **mill** and represents the thousandth part of a dollar, or one-tenth of one cent.

When the final result of a monetary number includes a mill, it is usually rounded to a whole number of cents. To round a number to the nearest cent, the third digit

(the mill) is dropped if it is less than 5. If that digit is 5 or more, another cent is added to the digit before it. For example:

$4.626 rounded to the nearest cent is $4.63, because 6 mills are more than 5.

$4.623 rounded to the nearest cent is $4.62, because 3 mills are less than 5.

$4.625 rounded to the nearest cent is $4.63, because the last digit is 5, which is 5 or more.

The mill is an important tool in the food service industry because the production cost of an item and the cost of a menu food item are figured to the mill to obtain the exact cost of the item in question. Knowing the exact cost is very important when figuring a menu or selling price. For example, when producing rolls, it is necessary to know that each roll may cost $0.043 to produce, making the cost of one dozen rolls $0.516, or $0.52. In the case of a menu item, the manager must determine the cost of a serving before he or she can determine a selling or menu price.

To Insure Perfect Solutions

When costing out ingredients in a recipe, each ingredient should be costed out to the mill. Next, the cost of each ingredient is added together, resulting in the total cost. The final step is rounding to the hundredths place using the mill.

Practice Problems 2–4   The Mill

Answer the following questions about the mill.

36. How many mills are contained in one cent? _____

37. How many mills are contained in 10 cents? _____

38. How many mills are contained in $1.00? _____

39. What is the rule to follow if the mill is 4 or less? _____.

40. 5 or more? _____

Solve the following problems. Round all answers to the hundredths place using the mill.

41. $0.035 _____

42. $0.591 _____

43. $0.069 _____

44. $0.052 _____

45. $0.081 _____

46. $0.074 _____

47. $0.027 _____

48. $0.134 _____

49. $592.713 _____

50. $8,425.793 _____

51. $729.139 _____

The Value of Rounding Up

In the food service industry, it is essential to make intelligent financial decisions to have a profitable business or maintain a budget in a nonprofit organization. Industry leaders often say, "Don't step over pennies to pick up nickels." Instead of stepping over pennies, pick them up and use them to make a profit or balance a budget! Those pennies that are picked up will assist in having a financially successful operation.

For instance, an owner of a fast-food operation selling french fries determines that each portion of fries costs 0.134 cents to produce. Now that she has figured out the raw food cost, the owner can set the menu price. Even though it is mathematically incorrect to round up when the hundredth place (the mill) is 4 or less, it makes sense business-wise to round up. Rounding off correctly in mathematic terms would result in each portion of fries costing 13 cents. However, the fast-food owner decides to round up the portion of fries to 14 cents because it makes better business sense. She also sets the desired food cost percentage to 20 percent. The formula to determine the menu price is raw food cost divided by the desired food cost percentage. The 13-cent portion of fries divided by 20 percent would create a menu price of 65 cents for each portion of fries. But if the owner rounds up to the next penny (14 cents), the menu price is now determined to be 70 cents. Selling a million orders of french fries would result in an income gain of $50,000!

Discussion Question 2-1

Why is the mill useful when costing out recipes?

three

Addition, Subtraction, Multiplication, and Division

Objectives

At the completion of this chapter, the student should be able to:

1. Find sums.
2. Find differences.
3. Check subtraction by adding.
4. Find products using the multiplication table.
5. Use a step-by-step procedure to find products.
6. Check the accuracy of the multiplication product.
7. Find quotients.
8. Find the remainder.
9. Check the accuracy of the division quotient.

Key Words

addition	difference	multiplier	divisor
sum	trading (borrowing or carrying)	product	quotient
subtraction		subproducts	remainder
minuend	multiplication	division	
subtrahend	multiplicand	dividend	

In this chapter, the four most basic, essential math functions—addition, subtraction, multiplication, and division—will be covered. In these pages, you will not only revisit the foundation of all computation, but you will also see how these computations are integral to food service operations.

"In our profession, the knowledge and application of math must be used every day. Our owners, chefs, and managers must know how to set prices correctly on their menus. They have to take into account the cost of raw food, labor, and all of their other expenses in order to set a fair menu price for their customers and still make a profit. I am amazed at the individuals who think that they can be successful knowing only one aspect of the business . . . how to cook or how to manage, but don't know how to determine a fair menu price. We have members who have leases that are extremely expensive. Some members have to pay $1,200,000 each month on renting space for their restaurants. These successful members are constantly using their math knowledge to set menu prices in order to cover their rent as well as all other expenses. Math is a subject that you will use daily in your professional and individual life."

Rick Sampson
President and Chief Executive Officer
New York State Restaurant Association

The New York State Restaurant Association (NYSRA) represents more than 8,500 restaurants in the state, in locations ranging from Montauk to New York City to Niagara Falls. New York State enjoys the culinary diversity of more than 36,000 eating and drinking establishments that include all segments of the industry, from formal, white-tablecloth restaurants to fast-food franchises. The food service division of the hospitality profession makes up the largest part of the state's tourism industry, with sales of more than $20 billion a year. In 1999, the NYSRA established an educational foundation that oversees and implements the National Restaurant Association's ProStart program, which is taught in 55 facilities to over 1,500 students. Each year, NYSRA sponsors the International Restaurant and Foodservice Show in New York City. Also included in the NYSRA is the New York Nightlife Association, which serves all the bars, lounges, and clubs in New York City.

Mr. Sampson's career began with the NYSRA in 1976, and in 1994, he became the leader of the organization. Rick is also chairman of the 22-member Council of Licensed Beverage Industry. This group consists of any business that manages, produces, or sells alcoholic beverages in the state of New York. Mr. Sampson is also the treasurer of the New York State Wine and Grape Foundation, which represents more than 209 wineries in the state. In addition, he is one of the five members of the New York State Department of Labor Wage Board and a director of the New York State Hospitality and Tourism Association.

Addition

Addition can be considered one of the most frequently used math functions in business because it means an increase is taking place. In any business venture, the operator always wants an increase to show up in the form of a nice profit.

Addition is the act of putting things together, or combining things or units that are alike, to obtain a total quantity. This total quantity is called the **sum**. If you have $6.00 and are given $10.00, you have a total of $16.00. This simple addition problem can be written two different ways. For example:

$$\$6.00 + \$10.00 = \$16.00$$

Written with the numbers placed in a row or line, this is called the *horizontal position*. The horizontal position is seldom used in a problem involving large numbers because the way the numbers are positioned makes it difficult to calculate the answer. This same problem can also be written in what is called the *vertical* or *column position*.

$$
\begin{array}{r}
\$\ \ 6.00 \\
+\ \ 10.00 \\
\hline
\$\ 16.00
\end{array}
$$

In both instances, the plus sign, a symbol of operation, is used to indicate that the numbers are to be added. Figure 3–1 shows an example of how addition is used in food service.

To Insure Perfect Solutions

Addend plus Addend equals Sum

or

Addend
+ Addend
Sum

Figure 3–1
How many servings of cappuccino do we need? Simple addition is used in food service every day (2 + 2 = 4).
© Cengage Learning 2012

As another example, when serving a sirloin steak dinner, if there are 25 steaks ready to be served, 18 cooking on the broiler, and 125 stored in the refrigerator, the food service establishment has a total of 168 steaks on hand. Because all the units to be added are alike, it is unnecessary to write out what they are. Therefore, the addition can be written in either of the following ways:

$$25 + 18 + 125 = 168 \quad \text{(or)} \quad \begin{array}{r} 25 \\ 18 \\ +\ 125 \\ \hline 168 \end{array}$$

Computing addition problems manually may be considered a task of the past because almost everyone uses calculators today. Nevertheless, it is still wise to understand the rules and proper steps for solving addition problems without mechanical help because situations may arise when a calculator is unavailable or, worse yet, when the battery goes dead while you are performing an important calculation. It is never wise to depend entirely on calculators or adding machines. Absorb the information and examples presented in this chapter so that you can add rapidly and accurately if automation should ever fail you.

Guidelines

There are several basic guidelines that you should follow when solving mathematical problems to save time and improve accuracy.

Be Neat

If you are interested in a food service career, neatness is essential in both your physical appearance and personal hygiene. Neatness is also important in math. It does not require additional time to write neatly and carefully, placing each number in the proper column directly under the number above it, as shown here:

$$\begin{array}{r} 2\ 1\ 5\ 8 \\ 3\ 6 \\ 5\ 2\ 6 \\ 2\ 0\ 9 \\ 8\ 5 \\ +\ 1\ 9\ 2\ 2 \\ \hline 4\ 9\ 3\ 6 \end{array}$$

Neatness is also important when trading (carrying) numbers over from one column to the next. The sum of the ones column in the preceding problem is 36, not 6. The 3 (which actually means 30) is traded (carried over) to the tens column. When the trade (carryover) 3 is written, it is placed neatly at the top of the tens column so that it is not overlooked when counting that column. The sum of the tens column is 23 (actually 230). The 2 is traded (carried over) to the hundreds column.

To Insure Proper Solutions

Remember that each digit must be placed in the proper column to give it the proper value.

To Insure Perfect Solutions

Always write down trades (carryovers).

Again, place the 2 neatly over the top of the hundreds column. Follow this procedure for each column in the problem as shown here:

```
  ① ② ③
  2 1 5 8
      3 6
    5 2 6
    2 0 9
      8 5
+ 1 9 2 2
  4 9 3 6
```

Check Your Work

All work must be checked, even when using a calculator, to be sure your addition is correct. Mistakes can be made even when calculating automatically. Even if you find, through checking, that your work is always correct, you should still continue the practice. The penalty for making mathematical errors in the classroom is only a lower grade; the penalty for making errors in a food service operation can result in a monetary loss for both you (because you could lose your job) and your employer (because the business could fail altogether).

The common method of checking addition is to add the individual columns in reverse order. For example, if you originally added the columns from top to bottom, which is the usual practice, you can check your work by adding a second time, from bottom to top. Just reverse your procedure.

Increase Your Accuracy and Speed

Addition is often simplified if numbers are combined and then added. For example, in the problem $7 + 3 + 8 + 2 + 5 + 3 = 28$, the addition is greatly simplified by combining 7 and 3 into 10, and 8 and 2 into 10, and then adding the two 10s to make 20. Adding the remaining numbers (5 and 3) gives 8, which, added to 20, makes a total of 28.

Eliminate unnecessary steps when adding. One method of increasing your speed and accuracy is that instead of thinking 7 plus 3 equals 10, automatically see the 7 and 3 combination as 10. When adding the problem in the previous paragraph, do not think that 10 plus 10 equals 20, plus 5 equals 25, plus 3 equals 28. Think 10, 20, 28.

If you follow these guidelines, they will help you ensure the accuracy and speed that are required for any type of addition problem, especially those related to food service. Some of these guidelines, such as neatness and checking your work, apply to all arithmetic operations.

To Insure Perfect Solutions

When using a calculator or computer, you need to check the numbers that you input to make certain an error doesn't occur in the entry process.

Practice Problems 3-1   Addition

Find the sum of each of the following addition problems. Use the methods and guidelines suggested in this chapter. To improve your math skills, calculate these problems manually and then check your work.

1.
```
    5
  + 8
```

2.
```
    4
    7
    6
  + 3
```

3. 2 + 9 + 1 + 18 = _____

4. 24 + 19 + 12 + 28 = _____

5.
```
    148
  + 699
```

6.
```
    338
    225
  + 648
```

7.
```
  $64.19
   49.08
   32.27
 + 19.53
```

8.
```
    312
    422
    345
    239
  + 751
```

9.
```
  $425.92
   333.33
   268.21
   599.99
 +111.06
```

10.
```
       8
      28
     335
    2765
     222
     589
      17
     259
   + 126
```

11.
```
  $57.01
   22.98
   36.36
   99.12
    1.03
   41.22
   67.19
   18.70
   26.98
 + 11.75
```

12.
```
  $555.25
   216.11
   140.18
   310.20
   713.14
   726.12
   289.82
   326.22
   129.10
 + 222.12
```

13. If a person's guest check includes an omelette @ $6.99, French toast @ $6.99, and coffee @ $2.25, how much is the total check? _____

14. When preparing a fruit salad bowl, the following items were used, at the following costs: oranges @ $1.98, apples @ $0.79, grapes @ $0.92, bananas @ $1.69, strawberries @ $2.68, peaches @ $1.47, and pineapple @ $0.98. What was the total cost of the fruit salad bowl? _____

15. The restaurant had 199 orders of chicken in the freezer, 110 in the walk-in refrigerator, and 59 in the reach-in refrigerator. How many orders of chicken did it have on hand?

_____

Subtraction

Subtraction means to take away. It is the removal of one number of things from another number of things (see Figure 3–2).

The word *subtract* is very seldom used except in its mathematical sense. The popular word used in the business world is *deduct,* which also means to take away. For example, instead of "He *subtracted* a discount of $2.00 from my bill," the statement would be "He *deducted* a discount of $2.00 from my bill."

If you have $12.00 and spend $8.25, the subtraction problem is written as follows:

$$\begin{array}{r} \$12.00 \\ -\ 8.25 \\ \hline \$\ 3.75 \end{array}$$

The minus sign (−) must always be used so that the problem is not confused with another mathematical operation.

Each of the factors in subtraction has a name. The original number, before subtraction or before anything is removed, is called the **minuend.** In the example above, the minuend is $12.00. The number removed from the minuend is called the **subtrahend.** Finally, the amount left over, or remaining after the problem is completed, is called the **difference.**

Figure 3–2
Subtraction is taking place when a serving portion is removed from a whole item (10 − 2 = 8).
© Cengage Learning 2012

$$\begin{array}{rl} 1585 & \text{Minuend} \\ -\ 742 & \text{Subtrahend} \\ \hline 843 & \text{Difference} \end{array}$$

Trading (Borrowing or Carrying)

Subtraction frequently requires **trading (borrowing or carrying).** When trading, add 10 to the ones column of the minuend as the example here illustrates. At the same time, diminish the number in the tens column by 1. Although the minuend is usually a larger number than the subtrahend, a particular digit in the minuend may be less than the digit beneath it in the subtrahend, so trading (borrowing) is required. Example: 1,723 − 688 = 1,038. When this problem is set up in the vertical position, it looks like this:

thousands	hundreds	tens	ones	
1	7	2	3	Minuend
−	6	8	8	Subtrahend
1	0	3	5	Difference

To Insure Perfect Solutions

Minuend minus Subtrahend equals Difference

or

Minuend
− Subtrahend
Difference

To Insure Perfect Solutions

Always write down trades (carryovers).

The minuend (1,723) is clearly a larger number than the subtrahend (688). However, the digit 8 in the ones column of the subtrahend is larger than the digit 3 in the ones column of the minuend. Since 8 cannot be subtracted from 3, it becomes necessary to trade (borrow) from the tens column.

To indicate that a 10 has been traded (borrowed), cross out the 2 in the tens column and write 1 above it. If this step is neglected, you may sometimes forget that you traded (borrowed).

```
      1 13
  1 7 2 3
-   6 8 8
```

Add the traded (borrowed) 10 to the 3 in the ones column, which increases the 3 to 13. Then subtract 13 − 8 = 5. The 5 is written beneath the bar in the ones column.

```
      1 13
  1 7 2 3
-   6 8 8
        5
```

In the tens column, 8 cannot be subtracted from 1 (actually 80 from 10), so it is necessary to trade (borrow) 100 from the hundreds column. This is done by crossing out the numeral 7 in the hundreds column and writing 6 above it.

```
   6 11 13
  1 7 2 3
-   6 8 8
        5
```

Return to the tens column, and subtract 8 from 11 (actually 80 from 110) to get 3 (actually 30). Write the 3 in the tens column beneath the bar.

```
   6 11 13
  1 7 2 3
-   6 8 8
      3 5
```

Moving to the hundreds column, 6 can be subtracted from 6 (which is actually 600 from 600). Even though nothing will remain, a zero is used to hold a place. Trading (borrowing), therefore, is unnecessary in this column.

```
   6 11 13
  1 7 2 3
-   6 8 8
    0 3 5
```

The problem is completed by bringing down the 1 that remains in the thousands column. The completed problem appears here:

```
   6 11 13
  1 7 2 3
-   6 8 8
  1 0 3 5
```

Checking Subtraction

Checking any math problem is always a wise step to take, even when using a calculator, because errors are so easily made. The common way of checking a subtraction answer is to add the subtrahend and the difference. The sum of these two numbers should equal the minuend.

Subtraction:

```
  3 6 4 2   Minuend
- 2 1 3 2   Subtrahend
  1 5 1 0   Difference
```

Check:

```
  2 1 3 2   Subtrahend
+ 1 5 1 0   Difference
  3 6 4 2   Minuend
```

Practice Problems 3–2   Subtraction

Find the difference in the following subtraction problems. Calculate these problems manually and then check your work.

16. 888 − 271 = _____   17.   688 − 520 = _____

18. 5,892 − 1,538 = _____

19.   743
     − 526

20.   736
     − 619

21.   5,197
   − 2,058

22. $36.22
   − 19.78

23. $76.32
   − 56.54

24. $127.86
  − 49.87

25. $7,333.64
  − 6,132.45

26. $462,004.01
  − 86,526.09

27. The bill for a wedding party came to $1,585.21. The bride and groom were given a discount of $121.00 because the guaranteed number of people attended. What was the total bill?

_____

28. The restaurant thought it had 32 live lobsters on hand. Taking a quick inventory, it was discovered that 9 were dead. How many live lobsters did the restaurant have left?

_____

29. A restaurant had 240 chickens in the freezer. It used 31 for a special party. How many did it have left? _____

30. A restaurant purchased 275 pounds of sirloin. A total of 48 pounds were lost in boning and trimming. How many pounds were left?

_____

To Insure Perfect Solutions

Multiplier times Multiplicand equals Product

or

Multiplier
× Multiplicand
Product

Multiplication

Multiplication is another math operation where an increase takes place. Methods that bring forth an increase, such as addition, seem to be most popular, especially if the increase is spelled "profit" or carries a dollar sign. Multiplication can be thought of as a shortcut for a certain type of addition problem. In **multiplication,** a whole number is added to itself a specified amount of times. For example, $4 \times 2 = 8$ is another way of expressing $4 + 4 = 8$. The number 4 is added to itself two times.

Because a relationship exists between addition and multiplication, it does not matter which operation is used in simple problems such as the one cited here. However, when the problem consists of problems involving large numbers (such as $4{,}531 \times 6{,}580 = ?$), addition is an impractical way of solving it. This is when multiplication becomes useful as a shortcut for addition. Working out the preceding problem is quite lengthy using multiplication, as shown in the following example. Now just imagine what would be involved if we tried to solve the problem using addition:

```
           6580
    ×      4531
           6580
          19740
         32900
        26320
       29813980
```

Each number involved in the multiplication process has a name. The number that is added to itself (the number 4 in the example $4 \times 2 = 8$) is called the **multiplicand** (which means "going to be multiplied"). The number representing the amount of times that the multiplicand is to be added to itself is called the **multiplier** (the number 2 in the example). The result of multiplying the multiplicand by the multiplier is called the **product.** The product in our example is 8.

The following example gives the names and functions of the various numbers involved in the multiplication operation:

```
      362    Multiplicand
    ×  32    Multiplier
      724    Subproduct
    10860    Subproduct
    11584    Product
```

Function	Name
Number to be added to itself	Multiplicand
Number of times to be added to itself	Multiplier
Product of the ones column	Subproduct
Product of the tens column	Subproduct
Final result (answer)	Product

In this example, subproducts are shown. **Subproducts** (*sub* meaning "under, below, or before"; *product* being the result of multiplying) occur whenever the multiplier consists of two or more digits. In this case, the multiplier is 32. The first subproduct (724) is the result of multiplying 362 × 2. The second subproduct (10,860) is the result of multiplying 362 × 30. The zero at the end of this sub-product is not normally put into the answer because 4 + 0 = 4. It does not affect the outcome of the problem, but it is shown here only to illustrate that the product of multiplying 362 × 30 is 10,860 and not 1,086. It also helps keep all the digits in their proper columns (ones in the ones column, tens in the tens column, and so forth), as mentioned earlier in relation to subtraction.

Once all the subproducts are determined, they are added together to obtain the final total or product (in this example, 11,584). The multiplication sign (also called the times sign) is always used in a multiplication problem to distinguish it from any other type of arithmetic operation.

The Multiplication Table

It has now been demonstrated through examples that multiplication is a shortcut for certain types of addition problems. A shortcut method is valuable only if it can be used efficiently and accurately. The key to using multiplication efficiently is the multiplication table (see Figure 3–3, showing products up to 12 × 12). Accuracy depends on your efforts and how well you have developed your multiplication skills.

Study the multiplication table until you have memorized it. To test how well you have memorized this table, write each problem on one side of an index card and the product on the other side. You should be able to look at a problem and know its answer within five seconds, without looking at the other side.

To Insure Perfect Solutions

Remember the old saying: practice makes perfect.

1	×	1	=	1	5	×	1	=	5	9	×	1	=	9

$1 \times 1 = 1$
$1 \times 2 = 2$
$1 \times 3 = 3$
$1 \times 4 = 4$
$1 \times 5 = 5$
$1 \times 6 = 6$
$1 \times 7 = 7$
$1 \times 8 = 8$
$1 \times 9 = 9$
$1 \times 10 = 10$
$1 \times 11 = 11$
$1 \times 12 = 12$

$5 \times 1 = 5$
$5 \times 2 = 10$
$5 \times 3 = 15$
$5 \times 4 = 20$
$5 \times 5 = 25$
$5 \times 6 = 30$
$5 \times 7 = 35$
$5 \times 8 = 40$
$5 \times 9 = 45$
$5 \times 10 = 50$
$5 \times 11 = 55$
$5 \times 12 = 60$

$9 \times 1 = 9$
$9 \times 2 = 18$
$9 \times 3 = 27$
$9 \times 4 = 36$
$9 \times 5 = 45$
$9 \times 6 = 54$
$9 \times 7 = 63$
$9 \times 8 = 72$
$9 \times 9 = 81$
$9 \times 10 = 90$
$9 \times 11 = 99$
$9 \times 12 = 108$

$2 \times 1 = 2$
$2 \times 2 = 4$
$2 \times 3 = 6$
$2 \times 4 = 8$
$2 \times 5 = 10$
$2 \times 6 = 12$
$2 \times 7 = 14$
$2 \times 8 = 16$
$2 \times 9 = 18$
$2 \times 10 = 20$
$2 \times 11 = 22$
$2 \times 12 = 24$

$6 \times 1 = 6$
$6 \times 2 = 12$
$6 \times 3 = 18$
$6 \times 4 = 24$
$6 \times 5 = 30$
$6 \times 6 = 36$
$6 \times 7 = 42$
$6 \times 8 = 48$
$6 \times 9 = 54$
$6 \times 10 = 60$
$6 \times 11 = 66$
$6 \times 12 = 72$

$10 \times 1 = 10$
$10 \times 2 = 20$
$10 \times 3 = 30$
$10 \times 4 = 40$
$10 \times 5 = 50$
$10 \times 6 = 60$
$10 \times 7 = 70$
$10 \times 8 = 80$
$10 \times 9 = 90$
$10 \times 10 = 100$
$10 \times 11 = 110$
$10 \times 12 = 120$

$3 \times 1 = 3$
$3 \times 2 = 6$
$3 \times 3 = 9$
$3 \times 4 = 12$
$3 \times 5 = 15$
$3 \times 6 = 18$
$3 \times 7 = 21$
$3 \times 8 = 24$
$3 \times 9 = 27$
$3 \times 10 = 30$
$3 \times 11 = 33$
$3 \times 12 = 36$

$7 \times 1 = 7$
$7 \times 2 = 14$
$7 \times 3 = 21$
$7 \times 4 = 28$
$7 \times 5 = 35$
$7 \times 6 = 42$
$7 \times 7 = 49$
$7 \times 8 = 56$
$7 \times 9 = 63$
$7 \times 10 = 70$
$7 \times 11 = 77$
$7 \times 12 = 84$

$11 \times 1 = 11$
$11 \times 2 = 22$
$11 \times 3 = 33$
$11 \times 4 = 44$
$11 \times 5 = 55$
$11 \times 6 = 66$
$11 \times 7 = 77$
$11 \times 8 = 88$
$11 \times 9 = 99$
$11 \times 10 = 110$
$11 \times 11 = 121$
$11 \times 12 = 132$

$4 \times 1 = 4$
$4 \times 2 = 8$
$4 \times 3 = 12$
$4 \times 4 = 16$
$4 \times 5 = 20$
$4 \times 6 = 24$
$4 \times 7 = 28$
$4 \times 8 = 32$
$4 \times 9 = 36$
$4 \times 10 = 40$
$4 \times 11 = 44$
$4 \times 12 = 48$

$8 \times 1 = 8$
$8 \times 2 = 16$
$8 \times 3 = 24$
$8 \times 4 = 32$
$8 \times 5 = 40$
$8 \times 6 = 48$
$8 \times 7 = 56$
$8 \times 8 = 64$
$8 \times 9 = 72$
$8 \times 10 = 80$
$8 \times 11 = 88$
$8 \times 12 = 96$

$12 \times 1 = 12$
$12 \times 2 = 24$
$12 \times 3 = 36$
$12 \times 4 = 48$
$12 \times 5 = 60$
$12 \times 6 = 72$
$12 \times 7 = 84$
$12 \times 8 = 96$
$12 \times 9 = 108$
$12 \times 10 = 120$
$12 \times 11 = 132$
$12 \times 12 = 144$

Figure 3–3
Multiplication table of numbers from 1 through 12.

1	2	3	4	5	6	7	8	9	10	11	12	13	14	15	16	17	18	19	20	21	22	23	24	25
2	4	6	8	10	12	14	16	18	20	22	24	26	28	30	32	34	36	38	40	42	44	46	48	50
3	6	9	12	15	18	21	24	27	30	33	36	39	42	45	48	51	54	57	60	63	66	69	72	75
4	8	12	16	20	24	28	32	36	40	44	48	52	56	60	64	68	72	76	80	84	88	92	96	100
5	10	15	20	25	30	35	40	45	50	55	60	65	70	75	80	85	90	95	100	105	110	115	120	125
6	12	18	24	30	36	42	48	54	60	66	72	78	84	90	96	102	108	114	120	126	132	138	144	150
7	14	21	28	35	42	49	56	63	70	77	84	91	98	105	112	119	126	133	140	147	154	161	168	175
8	16	24	32	40	48	56	64	72	80	88	96	104	112	120	128	136	144	152	160	168	176	184	192	200
9	18	27	36	45	54	63	72	81	90	99	108	117	126	135	144	153	162	171	180	189	198	207	216	225
10	20	30	40	50	60	70	80	90	100	110	120	130	140	150	160	170	180	190	200	210	220	230	240	250
11	22	33	44	55	66	77	88	99	110	121	132	143	154	165	176	187	198	209	220	231	242	253	264	275
12	24	36	48	60	72	84	96	108	120	132	144	156	168	180	192	204	216	228	240	252	264	276	288	300
13	26	39	52	65	78	91	104	117	130	143	156	169	182	195	208	221	234	247	260	273	286	299	312	325
14	28	42	56	70	84	98	112	126	140	154	168	182	196	210	224	238	252	266	280	294	308	322	336	350
15	30	45	60	75	90	105	120	135	150	165	180	195	210	225	240	255	270	285	300	315	330	345	360	375
16	32	48	64	80	96	112	128	144	160	176	192	208	224	240	256	272	288	304	320	336	352	368	384	400
17	34	51	68	85	102	119	136	153	170	187	204	221	238	255	272	289	306	323	340	357	374	391	408	425
18	36	54	72	90	108	126	144	162	180	198	216	234	252	270	288	306	324	342	360	378	396	414	432	450
19	38	57	76	95	114	133	152	171	190	209	228	247	266	285	304	323	342	361	380	399	418	437	456	475
20	40	60	80	100	120	140	160	180	200	220	240	260	280	300	320	340	360	380	400	420	440	460	480	500
21	42	63	84	105	126	147	168	189	210	231	252	273	294	315	336	357	378	399	420	441	462	483	504	525
22	44	66	88	110	132	154	176	198	220	242	264	286	308	330	352	374	396	418	440	462	484	506	528	550
23	46	69	92	115	138	161	184	207	230	253	276	299	322	345	368	391	414	437	460	483	506	529	552	575
24	48	72	96	120	144	168	192	216	240	264	288	312	336	360	384	408	432	456	480	504	528	552	576	600
25	50	75	100	125	150	175	200	225	250	275	300	325	350	375	400	425	450	475	500	525	550	575	600	625
1	2	3	4	5	6	7	8	9	10	11	12	13	14	15	16	17	18	19	20	21	22	23	24	25

Figure 3–4
Multiplication table of numbers from 1 through 25.
© Cengage Learning 2012

Another method of presenting the multiplication table is shown in Figure 3–4. This unique table gives the products of numbers up to $25 \times 25 = 625$. It is relatively simple to use. For example, to find the product of 8×9, locate the number 8 in the vertical (up-and-down) column to the far left. Then move your finger to the right until you reach the 9 located in the horizontal (left-to-right) column at the top of the table. The number 72 is in the place where the 8 column and the 9 column intersect. Therefore, 72 is the product of 8×9. Look one place below the 72 and find the number 81. This is the product of 9×9. Drop down another place to find that $10 \times 9 = 90$.

Simplifying Multiplication by a Step-by-Step Procedure

This multiplication example is intended to illustrate the step-by-step procedures involved in finding a product. As mentioned earlier, multiplication is a variation of, and has a very close association with, addition. In this example, it will be shown that the product of the problem is the result of adding the subproducts of each step of the problem.

To Insure Perfect Solutions

Placing a card or sheet of paper across the multiplication table horizontally is helpful in locating the products of the various numbers.

Example:

$$\begin{array}{r} 924 \\ \times\ 65 \end{array}$$

Ones Column:

Step 1.	$5 \times 4 =$	20
Step 2.	$5 \times 20 =$	100
Step 3.	$5 \times 900 =$	4,500
	Subproduct of ones column	4,620

Tens Column:

Step 4.	$60 \times 4 =$	240
Step 5.	$60 \times 20 =$	1,200
Step 6.	$60 \times 900 =$	54,000
	Subproduct of tens column	55,440

Add the subproducts:

Step 7.	$4,620 + 55,440 =$	60,060 (Product)

This example shows the steps in finding the product of 924×65. Generally when the problem is worked, the unneeded zeros are eliminated but carryover numbers are used, as shown in the following example:

9 2 4	Multiplicand
× 6 5	Multiplier
4 6 2 0	Subproduct of ones column
5 5 4 4	Subproduct of tens column
6 0 0 6 0	Product

2 is the carryover number for the ones column.
1 is the carryover number for the tens column.

Notice that the subproduct of the ones column in both methods of working the problem is 4,620. The same is true for the subproduct of the tens column, 55,440. The zero is left off the subproduct in the second method because its only purpose is to hold a place. So long as the other figures are in their proper places, the zero is unnecessary.

Checking the Product

The accepted and common method of checking the accuracy of a multiplication product is to invert, or switch, the multiplicand and the multiplier and work the problem from a reverse position.

Original Multiplication

3 4 8	Multiplicand
× 5 4	Multiplier
1 3 9 2	Subproduct
1 7 4 0	Subproduct
1 8 7 9 2	Product

Problem Checked

5 4	Multiplier
× 3 4 8	Multiplicand
4 3 2	Subproduct
2 1 6	Subproduct
1 6 2	Subproduct
1 8 7 9 2	Product

If the problem is worked accurately in both instances, the products will be the same. If two different products are obtained, invert the problem back to its original form and try again. Today, checking can be done on a calculator. However, it is a good practice to work problems through manually and then double-check the work on a calculator. Remember that doing problems manually sharpens your math skills, and that in additionally, times will arise when you must function without automation.

Guidelines

A few guidelines are offered here to help provide speed and accuracy to multiplication work.

Be Neat

Neatness is very important, as pointed out earlier in this chapter about addition. The customary method of multiplying eliminates end zeroes (zeroes that appear at the end of a number), and therefore you must be very careful to write each number in its proper place.

Be Careful with Carryover Numbers

Remember that carryover numbers are added to the product of the two numbers being multiplied. The carryover numbers are not multiplied, as pointed out in the following example.

$$
\begin{array}{r}
④ ⑤ \\
7\ 5\ 8 \\
\times\ 7 \\
\hline
5\ 3\ 0\ 6
\end{array}
$$

The first numbers to multiply are $7 \times 8 = 56$. Write the 6 in the ones column beneath the bar and carry the 5 over to the tens column. Next, $7 \times 5 = 35$. To this, we add the carryover number 5; $35 + 5 = 40$. Write the 0 in the tens column beneath the bar and carry the 4 to the hundreds column. The next step in proper order is $7 \times 7 = 49$. To this, add the carryover number 4; $49 + 4 = 53$. Write the 3 in the hundreds column beneath the bar and the 5 in the thousands column beneath the bar; $7 \times 758 = 5,306$.

To Insure Perfect Solutions
When the multiplier consists of two or more numerals, be careful to note the carryover numbers.

To Determine the Product Quickly when Multiplying by 10, 100, 1000, and so forth, Add the Correct Number of Zeroes to the Multiplicand

For example: $10 \times 222 = 2,220$. Because there is one zero in 10, add one zero to 222 to obtain the product. When multiplying by 100, two zeroes are added; $100 \times 222 = 22,200$. When multiplying by 1000, three zeroes are added.

Use Units in the Product when They Are Used in the Multiplicand

A unit was explained in a previous chapter as a single quantity of like things. Most multiplication problems in the world of work involve some sort of designated unit. If a chicken-processing plant has 15 separate pens with 45 chickens each, how many chickens does it have on hand? ($45 \times 15 = 675$) The product is not simply 675, but 675 chickens. This type of unit does not have to be written next to the multiplicand when working the problem, but remember what type of units are being multiplied so the result will be a certain number of those designated units.

Practice Problems 3-3 Multiplication

Find the answer to the following multiplication problems. If units are indicated, write the unit in the answer. Do these problems manually and then check your work. Round answers to the hundredths place.

31.   227
         × 4

32.   5,682
         × 76

33.   4,119
         × 37

34.   372
        × 121

35.   8,233
        × 1,956

36. $355.46
         × 32

37. $7,982.50
         × 45

38. $8,421.55
         × 1.69

39. A side of beef weighs 323 pounds and costs $4.59 per pound. How much does the side cost?

_____

40. If a foresaddle of veal weighs 46 pounds and costs $7.60 per pound, what is the total cost?

_____

41. Jim's catering truck gets 15 miles to every gallon of gas. How many miles can it travel on 132 gallons of gas? _____

42. When preparing meat loaf, it is required that 4 pounds of ground beef go into each loaf. How many pounds of ground beef must be ordered if you want to prepare 65 loaves?

_____

43. Ribs of beef weigh 24 pounds and cost $3.98 per pound. What is the total cost of the ribs? _____

44. A wedding reception is catered for 575 people. The caterer charges $25.75 per person. What is the total bill? _____

45. A cook earns $120.00 a day. How much does the cook earn in a year if she works 318 days? _____

Division

Division is the act of separating a whole quantity into parts. It is a sharing of that whole part, a process of dividing one number by another. Division is basically the method of finding out how many times one number is contained in another number. It is, in a sense, a reverse of multiplication, as shown here:

Multiplication	$5 \times 8 = 40$
Division	$40 \div 8 = 5$
	$40 \div 5 = 8$

Look at division from another viewpoint. Assume that your employer promises to pay you $8.00 per hour. After putting in eight difficult hours, you receive a check for only $56.00 (before deductions, of course). Just looking at the total, you know something is wrong. A simple division problem will show you that $56 \div 8 = 7. Either you were being paid only $7.00 an hour, or you were paid only for seven hours. Using division can thus help you determine that a mistake was made.

Division is frequently used in the food service business because foods are being divided constantly. A strip sirloin is divided into steaks, vegetables into portions, cakes into servings, and so forth (see Figure 3–5, which shows another example). An example illustrating the division of food can be seen by observing how a solution is found to the following problem:

A #10 can of applesauce contains about 105 ounces. How many guests can be served if each guest receives a 3-ounce portion?

$$105 \div 3 = 35$$

According to this equation, 35 guests can be served from the 105-ounce can of applesauce. Using division has helped the cook to know how many cans must be opened when serving a certain number of people.

To Insure Perfect Solutions

Dividend divided by Divisor equals Quotient

$$\text{Divisor}\overline{)\text{Dividend}}^{\text{Quotient}}$$

Figure 3–5
Division is the method of operation used when dividing roll dough into units.
© Cengage Learning 2012

To Insure Perfect Solutions

When dividing using the calculator, enter the dividend *first*. For their students, the authors have the students remember a BLT, or a bacon, lettuce, and tomato sandwich, to help them recognize what number is the dividend.

Quotient
Divisor)Dividend

In the first illustration here, the dividend is in what the authors call the Box, representing the word *Bacon* or *B*.

Dividend ÷ Divisor = Quotient

The second illustration shows the dividend on the left of the equation, representing the word *Lettuce* or *L*.

$$\frac{\text{Dividend}}{\text{Divisor}}$$

The third illustration shows the dividend on the top of the equation, representing the word *Tomato* or *T*.

Therefore, if readers think of a bacon, lettuce, and tomato sandwich or a BLT, it will assist them in remembering what number is entered into the calculator first when dividing.

In division, the number to be divided is called the **dividend.** In the problem $80 ÷ 4 = 20$, the number 80 is the dividend. The term for the number by which the dividend is divided (the number 4, in this example) is the **divisor.** The result of dividing the dividend by the divisor is called the **quotient.** The quotient in this example is the number 20.

In situations where the divisor is not contained in the dividend an equal or exact number of times, the figure left over is called the **remainder.** For example: $83 ÷ 4 = 20$ with 3 left over, because 4 is too large to be contained in 3. In this problem, 3 is the remainder.

Several division signs can be used when working division problems. Usually the sign selected depends on how long or difficult the problem may be. Up to this point in our examples of the division operation, division has been indicated by a bar with a dot above and below ($÷$). This symbol is mainly used when the problem is simple, or when first stating a division problem that is to be solved. Simple problems are also written using the fraction bar. For example, $84 ÷ 7 = 12$ can also be written $^{84}/_7 = 12$.

For what is known as a long-division problem, the accepted sign to use has the appearance of a closed parenthesis sign with a straight line coming out of the top, like this:

$$\overline{)}$$

Step-by-Step Division

When reviewing basic mathematical operations, division is usually discussed last because it involves both multiplication and subtraction in its operation (including carryover numbers and trading). For example: $8,295 ÷ 15 = ?$

Because this problem would be considered a lengthy one, the long-division form is used:

$$\begin{array}{c}\text{thousands hundreds tens ones}\\ \text{Divisor} \quad 15\overline{)8\ 2\ 9\ 5}\end{array} \quad \begin{array}{l}\text{Quotient goes here}\\ \text{Dividend}\end{array}$$

A long-division problem is started from the left, rather than from the right, as in addition, subtraction, and multiplication. The first step is to estimate how many times 15 is contained in 82 (which is actually 8,200). You know that $5 × 15 = 75$, so your first estimate is 5. The 5 is written above the division bar in the hundreds place:

$$\begin{array}{c}\text{thousands hundreds tens ones}\\ 5\\ 15\overline{)8\ 2\ 9\ 5}\end{array} \quad \begin{array}{l}\text{Start of quotient}\\ \text{Dividend}\end{array}$$

To make sure that 5 is the correct figure, it is multiplied by 15. The product is 75. The 7 is written in the thousands column, under the 8, and the 5 in the hundreds column, under the 2. Then 75 is subtracted from 82. If the difference is less than 15, the estimate of 5 in the hundreds place of the quotient is correct. $82 - 75 = 7$. Because 7 is less than 15, the estimate is correct:

```
      thousands
      hundreds
      tens
      ones
         5
15)8  2  9  5      Dividend
   7  5            Product of 5 × 15
      7            (82 − 75 = 7)
```

The next step is to bring the 9 in the tens place of the dividend down to the right of the 7, giving 79. We estimate that 79 contains 15 only 5 times. $79 - 75 = 4$, which is smaller than 15. (Note that sometimes the estimate is too low or too high. When this happens, the estimate must be increased or decreased accordingly.)

So far, our problem has advanced to this point:

```
      5  5
15)8  2  9  5      Dividend
   7  5
      7  9
      7  5         Product of 5 × 15
         4         (79 − 75 = 4)
```

The next step is to bring down the figure 5 from the ones column and place it to the right of the 4 (which is left over from subtracting 75 from 79). Again, estimate how many times 45 contains 15. It is easy to see that 3 should be the estimated figure, making the problem come out even. The completed problem is shown as follows:

```
      5  5  3      Quotient
15)8  2  9  5      Dividend
   7  5
      7  9
      7  5
         4  5
         4  5      Product of 3 × 15
```

The Remainder

As explained earlier, the figure in a division problem that may be left over when the dividend does not contain the divisor exactly is called the remainder. For example:

```
                 6  5      Quotient
Divisor    33)2  1  6  3   Dividend
              1  9  8      Product of 6 × 33 = 198
              1  8  3
              1  6  5      Product of 5 × 33 = 165
                 1  8      Remainder
```

At this point, there are no more numerals to bring down from the dividend, and 33 cannot be contained in the number 18. Therefore, the leftover 18 is called the remainder. Therefore, the solution is written as 65 R18. The remainder can also be written in fractional or decimal form, as shown here:

$$2{,}163 \div 33 = 65^{18}/_{33} \text{ (a fraction) or } 65.545 \text{ (a decimal)}$$

Checking Division

The common method of checking division is to multiply the quotient by the divisor. The product of multiplying the divisor and quotient should be the same as the dividend:

```
Division:                    1 3 2      Quotient
              Divisor    22)2 9 0 4      Dividend
                           2 2
                          _____
                             7 0
                             6 6
                            _____
                               4 4
                               4 4
                              _____
                                  0      Remainder
```

```
To check the division:      1 3 2       Quotient
                          ×     2 2      Divisor
                          _____
                            2 6 4
                          2 6 4
                          _____
                          2 9 0 4        Dividend
```

When the quotient includes a remainder, multiply the quotient by the divisor as shown in the previous example, and then add the remainder to the product:

```
                             2 7 5       Quotient
              Divisor    31)8 5 4 4       Dividend
                           6 2
                          _____
                           2 3 4
                           2 1 7
                          _____
                             1 7 4
                             1 5 5
                            _____
                               1 9       Remainder
```

To check the division with a remainder present:

```
                             2 7 5       Quotient
                          ×     3 1      Divisor
                          _____
                             2 7 5
                           8 2 5
                          _____
                           8 5 2 5       Product
                          +     1 9      Remainder
                          _____
                           8 5 4 4       Dividend
```

Practice Problems 3–4   Division

Find the quotient for the following division problems. Calculate these problems manually and then check all work. Round off all answers to the hundredths place.

46. $60 \div 15 =$ _____

47. $96 \div 3 =$ _____

48. $9\overline{)990}$

49. $8\overline{)1,696}$

50. $38\overline{)3,165}$

51. $58\overline{)896.74}$

52. $17\overline{)596.25}$

53. $344\overline{)988.42}$

54. A 480-pound side of beef is purchased for $1,250.40. What is the cost per pound?

_____

55. In one week, the Prime Time Catering Company's delivery truck traveled 336 miles. It used 24 gallons of gasoline. How many miles did it average per gallon? _____

56. The chef at the Starlight Restaurant earns $45,000 per year. If this chef works 48 weeks per year, how much does she earn in one week? _____

57. The preparation cook at the Blue Star Restaurant works five days a week and earns $356.00 per week. How much does he earn in one day? _____

58. A restaurant orders 406 pounds of pork loins. Each loin weighs 14 pounds. How many loins are contained in the shipment?

_____

59. The Deluxe Catering Company's delivery truck averages 13 miles per gallon of gasoline. During 30 days of operation, the truck travels 2,028 miles. How much gasoline is used? _____

60. One hundred twenty-eight fluid ounces of orange juice are contained in one gallon. How many 8-ounce glasses of juice can be served?

_____

Discussion Question 3-1

Why should a person in the food service profession know how to solve these problems without using a calculator or a computer?

Fractions, Decimals, Ratios, and Percents

Objectives

At the completion of this chapter, the student should be able to:

1. Simplify (or express) a fraction in lower terms without changing the value of the fraction.
2. Add, subtract, multiply, and divide fractions.
3. Change fractions to decimals.
4. Write decimals and mix decimal fractions in words.
5. Write numbers as decimals.
6. Find sums, differences, products, and quotients in decimal problems.
7. Solve problems by using given ratios.
8. Write common fractions as percents.
9. Write percents as common fractions, whole numbers, or mixed numbers.
10. Find the percents of meat cuts.

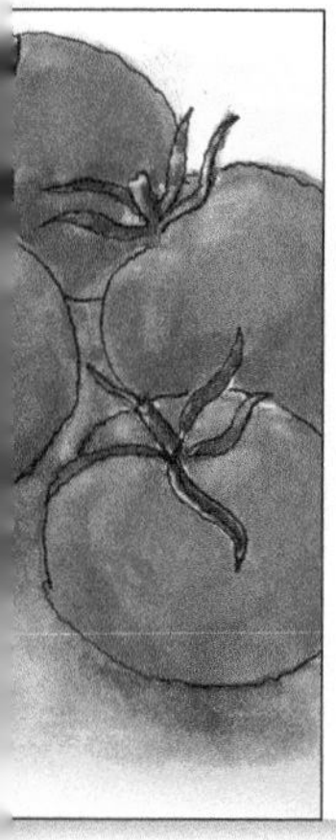

Key Words

fractions	improper fractions	least common denominator	mixed decimal fractions
numerator	mixed number	decimal	ciphers
denominator	simplification	decimal fractions	ratio
proper fractions	like fractions	decimal point	proportion
factor	unlike fractions		percent

Now that you have learned about the roles that addition, subtraction, multiplication, and division play in food service operations, it is time to learn about the equally important roles played by fractions, decimals, ratios, and percents.

Fractions

Fractions are sometimes used in a restaurant operation. They may play an important part when converting standard recipes, dealing with the contents of a scoop or dipper, and dividing certain items into serving portions, but compared to most other math operations, the use of fractions is limited. This does not mean, however, that the knowledge of fractions is unimportant. Situations will occur in your workplace and everyday life where knowledge of this subject will be required, so review this section just as intensely as the others.

A **fraction** indicates one or more equal parts of a unit. For example, a cake is usually divided into eight equal pieces. (See Figure 4–1.) If this is done, the following statements are true about the parts or slices of the cake:

One part is 1/8 of the cake.

Three parts are 3/8 of the cake.

Seven parts are 7/8 of the cake.

Eight parts are 8/8 of the cake, or the whole cake.

Another example of this same teaching tool is the division of a 9-inch pie into slices. A 9-inch pie is usually cut into seven equal servings. In this case, the fractional parts would be a little different, but the same theory for the sliced cake would hold true:

One part is 1/7 of the pie.

Three parts are 3/7 of the pie.

Six parts are 6/7 of the pie.

Seven parts are 7/7 of the pie, or the whole pie.

To Insure Perfect Solutions

The parts of a fraction are the numerator (top number) and the denominator (bottom number). Think of the letter *d* in denominator as the *d* in down (in other words, the bottom number):

$$\frac{\text{Numerator}}{\text{Denominator}}$$

Figure 4–1
An example of a fractional part is shown when cutting a cake. Usually $\frac{1}{8}$ is a serving portion.
© Cengage Learning 2012

Because fractions indicate the division of a whole unit into equal parts, the numeral placed above the division or fraction bar indicates the number of fractional units taken and is called the **numerator.** The numeral below the bar represents the number of equal parts into which the unit is divided and is called the **denominator.** Thus, if a cantaloupe is cut into eight equal wedges, but only five of those wedges are used on a fruit plate, the wedges used are represented by the fraction $\frac{5}{8}$.

A common fraction is written with a whole number above the division bar and a whole number below it. For example:

$$\frac{5}{8} \quad \frac{\text{Numerator}}{\text{Denominator}}$$

A **proper fraction** is a fraction whose numerator is smaller than its denominator. For example:

$$\frac{5}{8} \quad \frac{\text{Numerator}}{\text{Denominator}}$$

This type of fraction is in its lowest possible terms when the numerator and denominator contain no common factor. A **factor** refers to two or more numerals that, when multiplied, yield a given product. For example, 3 and 4 are factors of 12. The fraction $\frac{5}{8}$ is in its lowest possible terms because there is no common number by which both can be divided. (See the section entitled "The Simplification of Fractions," later in this chapter.)

An **improper fraction** is a fraction whose numerator is larger than its denominator, and whose value thus is greater than a whole unit. If, for instance, $1\frac{3}{4}$ hams is expressed as an improper fraction, it is expressed as $\frac{7}{4}$ because the one whole ham would be $\frac{4}{4}$, and the extra $\frac{3}{4}$ added to it makes it $\frac{7}{4}$. Such a fraction can be expressed as a mixed number by dividing the numerator by the denominator, as shown here:

$$\frac{7}{4} = 1\frac{3}{4} \text{ (mixed number)}$$

A **mixed number** is a whole number mixed with a fractional part. For example:

$$1\frac{1}{3},\ 3\frac{3}{4},\ \text{and } 8\frac{2}{3}$$

The Simplification of Fractions

Simplification is a method used to express a fraction in lower terms without changing the value of the fraction. This is achieved by dividing the numerator and denominator of a fraction by the greatest factor (number) common to both. For example:

$$\frac{12}{28} \quad \begin{array}{l}(\div\ 4 \text{ is the greatest factor}) = \\ (\div\ 4 \text{ is the greatest factor}) = \end{array} \quad \frac{3}{7}$$

$$\frac{16}{24} \quad \begin{array}{l}(\div\ 8 \text{ is the greatest factor}) = \\ (\div\ 8 \text{ is the greatest factor}) = \end{array} \quad \frac{2}{3}$$

The value of these fractions is unchanged, but they have been simplified, or reduced to their lowest possible terms.

A mixed number is usually expressed as an improper fraction when it is to be multiplied by another mixed number, a whole number, or a fraction. The first step is to express the mixed number as an improper fraction. This is done by multiplying the whole number by the denominator of the fraction and then adding the numerator to the result. The sum is written over the denominator of the fraction. For example:

$$1\tfrac{3}{4} \times 4\tfrac{1}{4} = \tfrac{7}{4} \times \tfrac{17}{4} = \tfrac{119}{16} = 7\tfrac{7}{16}$$

In this example, the whole number (1) is multiplied by the denominator of the fraction (4). To this result (4), the numerator (3) is added. The sum (7) is written over the denominator (4), creating the improper fraction $\tfrac{7}{4}$. The same procedure is followed in expressing the mixed number $4\tfrac{1}{4}$ as the improper fraction $\tfrac{17}{4}$. When the two mixed numbers are expressed as improper fractions, the product is found by multiplying the two numerators together and the two denominators together, resulting in the improper fraction $\tfrac{119}{16}$, and then simplifying (reducing) it to its lowest terms, $7\tfrac{7}{16}$.

Adding and Subtracting Fractions

Fractions are used most often to increase and decrease recipe ingredients. Ingredients such as herbs and spices generally appear in a recipe in fractional quantities. The addition and subtraction of fractions are used most often when adjusting recipes. However, all operations dealing with fractions will be required at some point on the job or in everyday activities. One example of the use of fractions in food service is illustrated in Figure 4–2.

Before fractions can be added or subtracted, they must have the same denominator. **Like fractions** are fractions that have the same denominator. To add or subtract like fractions, add or subtract the numerators and write the result over the common denominator. Examples of adding and subtracting like fractions are shown here:

$$\tfrac{2}{9} + \tfrac{5}{9} = \tfrac{7}{9} \qquad \tfrac{5}{9} - \tfrac{3}{9} = \tfrac{2}{9}$$

Note how simple it is to add and subtract like fractions. It is just like doing regular adding and subtracting. The next step, dealing with unlike fractions, becomes a little more difficult.

To Insure Perfect Solutions

When adding like fractions, add the numerators only (the top numbers of the fractions). The denominators (the bottom numbers of the fractions) remain unchanged.

When subtracting like fractions, subtract the numerators only (the top numbers). The denominators (the bottom numbers) remain unchanged.

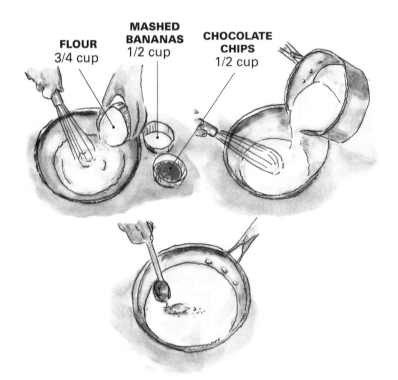

FLOUR
3/4 cup

MASHED BANANAS
1/2 cup

CHOCOLATE CHIPS
1/2 cup

Figure 4–2
Fractions are used in recipes, for example, by adding ¾ cup of flour +½ cup of mashed bananas + ½ cup of chocolate chips.
© Cengage Learning 2012

Unlike fractions have different denominators. They are more difficult to work with because only like things can be added or subtracted. Therefore, to add or subtract fractions that have unlike denominators, the fractions must first be expressed so the denominators are the same. To find this common denominator, multiply the two denominators ($5 \times 4 = 20$). The product will, of course, be common to both. For example:

$$\tfrac{2}{5} + \tfrac{3}{4} = \tfrac{?}{20}$$

When a number is found that is a multiple of both denominators, the fractions are then expressed in terms of the common denominator, so $\tfrac{2}{5}$ is $\tfrac{8}{20}$ and $\tfrac{3}{4}$ is $\tfrac{15}{20}$. These fractions have now become like fractions that can be added or subtracted without too much difficulty, as shown here:

Add		Subtract	
$\tfrac{2}{5}$ = $\tfrac{8}{20}$		$\tfrac{3}{4}$ = $\tfrac{15}{20}$	
+ $\tfrac{3}{4}$ = $\tfrac{15}{20}$		− $\tfrac{2}{5}$ = $\tfrac{8}{20}$	
$\tfrac{23}{20}$ = $1\tfrac{3}{20}$ Sum		Difference $\tfrac{7}{20}$	

In adding and subtracting unlike fractions, the common denominator may be any number that is a multiple of the original denominators. However, always use the least common denominator to simplify the work. The **least common denominator** is the smallest number that is a multiple of both denominators.

For example: if ⅓ and ⅖ are to be added, the least common denominator is 15 because it is the smallest multiple of both 3 and 5:

$$\begin{aligned} \tfrac{1}{3} &= \tfrac{5}{15} \\ + \tfrac{1}{5} &= \tfrac{3}{15} \\ \hline & \tfrac{8}{15} \end{aligned}$$

Be aware, however, that just multiplying the two denominators of the unlike fractions does not always result in the least common denominator. For example, $\tfrac{7}{12} - \tfrac{1}{2}$ has a common denominator of 24; but that is not the least common denominator. First, determine whether the 12 could actually be the least common denominator. Divide the 2 into the 24, and you discover that it is! A little practice and detective work in this area will help you determine the least common denominator. You may not guess the least common denominator the first time. Keep trying!

Multiplying Fractions

Multiplying fractions is considered the simplest operation involving fractions. When multiplying two fractions, multiply the two numerators and place the results over the result obtained by multiplying the two denominators. For example:

$$\tfrac{2}{3} \times \tfrac{7}{8} = \tfrac{14}{24} = \tfrac{7}{12}$$

Note: $\tfrac{14}{24}$ expressed in its lowest terms is $\tfrac{7}{12}$.

If multiplying a whole number by a fraction, multiply the whole number by the numerator of the fraction, place the result over the denominator of the fraction, and divide the new numerator by the denominator. For example:

$$\tfrac{17}{1} \times \tfrac{3}{4} = \tfrac{51}{4} = 12\tfrac{3}{4}$$

Sometimes it is possible to simplify the problem before multiplying. In the example shown here, 6 is a factor of 24 because 24 contains 6 exactly 4 times. This step is commonly called *canceling:*

$$\overset{4}{\cancel{\tfrac{24}{1}}} \times \tfrac{5}{\underset{1}{\cancel{6}}} = 20$$

Now the equation reads $4 \times 5 = 20$.

If the numerator and denominator can be divided evenly by the same number, simplify to the lowest terms. For example:

$\dfrac{32}{48}$ Numerator and denominator can be divided evenly by the common factor 16, resulting in: $\dfrac{2}{3}$

If multiplying by one or two mixed numbers, express the mixed number or numbers as improper fractions and proceed to multiply as you would two fractions. For example:

$$\tfrac{8}{1} \times 3\tfrac{5}{8} = \tfrac{8}{1} \times \tfrac{29}{8} = 29$$

$$2\tfrac{1}{3} \times 4\tfrac{3}{5} = \tfrac{7}{3} \times \tfrac{23}{5} = \tfrac{161}{15} = 10\tfrac{11}{15}$$

A note of caution: when dividing by a fraction (which is less than 1), the answer is greater than the dividend. For example, a serving of a hamburger is ⅓ pound. How many hamburgers can be obtained from 5 pounds of ground beef?

$$5 \div \tfrac{1}{3} = x$$

$$5 \times \tfrac{3}{1} = x$$

$$\tfrac{5}{1} \times \tfrac{3}{1} = x$$

$$15 = x$$

(You may have noticed that the fraction ⅓ was turned upside down, to ³⁄₁. This is called *inverting,* which is explained in the next section, "Dividing Fractions.")

From this result, you can see that from 5 pounds of ground beef, 15 hamburgers (weighing ⅓ pound each) can be obtained.

Dividing Fractions

Dividing fractions is perhaps the most difficult operation because it involves the process of inverting (turning over) the divisor. Always be careful to invert the correct fraction. Mistakes can be easily made when inverting takes place. After inverting the divisor, proceed to operate the same as you would when multiplying fractions.

Example A:

$$\tfrac{5}{8} \div \tfrac{1}{2} = \tfrac{5}{8} \times \tfrac{2}{1} = \tfrac{5}{4} \times \tfrac{1}{1} = \tfrac{5}{4} = 1\tfrac{1}{4}$$

Step 1:   The divisor is ½; invert it to ²⁄₁.

Step 2:   Cancel a factor of 2 from the 8 and 2.

Step 3:   Multiply ⁵⁄₄ × ¹⁄₁ to get ⁵⁄₄.

Step 4:   The result, ⁵⁄₄, is an improper fraction and must be reduced to a mixed number, which would be 1¼.

Example B:

$$\tfrac{14}{1} \div \tfrac{1}{2} = \tfrac{14}{1} \times \tfrac{2}{1} = 28$$

Step 1:   The divisor, ½, is inverted to ²⁄₁.

Step 2:   Multiply ¹⁴⁄₁ × ²⁄₁ = 28.

Example B results in a whole number so, of course, reducing is not necessary.

Practice Problems 4–1   Adding Fractions

Find the sum in each of the following addition problems. Simplify all answers to their lowest terms.

1. $\frac{5}{7}$
    $+ \frac{1}{7}$

    6/7

2. $\frac{4}{9}$
    $+ \frac{2}{9}$

    7/9

3. $\frac{5}{9}$
    $+ \frac{1}{9}$

    6/9

4. $\frac{1}{2}$
    $+ \frac{1}{8}$

    5/34

5. $\frac{4}{16}$
    $+ \frac{2}{4}$

    2/54

6. $\frac{3}{4}$
    $+ \frac{1}{8}$

    7/8

7. $1\frac{2}{16}$
    $+ 2\frac{3}{4}$

    29/64

8. $\frac{23}{32}$
    $+ \frac{15}{16}$

    53/27

9. $1\frac{1}{2}$
    $3\frac{2}{4}$
    $+ 7\frac{1}{8}$

    3 56/64

10. $\frac{4}{9}$
     $\frac{5}{12}$
     $+ \frac{5}{18}$

11. $\frac{1}{2}$
     $\frac{2}{3}$
     $+ \frac{4}{5}$

12. $6\frac{5}{6}$
     $10\frac{5}{12}$
     $+ 13\frac{2}{3}$

13. $14\frac{2}{5}$
     $26\frac{3}{15}$
     $+ 9\frac{6}{10}$

14. $12\frac{1}{6}$
     $9\frac{1}{3}$
     $+ 7\frac{1}{9}$

15. $12\frac{5}{8}$
     $6\frac{3}{4}$
     $+ 11\frac{1}{2}$

Practice Problems 4–2   Subtracting Fractions

Find the difference in each of the following subtraction problems. Simplify all answers to their lowest terms.

16. $\frac{3}{7}$
     $- \frac{1}{7}$

17. $\frac{5}{9}$
     $- \frac{2}{9}$

18. $\frac{7}{16}$
     $- \frac{3}{16}$

19. $\frac{3}{4}$
     $- \frac{2}{3}$

20. $3\frac{3}{4}$
     $- 1\frac{3}{16}$

21. $12\frac{1}{4}$
     $- 5\frac{5}{16}$

22. $14\frac{7}{24}$
     $- 6\frac{5}{16}$

23. $45\frac{5}{8}$
     $- 32\frac{7}{16}$

24. $18\frac{7}{16}$
     $- 13\frac{1}{4}$

25. $23\frac{5}{18}$
     $- 7\frac{5}{12}$

26. $42\frac{23}{32}$
     $- 23\frac{15}{16}$

27. $43\frac{5}{8}$
     $- 18\frac{1}{4}$

28. $21\frac{3}{16}$
     $- 16\frac{1}{8}$

29. $15\frac{5}{9}$
     $- 8\frac{2}{3}$

30. $25\frac{5}{12}$
     $- 12\frac{3}{16}$

Practice Problems 4–3   Multiplying Fractions

Find the product in each of the following multiplication problems. Simplify all answers to their lowest terms.

31. $\frac{3}{8} \times \frac{1}{2} =$ _____

32. $\frac{7}{8} \times \frac{2}{4} =$ _____

33. $4\frac{1}{4} \times 6\frac{1}{4} =$ _____

34. $1\frac{3}{4} \times 4\frac{5}{8} =$ _____

35. $36 \times 5\frac{3}{4} =$ _____

36. $45 \times 7\frac{1}{2} =$ _____

37. $4\frac{3}{4} \times 5\frac{1}{2} =$ _____

38. $18 \times 9\frac{5}{9} =$ _____

39. $\frac{2}{3} \times 12\frac{1}{3} =$ _____

40. $24\frac{1}{3} \times 7\frac{2}{3} =$ _____

41. $22\frac{5}{16} \times 4 =$ _____

42. $8\frac{2}{9} \times 3\frac{1}{2} =$ _____

43. $10\frac{3}{4} \times 3\frac{1}{2} =$ _____

44. $22 \times 5\frac{1}{4} =$ _____

45. $3\frac{5}{8} \times \frac{1}{2} =$ _____

Practice Problems 4–4   Dividing Fractions

Find the quotient in each of the following division problems. Simplify all answers to their lowest terms.

46. $^{15}\!/_{16} \div \frac{3}{4} =$ _____

47. $^{15}\!/_{16} \div 2 =$ _____

48. $\frac{3}{4} \div \frac{3}{16} =$ _____

49. $\frac{7}{16} \div \frac{3}{16} =$ _____

50. $1\frac{1}{2} \div 6 =$ _____

51. $2\frac{5}{8} \div 7 =$ _____

52. $\frac{1}{4} \div 10 =$ _____

53. $\frac{3}{4} \div 2 =$ _____

54. $\frac{5}{16} \div 3 =$ _____

55. $2\frac{1}{4} \div 1\frac{1}{2} =$ _____

56. $7\frac{5}{8} \div 2\frac{1}{4} =$ _____

57. $9\frac{3}{8} \div \frac{3}{4} =$ _____

58. $10\frac{2}{3} \div \frac{1}{2} =$ _____

59. $\frac{7}{8} \div \frac{1}{4} =$ _____

60. $12\frac{3}{4} \div \frac{2}{3} =$ _____

To Insure Perfect Solutions

A little trick to help remember the decimal: Keep in mind that a decade equals 10 years. Therefore, a decimal is based on the number 10.

Decimals

A decimal is based on the number 10. The decimal system refers to counting by 10s and powers of 10. The term **decimal** refers to decimal fractions. **Decimal fractions** are those fractions that are expressed with denominators of 10 or powers of 10. For example:

$$\frac{1}{10} \qquad \frac{9}{100} \qquad \frac{89}{1,000} \qquad \frac{321}{10,000}$$

Instead of writing a fraction, a point (.) called a **decimal point** is used to indicate a decimal fraction. For example:

$$\frac{1}{10} = 0.1 \qquad\qquad \frac{9}{100} = 0.09$$

$$\frac{89}{1,000} = 0.089 \qquad\qquad \frac{321}{10,000} = 0.0321$$

Individuals should know and memorize the relationship of decimals to common fractions as used in the food service industry. If a food service employee is working at a delicatessen and a customer asks for ½ pound of cheese, the employee must know that when the scale reads 0.5, that represents ½ pound, based on the decimal system. Table 4–1 illustrates common fractions that are used in the food service industry and their decimal equivalents. It is helpful for a food service professional to memorize this information.

Table 4–1
Relationship between fractions and decimals (© Cengage Learning 2012)

Fraction	Decimal Equivalent
⅛	0.125
⅕	0.2
¼	0.25
⅓	0.33333…
⅖	0.4
½	0.5
⅔	0.66666…
¾	0.75
⅞	0.875

Numbers go in both directions from the decimal point. The place value of the numbers to the left starts with the units or ones column, and each column (moving left) is an increasing multiple of 10.

Thousands	Hundreds	Tens	Units or Ones
1,000	100	10	1

How to Read and Understand Place Values of Decimal Numbers

Table 4–2
Place value of decimals (© Cengage Learning 2012)

.	3	5	4	6	9
Decimal Point	Tenths	Hundredths	Thousandths	Ten Thousandths	Hundred Thousandths

1. Read the number as if it were a whole number, from left to right, without the decimal. For example, the number 35,469 is read as "thirty-five thousand, four hundred sixty nine."

2. Next, identify the last digit in the number. In the number given in Table 4–2, the decimal number .35469, nine (9) is the last digit.

3. Note that the nine (9) is in the hundred thousandths place.

4. Now read the number again, adding the decimal words that correspond to the place value of the last number.

5. The number .35469 reads: Thirty five thousand, four hundred sixty nine *hundred-thousandths.*

To the right of the decimal point, each column is one-tenth of the number in the column immediately to its left. For example, one-tenth of 1 is $\frac{1}{10}$. Thus, the decimals to the right of the decimal point are 0.1, 0.01, 0.001, 0.0001, and so on. These numbers stated as decimal fractions are $\frac{1}{10}$, $\frac{1}{100}$, $\frac{1}{1,000}$, and $\frac{1}{10,000}$.

Decimal fractions differ from common fractions because they have 10 or a power of 10 as a denominator, whereas common fractions can have any number as the denominator. To simplify writing a decimal fraction, the decimal point is used. For example, to express the decimal fraction $\frac{725}{1,000}$ as its equivalent using a decimal point, perform the following steps:

1. Convert the decimal fraction to a decimal by writing the numerator (725).

2. Count the number of zeroes in the denominator and place the decimal point according to the number of zeroes. There must always be as many decimal places as there are zeroes in the denominator (0.725).

Often, when writing a decimal fraction as a decimal, it is necessary to add zeroes to the left of the numerator before placing the decimal point to indicate the value of the denominator. For example: $\frac{725}{10,000} = 0.0725$, which should be read as "seven hundred twenty-five ten thousandths."

When a number is made up of a whole number and a decimal fraction, it is referred to as a **mixed decimal fraction.** To write a mixed decimal fraction, the whole number is written to the left of the decimal point and the fractional part is on the right of the decimal point. For example: $7\frac{135}{1,000} = 7.135$. The decimal point is read as "and," so to read this mixed decimal fraction, the whole number is read first, then the decimal point as "and." Next, read the fraction as a whole number and state the denominator. Following this procedure, 7.135 is read "seven and one-hundred thirty-five thousandths."

To add or subtract decimal fractions, keep all whole numbers in their proper columns and all decimal fractions in their proper columns. Remember that the decimal point separates whole numbers from fractional parts. It is, therefore, very important that decimal points are directly in line with one another. For example, in adding decimal fractions:

$$
\begin{array}{ll}
2.135 & \text{Addend} \\
7.43 & \text{Addend} \\
4.008 & \text{Addend} \\
+\ 1.125 & \text{Addend} \\
\hline
14.698 & \text{Sum}
\end{array}
$$

Note that the decimal point in the sum goes under the decimal point of the other numbers.

When subtracting decimal fractions:

$$
\begin{array}{ll}
9.825 & \text{Minuend} \\
-\ 5.450 & \text{Subtrahend} \\
\hline
4.375 & \text{Difference}
\end{array}
$$

Note that the decimal point in the difference goes under the decimal point in the minuend and subtrahend.

To multiply decimal fractions, follow the same procedure as when multiplying whole numbers. To locate the decimal point in the product, count the number of decimal places in both the multiplicand and the multiplier. The number of decimal places counted in the product is equal to the sum of those in the multiplicand and multiplier. For example:

$$
\begin{array}{ll}
4.32 & \text{Multiplicand} \\
\times\ 0.06 & \text{Multiplier} \\
\hline
0.2592 & \text{Product}
\end{array}
$$

There are four decimal places in the multiplicand and multiplier. Therefore, four decimal places are counted from right to left in the product.

In many cases, the total number of decimal places in the multiplicand and multiplier exceeds the number of numerals that appear in the product. In such cases, **ciphers** (zeroes) are added to the left of the digits in the product to complete the decimal places needed:

$$
\begin{array}{ll}
0.445 & \text{Multiplicand} \\
\times\ \ 0.16 & \text{Multiplier} \\
\hline
2670 & \\
445 & \\
\hline
0.07120 & \text{Product}
\end{array}
$$

Note that a cipher is added to the product to complete the five decimal places required.

To divide decimal fractions, proceed as if the numbers were whole numbers and place the decimal point as follows:

1. When dividing by whole numbers, place the decimal point in the answer directly above the decimal point in the dividend.

$$\begin{array}{r} 0.06 \\ 6\overline{)0.36} \\ 0.36 \end{array}$$

Divisor 6)0.36 Dividend

0.06 — Quotient Use zeroes as needed in the quotient to hold a place.

$$\begin{array}{r} 0.8 \\ 5\overline{)4.0} \\ 4.0 \end{array}$$

Divisor 5)4.0 Dividend

0.8 — Quotient Zeroes are not needed in the quotient to hold a place.

To Insure Perfect Solutions

Dividend divided by Divisor equals Quotient

$$\text{Divisor} \overline{)\text{Dividend}}^{\text{Quotient}}$$

2. When dividing a whole number or mixed decimal by a mixed decimal or decimal fraction, change the divisor and dividend so the divisor becomes a whole number. This is accomplished by multiplying both the dividend and divisor by the same power of 10. The divisor and dividend can be multiplied by the same power of 10 without changing the value of the division:

$$\begin{array}{r} 12. \\ 0.25\overline{)3.00.} \\ 2\,5 \\ \overline{50} \\ \overline{50} \end{array}$$

Divisor 0.25)3.00. 12. — Quotient, Dividend

To Insure Perfect Solutions

When dividing using the calculator, enter the dividend *first*.

In the preceding example, the divisor 0.25 is made into the whole number 25 by multiplying by 100, moving the decimal point two places to the right. Because the dividend must also be multiplied by 100, the decimal point in the dividend is also moved two places to the right, so 3 becomes 300. The decimal point in the quotient is always placed directly over the decimal point in the dividend. The answer is 12, a whole number. Note that when moving a decimal point, we are using an arrow to show where the decimal point is to be moved.

Practice Problems 4–5 Decimals

Change the following fractions to decimals. Round to the nearest hundredths place using the mill.

61. $\frac{7}{10}$ = _____   66. $\frac{49}{100}$ = _____

62. $\frac{3}{10}$ = _____   67. $\frac{68}{100}$ = _____

63. $\frac{45}{100}$ = _____   68. $\frac{83}{100}$ = _____

64. $\frac{7}{10}$ = _____   69. $\frac{52}{100}$ = _____

65. $\frac{92}{100}$ = _____   70. $\frac{3}{10}$ = _____

Write the following decimals and mixed decimal fractions in words.

71. 0.4 _____   76. 0.67187 _____

72. 0.29 _____   77. 7.4 _____

73. 0.7481 _____   78. 7.42 _____

74. 0.002 _____   79. 8.236 _____

75. 0.0439 _____   80. 3.41 _____

Write each of the following numbers as decimals.

81. Five tenths _____

82. Fourteen hundredths _____

83. Sixteen hundredths _____

84. Sixty-eight ten thousandths _____

85. One hundred twenty-two thousandths _____

86. Sixty-four hundred thousandths _____

87. Three and five tenths _____

88. Sixteen hundred thousandths _____

89. One hundred thousandths _____

90. Eight and nine hundredths _____

Find the sum in each problem. Do not round the decimals.

91. 0.36 + 0.058 + 8.167 + 0.009 = _____

92. 0.58 + 0.675 + 6.225 + 9.323 = _____

93. 0.013 + 0.601 + 10.317 + 23.729 = _____

94. 0.056 + 0.015 + 0.711 + 6.25 + 16.37 = _____

95. 0.038 + 0.009 + 772 + 8.1675 = _____

Find the difference in each problem. Do not round the decimals.

96. $9.765 - 0.046 =$ _____

97. $8 - 0.451 =$ _____

98. $1 - 0.685 =$ _____

99. $0.0897 - 0.0536 =$ _____

100. $139.371 - 123.218 =$ _____

Find the product in each problem. Round the answers to the nearest hundredth.

101. $386 \times 0.63 =$ _____

102. $0.822 \times 1.52 =$ _____

103. $0.0159 \times 0.811 =$ _____

104. $6.53 \times 0.38 =$ _____

105. $5.322 \times 4.441 =$ _____

Find the quotient in each problem. Round the answers to the nearest hundredth.

106. $0.49 \div 7 =$ _____

107. $12 \div 4.8 =$ _____

108. $945 \div 500 =$ _____

109. $0.0660 \div 12 =$ _____

110. $46.76 \div 400 =$ _____

111. $6 \div 0.25 =$ _____

112. $2.65 \div 1.5 =$ _____

113. $9.5 \div 2.55 =$ _____

114. $45.5 \div 3.5 =$ _____

115. $52.10 \div 3.4 =$ _____

Ratios

The term *ratio* is used in food service to express a comparison between two numbers. A **ratio** between two quantities is the number of times that one contains the other. An example of using a ratio as a comparison is shown in the following problem:

> Last week, the Sirloin Steak Restaurant sold five times as many steaks as pork chops. How many steaks were sold last week?

To determine how many steaks were sold, the amount of pork chops sold must be known. The restaurant sold 425 orders of pork chops.

Multiplying the number of pork chops that were sold by the number 5 will solve this problem.

Mathematically, the problem will be set up this way:

$$425 \times 5 = 2{,}125$$

Therefore, 2,125 steaks were sold last week at the Sirloin Steak Restaurant.

Another way to state this fact is by saying that steaks outsold pork chops by 5 to 1.

To Insure Perfect Solutions

All answers should be checked for reasonableness. Think about and estimate what the correct answer should be before you start solving a problem. In the problem on the left, if your answer came out to be 425 or less, it would not be reasonable. If a ratio is set up the wrong way, the answer will not be reasonable.

Practice Problems 4–6 Ratios

Determine the answers to the following questions using ratios.

116. The Cabernet Café sold eight times as much Cabernet Sauvignon as Zinfandel. How many bottles of Cabernet Sauvignon were sold if the café sold 5 bottles of Zinfandel?

_____

117. Lanci's sold eight times as much osso bucco as veal marsala. How many orders of osso bucco were sold if Lanci's sold 33 orders of veal marsala?

_____

118. The Bears Restaurant sells 20 times as many orders of chateaubriand as chicken breasts. How many orders of chateaubriand were sold if 12 orders of chicken breasts were sold?

_____

119. The Casola Dining Room sold half as many orders of appetizers as desserts. How many appetizers were sold if the restaurant sold 250 desserts?

_____

120. Scotti's sold 15 times as many orders of sausage and cheese pizzas than cheese pizzas. How many sausage and cheese pizzas were sold if Scotti's sold 155 cheese pizzas?

_____

Proportions

Mathematical or word problems that include ratios may be solved by using proportions. A **proportion** is defined as a relation in size, number, amount, or degree of one thing compared to another. For example, when preparing baked rice, the ratio is 2 to 1—that is, 2 parts liquid to 1 part rice. If cooking 1 quart of raw rice, the formula calls for 2 quarts water or stock. The order in which the numbers are placed when expressing a ratio is important. If you say that the ratio when cooking barley is 4 to 1, meaning 4 parts water to 1 part barley, it is not the same as saying 1 to 4, which would reverse the ratio and mean 1 part water to every 4 parts of barley (which would cause the barley to scorch and burn).

How to Use Proportions to Solve Problems

The problem reads: How much water is needed to cook 8 quarts of barley using a liquid-to-barley ratio of 4 to 1?

Step 1
Set up a written equation.
Right now, you don't know how much water is needed to cook 8 quarts of barley.
Because the amount of water is an unknown, that unknown quantity will be named x.
(In this case, x is the amount of water to be determined; it does not mean to multiply.)
Facts that you must know to do a proportion:
The water is represented by x because that is the answer to be determined.
The expression "Is to" in a mathematical equation is represented by a colon (:).
The numbers on the outside of the equation are called *extremes*.
The numbers on the inside of the equation are called *means*.

Step 2
Set up a mathematical equation. In this case, it would be
$$x : 8 = 4 : 1$$

Step 3
Multiply the means ($8 \times 4 = 32$), and put the answer on the right of the = sign.
Then, multiply the extremes ($x \times 1 = 1x$), and put the answer on the left of the = sign.
The resulting mathematical equation looks like this: $1x = 32$.

Step 4
Divide both sides of the equation by the number next to the x. $1x / 1 = x$
(the 1 cancels out the 1), and $32/1 = 32$.
Therefore, $x = 32$, and so 32 quarts of water is needed to cook 8 quarts of barley.

Practice Problems 4–7   Proportions

Solve the following problems using the proportions given.

121. How much water is needed to bake ¾ gallon of rice using a liquid-to-rice ratio of 2 to 1?

_____

122. How many pounds of beef bones are needed to make 15 gallons of basic brown stock using a ratio of 12 pounds of beef bone to make 2 gallons of stock?

_____

123. How much water should be used to cook 1 pint of barley using a water-to-barley ratio of 4 to 1?

_____

124. How many pounds of green or yellow bell peppers are needed to make 8 pints of bell pepper coulis using a ratio of 4 pounds of green or yellow bell peppers to make 2.5 pints of coulis?

_____

125. How much water is needed to prepare lemonade using 1¾ pints of frozen lemonade and a water-to-lemonade ratio of 4 to 1?

_____

126. How many ounces of honeydew melons are needed to make 400 ounces of fruit salsa using a ratio of 8 ounces to make 32 ounces of salsa?

_____

127. How much water will it take to simmer 1¾ quarts of barley using a water-to-barley ratio of 4 to 1?

_____

128. How many saddles of lamb are needed to make 20 portions of lamb filet using a ratio of 2 saddles to make 8 portions?

_____

129. How much water is needed to prepare orange juice using 1¾ quarts of orange concentrate and a water-to-concentrate ratio of 4 to 1?

_____

130. How many pounds of pork tenderloin are needed to make 55 portions of chipotle marinated pork tenderloin using a ratio of 4 pounds of pork to make 10 portions?

_____

Percents

Percents play a big part in food service language. They are used to express a rate when dealing with important business matters such as food costs, labor costs, profits, and even that undesirable figure called losses. When management meets with food service employees and wishes to emphasize points that need improving, the message conveyed is usually done by expressing a percentage. For example: Last month, our food cost was 45 percent. We must bring this figure under control.

Percent (%) means "of each hundred." Thus, 5 percent means 5 out of every 100. This same 5 percent can also be written 0.05 in decimal form. In fraction form, it is ⁵⁄₁₀₀. The percent sign (%) is, in reality, a unique way of writing 100.

Percents are a special tool used to express a rate of each hundred. If 50 percent of the customers in a restaurant select a seafood entree, a rate of a whole is being expressed. The whole is represented by 100 percent, and all the customers entering the restaurant would represent the whole, or 100 percent. Another example of percent in food service is shown in Figure 4–3.

Figure 4–3
Here's an example of percent in food service—20 percent of the truffles are dark.
© Cengage Learning 2012

To find what percent one number is of another number, divide the number that represents the part by the number that represents the whole. For example, a hindquarter of beef weighs 240 pounds. The round cut weighs 52 pounds. What percent of the hindquarter is the round cut?

The 240-pound hindquarter represents the whole. The 52-pound round cut represents only a fractional part of the hindquarter. As a fraction, it is written $52/240$. Simplified, or reduced to its lowest terms, it is $13/60$. To express a common fraction as a percent, the numerator is divided by the denominator. The division must be carried out to two places (that is, the hundredths place) to get the percent. Carrying the division three places behind the decimal gives the tenth of a percent, which makes the percent more accurate. The finished problem using the $52/240$ fraction looks like this:

$$
\begin{array}{r}
0.2166 \text{ is equal to } 21.7\% \\
240\overline{)52.0000} \\
-48\,0 \\ \hline
4\,00 \\
-2\,40 \\ \hline
1\,600 \\
-1\,440 \\ \hline
1600 \\
-1440 \\ \hline
160
\end{array}
$$

Percent means hundredths, so the decimal is moved two places to the right when the percent sign is used.

This same percent could be obtained by converting the fraction $13/60$ into a percent by dividing the denominator into the numerator, as shown in the following example:

$$
\begin{array}{r}
0.2166 \text{ is equal to } 21.7\% \\
60\overline{)13.0000} \\
-12\,0 \\ \hline
1\,00 \\
-\ 60 \\ \hline
400 \\
-\ 360 \\ \hline
400 \\
-360 \\ \hline
40
\end{array}
$$

When a percent is expressed as a common fraction, the given percent is the numerator and 100 is the denominator. For example:

$$40\% = \frac{40}{100} \text{ or } \frac{2}{5}$$

$$20\% = \frac{20}{100} \text{ or } \frac{1}{5}$$

When a percent is changed to a decimal fraction, the percent sign is removed and the decimal point is moved two places to the left. For example:

$$24.5\% = 0.245$$
$$75.7\% = 0.757$$

When a decimal fraction is expressed as a percent, move the decimal point two places to the right and place the percent sign to the right of the last figure. For example:

$$0.234 = 23.4\%$$
$$0.826 = 82.6\%$$

The preceding percents are read as "twenty-three and four-tenths percent" and "eighty-two and six-tenths percent."

Remember the following points when dealing with percents:

- When a number is compared with a number larger than itself, the result is always less than 100 percent. For example, 72 is 80 percent of 90 because $^{72}/_{90} = ^{4}/_{5} = 80\%$.

- When a number is compared with itself, the result is always 100 percent. For example, 72 is 100 percent of 72 because $^{72}/_{72} = 1 = 100$ percent.

- To find a percent of a whole number, the method of operation used is multiplication. For example, if a restaurant takes in $9,462 in one week, but only 23 percent of that amount is profit, what is the profit? Here's how to find this answer:

$$
\begin{array}{r}
\$\,9{,}462 \\
\times\ \ 0.23 \\
\hline
28386 \\
18924 \\
\hline
\$2{,}176.26 \quad \text{Profit}
\end{array}
$$

Finding Percents of Meat Cuts

The use of percents in expressing a rate is a common practice in the food service business. This exercise, therefore, serves two purposes: first, to show the student how the sides of beef, veal, pork, and lamb are blocked out into wholesale or primal cuts, and second, to provide another opportunity to practice and understand percents.

A side is half of a complete carcass. A saddle, used in reference to the lamb carcass, is the front or hind half of the complete carcass, and it is cut between the twelfth and thirteenth ribs of the lamb. The side or saddle is blocked out into wholesale or primal cuts at the meat processing plant.

Figure 4–4 shows a blocked-out side of beef and how the percentage of each wholesale cut is found. For the side of beef in Figure 4–4, find the percentage of each wholesale cut.

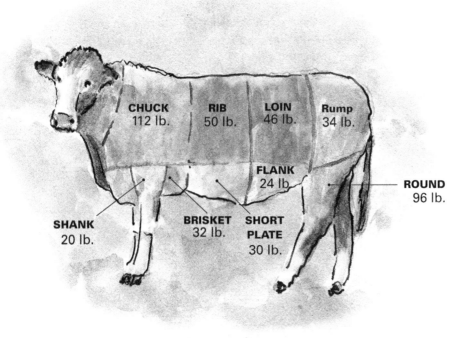

Figure 4–4
A side of beef divided into cuts.
© Cengage Learning 2012

To find a percentage, divide the whole into the part. In this case, the whole is represented by the total weight of the side of beef, 444 pounds. The part is represented by the weight of each individual wholesale cut. For example, the percentage of chuck is found as follows:

$$
\begin{array}{r}
0.252 \text{ is equal to } 25.2\% \quad \text{Percentage of chuck} \\
\text{Total weight of side of beef } 444\overline{)112.000} \quad \text{Weight of chuck} \\
-88\ 8 \\ \hline
23\ 20 \\
-22\ 20 \\ \hline
1\ 000 \\
888 \\ \hline
112
\end{array}
$$

The percentages of the other eight beef cuts are found by following the same procedure. Carry three places to the right of the decimal. When the exercise is completed and the percentages are totaled, the result should be 99 percent plus a figure representing a tenth of a percent. In the following example, the figure expressing the sum is 99.7 percent. A 100 percent result is unlikely because the individual percents will almost never figure out evenly.

25.2%	Chuck
4.5%	Shank
7.2%	Brisket
6.7%	Short plate
11.2%	Rib
10.3%	Sirloin
5.4%	Flank
7.6%	Rump
21.6%	Round
99.7%	**Total**

Practice Problems 4–8   Percents

Express the following common fractions as percents. Round to the hundredths place when necessary.

131. $\frac{2}{8}$ = _____   136. $\frac{5}{8}$ = _____

132. $\frac{5}{9}$ = _____   137. $\frac{4}{6}$ = _____

133. $\frac{9}{10}$ = _____   138. $\frac{4}{9}$ = _____

134. $\frac{5}{12}$ = _____   139. $\frac{1}{3}$ = _____

135. $\frac{5}{16}$ = _____   140. $\frac{3}{4}$ = _____

Express the following percents as common fractions, whole numbers, or mixed numbers. Reduce to the lowest common denominator.

141.   4% = _____   146.   38% = _____

142.   40% = _____   147.   63% = _____

143.   65% = _____   148.   200% = _____

144.   60% = _____   149.   45% = _____

145.   90% = _____   150.   140% = _____

Solve the following problems. Round answers to the nearest hundredth.

151.   5% of 75 = _____

152.   30% of 678 = _____

153.   42% of 800 = _____

154.   14.5% of 92 = _____

155.   49% of $38.20 = _____

156.   75% of $750.00 = _____

157.   47% of $468.00 = _____

158. 65% of $2,480.00 = _____

159. 24% of $4,680.00 = _____

160. 79% of $2,285.00 = _____

161. A 524-pound side of beef is ordered. The chuck cut weighs 75 pounds and the round cut weighs 58 pounds. What percent of the side is the chuck?_____ What percent is the round? _____

_____

162. A party for 325 people is booked. The cost of the party is $8,125. If the party's hosts are given an 8 percent discount on their total bill, what is the cost of the party?

_____

163. A party for 120 people is booked. The cost of the party is $3,600. If the party's hosts are given a 12 percent discount on their total bill, what is the cost of the party?

_____

164. If a restaurant takes in $25,680 in one week, and 26 percent of that amount is profit, how much is the profit?

_____

165. Mrs. Hill purchased four new coffee urns at $1,695 each. For buying in quantity, she is given a 3½ percent discount on the total bill. What is the amount she paid?

_____

166. If a 48-pound beef round is roasted, and 9 pounds are lost through shrinkage, what percent of the round is lost through shrinkage?

_____

167. The food cost percentage for a restaurant for the month is 36 percent. If $29,580 was taken in that month, how much of that amount went for the cost of food?

_____

168. If a restaurant's gross receipts for one week total $12,000, of which $8,000 is profit, what percent of the gross receipts is profit?

_____

169. If a restaurant's gross receipts for one day total $39,500, of which $5,600 are expenses, what percent of the gross receipts are expenses?

_____

170. If a 45-pound round of beef is roasted, and 9 pounds are lost through shrinkage, what percent of the round is lost through shrinkage?

_____

171. If a restaurant's gross receipts for one week total $35,090, but only 23 percent of that amount is profit, how much are expenses?

_____

172. If a 52-pound round is roasted, and 9 pounds are lost through shrinkage, what percent of the round roast is lost through shrinkage?

_____

173. If a restaurant's gross receipts for one week is $150,595, and 26 percent of that amount is for labor, 37 percent for food cost, and 15 percent for miscellaneous items, how much is the profit?

_____

Find the percentage of beef and pork wholesale cuts in the following problems. Round to the hundredths place.

174. Find the percentage of each cut of beef that makes up the side of beef shown in the figure.

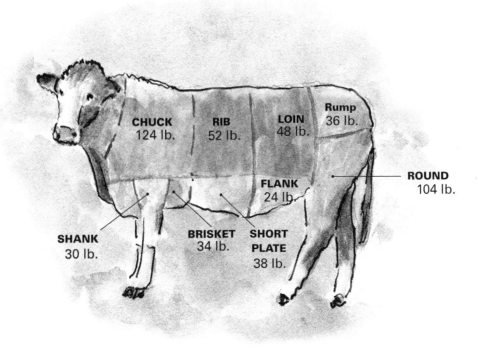

_____ % Chuck   Total weight of the side _____

_____ % Shank

_____ % Brisket

_____ % Short Plate

_____ % Rib

_____ % Loin

_____ % Flank

_____ % Rump

_____ % Round

175. Find the percentage of each cut of pork that makes up the side of pork shown in the figure.

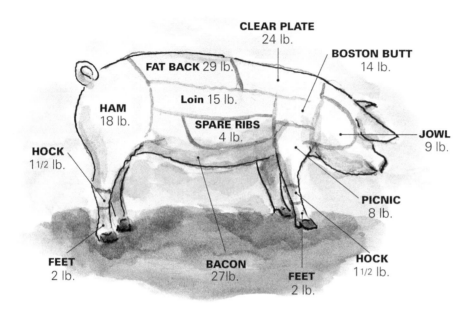

CLEAR PLATE
24 lb.

BOSTON BUTT
14 lb.

FAT BACK 29 lb.

Loin 15 lb.

HAM
18 lb.

SPARE RIBS
4 lb.

JOWL
9 lb.

HOCK
1 1/2 lb.

PICNIC
8 lb.

FEET
2 lb.

BACON
27lb.

FEET
2 lb.

HOCK
1 1/2 lb.

_____ % Jowl   Total weight of the side _____

_____ % Boston Butt

_____ % Clear Plate

_____ % Ham

_____ % Picnic

_____ % Hock

_____ % Feet

_____ % Loin

_____ % Bacon

_____ % Spare Ribs

_____ % Fat Back

Discussion Question 4-1

Why is it necessary to be able to compute fractions in the food service profession?

three

Math Essentials and Cost Controls in Food Preparation

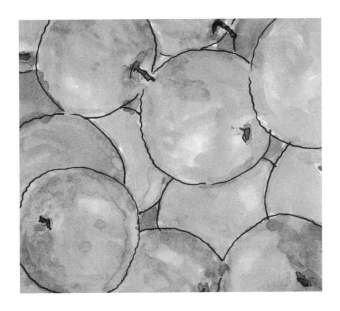

Now that the review is completed and you have refreshed your math skills, it is time to approach the math functions used in kitchen production by the preparation crew.

In the past, the preparation crew was hired to perform individual production tasks such as broiling, sauteing, and roasting. Other details concerned with math skills were the responsibility of management. In addition, management set standards for controlling portions, converted recipes, and wrote food production reports. Today, controls in all areas of production have become everyone's job. Math skills must be learned and developed by all personnel. This is the only way that management can control the high cost of food and labor as well as keep menu prices competitive. Developing math skills is also a step in moving up the ladder to a management position or from employee to employer.

There are a number of daily situations in the preparation area of a commercial kitchen where math skills are required for the operation to run efficiently. These situations require the attention of each member of the crew.

Because more products are being packaged and more recipes are being written using the metric system, this part of the book includes a chapter explaining the importance of understanding and using the metric system of measure.

Kitchen personnel responsible for food preparation usually consist of the chef, sous-chef, cook, butcher, baker, and pantry or salad worker. Every member of this crew should understand the math functions presented in this section of the text. Remember that the steps up the ladder of promotion and success are not difficult ones to climb if you are prepared when the opportunity arrives.

five

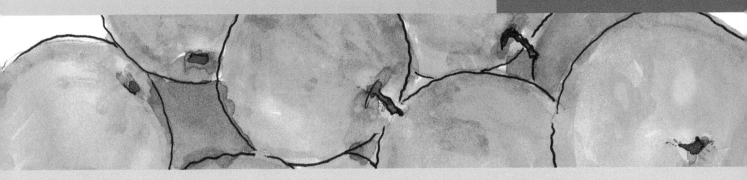

Weights and Measures

Objectives

At the completion of this chapter, the student should be able to:

1. Identify the equivalent measures commonly used in food service operations.
2. Find equivalent measures.
3. Tell what the terms *As Purchased (A.P.)* and *Edible Portion (E.P.)* mean.
4. Identify abbreviations of weights and measures.
5. Use a baker's balance scale.
6. Demonstrate how to convert decimal weights into ounces.
7. Identify different types of portion scales (dial and digital) and know how to use them.
8. Be able to explain the difference between fluid ounces and avoirdupois ounces.

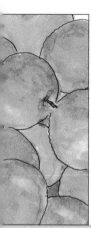

Key Words

avoirdupois ounces	Edible Portion (E.P.)	ladles	portions
scaling	drained weight test	baker's balance scale	portion scale
fluid ounces	scoops	volume	
As Purchased (A.P.)	dippers		

The careful use of weights and measures is an essential part of a food service operation. It is a method used to obtain accuracy and consistent quality in all food products and to control cost. Uniform products mean repeat sales.

There are two essential kinds of measurement practiced in a food service operation. Both are extremely important for having and maintaining a successful operation. They are:

- Ingredient measurement
- Portion measurement

In this chapter, the equipment used in weighing and measuring ingredients is shown using U.S. measurements. The use of these measurement devices is explained and the two basic kinds of measurement, fluid ounces and avoirdupois ounces, are discussed. In the following chapters, portion measurement, normally referred to as portion control, and the metric system of measurement will be emphasized and clarified.

"As a professional pastry chef and restaurateur, my best friend in the kitchen is math. I use it to scale up recipes, understand ratios and relationships between ingredients, and find out the food costs and labor costs for my dishes. Then I can use math to multiply and get my retail prices for those units."

Gale Gand
Executive Pastry Chef/Partner
TRU
Chicago, Illinois

Chef Gale Gand co-owns the award-winning restaurant TRU. Her restaurant has received four stars from Mobil, five diamonds from AAA, and a Grand Award from *Wine Spectator* magazine for its wine list. She was host of the Food Network's *Sweet Dreams*, which aired for eight years, and is the author of seven books. Her most recent cookbook is entitled *Gale Gand's Brunch!* She regularly appears on television to demonstrate her pastry skills. She has been a contestant on *Iron Chef America* and has been a judge for pastry competitions aired on the Food Network. She is a James Beard Foundation Outstanding Pastry Chef and has been a judge on *Top Chef*. She also has her own root beer company.

The Use of Weights and Measures

Recipes or formulas used in food establishments are stated using measurements. Culinary professionals generally use recipes in cooking and formulas in baking. Most culinary professionals think of cooking as an art and baking as a science. Recipes may have both dry ingredients that must be weighed and fluids that must be measured in ounces.

It is imperative that cooks recognize and understand the difference between avoirdupois ounces, used to measure items that must be weighed, and fluid ounces, which are used to measure liquids. Unfortunately, over the years many cooks have not understood the difference between avoirdupois and fluid ounces, nor when and how to use them in recipes. Many people use the term *ounce* to mean both fluid and avoirdupois ounces.

When cooking, as opposed to baking, ingredient measurements are not always exact. An extra ounce of beef stock in a soup will not cause the soup to be a failure; on the other hand, when baking a cake, the recipe must be followed exactly or the product's quality will be adversely affected. If the baker measures ingredients without weighing them, the cake may not bake properly and will not look or taste good. There is a *huge* difference between avoirdupois and fluid ounces, and the culinary professional must know the difference.

Avoirdupois ounces are used to measure weight. Because their measurements in a recipe must be exact, bakers weigh their ingredients using a scale. The term for the weighing of ingredients in the baking profession is called **scaling.** To illustrate this point, think about two bakers making pancakes. The recipe calls for 8 ounces of pastry flour. Our first baker pours the pastry flour into a cup that holds 8 fluid ounces, but the flour may not weigh exactly 8 ounces because it is not packed firmly or it's packed too firmly. Our second baker weighs 8 ounces of pastry flour. The pancakes made by the two bakers will most likely not weigh the same, and the pancakes made with the two different batters will not be standard or uniform.

Fluid ounces are used to measure volume. Volume can be thought of as taking up space. A quart of orange juice, for example, has 32 fluid ounces. This orange juice fills up the space in a quart container. Some other common fluid ounce measurements are cups, pints, and gallons.

To further illustrate the difference between fluid and avoirdupois ounces, picture a cup that measures 8 fluid ounces of liquid. Let's just pretend that a recipe calls for 8 ounces of rocks and 8 ounces of feathers (yum). If the cook used a container that measured fluid ounces, the difference between the two would be enormous. There would be not enough feathers for the recipe because the feathers would fill the volume of the cup but not weigh 8 ounces.

As stated previously, the correct term to use when measuring an ingredient by weight is *avoirdupois ounces;* however, many professionals over the years have shortened the term to just *ounce,* which has sometimes confused the beginning cook. In this textbook, the authors will use the term *fluid ounces* when referring to items that measure volume and the term *ounces* when referring to avoirdupois ounces, which measure weight.

Baking recipes are stated in weights. The baker scales the ingredients using a balanced baker's scale, which is described later in this chapter. Using the balanced baker's scale, ingredient amounts can be weighed accurately and the baked products will turn out consistently.

The baker does not have to weigh *every* kind of ingredient, though. When a recipe calls for water or any other item with the same consistency as water such as milk, vanilla, or eggs, the baker will use fluid ounces. This is because these ingredients weigh and measure the same. A cup of water or vanilla weighs 8 ounces and measures 8 fluid ounces. Therefore, it is quicker for the baker to measure those ingredients rather then weighing them. Also, when the amount of a dry ingredient is too small to weigh, such as a ¼ teaspoon of salt or ½ teaspoon of cinnamon, the baker may measure them using volume measures. In the United States, we are seeing a trend of bakers using the metric system of measurements because they want their products to be uniform. The metric system of measurements is covered in Chapter 6.

The common measures used in cooking and baking are teaspoons, tablespoons, ounces, cups, pints, quarts, and gallons. These are usually abbreviated when stated in recipes. Figure 5–1 gives the common abbreviations used.

Figure 5–1
Common abbreviations of weights and measures.
© Cengage Learning 2012

tsp. or small "t"	teaspoon
tbsp. or large "T"	tablespoon
C.	cup
pt.	pint
qt.	quart
gal.	gallon
oz.	ounce
lb.	pound
bch.	bunch
doz.	dozen
ea.	each
crt.	crate

To reinforce the terminology, a fluid ounce refers to how much space or volume the ingredients must take up. An avoirdupois ounce or an ounce refers to how much the ingredient weighs.

As Purchased (A.P.) Versus Edible Portion (E.P.)

As stated previously, it is imperative in baking to weigh the ingredients using an accurate scale. All culinary professionals must know the difference between A.P. (As Purchased) weight or E.P. (Edible Portion) weight.

- **As Purchased, abbreviated A.P.,** is a term used to refer to the weight of a product as it was purchased.
- **Edible Portion, abbreviated E.P.,** is a term used to refer to the weight of a product after it has been cleaned, trimmed, boned (in the case of meat, fish, and poultry), and so forth. At this point, all the nonedible parts have been removed.

A recipe or formula should indicate which weight is being referred to by using A.P. or E.P. when listing ingredients. If this step is neglected, the culinary professional must attempt to judge from the instructions in the method of preparation. When the instructions state that the item must first be trimmed, peeled, and boned, then the cook can be certain that A.P. weight is stated. If the instructions indicate the item has already been cleaned, trimmed, and peeled, the cook knows E.P. weight is called for.

To Insure Perfect Solutions

When weighing liquids, be aware that all liquids do not weigh the same. A cup of water does not weigh the same as a cup of oil. Therefore, the old saying "a pint is a pound the world around" *is NOT true*!

Equivalents of Weights and Measures

To compete in the culinary world, a chef or culinarian must be able to weigh and measure ingredients used for recipes. Being knowledgeable about how to use mathematics to convert ingredients for different recipes is essential for success in this industry. The culinarian must know how many ounces make up a pound; how many ounces are in a #10 can, and so on. The professional must know how many quarts make up a gallon, how many fluid ounces are in a quart, and so on. Figure 5–2 is a useful tool that was developed and used by Professor Gary Brenenstuhl to teach culinary arts students at Schenectady County Community College. The large G signifies a gallon of liquid. Inside the G are four Qs, which signify that 4 quarts make up 1 gallon. Inside each Q are two Ps, which signify that 2 pints make up 1 quart. Each P has two Cs, which signify that 2 cups are equal to 1 pint.

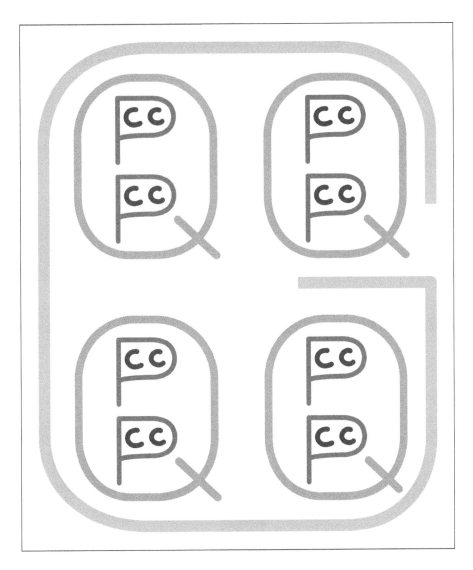

Figure 5–2
Professor Brenenstuhl's useful measurement tool.
Courtesy of Gary Brenenstuhl

Another useful tool that was suggested by two reviewers is the Big Ounce which refers to the fluid ounce, in other words water, milk, and liquids of a like consistency. The Big Ounce uses illustrations to emphasize the relationships between teaspoons and tablespoons and an ounce. In the first three illustrations, a large circle is drawn representing one ounce with a vertical line drawn down the middle of the circle. In the first illustration (Figure 5–3) on either side of the vertical line is one T (Tablespoon). The two T's are equal to one ounce. In the next illustration (Figure 5–4), suggested by Steven Rascoe of Sullivan University, a T is on the left side of the vertical line and 3 small t's are on the right side of the line. This shows that 3 teaspoons are equal to one tablespoon which ultimately represent the Big Ounce. In the last illustration (Figure 5–5) 3 t's are on both sides of the vertical line representing the fact that 6 t's are equal to the Big Ounce.

A word of caution: Not all items weigh the same. For example, 2 tablespoons of corn syrup weigh an ounce and a half. That is why the Big Ounce only works for items of waterlike consistency.

To further illustrate why we recommend this visual for fluid ounces instead of avoirdupois ounces is because of the following example. Two tablespoons of allspice weigh a total of a ½ ounce (they do not weigh an ounce as shown in the Big Ounce). We suggest that you consult figure 5–17 for the exact weights of items. In spite of this fact, for most cooked items the difference in weight with this small of measure will probably be inconsequential. However, as stated before, the culinarian should be extremely cautious and use the preferred method of weighing ingredients when baking to make certain that the baked product will be a success.

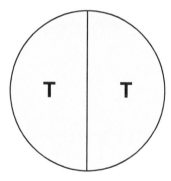

Figure 5–3
2 tablespoons equal 1 ounce.
© Cengage Learning 2012

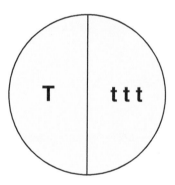

Figure 5–4
3 teaspoons equal
1 tablespoon. That equals
½ ounce.
Courtesy of Steven Rascoe and the
math faculty of Sullivan University

Figure 5–5
6 teaspoons equal 1 ounce.
© Cengage Learning 2012

Another memory device for remembering the "Big Ounce" concept is shown in figure 5–6. This memory device was developed by Kimberly Otis of Schenectady County Community College. In this diagram a capital T is used to illustrate a Tablespoon. There are three small circles on the tips of each end of the Tablespoon to represent the fact that there are 3 teaspoons in a Tablespoon. Two of these Tablespoons with circles are drawn side by side and then a large circle is drawn around them to represent one ounce.

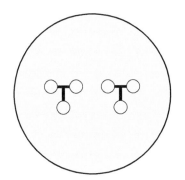

Figure 5–6
The three small circles represent 3 teaspoons in a Tablespoon. An ounce has 2 Tablespoons.
Courtesy of Kimberly Otis, Schenectady County Community College

Figure 5–7 illustrates the amount of fluid ounces and the relationship of the common equivalent fluid ounces to each other.

Unit of measure	Number of fluid ounces	Equivalent relationship
1 gallon	128	2 half gallons or 4 quarts
½ gallon	64	2 quarts
1 quart	32	2 pints
1 pint	16	2 cups
1 cup	8	

Figure 5–7
Relationships among gallons, quarts, pints, and cups in measurements.
© Cengage Learning 2012

A culinarian can use this information to control food costs and use products that may spoil and have to be thrown out. For example, at an elementary school, the cook has to prepare a recipe that calls for a gallon of milk. The cook, after taking inventory of milk, discovers that there is an excess of 8-oz. containers of milk that, if not used, would spoil in a day. Instead of opening up a new gallon container of milk, the cook uses 16 of the 8-oz. containers of milk. Mathematically, the equation is $16 \times 8 = 128$. This result, 128, represents the number of fluid ounces in a gallon of milk.

The relationship of common equivalents is given in Figure 5–8. The information in Figure 5–8 can be used to save production time. For example, if 2 pounds of liquid milk are required in a recipe, this can be measured quickly by volume as 1 fluid quart because 2 pounds of liquid equals 1 fluid quart; if 1 pound of whole eggs is needed, this can be measured as a fluid pint.

Volume Equivalents

Item	Equals	Item
1 pinch	=	⅛ teaspoon (approximately)
3 teaspoons	=	1 tablespoon
4 tablespoons	=	¼ cup
8 tablespoons	=	½ cup
12 tablespoons	=	¾ cup
16 tablespoons	=	1 cup
2 cups	=	1 pint
4 cups	=	1 quart
16 cups	=	1 gallon
2 pints	=	1 quart
4 quarts	=	1 gallon

Count Equivalents

Item	Equals	Item
12 items	=	1 dozen
12 dozen	=	1 gross
8 quarts	=	1 peck
4 pecks	=	1 bushel

Weight-to-Volume Equivalents

Please note that these equivalents are valid only for items where U.S. avoirdupois and fluid ounces are equal, like water, eggs, and milk.

Weight	Equals	Volume
1 pound	=	1 fluid pint
2 pounds	=	1 fluid quart
8 pounds	=	1 fluid gallon

Miscellaneous Equivalents

Item	Equals	Weight
6 teaspoons	=	1 ounce
2 tablespoons	=	1 ounce
16 ounces	=	1 pound

Discussion Question 5-1

A recipe calls for ½ gallon of milk. Using the information from Figure 5–6, calculate the possible solutions if the restaurant only has the following containers of milk: quarts; pints; cups.

Practice Problems 5–1   The Use of Weights and Measures

Fill in the correct measure using the information found in Figures 5–3 through 5–8.

1. 12 teaspoons   equal   _____ tablespoons

2. 8 tablespoons   equal   _____ cup

3. 3 pinches   equal   _____ teaspoon(s)

4. 16 tablespoons   equal   _____ cup(s)

5. 124 quarts   equal   _____ gallons

6. 1 gallon   equals   _____ quarts

7. 10 pounds   equal   _____ fluid quarts

8. 64 ounces   equal   _____ quarts

9. 30 gallons   equal   _____ quarts

10. 1 peck   equals   _____ quarts

11. 16 pints   equal   _____ quarts

12. 64 ounces   equal   _____ pounds

13. 6 cups   equal   _____ ounces

14. 1 bushel   equals   _____ pecks

15. 16 cups   equal   _____ pints

In food preparation and baking, a recipe or formula will call for so many pounds or ounces of liquid and a scale may not be available, or it would be more convenient to measure the liquid. Assume that this is the situation for the following problems. For each, state the amount of volume measure you would use.

16. The recipe calls for 1 pound 8 ounces of water. ___1 f l u___

17. The recipe calls for 4 pounds of apple juice. ___60 ounces___

18. The recipe calls for 5 pounds of apple juice. _____

19. The recipe calls for 2 pounds and 12 oz. milk. _____

20. The recipe calls for 6 pounds of skim milk. _____

Discussion Question 5-2

Why does a food service professional have to know how to convert measurements to equivalent weights and measures? Give two examples of how this knowledge would be used in a food service operation.

Size of Cans

In the food service industry, many products are packed in cans. A culinarian has to know how much is in each can. Figure 5–9 shows can numbers and their equivalent measurements. Because a can of vegetables or fruit has a varying amount of liquid, measurements are not exact. The food service operator must perform a "can cutting" to determine the quality of the product, how much of the ingredients of the can is product, and how much is liquid. This is called a **drained weight test.** For example, the operator will open up a #10 can of tomatoes, pour the liquid into one container, and pour the tomatoes into another. Both containers are weighed, which shows the operator the liquid weight and the tomato weight separately. This will explain why there is a variation in the amount of measurements in the can.

Figure 5–9
Common can numbers and their equivalents.
© Cengage Learning 2012

Size of Can—Number	Customary Measurement	Equivalent Ounces	Equivalent Metrics
1 or Picnic	1 ¼ cups	10.5 to 12	297.67 to 340.1943 grams
300	1 ¾ cups	14 to 16	396.8933 to 453.5924 grams
303	2 cups	16 to 17	453.5924 to 481.9419 grams
2	2 ½ cups	20	566.9905 grams
2 and ½	3 ¾ cups	27 to 29	765.4371 to 822.1362 grams
3	5 ¾ cups	51 to 52	1,445.826 grams or (1 kilogram and 445.826 grams) to 1,474.175 grams or (1 kilogram and 474.175 grams)
10	3 quarts	104 ounces (6 pounds 8 ounces) to 117 ounces (7 pounds 5 ounces)	2,948.35 grams or (2 kilograms and 948.35 grams) to 3,316.894 grams or (3 kilograms and 316.894 grams)

Practice Problems 5–2   The Use of Weights and Measures

Fill in the correct measure using the information in Figure 5–9 and making conversions where needed.

21. What is the range of ounces in a #10 can? _____ to _____.

22. How many pints are in a #10 can? _____ to _____.

23. How many tablespoons are in a #303 can? _____.

24. How many quarts are in a #3 can? _____

25. How many teaspoons are in a #1 can?_____

Measuring and Weighing Devices

There are many measuring and weighing instruments used in food service operations. They include an assortment of cups, spoons, ladles, dippers, and scoops; baker's balance scales, digital platform scales, and portion scales; kitchen and serving spoons; and pints, quarts, and gallons that are used as a substitute for weighing liquid measures. Some of these are illustrated in Figures 5–10 through 5–16 and described in this chapter.

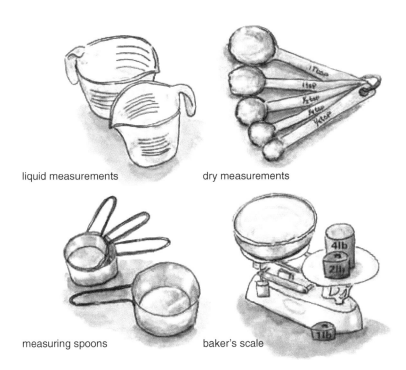

liquid measurements   dry measurements

measuring spoons   baker's scale

Figure 5–10
An assortment of measuring and weighing utensils used in food service operations.
© Cengage Learning 2012

Scoops or Dippers

Scoops or **dippers** are used to serve many foods, as well as to control the portion size. The various sizes are designated by a number that appears on the lever that mechanically releases the item from the scoop. The number that appears on the lever indicates the number of level scoops that it will take to fill a quart (32 liquid ounces). Figure 5–11 shows the relationship of the scoop number to the capacity in volume content for both customary and metric measure.

Figure 5–11
Scoop or dipper sizes and approximate weights and measures in both customary and metric units. Different foods will vary in weight; therefore, this chart should be used only as a guide.
© Cengage Learning 2012

Scoop Number	Approximate Volume Customary	Approximate Volume Metric	Approximate Weight Customary	Approximate Weight Metric
6	5.33 fl. oz.	160 ml	5 oz.	140 g
8	4 fl. oz.	120 ml	4 oz.	110 g
10	3.2 fl. oz.	90 ml	3.25 oz.	92 g
12	2.66 fl. oz.	80 ml	2.75 oz.	78 g
16	2 fl. oz.	60 ml	2.25 oz.	58 g
20	1.6 fl. oz.	45 ml	1.67 oz.	46 g
24	1.33 fl. oz.	40 ml	1.5 oz.	38 g
30	1.07 fl. oz.	30 ml	1.25 oz.	31 g
40	0.8 fl. oz.	24 ml	1 oz.	23 g

Ladles

Ladles are used to serve stews, soups, sauces, gravies, dressings, cream dishes, and other liquids or semiliquids when portioning and uniform servings are desired or required. (See Figure 5–12.) They come in assorted sizes, holding from 2 to 8 ounces. The size, in ounces, is stamped on the handle. Figure 5–13 shows the ladle sizes most frequently used.

Figure 5–12
This chef is using a ladle to measure an exact serving of sauce.
© Cengage Learning 2012

Size	Weight
¼ cup	2 oz.
½ cup	4 oz.
¾ cup	6 oz.
1 cup	8 oz.

Figure 5–13
Ladle sizes.
© Cengage Learning 2012

Discussion Question 5-3

Why does a food service professional have to know the sizes of scoops and ladles? How will this affect the cost of food and the appearance of the plates?

The Baker's Balance Scale

The **baker's balance scale** is the best type of scale to use because it ensures accuracy when weighing ingredients. The scale has a twin platform. (See Figure 5–14.) On the platform to the left is placed a metal scoop, in which the food to be weighed is placed. On the platform to the right is placed a special weight equal to the weight of the scoop. (See Figure 5–16.) If another container is used on the left platform, balance the scale by placing counterweights on the right side or by adjusting the ounce weight on the horizontal beam. This horizontal beam runs across the front of the scale. The beam has a weight attached to it and is graduated in ¼ ounces. The weight is placed on the number of ounces that one wishes to weigh. The ounce weight can be graduated up to 16 ounces (1 pound). (See Figure 5–15.) This scale can be used to weigh ingredients up to 10 pounds.

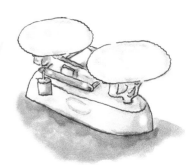

Figure 5–14
A measuring scale.
© Cengage Learning 2012

Figure 5–15
A baker's scale beam graduated in ¼ ounces up to 16 ounces (1 pound).
© Cengage Learning 2012

If a larger amount of food is to be weighed, additional metal weights of 1, 2, and 4 pounds are provided. When using this scale, always balance it before setting the weights for a given amount. It must balance again after the ingredients are placed on the scale.

For example, when weighing 8 ounces of egg yolks, place a container large enough to hold the yolks on the left platform and balance the scale. Next, adjust the weight on the horizontal beam 8 additional ounces. Then add the yolks to the container until the scale balances again.

If 1 pound, 6½ ounces of flour are to be weighed, place the metal scoop on the left platform and the special balance weight on the right platform. This brings the two platforms to a complete balance. The 1-pound weight is placed on the platform to the right, and the weight on the scaling beam is set on 6½ ounces. Then flour is placed in the metal scoop until the two platforms balance a second time. For weighing small amounts, such as 1¾ ounces of baking powder, a piece of paper or a small paper plate should be placed on both platforms. To weigh the baking powder, slide the hanging weight (the weight on the horizontal beam attached to the scale) to 1¾ ounces. Pour the baking powder onto the paper on the left platform until it balances.

Figure 5–16
An example of a baker's scale to determine quantities.
© Cengage Learning 2012

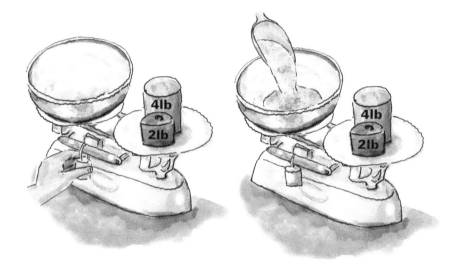

To Insure Perfect Solutions

The weight of 1 cup of cotton balls *does not* equal the weight of 1 cup of crushed stone.

Why the Baker's Balance Scale Is Important

A major challenge in baking is realizing that volume measures and measures of weights are different. For instance, if a recipe is written in **volume** (that is, the recipe says to add 2 cups of flour), then the baker would measure 2 cups of flour by volume. But if the recipe calls for weighing out 16 ounces of flour, that may or may not be the same amount as the 2 cups of volume measure. The baker has to have the skill to use the balance scale accurately for the finished product to be a success.

To prove our point, obtain two 8-ounce measuring cups. Fill one with cotton balls and the other with crushed stone. Both of them measure 8 ounces of ingredients by volume, but do they both weigh the same amount? Of course not! To check our conclusion, weigh both items using a baker's balance scale.

In the workplace, you will be expected to be able to use the baker's scale correctly. Practice is necessary to become competent, so whenever possible, set the scale at various settings and weigh whatever items are on hand, such as flour, salt, sugar, rice, and water. (See Figure 5–16.)

The weights of ingredients are different as illustrated in Figure 5–17, which gives the approximate weights and measures of common foods. For instance, compare the weight of a cup of cooked diced beef with a cup of fresh bread crumbs. A cup of beef weighs 5½ ounces, while a cup of bread crumbs weighs 2 ounces.

Food Product	Tbsp.	Cup	Pt.	Qt.
Allspice	¼ oz.	4 oz.	8 oz.	1 lb.
Apples, fresh, diced	½ oz.	8 oz.	1 lb.	2 lbs.
Bacon, raw, diced	½ oz.	8 oz.	1 lb.	2 lbs.
Bacon, cooked, diced	⅔ oz.	10 ½ oz.	1 lb., 5 oz.	2 lbs., 10 oz.
Baking powder	⅜ oz.	6 oz.	12 oz.	1 lb., 8 oz.
Baking soda	⅜ oz.	6 oz.	12 oz.	1 lb., 8 oz.
Bananas, sliced	½ oz.	8 oz.	1 lb.	2 lbs.
Barley	—	8 oz.	1 lb.	2 lbs.
Beef, cooked, diced	⅜ oz.	5 ½ oz.	11 oz.	1 lb., 6 oz.
Beef, raw, ground	½ oz.	8 oz.	1 lb.	2 lbs.
Bread crumbs, dry	¼ oz.	4 oz.	8 oz.	1 lb.
Bread crumbs, fresh	⅛ oz.	2 oz.	4 oz.	8 oz.
Butter	½ oz.	8 oz.	1 lb.	2 lbs.
Cabbage, shredded	¼ oz.	4 oz.	8 oz.	1 lb.
Carrots, raw, diced	⁵⁄₁₆ oz.	5 oz.	10 oz.	1 lb., 4 oz.
Celery, raw, diced	¼ oz.	4 oz.	8 oz.	1 lb.
Cheese, diced	—	5 ½ oz.	11 oz.	1 lb., 6 oz.
Cheese, grated	¼ oz.	4 oz.	8 oz.	1 lb.
Cheese, shredded	¼ oz.	4 oz.	8 oz.	1 lb.
Chocolate, grated	¼ oz.	4 oz.	8 oz.	1 lb.
Chocolate, melted	½ oz.	8 oz.	1 lb.	2 lbs.
Cinnamon, ground	¼ oz.	3 ½ oz.	7 oz.	14 oz.
Cloves, ground	¼ oz.	4 oz.	8 oz.	1 lb.
Cloves, whole	³⁄₁₆ oz.	3 oz.	6 oz.	12 oz.
Cocoa	³⁄₁₆ oz.	3 ½ oz.	7 oz.	14 oz.
Coconut, macaroon, packed	³⁄₁₆ oz.	3 oz.	6 oz.	12 oz.
Coconut, shredded, packed	³⁄₁₆ oz.	3 ½ oz.	7 oz.	14 oz.
Coffee, ground	³⁄₁₆ oz.	3 oz.	6 oz.	12 oz.
Cornmeal	⁵⁄₁₆ oz.	4 ¾ oz.	9 ½ oz.	1 lb., 3 oz.
Cornstarch	⅓ oz.	5 ⅓ oz.	10 ½ oz.	1 lb., 5 oz.
Corn syrup	¾ oz.	12 oz.	1 lb., 8 oz.	3 lbs.
Cracker crumbs	¼ oz.	4 oz.	8 oz.	1 lb.
Cranberries, raw	—	4 oz.	8 oz.	1 lb.
Currants, dried	⅓ oz.	5 ⅓ oz.	11 oz.	1 lb., 6 oz.
Curry powder	³⁄₁₆ oz.	3 ½ oz	—	—

Figure 5–17
Approximate weights and measures of common foods. (*continued*)
© Cengage Learning 2012

Food Product	Tbsp.	Cup	Pt.	Qt.
Dates, pitted	5/16 oz.	5 ½ oz.	11 oz.	1 lb., 6 oz.
Eggs, whole	½ oz.	8 oz.	1 lb.	2 lbs.
Egg whites	½ oz.	8 oz.	1 lb.	2 lbs.
Egg yolks	½ oz.	8 oz.	1 lb.	2 lbs.
Extracts	½ oz.	8 oz.	1 lb.	2 lbs.
Flour, bread	5/16 oz.	5 oz.	10 oz.	1 lb., 4 oz.
Flour, cake	¼ oz.	4 ¾ oz.	9 ½ oz.	1 lb., 3 oz.
Flour, pastry	5/16 oz.	5 oz.	10 oz.	1 lb., 4 oz.
Gelatin, flavored	⅜ oz.	6 ½ oz.	13 oz.	1 lb., 10 oz.
Gelatin, plain	5/16 oz.	5 oz.	10 oz.	1 lb., 4 oz.
Ginger	3/16 oz.	3 ¼ oz.	6 ½ oz.	13 oz.
Glucose	¾ oz.	12 oz.	1 lb., 8 oz.	3 lbs.
Green peppers, diced	¼ oz.	4 oz.	8 oz.	1 lb.
Ham, cooked, diced	5/16 oz.	5 ¼ oz.	10 ½ oz.	1 lb., 5 oz.
Horseradish, prepared	½ oz.	8 oz.	1 lb.	2 lbs.
Jam	⅝ oz.	10 oz.	1 lb. 4 oz.	2 lbs., 8 oz.
Lemon juice	½ oz.	8 oz.	1 lb.	2 lbs.
Lemon rind	¼ oz.	4 oz.	8 oz.	1 lb.
Mace	¼ oz.	3 ¼ oz.	6 ½ oz.	13 oz.
Mayonnaise	½ oz.	8 oz.	1 lb.	2 lbs.
Milk, liquid	½ oz.	8 oz.	1 lb.	2 lbs.
Milk, powdered	5/16 oz.	5 ¼ oz.	10 ½ oz.	1 lb., 5 oz.
Molasses	¾ oz.	12 oz.	1 lb.	3 lbs.
Mustard, ground	¼ oz.	3 ½ oz.	6 ½ oz.	13 oz.
Mustard, prepared	¼ oz	4 oz.	8 oz.	1 lb.
Nutmeats	¼ oz.	4 oz.	8 oz.	1 lb.
Nutmeg, ground	¼ oz.	4 ¼ oz.	8 ½ oz.	1 lb., 1 oz.
Oats, rolled	3/16 oz.	3 oz.	6 oz.	12 oz.
Oil, salad	½ oz.	8 oz.	1 lb.	2 lbs.
Onions	⅓ oz.	5 ½ oz.	11 oz.	1 lb., 6 oz.
Peaches, canned	½ oz.	8 oz.	1 lb.	2 lbs.
Peas, dry, split	7/16 oz.	7 oz.	14 oz.	1 lb., 12 oz.
Pickle relish	5/16 oz.	5 ¼ oz.	10 ½ oz.	1 lb., 5 oz.
Pickles, chopped	¼ oz.	5 ¼ oz.	10 ½ oz.	1 lb., 5 oz.
Pimentos, chopped	½ oz.	7 oz.	14 oz.	1 lb., 12 oz.
Pineapple, diced	½ oz.	8 oz.	1 lb.	2 lbs.
Potatoes, cooked, diced	—	6 ½ oz.	13 oz.	1 lb., 10 oz.
Prunes, dry	—	5 ½ oz.	11 oz.	1 lb., 6 oz.
Raisins, seedless	⅓ oz.	5 ⅓ oz.	10 ¾ oz.	1 lb., 5 oz.
Rice, raw	½ oz.	8 oz.	1 lb.	2 lbs.
Sage, ground	⅛ oz.	2 ¼ oz.	4 ½ oz.	9 oz.
Salmon, flaked	½ oz.	8 oz.	1 lb.	2 lbs.

Figure 5–17

Approximate weights and measures of common foods. (*continued*)

Food Product	Tbsp.	Cup	Pt.	Qt.
Salt	½ oz.	8 oz.	1 lb.	2 lbs.
Savory	⅛ oz.	2 oz.	4 oz.	8 oz.
Shortening	½ oz.	8 oz.	1 lb.	2 lbs.
Soda	7⁄16 oz.	7 oz.	14 oz.	1 lb., 12 oz.
Sugar, brown, packed	½ oz.	8 oz.	1 lb.	2 lbs.
Sugar, granulated	7⁄16 oz.	7 ½ oz.	15 oz.	1 lb., 14 oz.
Sugar, powdered	5⁄16 oz.	4 ¾ oz.	9 ½ oz.	1 lb., 3 oz.
Tapioca, pearl	¼ oz.	4 oz.	8 oz.	1 lb.
Tea	⅙ oz.	2 ½ oz.	5 oz.	10 oz.
Tomatoes	½ oz.	8 oz.	1 lb.	2 lbs.
Tuna fish, flaked	½ oz.	8 oz.	1 lb.	2 lbs.
Vanilla, imitation	½ oz.	8 oz.	1 lb.	2 lbs.
Vinegar	½ oz.	8 oz.	1 lb.	2 lbs.
Water	½ oz.	8 oz.	1 lb.	2 lbs.

Figure 5–17
Approximate weights and measures of common foods. (*continued*)

Discussion Question 5-4

Using Figure 5–17, give other examples of cups of food that do not equal each other in weight.

Practice Problems 5–3   The Baker's Balance Scale

Total the amounts of each ingredient in the five formulas given and write the total below each formula.

For Example:

Ingredients	Pounds	Ounces	Total
Sugar	1	8	
Flour	4	6	
Salt	—	1	
Shortening	1	12	
TOTAL	**6 lbs.** plus	**27 oz** =	**7 lbs. 11 oz.**

(*Note: There are 16 ounces in a pound, so for each 16 ounces, carry 1 pound to the pound column. Twenty-seven ounces equals 1 pound, 11 ounces, so 6 pounds, 27 ounces equals 7 pounds, 11 ounces.*)

Then, for hands-on practice, weigh each ingredient separately, using sugar or rice to represent each ingredient. When this is done, add up the total amount of all the ingredients weighed. The amount should equal the sum of all the weights of the ingredients listed.

26.

Ingredients	Pounds	Ounces
Shortening	1	6
Bread Flour	3	12
Salt	—	1
Sugar	2	10
Baking Powder	—	3
TOTAL		

27.

Ingredients	Pounds	Ounces
Shortening	1	8
Pastry Flour	2	10
Baking Powder	—	4
Baking Soda	—	½
Sugar	1	12
Salt	—	2¼
TOTAL		

28.

Ingredients	Pounds	Ounces
Sugar	2	6
Baking Powder	—	¾
Salt	—	½
Flour	4	10
Cornstarch	—	5
TOTAL		

29.

Ingredients	Pounds	Ounces
Butter	1	12
Pastry Flour	4	6
Dry Milk	—	3½
Shortening	1	6
Sugar	2	10
Salt	—	¾
TOTAL		

30.

Ingredients	Pounds	Ounces
Butter	—	12
Cake Flour	—	10
Sugar	2	14
Baking Powder	1	1¾
Dry Milk	—	6
Water	1	11
TOTAL		

"In bread and roll production, the student must weigh out ingredients. This is an important step because of:

A. Balanced formula—varying the percent of ingredients will change the formula;

B. Consistent production of the required quantity—varying the ingredients may result in too large or too small a quantity;

C. Consistent production of quality;

D. Uniformity regardless of changes in mixing personnel;

E. Uniformity in fermentation times;

F. Control of costs."

Chef Noble Masi, Certified Master Baker,
Emissary & Heritage Professor
The Culinary Institute of America
Hyde Park, NY

Noble Masi was the 1999 American Culinary Chef (ACF) of the Year. He was a professor of baking and pastry at The Culinary Institute of America. He was also the recipient of the 1996 ACF Chef Professionalism Award. He is an ACF-certified judge and a frequent speaker at seminars. He presented a seminar on signature breads at the American Culinary Federation National Convention.

The Portion Scale

A portion scale is used for measuring food servings, or **portions.** Sometimes ingredients are measured with a portion scale as well if a baker's balance scale is not available. However, a **portion scale** is operated by the use of a spring and can be unbalanced easily, so it is recommended that ingredients be weighed using the baker's balance scale if at all possible.

Portioning foods for service is a control method used in industry to ensure that the correct amount of an item or preparation is acquired and served. The scale would be used to portion a 3-ounce serving of baked ham, a 2½-ounce serving of roast turkey, a 5-ounce hamburger steak, or a 4½-ounce patty of pork sausage. If the exact cost of each item sold is to be determined, it is necessary to know the yield of each food. For example, if 15 pounds of beef round cost $27.75, the cost per serving cannot be determined until a serving portion and yield are established after the meat has been roasted.

The portion scale shown in Figure 5–18 is used to weigh quantities up to 32 ounces (2 pounds). Each number on the movable dial represents 1 ounce. Each mark between the numbers represents ¼ ounce. For instance, the first mark past the pointer is ¼ ounce. The longer line next to it is ½ ounce. The short line next in order is ¾ ounce, and the long line that comes next is 1 full ounce.

The platform at the top of the portion scale is attached to a metal stem that fits into the scale. It is made of stainless steel and can be removed for washing, but care must be taken when replacing it to ensure that it fits properly and performs accurately. When the platform is properly placed, the pointer rests on 0, which also represents 32 ounces when weighing takes place. When weighing amounts that fit on the platform, first place waxed paper or some type of patty paper on the platform. Then, using the handle to move the scale dial, move the dial to the left until the pointer is again at zero. This action accounts for the weight of the paper. Place enough of the item being weighed on the paper until the pointer is exactly at the amount needed. For example, if portioning a 3-ounce crab cake, place enough of the mixture on the platform so that the pointer points directly at the 3, indicating that 3 ounces have been obtained. When weighing amounts that do not fit properly on the platform, use a light aluminum cake or pie pan to hold the item. Before weighing the item, however, be sure to balance the pan using the same method as for balancing the paper.

Figure 5–18
Measuring meat on a portion scale helps control serving size and cost.
© Cengage Learning 2012

Discussion Question 5-5

What is the most important thing to remember about measuring volume and weight?

Practice Problems 5–4   The Portion Scale

Determine both the weight and the cost of the food product for the following problems. Round answers to the hundredths place, if necessary.

31. Determine the cost of a hamburger if the dial pointer on the portion scale points to the second mark beyond the 5 and the cost of 1 pound of lean ground beef is $3.99.

    _____

32. Determine the cost of a portion of cooked corned beef if the dial on the portion scale points to the third mark beyond the 2 and the cost of 1 pound of cooked corned beef is $5.25.

    _____

33. Determine the cost of a portion of cooked ham if the dial pointer on the portion scale points to the first mark beyond the 3 and the cost of 1 pound of cooked ham is $3.45.

    _____

34. Determine the cost of a portion of roast loin of pork if the dial pointer on the portion scale points to the second mark beyond the 4 and the cost of 1 pound of roasted pork loin is $3.99. _____

35. Determine the cost of a filet mignon if the dial pointer on the portion scale points to the second mark beyond the 8 and the cost of 1 pound of beef tenderloin is $9.95.

    _____

Converting Decimal Weights into Ounces

As the food service industry moves toward using weights of ingredients based on the decimal system, the professional must know how to convert the amount of a decimal into various units of weight.

Manufacturers are selling scales based upon the decimal system, where the base number is 10. This causes people to become confused because 0.5 is actually 8 ounces (0.5 × 16 = 8)—0.5 is not 5 ounces.

Many recipes state ingredients in ounces. For example, a soup recipe requires 5 ounces of pepperoni, or a salad dressing requires 6 ounces of blue cheese. In the past, the food service professional used the ounce scale. It was, and still is, easy to weigh the ingredients on this scale. However, purveyors are beginning to sell and price ingredients based on the decimal system. It is common to have food products listed on invoices in pounds using decimal numbers. The amount of blue cheese may be listed on an invoice as 5.637 pounds. How will the chef determine how many ounces have been received in this case? He must be convert this measurement to ounces. There are 16 ounces in a pound. Therefore, 5 pounds × 16 = 80 ounces. That is the easy part. But how many ounces of blue cheese does the 0.637 represent? To find the answer, 16 must be multiplied by 0.637 ounces, which equals 10.192 ounces.

To Insure Perfect Solutions

The food service professional must realize that 0.5 on a digital scale is not 5 ounces, but instead equals 8 ounces or half of a pound (16 × 0.5 = 8 ounces).

Decimal on the Scale	Amount of Ounces
0.1	1.6
0.2	3.2
0.3	4.8
0.4	6.4
0.5	8
0.6	9.6
0.7	11.2
0.8	12.8
0.9	14.4
1	16

Figure 5–19
The relationship between decimal numbers and ounces in a pound.
© Cengage Learning 2012

Here's how to calculate the math:

Decimal amount of ounces	0.637
Number of ounces in a pound	× 16
Total ounces	10.192 ounces

Add this amount to the 5 pounds, which equals 80 ounces. The 80 ounces plus the 10.192 ounces adds up to 90.192 ounces.

Discussion Question 5-6

Is 1.5 pounds of cheese the same as 24 ounces of cheese? If not, which is more? Explain how you arrived at your answer.

Figure 5–19 shows the relationship between decimal numbers and ounces in a pound.

Practice Problems 5–5   Converting Decimal Weights into Ounces

Find the number of ounces in the following problems. Do not round the answers.

36. 0.55 lb. _____

37. 0.75 lb. _____

38. 0.15 lb. _____

39. 0.333 lb. _____

40. 0.697 lb. _____

41. 0.737 lb. _____

42. 0.985 lb. _____

43. 0.279 lb. _____

44. Chef Bhutta orders and receives 256.75 ounces of chicken. If each guest receives a 8-ounce portion of chicken, how many guests can be served?

_____

45. The Merlot Restaurant receives 10 ribs of beef weighing 22.72 pounds each. How many ounces of beef does this represent? _____

six

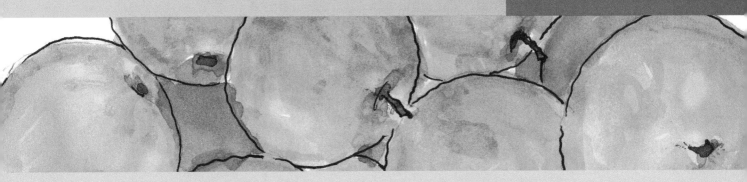

Using the Metric System of Measure

Objectives

At the completion of this chapter, the student should be able to:

1. Recite the basic units of measure of the metric system.
2. Compute length using meters.
3. Compute mass or weight using kilograms or grams.
4. Compute volume using liters.
5. Compute temperature using degrees Celsius.
6. Recognize the increase in the use of metrics in the U.S. food service industry.
7. Change measurements from the customary system to the metric system.
8. Find the cost of food and beverage products using the metric system.

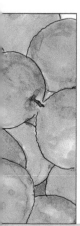

Key Words

metric system	kilograms	prefixes	dekameter
milliliters	liters or cubic	decimeter	hectometer
grams	meters	centimeter	kilometer
meters	degrees Celsius	millimeter	cubic centimeter

History of the Metric System in the United States

What Is the Metric System?

The **metric system** of measure is a decimal system based on the number 10. It is difficult to understand why this system of measure has never been adopted for exclusive use in the United States. This system is more accurate than the system that is used in the United States, which relies on quarts, pounds, ounces, and so forth. It is especially useful in baking because baking is a science where exact measurements are needed to produce consistent-quality baked products.

France introduced the metric system to the world during the French Revolution. France's lawmakers, during that period of history, asked the country's scientists to develop a system of measurement based on science rather than custom. They developed a system of measurement that was based upon a length called the *meter.*

The metric system has been used in a limited capacity over the last 40 years in the United States, but never to its fullest extent. Perhaps it can be blamed on the fact that most people resist change. There have been attempts over the years to bring about the change. In 1971, the Department of Commerce recommended that the United States adopt the system in a report made to Congress. The report stated that the question was not whether the United States should go metric but how the switch should take place. It proposed that the switch be made over a 10-year period, as Great Britain and Canada did. A key element in the Great Britain and Canadian conversion was education. It became the only system taught in the primary schools. The general public was taught the metric system and terms by means of magazines, posters, television, newspapers, radio, and so forth. A demonstration center was even set up so that the public could practice purchasing food using the metric system. In the United States, little action was taken on this report until December 23, 1975. At that time, President Gerald Ford signed into law the Metric Conversion Act, establishing a national policy in support of the metric system and supposedly ending the dilemma that had continued for so long.

With the signing of the new law, it was understood that, through a national policy of coordinating the increasing use of metrics in the United States, the conversion to the metric system would be done on a voluntary basis. The government also created a metric board, appointed by the president with the advice and consent of the Senate. The board was made up of individuals from the various economic sectors that would be influenced most by the metric changeover. Included were people representing labor, science, consumers, manufacturing, construction, and so forth. The function of this board was to create and carry out a program that would allow the development of a sensible plan for a voluntary changeover. This all took place in the 1970s. Today, little is heard of this law or program, although some progress is being made slowly. In 1988, President George H. W. Bush ordered every federal agency to go metric. However, again the president was not specific as to when the change should occur. No timetable was set—the president left it to each individual federal agency. Some of these agencies have set a date for the change, while others have not. The Federal Highway Administration, for example, moved forward and ordered states to use the metric system in designing all roads that were built after September 30, 1996. If states did not comply, a penalty was assessed.

Industries That Use the Metric System

Some industries, notably in science, pharmaceuticals, engineering, and automotive, have found it necessary to go metric to participate in world trade. The medical field has also joined in the use of metric terminology. Doctors learn early in their training to specify drug dosage in metric units. Today, over *90 percent* of the world's population uses the metric system. It is also used by over *nine-tenths* of the world's *nations*.

In the United States, metric measurements are gradually being introduced and used in many industries, among them the food and beverage industry. For example, when a person buys a beverage (soda, coffee, etc.), the measurement often appears on the package in both metric terms and the customary measurements that have always been used. For instance, the authors purchased a "to go" cup of coffee, and on the paper cup was printed "12 ounces," along with the metric measurement of "355 ml" (which stands for **milliliters**). When the authors received a package of potato chips with their sandwich, the package listed the weight as 1 oz. or 28 g (which stands for **grams**). Because the metric system is exact, it is better to use it in baking because ingredients are usually weighed rather than measured. The textbook *Professional Baking,* by Wayne Gisslen, gives recipes in customary (or, as he calls it, "U.S.") measurements along with metric measurements.

Therefore, as the United States changes to the metric system, the people who will be affected most are those whose jobs are concerned with weights and measures. This is certainly the case for food service workers. Instead of pints, quarts, and gallons, they will have to adjust to liters, milliliters, and so on. The change has been integrated slowly into our industry, especially with bottles of wine. There are very few bottles of wine that are sold in the United States today using the customary U.S. measures. Instead of pounds and ounces, the industry will use kilograms and grams; and instead of degrees Fahrenheit, temperature will be in degrees *Celsius* (previously known as *Centigrade*). The purpose of this chapter, therefore, is to make these terms and others dealing with the metric system more familiar to the food service student.

Discussion Question 6-1

Find five food or beverage products that you have at home that have their contents listed in metric measurements. Why are companies listing their contents in metric terms?

In recent years, food service students in the United States have been exchanged with students from foreign countries in similar programs. When an exchange like this takes place, certainly recipes and formulas are exchanged, making knowledge of the metric system an asset. The student should be able to convert recipes and formulas both ways; that is, from customary to metric and vice versa.

As stated before, the metric system is a decimal system based on the number 10. For example, when the meter is divided by 10, it produces 10 *decimeters;* a decimeter divided by 10 produces 10 *centimeters;* and a centimeter divided by 10 produces 10 *millimeters.* To put it another way, one meter equals 1,000 millimeters, or 100 centimeters, or 10 decimeters. This system of measure seems more practical when compared to our customary units of measure—the yard, which is divided into 3 feet (or 36 inches); and the foot, which is divided into 12 inches.

To Insure Perfect Solutions

Meters (m) measure lengths; **liters** (l) measure volume; **grams** (g) measure weight; and temperature is measured in **Celsius (°C).**

The metric system also provides standard rules for communicating the amounts of its units through prefixes. For example, *a milligram* is one-thousandth of a gram (weight), *a milliliter* is one-thousandth of a liter (volume), and a *millimeter* is one-thousandth of a meter (length). When the unit is increased and the prefix *kilo* is added, a *kilogram* is 1,000 grams and a *kilometer* is 1,000 meters. The customary system lacks this kind of uniformity and predictability.

"The knowledge of mathematics is so important in baking because it ensures the result is the same with each formula produced, regardless of its amount or volume. Scaling and measuring accurately are absolutely imperative.

"The United States is the only major country that uses a complex system of measurements (pounds, ounces, etc.). The rest of the world uses the metric system. Most people think the metric system is harder than it actually is. Metric kitchens do not work with impractical numbers, such as 454 g = 1 lb., 28.35 g = 1 oz., or 191°C. No surprise, most people are scared of the metric system. American industry will probably adopt the metric system sometime in the future."

Richard Wagner
Pastry Chef

Chef Richard Wagner has been the executive pastry chef at the Oahu Country Club in Honolulu, Hawaii. Chef Wagner has had a vast amount of experience as a pastry chef on cruise ships and in first-class hotels and pastry shops, both domestic and international. Chef Wagner is also a chef/instructor/lecturer at community colleges in Hawaii. Chef Wagner was awarded a master's degree in patisserie and confiserie from the Culinary Institute of Vienna in 1972.

Units of Measure in the Metric System

The best way to learn the metric system is to forget all about the customary measurements and simply think metric. To "think metric" is to think in terms of 10 and to understand the following basics: the **meter** represents *length;* **grams,** or, in most cases, **kilograms**, represent *mass or weight;* **liters or cubic meters** represent *volume;* and **degrees Celsius** deals with *temperature.* To compare these new units of measure with familiar ones, a meter is about 39 inches, which is slightly longer than a yard. The gram is a very small unit of mass; it measures 0.03527396 of an ounce, so to make a comparison, it is necessary to take 1,000 grams or 1 kilogram, which is equal to 2.204623 pounds. A liter is equal to 1.056 U.S. quarts or 33.814 fluid ounces, which means it is about 5 percent larger than a quart. There are other units of measure in the metric system, but the ones mentioned are those that will be of most concern to the people involved in food service.

Length

It was stated that to think metric is to think in terms of 10. To show how this is done, take the base unit of length (the *meter*), and multiply or divide it by 10. Each time the meter is multiplied or divided by 10, special names are attached on the front of the word to indicate the value. These names are called **prefixes.** Lengths smaller than a meter are divided by 10, and the result is called a **decimeter.** Dividing a decimeter by 10 gives a **centimeter.** When the centimeter is divided by 10, it is called a **millimeter.**

    1 decimeter = 0.1 meter (a tenth of a meter)
    1 centimeter = 0.01 meter (a hundredth of a meter)
    1 millimeter = 0.001 meter (a thousandth of a meter)

So for units smaller than a meter, the prefixes are *deci* (a tenth of a meter), *centi* (a hundredth of a meter), and *milli* (a thousandth of a meter).

For lengths larger than a meter, multiply by 10. For 10 meters, the prefix *deka* is used. For 100 meters, the prefix is *hecto.* The prefix for 1,000 is *kilo.* So 10 meters are called a **dekameter,** 100 meters a **hectometer,** and 1,000 meters a **kilometer.** *Kilo* is a familiar prefix because distances on roadways in the United States are sometimes given in kilometers along with miles.

    1 kilometer   = 1,000 meters
    1 hectometer = 100 meters
    1 dekameter = 10 meters

To Insure Perfect Solutions

The length of a *meter* is about *one giant step.*

Volume and Capacity

When measuring volume and capacity, it is first necessary to understand what a cubic meter is before learning what a liter represents. A *cubic meter* is a cube with each side being 1 meter long. In other words, a cubic meter equals the length of 1 meter, the width of 1 meter, and the height of 1 meter. If a metal container is ¹⁄₁₀ of a meter (one decimeter) on each side, it is referred to as 1 *liter.* It would contain

1 liter of liquid, which the U.S. system refers to as fluid ounces. As you have learned in Chapter 5, however, not all liquids weigh the same. So a liter measures volume or fluid ounces, not weight. Common sizes of bottles of wine are 375 ml, which holds 12.7 fluid ounces; 750 ml, which holds 25.4 fluid ounces; and 1.5 liters, which hold 50.7 fluid ounces. This knowledge becomes important when a food service manager has to determine how many glasses of wine can be obtained from a specific-sized bottle based on how many ounces a specific glass can hold. For units smaller than a liter, a container that has sides of 1 centimeter long is called a **cubic centimeter.** It would hold 1 milliliter of water, and 1 milliliter weighs 1 gram of water (or a liquid of water-like consistency) . From this, you can see that, in the metric system, there is a very direct relationship among length, volume, and mass.

Mass or Weight

The base unit for mass is the gram, but (as stated before) the gram is such a small unit of weight that it did not prove practical for application, so the kilogram (1,000 grams) is used as the base unit. It is the only base unit that contains a prefix. When the metric system is adopted, weights may be given in grams or kilograms. Because the kilogram is a fairly large unit, it may be too large to be a convenient unit for packing most foodstuffs, so the half-kilo (500 grams) may become a more familiar unit. Prefixes such as *deci, centi, milli, hecto,* and *deka* may be used with the gram, but they are not practical in everyday life, so the gram and kilogram are the common terms used.

When using the metric system, it is sometimes more efficient and practical to use abbreviations. (See Figure 6–1.)

To Insure Perfect Solutions

One **gram** is about the weight of a medium paper clip. One **kilogram** is about the weight of a large book or dictionary.

Quantity	Unit	Symbol
Length	meter	m
	decimeter	dm
	centimeter	cm
	millimeter	mm
	kilometer	km
	hectometer	hm
	dekameter	dam
Volume	cubic centimeter	cm³
	cubic meter	m³
Capacity	milliliter	ml
	liter	l
Mass	gram	g
	kilogram	kg
Temperature	degrees Celsius	°C

Figure 6–1
Metric units and their symbols.
© Cengage Learning 2012

Temperature

In the metric system, temperature is measured in degrees Celsius (°C). On the Celsius scale, the boiling point of water is 100° and the freezing point is 0°. On the Fahrenheit (F) scale, the boiling point is 212° and the freezing point is 32°.

(See Figure 6–2.) Actually, the official metric temperature scale is the Kelvin scale, which has its zero point at absolute zero. Absolute zero is the coldest possible temperature in the universe. The Kelvin scale is used often by scientists and very seldom, if ever, in everyday life.

To convert Fahrenheit temperature to degrees Celsius: Subtract 32 from the given Fahrenheit temperature and multiply the result by ⁵⁄₉.

For example, your restaurant calls for cooking hamburgers to 155°F. What is the temperature in degrees Celsius?

Step 1:	Subtract 32 from the given Fahrenheit temperature	$155 - 32 = 123$
Step 2:	Multiply the result by ⁵⁄₉	$123 \times ⁵⁄₉ = ⁶¹⁵⁄₉$
Step 3:	Divide by 9	$⁶¹⁵⁄₉ = 68.33$
Step 4:	The answer is	68.33°C

To Insure Perfect Solutions
Pay attention to the scale increments when reading a thermometer.

To convert Celsius degrees to Fahrenheit: Multiply the Celsius temperature by ⁹⁄₅ and add 32 to the result.

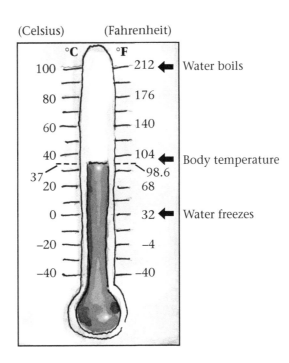

Figure 6–2
Some common temperatures expressed in Fahrenheit and Celsius.
© Cengage Learning 2012

Your new job is in a country that gives the temperature in Celsius degrees. What is the Fahrenheit temperature when it is reported to be 25°C?

Step 1:	Multiply the Celsius temperature by ⁹⁄₅	$25 \times ⁹⁄₅ = 45$
Step 2:	Add 32 to the results	$45 + 32 = 77$
	The answer: 25°C is 77 °F	77°F

Discussion Question 6-2

Why is it important to know metric information as a culinarian?

Practice Problems 6–1 Temperature

Converting Fahrenheit to Celsius

Convert the following Fahrenheit temperatures to Celsius. Round off all answers to the hundredths place.

1. 46 _____

2. 41 _____

3. 22 _____

4. 140 _____

5. 80 _____

6. 200 _____

7. 250 _____

8. 350 _____

9. 315 _____

10. −10 _____

Converting Celsius to Fahrenheit

Convert the following Celsius temperatures to Fahrenheit. Round off all answers to the hundredths place.

11. 7 _____

12. 3 _____

13. 25 _____

14. 56 _____

15. 13 _____

16. 75 _____

17. 19 _____

18. 12 _____

19. 42 _____

20. 4 _____

Converting Recipes from Customary Measurements to the Metric System

A tremendous amount of recipes have been written since this country was founded. Almost all these recipes are written in customary measurements. Some of these recipes are family favorites that the culinarian would like to duplicate in the food service occupation in which he or she works. To assist in helping U.S. cooks learn about both the customary and metric systems, companies like Ohaus are developing and selling scales that weigh by the pound, decimal ounce, fractional ounce, gram, and kilogram.

Figure 6–3 is a chart that provides the multipliers to the culinarian to convert customary measurements to metric units.

Using the information from Figure 6–3, we will illustrate how to convert a fricassee of veal recipe, as shown in Figure 6–4.

The first ingredient (18 pounds of veal) is multiplied by the kilogram multiplier of 0.4535937, found in the "Mass or Weight" row in Figure 6–3. The result is 8.1646866 kilograms. The last item, flour, is converted to ounces and multiplied by the grams multiplier. When Figure 6–3 is consulted, notice that we are multiplying like amounts; for instance, we multiply pounds by the multiplier for kilograms; we do not multiply pounds by the multiplier for grams. It is necessary to change items into the correct categories—otherwise, the answer will be wrong. Follow this same procedure to convert a recipe from the metric system to the customary system, as shown in Figure 6–6.

Figure 6–3
Conversion from customary to metric units.
© Cengage Learning 2012

Measurement Conversion: Converting U. S. Measurements to Metric Units

	When you know	Multiply by	To find	Symbol
Length	Inches	2.54	Centimeters	cm
	Feet	0.3048	Centimeters	cm
	Yards	0.9144	Meters	m
	Miles	1.609347	Kilometers	km
Capacity	Teaspoons	4.92892	Milliliters	ml
	Tablespoons	14.78677	Milliliters	ml
	Fluid Ounces	29.57353	Milliliters	ml
	Fluid Ounces	0.2957353	Liters	1
	Fluid Cups	0.236588	Liters	1
	Fluid Pints	0.0473176	Liters	1
	Fluid Quarts	0.94635	Liters	1
	Fluid Gallons	3.785412	Liters	1
Mass or Weight	Ounces	28.349523125	Grams	g
	Pounds	0.4535937	Kilograms	kg

Ingredients	Multiply by		Metric
18 lbs. of veal shoulder cut into 1-inch cubes			
To solve the problem: multiply 18 times (×)	0.4535937	=	8.1646866 kilograms
3 gallons of water	3.785412	=	11.356236 liters
2 lbs. of shortening	0.4535937	=	0.9071874 kilograms
1 lb., 8 oz. of flour (change this to ounces)			
1 lb. = 16 oz. + 8 = 24 oz.			
To solve the problem: multiply 24 times (×)	28.349523125	=	680.388555 grams
Salt and pepper to taste			

Figure 6–4
Converting a recipe from customary measurements to metric measurements.
© Cengage Learning 2012

Figure 6–5 is a table for converting metric measurements to customary measurements. Figure 6–6 illustrates how to convert an éclair dough recipe from metric to customary measurements. This also demonstrates why metric measurements are better to use. When converting the butter, the metric measurement is exact at 450 g, but to weigh out 15.2163 oz. is difficult, so if the baker were relying on customary measurements, he would likely just add a pound of butter, which would be inaccurate. The same is true for all the measurements. This illustration again emphasizes why metrics are more accurate in baking than the customary U.S. measurements.

Figure 6–5
Conversion from metric measurements to customary measurements.
© Cengage Learning 2012

Measurement Conversion: Converting Metric Units to U.S. Measurements

	When you know	Multiply by	To find	Symbol
Length	Centimeters	0.3937	Inches	in.
	Meters	3.28	Feet	ft.
	Meters	1.09361	Yards	yd.
	Kilometers	0.62	Miles	mi.
Capacity	Milliliters	0.20288	Teaspoons	tsp.
	Milliliters	0.067628	Tablespoons	tbsp.
	Milliliters	0.033814	Fluid ounces	fl. oz.
	Liters	33.814	Fluid ounces	fl. oz.
	Liters	4.22675	Fluid cups	C.
	Liters	2.113	Fluid pints	pt.
	Liters	1.05669	Fluid quarts	qt.
	Liters	0.26417	Fluid gallons	gal.
Mass or Weight	Grams	0.035274	Ounces	oz.
	Kilograms	2.204623	Pounds	lb.

Ingredients in metric	Multiply by		Customary
500 ml water			
To solve the problem: multiply 500 times (×)	0.033814	=	16.907 fl. oz.
5 ml salt	0.20288	=	1.0144 tsp or t.
22 ml sugar	0.067628	=	1.487816 tbsp
450 g butter or margarine	0.033814	=	15.2163 oz.
450 g bread flour	0.033814	=	15.2163 oz.
16 eggs			16 eggs

Figure 6–6
Recipe conversion from metric to customary measurements.
© Cengage Learning 2012

Metric		Customary
1 gram	=	0.03527396 ounce
1 kilogram	=	2.204623 pounds
28.34952313 grams	=	1 ounce
453.59237 grams	=	1 pound
4.92892 milliliters	=	1 teaspoon
14.78680 milliliters	=	1 tablespoon
236.58824 milliliters	=	1 cup
473.17648 milliliters	=	1 pint
946.3529 milliliters	=	1 quart
375 milliliters	=	12.7 fluid ounces
750 milliliters	=	25.4 fluid ounces
1 liter	=	33.814 fluid ounces
1.5 liters	=	50.7 fluid ounces
2 liters	=	67.628 fluid ounces

Figure 6–7
Weights and measures equivalents.
© Cengage Learning 2012

Figure 6–7 provides equivalents of weights and measures between the customary and metric measurements that may be used as a quick reference and may prove helpful to the food service professional.

Practice Problems 6–2 Converting Recipes

Converting Recipes from Customary Measurements to the Metric System

Convert recipes A through E from the U.S. customary system to the metric system. Use the conversion table shown in Figure 6–3. Round off all answers to the hundredths place.

A. White cream icing ingredients

1 lb., 4 oz. shortening	21._____ g
¼ oz. salt	22._____ g
5 oz. dry milk	23._____ g
14 fl. oz. water	24._____ ml
5 lbs. powdered sugar	25._____ kg
vanilla to taste	26._____ to taste

B. Yellow cake ingredients

2 lbs., 8 oz. cake flour	27._____ kg
1 lb., 6 oz. shortening	28._____ g
3 lbs., 2 oz. granulated sugar	29._____ kg
1 oz. salt	30._____ g
1¾ oz. baking powder	31._____ g
4 oz. dry milk	32._____ g
1 lb., 4 oz. water	33._____ g
1 lb., 10 oz. whole eggs	34._____ g
12 fl. oz. water	35._____ ml
vanilla to taste	36._____ to taste

C. Italian meringue ingredients

1 lb. egg whites	37._____ g
1 lb., 8 oz. water	38._____ ml
1 lb., 12 oz. sugar	39._____ g
1½ oz. egg white stabilizer	40._____ ml
⅛ oz. vanilla	41._____ ml

D. Vanilla pie filling ingredients

12 lbs. liquid milk	42._____ kg
4 lbs. granulated sugar	43._____ kg
1 lb. cornstarch	44._____ g
¼ oz. salt	45._____ g
2 lbs. whole eggs	46._____ g
6 oz. butter	47._____ g
vanilla to taste	48._____ to taste

E. Fruit glaze ingredients

2 lbs. water	49._____ g
2 lbs., 8 oz. granulated sugar	50._____ kg
8 fl. oz. water	51._____ ml
4 oz. modified starch	52._____ g
4 fl. oz. corn syrup	53._____ ml
1 fl. oz. lemon juice	54._____ ml
food color as desired	

Converting Recipes from the Metric System to the Customary System

Convert recipes F through J from the metric system to the U.S. customary system. Use the conversion table shown in Figure 6–5. Answers should be rounded to the hundredths place.

F. Chicken à la king ingredients

4.5 kilograms boiled chicken or turkey, diced	55._____ lb.
0.45 kilograms green peppers, diced	56._____ lb.
227 grams pimentos, diced	57._____ oz.
0.9 kilograms mushrooms, diced	58._____ lb.
2.8 liters chicken stock	59._____ qt.
0.74 kilograms flour	60._____ lb.
0.9 kilograms shortening	61._____ lb.
2.8 liters milk	62._____ qt.
240 milliliters sherry wine	63._____ fl. oz.

G. Tartar sauce ingredients

110 grams dill pickles, chopped fine   64._____ oz.

60 grams onions, chopped fine   65._____ oz.

0.14 grams parsley, chopped fine   66._____ oz.

1 liter mayonnaise   67._____ qt.

5 milliliters lemon juice   68._____ tsp.

H. Cocktail sauce ingredients

0.95 liters catsup   69._____ qt.

0.6 liters chili sauce   70._____ oz.

0.24 liters prepared horseradish   71._____ oz.

120 milliliters lemon juice   72._____ fl. oz.

30 milliliters Worcestershire sauce   73._____ fl.oz.

hot sauce to taste   74._____ to taste

I. Spicy peach mold ingredients

0.95 liters peaches, canned, sliced, drained   75._____ qt.

0.45 liters peach syrup   76._____ fl. oz.

0.45 liters hot water   77._____ fl. oz.

0.95 liters cold water   78._____ fl.oz.

0.24 liters vinegar   79._____ fl. oz.

0.36 liters sugar   80._____ C.

28 grams cinnamon stick   81._____ oz.

15 milliliters whole cloves   82._____ tsp.

392 grams orange gelatin   83._____ oz.

J. Brussels sprouts and sour cream ingredients

2.7 kilograms brussels sprouts   84._____ lb.

30 milliliters salt   85._____ tsp.

112 grams onions, minced   86._____ oz.

140 grams butter   87._____ oz.

0.90 kilograms sour cream   88._____ oz.

water to cover, boiling

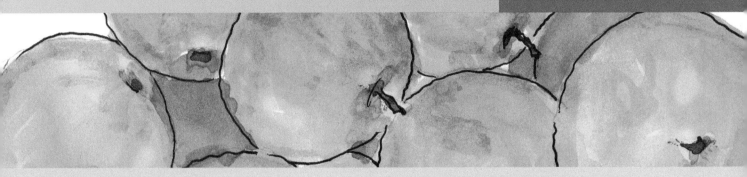

Portion Control

Objectives

At the completion of this chapter, the student should be able to:

1. Identify methods of controlling portion size.
2. Identify portion sizes.
3. Find the cost per serving.
4. Identify portion sizes using scoops and ladles.
5. Identify and find amounts of food to prepare.
6. Define and identify the terms E.P. (Edible Portion) and A.P. (As Purchased).
7. Find the approximate number of serving portions.
8. Find the amount of food to order.
9. Find the amount of cost per portion.
10. Be able to conduct and determine a yield test.

Key Words

portion control	As Purchased (A.P.)	yield	yield test
convenience foods	fabrication	drained weight test	(sometimes called butcher's yield)
portion size	Edible Portion (E.P.)	yield percentage	
cost per serving	shrinkage		

There is a saying in food service that a good, rich stock is the key to kitchen production. However, portion control is the key to profits.

Portion control is a term used in the food service industry to ensure that a specific or designated amount of an item is served to the guest. It is also the method used to acquire the correct number of servings from a standardized recipe, roast, vegetable preparation, cake, or pie. In addition, portion control is helpful in controlling food production, pricing the menu, purchasing, and controlling food cost.

Achieving Portion Control

The best way to control portions is to use standardized recipes that state the number of servings that a preparation will produce. However, a standardized recipe gives only the stated number of portions if the servings have a uniform size. To ensure uniform servings or portions, the food or baking preparation crew and serving personnel must be instructed in the proper use of ladles, scoops, scales, spoons, and similar measuring devices when portioning food (see Figure 7–1).

Another method of achieving a successful portion control program is intelligent buying. Foods should be bought in sizes that portion well. Work out buying specifications that suit the portion need. For example, cooked smoked ham can be purchased in many types and sizes. Purchase the kind that will produce a ham steak of the desired diameter and one that produces little or no waste. Most link sausage, such as wieners, pork links, and frankfurters, can be purchased at a certain number (6, 8, or 10) to each pound. Purchase the count per pound that best suits the portion requirement. Select veal, pork, lamb, and beef ribs and loins that provide the size chop or slice desired. Appearance is important. If the food does not look appetizing, the first bite may never be taken.

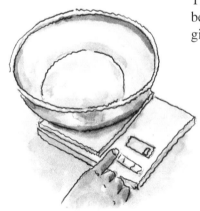

Figure 7–1
The chef is converting a recipe to determine the amounts needed to produce the required number of servings.
© Cengage Learning 2012

Many foods can be purchased ready-to-cook and are purchased for absolute portion control. They are referred to as **convenience foods.** This is another controlling device to consider. Fish fillets, steaks, chops, and cutlets are all cut to the exact ounce desired. (See Figure 7–4, later in this chapter.) The cost per pound is much higher because the more labor involved in fabricating a product, the higher the cost. To many food service operators, the final cost of buying convenience foods is actually lower when considering the following factors:

- no leftovers
- less storage required
- no waste
- no cutting equipment to purchase
- less labor cost

To Insure Perfect Solutions

Always know the exact cost of the food that is placed on the plate in front of a guest.

Methods of Controlling Portion Size

There are five basic methods used in the food service industry to control portion size. They are listed in Figure 7–2 with a few examples of how each can be achieved.

Method	Examples
Weight	5 oz. veal cutlet 8 oz. roast beef 6 oz. roast pork
Count	8 scallops per order 2 Italian meatballs per order 3 corn fritters per order
Volume	2 fluid oz. portion of Hollandaise sauce over vegetables #12 scoop of baked rice 3 oz. slotted spoonful of green beans
Equal portions	Cake cut into 8 equal slices Pie cut into 7 equal wedges Pan of baked lasagna cut into 12 equal servings
Portioned fill	8 oz. casserole of chicken pot pie 5 oz. glass of apple juice 4 oz. cup of chocolate mousse

Figure 7–2
Methods of portion control.
© Cengage Learning 2012

Portioning Food

Each food and beverage item that is served to guests needs to be the same exact size. **Portion size** is defined as the amount or quantity of prepared food or beverage served to an individual guest. When portioning food for a particular establishment, remember that portions can be too large as well as too small. Therefore, before a portion policy is established, the manager (as well as the chef) should know the customers. This knowledge can be acquired by carefully observing the plates brought into the dishwashing area. Too much uneaten food left in a bowl or on a plate indicates that a portion is too large or that the quality of the food does not satisfy the customer. In either case, the situation tells a story and must be corrected to improve customer satisfaction and control food cost. Too small a portion is usually indicated by plates and bowls that are scraped entirely clean.

When portioning food by weight, it is easy to find how much raw food is needed and how much should be prepared for a specific number of people. (See Figure 7–3.)

As an example, the Raven's Nest Restaurant expects to serve 325 hamburgers on Saturday evening. Each hamburger weighs 8 ounces before it is cooked. The chef at the Raven's Nest orders ground beef in bulk from the meat company, ready to be formed into hamburger patties by the staff at the Raven's Nest. Figure 7–3 illustrates how to determine how much raw hamburger to order.

Figure 7–3
How to calculate amount of meat to order for hamburgers at the Raven's Nest.
© Cengage Learning 2012

Step 1
Number to be served = 325 hamburgers

Step 2
Multiply this number by the raw weight of each hamburger, 8 ounces

Step 3
325 × 8 = 2,600 ounces

Step 4
Divide the 2,600 by 16 (ounces in one pound)

Step 5
The answer is 162.5 pounds, or 162 pounds and 8 ounces
Therefore, the formulas are as follows:
Number to be served × portion size = number of ounces needed
Number of ounces needed ÷ 16 (ounces in one pound) = number of pounds needed

Figure 7–4
Precise portion control results in cost management.
© Cengage Learning 2012

Once portion sizes are established for each menu item, the amount of food to prepare is easy to determine. Standardized recipes, which include standardized portion sizes, as illustrated in Figure 7–4 must be available to the kitchen staff so they may determine how much food to prepare. Standardized recipes can be posted, or placed in a recipe book, or loaded onto a computer which the staff has access to in the food preparation area. By observing portion control charts in the preparation area and doing some simple figuring, employees can determine how much food to prepare. Examples of typical portions are shown in the chart in Figure 7–5.

STEWS, BLANQUETTES, HASHES, ETC.

Beef goulash	7 oz.
Beef stew	7 oz.
Veal blanquette	6 oz.
Lamb blanquette	7 oz.
Lamb stew	7 oz.
Veal stew	7 oz.
Oxtail stew	10 oz.
Roast beef hash	6 oz.
Corned beef hash	6 oz.
Chicken hash	6 oz.
Beef stroganoff	7 oz.
Beef à la Deutsch	7 oz.

STARCH AND POTATO PREPARATIONS

Baked	6 oz.
Au gratin	4 oz.
Delmonico	4 oz.
French-fried	5 oz.
Mashed	5 oz.
Julienne	4 oz.
Lyonnaise	5 oz.
Croquette	5 oz.
Hash brown	5 oz.
Escallop	4 oz.
Candied sweet	5 oz.
Rice	4 oz.

VEGETABLES

Asparagus, spears	4 or 5 spears
Asparagus, cut	4 oz.
Beans, limas	4 oz.
Beans, string	4 oz.
Beans, wax	4 oz.
Beets	4 oz.
Brussels sprouts	5 oz.
Cabbage	5 oz.
Cauliflower	5 oz.
Carrots	4 oz.
Corn on the cob	1 cob
Corn, whole kernel	4 oz.
Corn, cream-style	5 oz.
Mushrooms, whole	4 oz.
Onions	5 oz.
Peas	4 oz.
Squash	4 oz.
Succotash	3 oz.
Tomatoes, stewed	4 oz.
Eggplant	4 oz.

DESSERTS

Baked Alaska	1 slice—per Alaska
Compotes	5 oz.
Cake	1 slice—8 per cake
Ice cream	4 oz.
Jubilee	5 oz. ice cream, 2 oz. cherries
Parfaits	5 oz. ice cream, 3 oz. sauce
Pie	1 slice—6 per pie
Pudding	5 oz.
Sherbets	4 oz.

SALADS

Cole slaw	4 oz.
Garden	5 oz.
Ham	5 oz.
Julienne	5 oz.
Macaroni	4 oz.
Potato	5 oz.
Toss	5 oz.
Waldorf	5 oz.

STEAKS

Chateaubriand (for 2 guests)	16 oz.
Filet mignon	8 oz.
Sirloin	10 oz.
N.Y. strip	12 oz.
T-bone	12 oz.
Club	10 oz.
Porterhouse	14 oz.
Salisbury	8 oz.
Ham	6 oz.
Veal	6 oz.
Lamb	7 oz.

CHOPS AND CUTLETS

Pork chops (2)	4 oz. each
Lamb chops (2)	4 oz. each
Veal chop	6 oz.
English lamb chop	6 oz.
Veal cutlet	6 oz.
Pork cutlet	6 oz.
Escallop of veal	7 oz.
Noisette of lamb (2)	3½ oz. each
Pork tenderloin	8 oz.
Beef tournedos (2)	4 oz. each

Figure 7–5
Standardized portion chart. (*continued*)
© Cengage Learning 2012

POULTRY

Fried chicken	½ fryer (3½ lbs. chicken)
Broiled chicken	½ broiler (2 lbs. chicken)
Roast chicken	½ chicken (3 lbs. chicken)
Roast turkey	2½ oz. white meat (3 oz. dark)
Turkey steak	5 oz. white meat
Boneless turkey wings	2 wings
Chicken a la king	6 oz.
Chicken pot pie	8 oz. plus crust
Chicken a la Maryland	½ fryer, 1 oz. bacon, 2 oz. cream sauce, 2 oz. corn fritters, 2 croquettes, 6 oz.
Chicken cutlets (2)	6 oz.
Roast duck	8 oz.
Roast squab	1 bird
Roast boneless chicken breast	5 oz. breast
Baked stuffed chicken leg	1 leg, 3 oz. stuffing

SEAFOOD

Lobster, broiled whole	16 oz.
Lobster Newburg	5 oz. meat
Fried shrimp	6 jumbo—8 medium
Shrimp Newburg	7 medium
Sauteed shrimp	6 jumbo—8 medium
Softshell crabs	2 crabs
Clam roast	8 cherrystone
Steamed clams	8 cherrystone
Fried clams	8 cherrystone
Fried oysters	7 select
Oyster stews	6 select
Fried scallops	8 small—6 large
Sauteed scallops	8 small—6 large
Halibut	7 oz.
Cod	7 oz.
Sea bass	7 oz.
Pampano	7 oz.
Red snapper	6 oz.
Frog legs	8 oz.
Mahi mahi	7 oz.
Lake trout	7 oz.
Rainbow trout	8 oz.
Brook trout	8 oz.
Smelt	6 fish, about 7 oz.
Salmon	7 oz.
Shad roe	4 oz.
English and Dover sole	7 oz.

ROASTED MEATS

Roast rib of beef	8 oz.
Roast tenderloin of beef	6 oz.
Roast sirloin of beef	6 oz.
Roast round of beef	5 oz.
Roast leg of lamb	5 oz.
Roast loin of pork	6 oz.
Roast leg of veal	5 oz.
Roasted fresh ham	6 oz.
Baked ham	6 oz.

Figure 7–5
Standardized portion chart. (*continued*)

"Math is the most important subject to learn because, as a chef/owner, I use it all the time. I have to use math to price my prix fixe menu at a cost that will allow me to make a profit. It also has to be priced so my guests perceive a value, so they will return to the inn. I must keep a guest history of what items sell the best on my menu, so I can forecast how many of each appetizer, entrée, and dessert we will sell. Once I forecast my menu, I have to purchase the correct amount of food so I don't have too much (which would result in spoiled food) or too little (which would result in unhappy guests). The success of the Andrie Rose Inn is dependent on my culinary skills, along with a correct understanding and use of math."

Irene Maston
Certified Executive Chef
American Academy of Chefs
The Andrie Rose Inn
Ludlow, Vermont

Chef Maston and her husband, Michael, are the owners and innkeepers of The Andrie Rose Inn. They provide gracious accommodations in a circa-1829 country village inn with luxury suites. The Andrie Rose Inn has received the three-diamond rating from the American Automobile Association and an A+ Triple Crown excellent rating from the American Bed and Breakfast Association's *Inspected, Rated & Approved Bed & Breakfasts and Country Inns. New York* magazine called it "a place not to be missed," and *USA Today* selected The Andrie Rose Inn as one of the "Top 10 Romantic Inns in the USA." It has also been selected as the most romantic inn in Vermont by Bill Gleenson in *Weekends for Two in New England, 50 Romantic Getaways*. Chef Maston serves a four-course meal every Friday and Saturday, and changes her menu seasonally.

A point to remember when figuring portion sizes is that the average human stomach can only hold approximately 2½ pounds of solid and liquid food comfortably. Therefore, oversized portions do not make customers satisfied and usually create more waste. The intelligent restaurant operator figures portion sizes so that the customer has room left for dessert. An example of how the portion sizes for one meal should add up is given in Figure 7–6. However, this is just a guideline of total portion sizes. Each restaurant owner or manager must determine the mix of what guests will order. Some guests may prefer to have an alcoholic beverage with their meal and skip dessert. Others will have a bottle of wine, which tends to increase the amount of total intake of food and beverages. The portion size that must be determined for a twenty-three-year-old professional football player at training camp and an eighty-year-old person in an assisted living residence is probably vastly different. Each establishment must decide the appropriate size for its particular situation.

Example:

Appetizer	4 oz.
Salad	4 oz.
Entree	8 oz.
Potato	4 oz.
Vegetable	4 oz.
Bread & butter	3 oz.
Dessert	6 oz.
Beverage	7 fl. oz.
	40 oz. = 2½ pounds

Figure 7–6
Ideal portion sizes for one meal.
© Cengage Learning 2012

Cost per Serving

Once the portion sizes have been determined, finding the cost per serving is the next step. To find the **cost per serving,** the total weight or fluid ounces of the item when purchased is converted into avoirdupois ounces or fluid ounces. The ounces are then divided into the total cost of the item purchased to determine the cost of one avoirdupois ounce or one fluid ounce of the item. The cost of one avoirdupois ounce or fluid ounce is multiplied by the number of ounces being served to the guests as a portion. See the following formula to simplify this explanation:

Total weight × 16 = total ounces

Total cost ÷ by total ounces = cost of 1 ounce

Cost of 1 ounce × number of ounces served = cost per serving

Example: A 5-pound box of frozen lima beans costs $6.24. How much does a 4-ounce serving cost?

Weight 5 lbs. × 16 = 80 ounces

$6.24 (total cost) ÷ 80 (ounces) = 0.078 cost of 1 ounce

0.078 (cost of 1 ounce) × 4 (ounces served) = 0.312 × $0.31

(cost of a 4-ounce serving)

The division is carried to three places to the right of the decimal point. Remember that the third digit to the right of the decimal point is the thousandths place or the mill. The next step is to round off to the hundredths place using the mill (thousdandths place) as has been stated in previous chapters.

Of course, if a cost per pound is given rather than a total, the number of pounds given must be multiplied by the cost per pound to find a total cost.

Example: Find the cost of a 3-ounce serving of succotash (mixture of two vegetables) if the following ingredients are used:

5-pound box lima beans @ $1.23 per pound.

2½-pound box corn @ $0.58 per pound.

To state this function as a math formula, it would be expressed as:

Total weight × unit price = total cost.

5 pounds × $1.23 = $6.15 total cost of lima beans.

2½ pounds × $0.58 = $1.45 total cost of corn.

$6.15 + $1.45 = $7.60 total cost of succotash.

To complete the problem, follow the same steps explained in the previous example:

7½ pounds × 16 = 120 ounces.

$7.60 total cost ÷ 120 ounces = $0.063 cost of 1 ounce.

$0.063 cost of 1 ounce × 3 ounces = $0.189 or $0.19 cost of a 3-ounce serving.

These examples are calculated when the product yields 100 percent usable product for a recipe; in other words, there is no waste and the entire contents can be used in serving the guest. Later in this chapter, we will explain the concept of yield testing. In the following chapters, costs will be calculated taking into account how much product can be used for a menu item and how much of the original product is not usable.

Practice Problems 7–1   Cost per Serving

Round answers to the hundredths place.

1. A 2½-pound box of frozen corn costs $1.65. How much does a 4-ounce serving cost?

   _____

2. When preparing succotash, a 2½-pound box of frozen corn costs $0.58 per pound, and a 5-pound box of frozen lima beans costs $1.18 per pound. How much does a 3-ounce serving cost?

   _____

3. A 2½-pound box of frozen peas and onions costs $0.89 per pound. How much does a 3½-ounce serving cost? _____

4. If frozen asparagus spears cost $11.95 for a 5-pound box, how much does a 3-ounce serving cost?

   _____

5. If a 2½-pound box of frozen cut broccoli costs $1.95, what is the cost of a 3½-ounce serving?
   _____   40 onz   0.04875 _____

6. A 5-pound box of frozen asparagus spears costs $2.39 per pound. How much does a 2½-ounce serving cost? _____

7. A 2½-pound bag of frozen oriental vegetable mix costs $1.59 per pound. How much does a 4-ounce serving cost? _____

8. A 3-pound bag of frozen Scandinavian vegetable mix costs $1.29 per pound. How much does a 3½-ounce serving cost? __48____ 0.026875____

9. A 2-pound bag of frozen whole baby carrots costs $1.45 per pound. How much does a 3-ounce serving cost? _____

10. Find the cost of a 5½-ounce serving of a beef stir-fry if the following items were used:
    3-pound bag frozen stir-fry vegetables @ $1.45 per pound.
    5 pounds of sliced fresh beef @ $3.80 per pound.
    ____48____ 6.030 _____

Portioning with Scoops or Ladles

Scoops, as mentioned in Chapter 5, are used to serve and portion such foods as dressings, rice, meat patties, croquette mixtures, ice cream, and muffin batters. Two examples are shown in Figure 7–7. They have a metal bowl or cup of known capacity, an extended handle, and a thumb-operated lever to release the item being portioned or served. A movable strip of metal on the inside of the bowl releases its contents. This metal strip contains a number to indicate the size of the metal cup; the larger the number, the smaller the cup. The number indicates the number of scoops it will take to make a quart. Figure 7–8 relates each scoop number to its approximate capacity in ounces and also to the approximate content of each scoop size in cups or tablespoons.

Figure 7–7
Two examples of food scoops.
© Cengage Learning 2012

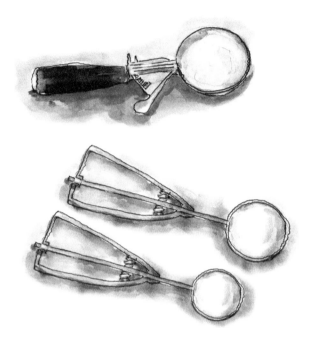

Figure 7–8
Scoop or dipper sizes and approximate weights and measures in both customary and metric units. Different foods will vary in weight, so this chart should be used only as a guide.
© Cengage Learning 2012

Scoop Number	Approximate Volume (Customary)	Approximate Volume (Metric)	Approximate Weight (Customary)	Approximate Weight (Metric)
6	5.33 fl. oz	160 ml	5 oz.	140 g
8	4 fl. oz.	120 ml	4 oz.	110 g
10	3.2 fl. oz.	90 ml	3.25 oz.	92 g
12	2.66 fl. oz.	80 ml	2.75 oz.	78 g
16	2 fl. oz.	60 ml	2.25 oz.	58 g
20	1.6 fl. oz.	45 ml	1.67 oz.	46 g
24	1.33 fl. oz.	40 ml	1.5 oz.	38 g
30	1.07 fl. oz.	30 ml	1.25 oz.	31 g
40	0.8 fl. oz.	24 ml	1 oz.	23 g

Ladle Sizes

Size	Fluid Ounces
¼ cup	2
½ cup	4
¾ cup	6
1 cup	8

Figure 7–9
Ladle sizes.
© Cengage Learning 2012

Ladles are used to portion sauces, gravies, soups, and other liquids. They come in assorted sizes, holding from 2 to 8 ounces. When ladles are used, portions will be consistent. The size, in ounces, is stamped on the handle. Figure 7–9 shows the ladle sizes most frequently used.

Determining the Number of Servings Using Scoops or Ladles

Chefs and cooks must portion food out uniformly for both customer satisfaction and cost control. To find the number of servings of a particular amount of food or liquid when portioning with a scoop or ladle, divide the amount contained in the scoop or ladle into the amount being served. This function, as a formula, appears as follows:

Amount portioned ÷ scoop or ladle content = number of servings

Example: How many servings can be obtained from 4 gallons of ice cream if a #8 scoop is used to portion out the ice cream?

Step 1: Consult the chart in Figure 7–8 and find the #8 scoop. The chart says that the volume will result in 4 U.S. fluid ounces or ½ (0.5) cup. Note: We use the volume (fluid ounces), rather than the weight, because different foods weigh different amounts. As we said in Chapter 5, the weight of one cup of cotton balls does *not* equal the weight of one cup of crushed stone.

Step 2: Because the volume of a #8 scoop is expressed in cups, we must convert the 4 gallons of ice cream to cups; to divide, like amounts are necessary. In other words, we can't divide cups into gallons; cups have to be divided into cups.

1 gallon contains 16 cups

4 gallons times (×) 16 = 64 cups

64 cups are in 4 gallons

Step 3: Cups are divided by the volume size of the scoop.

64 divided by (÷) 0.5, which represents ½ cup

$\frac{64}{1} \times \frac{2}{1} = 128$ servings

Example: How many servings of soup can be obtained from 5 gallons of soup using a ¾-cup ladle?

Step 1: Consult the chart in Figure 7–9 and find the ¾-cup ladle. The chart says that the volume will result in 6 fluid ounces.

Step 2: Because the volume of a ¾-cup ladle is expressed in cups and ounces, we must convert the 5 fluid gallons of soup into fluid cups or fluid ounces; to divide, like amounts are necessary. In other words, we can't divide cups into gallons; cups have to be divided into cups.

1 gallon contains 16 cups

5 gallons times (×) 16 = 80 cups

80 cups are in 5 gallons

or

1 gallon contains 128 fluid ounces

5 gallons times (×) 128 ÷ 640 fluid ounces

640 fluid ounces are in 5 gallons

Step 3:   Cups are divided by the volume size of the ladle.
           80 divided by (÷) ¾ cup

$$^{80}\!/_1 \times ^4\!/_3 = ^{320}\!/_3 = 106.67 \text{ servings}$$

We can obtain 106 servings; the remainder is dropped because it is not a complete portion.

or

Fluid ounces are divided by the fluid ounce size of the ladle:

640 fluid ounces divided by (÷) 6 fluid ounces = 106.67 servings

We can obtain 106 servings; the remainder is dropped, because it is not a complete portion.

Practice Problems 7–2   Determining the Number of Servings Using Scoops and Ladles

Use information from Figures 7–8 and 7–9 to solve the following problems. Only record complete servings; drop any remainders. For example, if in question 11 the answer is 72.333 cups (which it is not), the food service establishment has only 72 cups of soup to serve, so 72 would be the answer.

11. How many servings can be obtained from 16 gallons of soup if a ¾-cup ladle is used?

_____

12. How many servings can be obtained from a quart of Cabernet Sauvignon reduction if a ¼-cup ladle is used? _____

13. Determine how many servings can be obtained from 18 pounds of bread pudding if a #10 scoop is used to portion. _____

14. How many servings can be obtained from 5 quarts of strawberry mousse if a #6 scoop is used to portion? _____

15. How many individual salads can be obtained from 12 pounds of tuna fish salad if a #10 scoop is used to portion? _____

16. How many clam fritters can be obtained from 5 pounds of batter if a #24 scoop is used to portion?

_____

17. How many blueberry muffins can be obtained from 4½ gallons of batter if a #12 scoop is used to portion? _____

18. How many servings can be obtained from ½ gallon of cold pack cheese if a #16 scoop is used to portion? _____

19. How many hush puppies can be obtained from 5½ pounds of batter if a #30 scoop is used to portion? _____

20. How many servings can be obtained from 12 pounds of mashed potatoes if a #8 scoop is used to portion? _____

Figuring Amounts to Prepare

In any food service operation, it is constantly necessary to figure how many cans, boxes, or packages of certain food items are needed or must be opened to have enough food to serve a given number of people. This problem is solved by multiplying the number of people to be served by the portion size, resulting in the number of ounces needed. Next, the weight of the can, box, or package is converted into ounces, and the given amount is divided into the number of ounces needed. If a remainder results from the division, an additional container must be opened. By using mathematics in this situation, guesswork can be eliminated and food preparation can be controlled.

Example: How many #10 cans of green beans are needed to serve a party of 260 people if each person is to receive a 3-ounce serving and each can contains 4 pounds, 6 ounces of green beans after the liquid has been drained from the can?

Steps to simplify this function are as follows:

Step 1:
Determine how many people must be served: 260 people.

Determine the portion size each person will receive: 3 ounces.

Number of people to be served × portion size = ounces needed to serve 260 people.
260 × 3 ounces = 780 ounces

Step 2:
Determine the amount of usable green beans in the can and convert the weight into ounces.

Each can weighs 4 pounds and 6 ounces.

Convert the weight of the total usable green beans into ounces.

First, convert the pounds to ounces:

$$4 \text{ pounds} \times 16 \text{ ounces in a pound} = 64 \text{ ounces}$$

Add the additional 6 ounces:

$$64 \text{ ounces} + 6 = 70 \text{ ounces}$$

70 ounces = content of 1 container.

Step 3:
Determine the amount of servings needed to serve 260 guests:

Ounces needed to serve 260 people ÷ content of one can in ounces = number of cans needed to be ordered to serve 260 guests.
780 ounces ÷ 70 ounces = 11.14 cans

The preceding example shows that 12 #10 cans are needed to serve each of the 260 people a 3-ounce serving. When dividing the content of the can into the number of ounces needed, a remainder resulted, so an additional can must be ordered because many purveyors will not sell the food service establishment a portion of a can.

Practice Problems 7–3   Figuring Amounts to Prepare

Solve the following problems. Round off to the next highest whole number. For example, if question 21 results in the answer of 32.23 boxes (which it does not), round up to 33 boxes.

21. A 3-ounce serving of peas is to be served to each of 150 people. How many boxes of frozen peas should be cooked if each box has 2½ pounds of peas? _____

22. A 3-ounce serving of wax beans is to be served to each of 55 people. How many cans of wax beans are needed if each can has 14 ounces of wax beans? _____

23. How many #2½ cans of pork and beans are required to serve 95 people if each can weighs 1 pound, 10 ounces, and each serving is 6 ounces? _____

24. A 3-ounce serving of peas is to be served to each of 110 people. How many boxes of frozen peas are needed if each box has 5 pounds of peas? _____

25. How many #10 cans of green beans are needed to serve a party of 360 people if each person is to receive a 3½-ounce serving and each can contains 4 pounds, 4 ounces of green beans?

_____

26. How many #5 cans of potato salad are required to serve 96 people if each can weighs 3 pounds, 6 ounces, and each serving is 5½ ounces? _____

27. How many 2½-pound bags of corn will be needed to serve 270 people if each person is to receive a 3½-ounce serving? _____

28. How many boxes of frozen chopped spinach are needed to serve a party of 186 people if each person is to receive a 3-ounce serving and each box weighs 4 pounds? _____

29. How many 5-pound boxes of frozen lima beans are needed to serve a party of 175 people if each person is to receive a 4-ounce serving? _____

30. A 3½-ounce serving of frozen peas and pearl onions is to be served to 145 people. How many 5-pound boxes will be needed? _____

31. How many #10 cans of cut green beans are needed to serve a party of 200 people if each person is to receive a 3-ounce serving and each can contains 5 pounds, 10 ounces of green beans?

_____

32. How many 2-pound bags of Scandinavian vegetable mix will be required to serve a party of 85 people if each person is to receive a 4-ounce serving? _____

33. How many #2½ cans of diced beets are needed to serve a party of 86 people if each person is to receive a 4-ounce serving and each can contains 2 pounds, 5 ounces of beets?

_____

34. How many #5 cans of tomato juice will be needed to serve 132 people if each person is to receive a glass of 4 fluid ounces and each can contains 48 fluid ounces?

_____

35. How many #2½ cans of diced carrots are needed to serve a party of 230 people if each person is to receive a 3-ounce serving and each can contains 1 pound, 12 ounces of diced carrots? _____

Finding the Approximate Number of Serving Portions

Finding approximately how many servings can be acquired from a given amount of food (as shown in Figure 7–10) is another portion control concern. The food service professional must be able to use mathematics to determine how much food to order so the establishment will have the proper amount of food needed for the business. The business has to think like Goldilocks: you can't order too much, and you can't order too little; you have to order enough food so it is JUST RIGHT! For example, how many 12-ounce strip steaks can be cut from a short loin? How many 2-ounce meatballs can be made from a certain amount of ground beef? How many pounds of fish steaks must be ordered for a party of 80 people? How many gallons of orange juice must be ordered to serve a party of 250 people?

Figure 7–10
The picture on the left illustrates appropriate portion control. The picture on the right illustrates an unappealing presentation and inappropriate portion control.
© Cengage Learning 2012

The arithmetic involved in these problems is an essential part of a food service operation. This arithmetic must be accurate to keep inventories at a minimum, to control waste, and to maintain an effective portion control program. Before learning how to do the math to determine the approximate number of serving portions to prepare, the food service professional must know the difference between As Purchased (A.P.) and Edible Portion (E.P.).

As Purchased (A.P.)

When a raw food product is purchased in its natural state, this is called **As Purchased (A.P.).** Before serving the food to guests, an employee has to clean the product and prepare it for consumption. In the cleaning and preparation of the product, there will be a portion of the product that is discarded or can't be used. This is true of many products, whether it is meat (tenderloin of beef), poultry (whole turkey), vegetables (case of romaine lettuce), or fruits (for fruit salad). The tenderloin of beef cannot be taken from the case and cooked as filet mignon. It must be fabricated before it is ready to be cooked. **Fabrication** means that the cook must trim the meat, getting rid of nonusable parts of the tenderloin that cannot be served to guests. In addition, the cook will have to cut the tenderloin into standard-sized portions of filet mignon.

Edible Portion (E.P.)

A product that is ready to be served to guests is called an **Edible Portion (E.P.)**. There are many products offered to the food service industry that are ready to cook and serve without any waste.

Types of Edible Portion (E.P.) Products

Edible Portion (E.P.) products can be described in three ways. The easiest to understand and deal with are products that are purchased already fabricated and ready to be cooked. The second and third types of E.P. product begin as A.P. products and are converted to E.P. The second type of E.P. product is when a chef purchases a product and has to trim it and fabricate it into equal portions. The third type of E.P. product occurs after food (generally meat) is roasted. It is removed from the oven and cut into equal portions.

The first example of an E.P. is when a chef has to order chicken breasts for a banquet of 300 guests. Each guest will receive one chicken breast weighing 8 ounces. The only preparation needed before the breast is cooked is for the chef to add his or her special ingredients or marinades. There is no waste in buying the product. The chef knows the exact cost, weight, and portion size of all 300 breasts when purchased.

The second example can be described as follows: A chef purchases a short loin of beef. After fabricating the short loin, the loin is cut into steaks. The chef now has steaks that are in the E.P. state. They can be grilled and served to the guests.

In an example of the third type, when a chef roasts a prime rib of beef, a certain percentage of the weight of the product is lost through cooking (this is called **shrinkage**). After the roast is taken from the oven and rests the proper time, it is cut into desired portion weights and served to the guests in an E.P. state.

Therefore, the food service professional can purchase products As Purchased (A.P.) and fabricate them to get them to their desired state of Edible Portion (E.P.), or buy products ready to cook or even, in some instances, ready to be served directly to the guests without any preparation.

It is critical that food service professionals know how to determine the E.P. of products, both for determining serving portions and figuring out the food cost of the product. Two key factors that must be considered in the E.P. are *shrinkage* and *yield*.

How to Determine the Number of Servings (Yield)

To find out how many servings can be obtained from a given product (the **yield**), the amount of the E.P. product must first be established. Using our three examples previously discussed, we will illustrate how to obtain the yield.

In the first example, the chef simply has to place an order for the 300 chicken breasts. The chef knows that the yield will result in 300 (8-oz.) chicken breasts.

For the second example, the restaurant purchases an 18-pound short loin of beef in the A.P. state. When the prep cook trims and bones the short loin, the resulting waste of bone, fat, and skin cannot be used; in effect, they are lost to the restaurant. This loss amounts to 2 pounds and 10 ounces. When the cook weighs the trimmed short loin, it now weighs 15 pounds and 6 ounces (18 pounds − 2 pounds and 10 ounces). The amount of short loin left is the E.P. before cooking. Once the cook knows the E.P., the amount of servings can be determined. The formula is as follows:

Edible Portion (E.P.) divided by (÷) serving portion = number of servings

Using our short loin example, we will illustrate how to determine the number of servings that the prep cook will obtain.

Step 1: Convert the A.P. 18-pound short loin into ounces (16 ounces in a pound).
18 times (×) 16 = 288 ounces As Purchased (A.P.)

$32 \times 16 = 512$

Step 2: Convert the resulting waste from the short loin, 2 pounds and 10 ounces, into ounces.
2 times (×) 16 = 32 + 10 = 42 ounces of waste

Step 3: Subtract the waste (42 ounces) from the A.P. ounces (288).
288 minus − 42 = 246 ounces. This is now the Edible Portion (E.P.).

Step 4: The portion size of the steak is determined based upon restaurant specifications (12 ounces). This is the E.P. value for one steak.

Step 5: The Edible Portion (E.P.) of the short loin (246 ounces) is divided by the portion size of one steak (12 ounces).
246 divided by (÷) 12 = 20.5 steaks

Therefore, 20 (12-ounce) steaks is the yield that results from this E.P., which equals 240 ounces. This leaves 6 ounces from the short loin that cannot be used because it is not the correct portion size.

Shown as long division:

$$\begin{array}{r} 20.5 \\ 12\overline{)246.0} \\ \underline{24} \\ 60 \\ \underline{60} \end{array}$$ **E.P.** Amount

Each steak is to weigh 12 ounces, so the weight of each steak is divided into 246 ounces, the E.P. amount. This shows that 20 steaks can be cut from the sirloin. It was necessary to convert the E.P. amount to ounces because you can only divide like amounts.

In the third example, the chef will roast a pork loin after it has been fabricated. The pork loin weighs 13 pounds. One pound and 2 ounces are lost through shrinkage. How many 8-ounce portions can be obtained after cooking?

Step 1: Convert the fabricated pork loin into ounces (16 ounces in a pound).
13 times (×) 16 = 208 ounces

$32 \times 16 = 512$

$16 + 1.5 = 17.5$

Step 2: Convert the amount of shrinkage into ounces.
One pound = 16 ounces + 2 ounces = 18 ounces of shrinkage

494.5

Step 3: Subtract the shrinkage from the fabricated pork loin.
208 ounces minus (−) 18 ounces = 190 ounces

Step 4:   The E.P. of the pork loin (190 ounces) is divided by the portion size (8 ounces).

190 divided by 8 (or 190 ÷ 8) = 23.75 portions

Therefore, 23 (8-oz). portions is the yield that results from this E.P., which equals 184 ounces. This leaves 6 ounces from the pork loin that cannot be used because it is not the correct portion size.

Practice Problems 7–4   Finding the Approximate Number of Serving Portions

Solve the following problems. Record answers only as whole numbers; drop any remainders. For example, if in question 36 the answer is 72.333 filets (which it is not), the food service establishment will be able to serve only 72 filets.

36. A 6-pound A.P. beef tenderloin is trimmed; 9 ounces are lost. How many 6-ounce filet mignons can be cut from the tenderloin? _____

37. How many 5-ounce pork chops can be cut from a pork loin weighing 15 pounds A.P. if the tenderloin, which is removed, weighed 9 ounces, and 3 pounds, 5 ounces are lost through boning and trimming?

_____

38. How many orders of meatballs can be obtained from 60 pounds E.P. of ground beef if each meatball is to weigh 1.5 ounces and two meatballs are served per order?

_____

39. How many orders of Swedish meatballs can be obtained from 32 pounds E.P. of ground pork and veal if each meatball weighs 1½ ounces and four meatballs are served with each order?

_____

40. How many 6-ounce Swiss steaks can be cut from a beef round weighing 38 pounds A.P. if 4 pounds, 3 ounces are lost in boning and trimming? _____

41. When preparing pork sausage, 16 pounds A.P. of pork picnic is purchased. One-fourth of the amount is lost through boning and trimming. How many 4-ounce patties can be obtained?

_____

42. How many 6-fluid ounce glasses of orange juice can be obtained from 2 gallons of orange juice?

_____

43. A total of 46 pounds (A.P.) of turkey breast are purchased, and 4 pounds, 4 ounces are lost through boning and skinning. How many turkey steaks can be obtained if each steak is to weigh 5 ounces?

_____

44. A 13-pound (A.P.) pork loin is roasted, and 1 pound, 2 ounces is lost through waste. How many 2½-ounce servings can be obtained from the cooked loin?

_____

45. A 14-pound (A.P.) ham is trimmed, and 12 ounces are lost. How many ham steaks can be cut from the ham if each steak is to weigh 6 ounces? _____

46. A 19-pound (A.P.) rib eye is purchased, and 2 pounds, 14 ounces are lost through trimming. How many rib steaks can be cut from the rib eye if each steak is to weigh 8 ounces?

_____

47. A 12-pound (E.P.) pork loin is purchased. How many 4½-ounce pork cutlets can be cut from the loin?

48. A total of 15 pounds of chicken croquette mixture is prepared. How many croquettes will the mixture produce if each croquette is to weigh 2½ ounces?

49. A 20-pound (A.P.) leg of veal is purchased, and 6 pounds, 6 ounces are lost through trimming and boning. How many 5-ounce veal cutlets can be obtained from the leg of veal?

50. How many 8-ounce hamburgers can be obtained from 45 pounds (E.P.) of ground chuck?

Ordering Food

Controlling amounts to order is another important food service function. Ordering close to the proper amount needed will reduce inventories and help control food cost and waste. When ordering food for a specific number of people, the amount to order can be found by multiplying the amount of the serving portion by the number of people to be served. The result will be the number of ounces required. Next, convert the common purchasing quantity into ounces and divide this amount into the number of ounces needed. (Of course, in the case of meat, fish, etc., consideration must be given to the amount that may be lost through boning and trimming, as already discussed.) A suggested formula is as follows:

> **Amount of portion × number of people served**
> **= number of ounces required**
> **Common purchase quantity × 16**
> **= number of ounces in pound**
> **Number of ounces required ÷ ounces in pound**
> **= number to order**

Example: How many pounds of ground chuck E.P. should be ordered if 42 people are to be served and each person is to receive a 5-ounce portion?

Step 1:

> 5 ounces × 42 = 210 ounces
> Amount of portion × number to be served
> = number of ounces required to serve 42 people

840

Step 2:

> 210 ounces ÷ 16 ounces = 13⅛ = 14 pounds
> Number of ounces required ÷ 16 ounces in one pound
> = amount to order

This example can also be shown as follows:

$$\begin{array}{rl} 42 & \text{Number of people to be served} \\ \times\ 5 & \text{serving portion 5 ounces} \\ \hline 210 & \text{Number of ounces to serve 42 people} \\ \end{array}$$

$$\begin{array}{r} 13\frac{1}{8} \quad \text{14 pounds must be ordered} \\ 16\overline{)210\ \text{oz.}} \\ \underline{16} \\ 50 \\ \underline{48} \\ 2 \end{array}$$

A total of 210 ounces will be required to serve 42 people. The common purchase quantity for meat is pounds. Because there are 16 ounces in a pound, 16 is divided into the number of ounces required. The result is 13 with $\frac{1}{8}$ remaining, so the actual number of pounds to be ordered must be 14 pounds. The remainder indicates that 13 pounds will not produce enough portions to serve 42 people.

Practice Problems 7–5 Ordering Food

Solve the following problems. Round off to the next highest whole number. For example, if question 51 results in the answer of 32.23 sirloins (which it does not), round up to 33 sirloins.

51. For a wedding of 270 guests, an E.P. 8-oz. sirloin steak will be served. If each fabricated sirloin weighs 16 pounds, how many sirloins must be ordered? _____

52. Salisbury steak is to be served to a party of 195 people. Each portion is to weigh 7 ounces. How many E.P. pounds of ground beef must be ordered? _____

53. How many E.P. pounds of pork sausage should be ordered for 68 people if each person is to receive two 2½-ounce patties? _____

54. How many gallons of orange juice must be ordered for a party of 175 people if each person is to receive a 5-fluid-ounce glass? _____

55. How many pounds of bacon should be ordered when serving a breakfast party of 125 people if each person is to receive 3 slices of bacon and there are 16 slices of bacon to each pound?
    _____ 0.12 _____

56. When preparing a breakfast for 220 people, how many pounds of link sausage must be ordered if each person is to receive three sausages and there are eight sausages to each pound?

    _____

57. How many E.P. pounds of short ribs should be ordered when preparing for 80 people if each person is to receive a 12-ounce portion? _____

58. How many pounds of ground beef must be ordered to serve spaghetti and meatballs to 130 people if each person is to receive two 2½-ounce meatballs? _____

59. Pot roast of beef is being served to 110 people. Each person is to receive a 5-ounce serving. It is estimated that 3 pounds will be lost in shrinkage. How many A.P. pounds of beef brisket should be ordered? _____

60. When preparing a breakfast for 138 people, how many pounds of Canadian bacon must be ordered if each person is to receive a 2½-ounce portion? _____

61. How many pounds of ground beef must be ordered when preparing meat loaf for 76 people if each person is to receive a 5½-ounce serving? _____

62. How many gallons of apple juice must be ordered to serve a party of 115 people if each person is to receive a 4-fluid-ounce glass of juice? _____

63. How many E.P. pounds of pork loin must be ordered when serving 4-ounce breaded pork chops to a party of 210 people? _____

64. How many E.P. pounds of spare ribs should be ordered when preparing for 65 people if each person is to receive a 12-ounce portion? _____

65. How many A.P. pounds of beef tenderloin should be ordered to serve a party of 105 people if each person is served a 6-ounce tenderloin steak and 1 pound, 7 ounces are allowed for trimming? _____

$6. \times 105 = 630$

112

Purchasing Fresh Fish

The quantity of fresh fish to purchase depends on three things: the number of people being served, the portion size, and the market form desired. Figure 7–11 is a suggested guide associating the market form to the amount to purchase.

The formula shown here will simplify the ordering procedure:

Amount per person × number served = amount to order

Example 1: How many pounds of fish steaks must be ordered for serving a party of 84 people? (Use Figure 7–11 as a guide.)

$$\tfrac{1}{3} \times \tfrac{84}{1} = 28 \text{ pounds}$$

Example 2: How many pounds of dressed fish should be ordered when preparing for a group of 72 people? (Use Figure 7–11 as a guide.)

$$\tfrac{1}{2} \times \tfrac{72}{1} = 36 \text{ pounds}$$

Example 3: How many pounds of drawn fish should be ordered when preparing for a party of 56 people? (Use Figure 7–11 as a guide.)

$$\tfrac{3}{4} \times \tfrac{56}{1} = 42 \text{ pounds}$$

Market Form Guide	Amount per Person
Fish sticks, steaks & fillets (E.P.)	¼ pound
Dressed fish (E.P.)	½ pound
Drawn fish (A.P.)	¾ pound
Whole fish or fish in the round (just as it comes from the water) (A.P.)	1 pound

Figure 7–11
Chart for purchasing fresh fish.
© Cengage Learning 2012

254

195

48 390

$\dfrac{3}{4} \times \dfrac{260}{1} = \dfrac{780}{4}$

$\dfrac{4}{2}$

1

Practice Problems 7–6   Purchasing Fresh Fish

Determine the answers to the following 10 questions using the information from Figure 7–11. Round off to the next highest whole number; for example, if question 66 results in the answer of 32.23 pounds of drawn fish (which it does not), round up to 33 pounds.

66. How many pounds of drawn fish should be ordered when preparing for a party of 140 people?

_____

67. How many pounds of fish steaks should be ordered when preparing for a group of 78 people?

_____

68. How many pounds of fish fillets should be ordered when preparing for a party of 90 people?

_____

69. How many pounds of fish sticks should be purchased when preparing for a group of 96 people?

_____

70. How many pounds of drawn fish should be purchased when preparing for a party of 210 people?

_____

71. How many pounds of dressed fish should be purchased when preparing for a party of 94 people?

_____

72. How many pounds of fish steaks should be ordered when preparing for a group of 160 people?

_____

73. How many pounds of fish fillets should be ordered when preparing for a party of 114 people? _____

74. How many pounds of fish sticks should be purchased when preparing for a group of 123 people? _____

75. How many pounds of drawn fish should be ordered when preparing for a party of 260 people? _____

Yield Percentage of an A.P. Product

A food service professional must realize that many products that are bought have parts that cannot be served to the guests, thereby reducing the amount of food available to be served or the yield of the product. There are some products that yield 100 percent and have no waste, such as packets of grape jelly or packets of butter. If each guest is to receive one packet of grape jelly and one packet of butter, the food service professional simply opens up a case and serves a packet of each to the guests.

Another example is an ear of corn. If 200 guests were attending a clambake and each guest was to receive one ear of corn, 200 ears of corn would have to be ordered. Certainly there is waste with the cornsilk and the husk, but that will not affect the number of ears of corn that must be purchased. Even after the corn was prepared for the clambake, the yield would still be 200 ears of corn.

Compare our corn at a clambake with corn kernels already taken off the cob to be served as the vegetable for a meal. Our food purchaser buys #10 cans of corn. The cook simply opens up the can and cooks the corn. However, the weight of a #10 can varies from 6 pounds, 8 ounces, to 7 pounds, 5 ounces. The reason why the variation occurs is because many products are packed in some type of liquid, so the purchaser is buying the food product along with the liquid. This liquid most likely will not be served to the guest. The food service manager must determine how much of the weight of the can is product and how much is liquid. This is called a **drained weight test.** For example, the food service professional will open up a #10 can of corn, pour the liquid into one container, and pour the corn into another. Both containers are weighed, resulting in the liquid weight and the corn weight separately. This will explain why there is a variation in the amount of usable product in a #10 can. The formula for determining how much canned product to order is as follows:

Weight of original can — weight of the liquid = drained weight of the food

Using the corn from the previous example, here is how this is solved:

A #10 can of whole kernel corn weighs 6 pounds, 11 ounces, or 107 ounces.

The liquid in the can weighs 2 pounds, 3 ounces, or 35 ounces.

Weight of original can − weight of the liquid = drained weight of the food.

107 ounces − 35 ounces = 72 ounces of E.P. corn.

Discussion Question 7-1

Why is it important to do drained weight tests on canned products that are packed in liquid? What could happen to your business if you do not conduct these tests?

Once it has been determined how much of an A.P. product is drained weight or waste and how much is E.P., the person ordering food can convert this to a yield and determine a **yield percentage.** The purchaser can keep records of the yield percentage of items used and will know how much to purchase for future orders. Here is the formula for doing this:

Edible Portion (E.P.) divided by (÷) As Purchased (A.P.) = yield percentage

In the previous problem with the corn, the yield percentage would be 67.29 percent, as determined here:

The E.P. (72 ounces) divided by the A.P. (102 ounces) results in 0.67289 or 67.29 percent.

Butcher's Test or Butcher's Yield

Because much unusable product is created when fabricating meat, it is essential that a food service professional realizes the actual yield from meat that is purchased.

As an example, we will use the information from our 18-pound short loin of beef in the A.P. state. We discovered that, when the prep cook trimmed and boned the short loin, the resulting loss in waste amounted to 2 pounds and 10 ounces. The remaining trimmed short loin weighs 15 pounds and 6 ounces (18 pounds − 2 pounds and 10 ounces). The yield percentage of the short loin is determined in this manner:

Step 1: Convert the A.P. 18-pound short loin into ounces (16 ounces in a pound).

18 times (×) 16 = 288 ounces A.P.

Step 2: Convert the resulting waste from the short loin, 2 pounds and 10 ounces, into ounces.

2 times (×) 16 = 32 + 10 = 42 ounces of waste

Step 3: Subtract the waste (42 ounces) from the A.P. ounces (288)

288 minus (−) 42 = 246 ounces. This is now the E.P.

Step 4: Divide the E.P. by the A.P. to equal the yield percentage.

246 ÷ 288 = 85.42 percent yield percentage

How to Use the Yield Percentage

Once the purchaser knows how to determine the yield percentage of products, each product should be tested for the yield percentage. When the yield percentage is determined, this number must be saved for future ordering. The individual purchasing the product will have to take the yield percentage into account when purchasing products.

To figure out the amount of food to order, we will continue with our short loin example. For instance, your chef tells you to order enough short loin to serve each of 100 guests an 8-oz. portion. The purchaser has determined, through previous experiences, that a short loin results in a yield percentage of 85.42 percent. This can be solved by figuring out the amount of E.P. that is needed, and then dividing it by the yield percentage.

Step 1: Determine the amount of E.P. of short loin needed for the 100 guests.

100 guests × 8 oz. portion = 800 ounces of E.P. needed

Step 2: Number of ounces needed by E.P. divided by (÷) yield percentage = number of ounces of short loin needed.

800 ounces ÷ 85.42% = 936.54881 ounces of short loin needed

Step 3: Convert the ounces into pounds by dividing the amount of ounces needed by 16.

936.54881 ÷ 16 = 58.5343 pounds

Step 4: The purchaser would order 59 pounds of short loin.

It becomes helpful to put this information into a table form when conducting yield or butcher tests. Using the information from our short loin example, the table appears as follows:

Item	Pounds	Ounces	Total Ounces	Percent of the Original Weight
Short loin of beef	18	0	288	100%
Fat loss	0	10	10	3.47%
Unusable meat	2	0	32	11.11%
Bone loss	0	0	0	0%
Cooking and carving loss	0	0	0	0%
Total production loss			42	14.58%
E.P. weight			246	85.42%

Formulas from this table:

E.P. weight (246) = Original weight (288) − Total production loss (42).
Percentage of weight = ounces of item divided by the original weight, which was 288 ounces.
Total production loss % or Waste % (14.58%) = Total production loss in ounces (42) / A.P. weight in ounces (288).
Yield percentage (85.42%) = 100% − Total production loss % (14.58%).

In this example, after a yield or butcher test is done, a purchasing agent will know that when an A.P. short loin of beef is purchased, the yield will be 85.42 percent of E.P. meat. Therefore, if each guest is to receive a 8 oz. portion of meat, the purchasing agent will use the formula for ordering product as shown here. The forecast for the restaurant is for 100 guests to order this menu item.

Number of guests × 8 oz. = E.P. portion
100 × 8 oz. = 800 oz. of E.P. meat.
Edible portion required/Yield Percentage = A.P. required.
800 oz. / 85.42% = 936.54881 ounces.

Because there are 16 ounces in a pound, the purchasing agent must divide the number of ounces by 16 = 58.53, which is rounded to 59 pounds. Therefore, the purchasing agent must order 59 pounds of short loin to have enough E.P. product to serve the 100 guests.

Based on the authors' research, most purchasers and chefs determine the yield percentage one time and then they order based on experience. For example, one chef told us that for every prime rib he roasts, he obtains 17 regular cuts and 20 English cuts from the size of the rib that he specifies. When he has a party for 200 guests, he divides the 200 by 17 and determines that he must order 12 prime ribs. Another purchasing agent told us he has determined that when romaine salad is on the menu, the cooks will obtain 100 portions from a case of romaine lettuce that he buys. Therefore, if he plans to serve 300 romaine salads, he orders three cases of romaine lettuce. Being able to conduct and determine yield percentage is necessary to cost out recipes. This procedure will be shown in later chapters.

Practice Problems 7–7   Yield Percentage of an A.P. Product

Answers should be shown in this manner: 98.12%. Round answers to the hundredths place.

76. What is the yield percentage of a 22-pound turkey? The turkey lost 8 pounds, 5 ounces after fabrication and shrinkage. _____

77. What is the yield percentage of an 8-pound pork tenderloin? The tenderloin lost 1 pound, 5 ounces after fabrication and shrinkage. _____

78. What is the yield percentage of 80 pounds of potatoes? The potatoes lost 6 pounds, 3 ounces after fabrication. _____ 90.74 _____

79. What is the yield percentage of a 15-pound salmon? The salmon lost 3 pounds, 9 ounces after fabrication and shrinkage. _____

80. What is the yield percentage of a 8-pound chicken? The chicken lost 4 pounds, 2 ounces after fabrication and shrinkage. _____

Questions 81 through 85 have to be solved using the yield percentage for ordering food. Round up your answers to the next whole number.

81. If the yield percentage for a prime rib roast is 50 percent, how many pounds will have to be ordered to serve 300 guests? Each guest will receive an 8-ounce portion.

     _____ 300 _____

82. If the yield percentage for a chicken breast is 30.5 percent, how many pounds will have to be ordered to serve 210 guests? Each guest will receive a 6-ounce portion.

     _____

83. If the yield percentage for salmon is 45 percent, how many pounds will have to be ordered to serve 150 guests? Each guest will receive a 7-ounce portion. 146

     _____

84. If the yield percentage for a cantaloupe melon is 62.2 percent, how many pounds will have to be ordered to serve 75 guests? Each guest will receive a 6-ounce portion.

     _____

85. If the yield percentage for strawberries is 91.9 percent, how many pounds will have to be ordered to serve 300 guests? Each guest will receive a 3-ounce portion.

     _____

Questions 86 to 90 concern the amount of food to order after calculating the drained weight of each problem. Round up your answers to the next whole number.

86. How many #10 cans of cut green beans are needed to serve a party of 200 people if each person is to receive a 3-ounce serving and each can weighs 5 pounds, 10 ounces, with 9 ounces of that as liquid? _____

87. How many cans of corn are required to serve a party of 85 people if each person is to receive a 4-ounce serving? Each can has 1 pound, 7 ounces of liquid. _____

88. How many #2½ cans of diced beets are needed to serve a party of 86 people if each person is to receive a 4-ounce serving and each can weighs 2 pounds, 5 ounces, with 4 ounces of liquid in each can?

_____

89. How many #5 cans of spaghetti sauce will be needed to serve 132 people if each person is to receive 2 ounces of sauce and each can contains 48 fluid ounces? _____

90. How many #2½ cans of diced carrots are needed to serve a party of 230 people if each person is to receive a 3-ounce serving and each can weighs 1 pound, 12 ounces, with 7 ounces of liquid?

_____

For questions 91 to 95, find how much meat or fish must be ordered after determining the yield percentage. Round up your answers to the next whole number.

91. What is the yield percentage of a 24-pound turkey? The turkey lost 9 pounds, 5 ounces after fabrication and shrinkage. How many turkeys must be ordered to serve 300 guests if each guest receives an 8-ounce portion? _____

92. What is the yield percentage of a 7-pound beef tenderloin? The tenderloin lost 1 pound, 5 ounces after fabrication and shrinkage. How many pounds of beef tenderloin must be ordered to serve 75 guests if each guest receives an 8-ounce portion? _____

93. What is the yield percentage of 90 pounds of potatoes? The potatoes lose 6 pounds, 3 ounces after fabrication. How many pounds of potatoes must be ordered to obtain 100 portions, each weighing 0.5 ounce? _____

94. What is the yield percentage of a 25-pound salmon? The salmon lost 3 pounds, 9 ounces after fabrication. How many salmon must be ordered to serve 400 guests at a banquet if each guest receives an 8-ounce portion?

_____

95. What is the yield percentage of a 12-pound tenderloin? The tenderloin loses 2 pounds, 6 ounces after fabrication. How many pounds of tenderloin will be needed to serve the 400 guests at the annual Sons of Saint Patrick dinner if each guest receives an 8-ounce portion? _____

Discussion Question 7-2

A produce salesman offers to sell you bags of salad ingredients (cleaned and ready to eat). You have been buying the ingredients individually, and cleaning and preparing them with your current workforce. What considerations will you take into account when determining whether you should purchase ready-to-serve salad ingredients versus ones that your staff will have to clean and prepare? Provide three considerations.

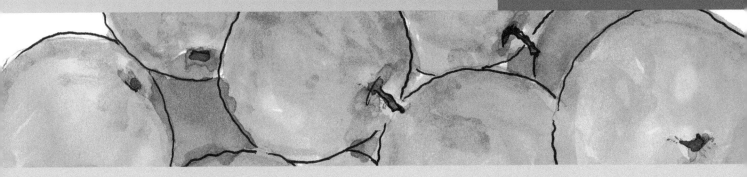

eight

Converting Recipes, Yields, and Baking Formulas

Objectives

At the completion of this chapter, the student should be able to:

1. Find the working factor to convert recipes.
2. Convert standard recipes from larger to smaller amounts, or from smaller to larger amounts.
3. Find approximate recipe yields.
4. Use ratios and proportions to convert ingredients for recipes.
5. Find percents for baker's percentage.

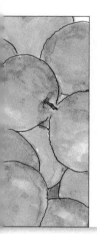

Key Words

standardized recipe	working factor yield	ratio proportion	baker's percentage

During your food service career, occasions will frequently occur when you will be required to convert recipes to amounts that will differ from the original recipe. These amounts may be more or less than the recipe yield. For example, the recipe that you have may yield 50 portions, but the need is for 25 or 100 portions.

Some food service establishments produce food from what is referred to as a **standardized recipe.** This is a recipe that will produce the same quality and quantity each and every time. Standardized recipes are ideal for food service operations such as nursing homes, retirement villages, and some school cafeterias. However, food production will vary in many food service operations, especially restaurants and catering operations, so converting recipes is a very important technique to master. (See Figure 8–1.)

Figure 8–1
The chef is converting a recipe to determine the amounts needed to produce the required number of servings.
© Cengage Learning 2012

Converting Standard Recipes

It is a simple matter to double or cut a recipe in half. Many times this can be done mentally with little or no effort. However, when it becomes necessary to change a recipe from 12 to 20 portions or from 50 to 28, it appears to be more complicated. Actually, the procedure is the same for both and involves a fairly simple function of finding a **working factor** and multiplying each ingredient quantity by the working factor. The working factor is the number that will be used to multiply the amount of the original ingredients in a recipe to either increase or decrease a recipe.

The first step in converting a recipe is to find the **working factor.** This is done as follows:

Step 1:   Divide the yield desired by original recipe yield.

$$\frac{\text{New yield}}{\text{Old yield}} = \text{Working factor}$$

Step 2:   Multiply each ingredient in the original recipe by the working factor.

Working factor $\times$ old quantity = new quantity (desired quantity)

To simplify this procedure, change ingredient pounds to ounces before starting to multiply. This way, it is only necessary to multiply ounces. After multiplying, convert the product back to pounds and ounces. (If you are using the metric system, this step is not necessary.)

Example: A standardized recipe yields 40 portions. Only 30 portions are desired.

First, you must find the working factor by following the formula given in Step 1.

$$\frac{30 \text{ New yield}}{40 \text{ Old yield}} = \text{¾ Working factor or } 0.75$$

Next, convert the quantity of each ingredient in the original recipe to ounces and multiply each ingredient by ¾ or 0.75, the working factor, as stated in Step 2. Convert new amounts back to pounds and ounces.

Example: A standardized recipe yields 75 portions. A large party is booked, and 225 portions are required.

First, you must find the working factor by following the formula given in Step 1:

$$\frac{225 \text{ New yield}}{75 \text{ Old yield}} = 3 \text{ Working factor}$$

Next, convert the quantity of each ingredient in the original recipe to ounces and multiply each ingredient by 3, the working factor, as stated in Step 2. Convert new amounts back to pounds and ounces.

To Insure Perfect Solutions

When figuring out a working factor, remember the acronym NO, which stands for "*New yield* on top, *old yield* on the bottom."

To Insure Perfect Solutions

When converting recipes to *more portions*, realize that the working factor will be *greater than 1*. When converting recipes to *fewer portions*, realize that the working factor will be *less than 1*.

Practice Problems 8–1   Find the Working Factor

Find the working factor for each problem. Round to the hundredths place.

1. The standardized recipe is for 40 portions. The party is for 310 guests. _____

2. The standardized recipe is for 50 portions. The party is for 35 guests. _____

3. The standardized recipe is for 75 portions. The party is for 290 guests. _____

4. The standardized recipe is for 10 portions. The party is for 193 guests. _____

5. The standardized recipe is for 50 portions. The party is for 12 guests. _____

6. The standardized recipe is for 30 portions. The party is for 350 guests. _____

7. The standardized recipe is for 90 portions. The party is for 30 guests.

_____

8. The standardized recipe is for 65 portions. The party is for 185 guests.

_____

9. The standardized recipe is for 25 portions. The party is for 5 guests.

_____

10. The standardized recipe is for 4 portions. The party is for 160 guests.

_____

When working a recipe after a conversion has taken place, some common sense must also be applied. You might think of this common sense or judgment as an extra ingredient. For instance, the recipe may not account for how fresh or old the spices or herbs are, or how hot the kitchen or bake shop is when mixing a yeast dough. Common sense or judgment must be applied when converting any recipe because it may not be practical to increase or decrease the quantity of each ingredient by the exact same rate. Many spices and herbs cannot be increased or decreased at the same rate as other ingredients. This may also be true of salt, garlic, and sugar in certain situations. Use good judgment in these situations and carry out tests before deciding on amounts.

Example: The following recipe yields 12 dozen hard rolls. It must be converted to yield 9 dozen rolls.

Ingredients for 12 dozen rolls	Amount of conversion	Amount needed to yield 9 dozen rolls
7 lbs. 8 oz. bread flour	¾	5 lbs. 10 oz.
3 oz. salt		2¼ oz.
3½ oz. granulated sugar		2⅝ oz.
3 oz. shortening		2¼ oz.
3 oz. egg whites		2¼ oz.
4 lbs. 8 oz. water (variable)		3 lbs. 6 oz.
4½ oz. yeast, compressed		3⅜ oz.

handwritten margin notes: 3 sabve fica; $\frac{9}{12} = 3/4$ working factor; 4; $3\frac{1}{2} \times \frac{3}{4}$

Step 1: Find the working factor.

$$\frac{9 \text{ dozen new yield}}{12 \text{ dozen old yield}} = \frac{3}{4} \text{ Is the working factor}$$

The quantity of each ingredient in the original recipe is multiplied by ¾ (the working factor).

Step 2: Convert all ingredients.

    Example: 7 pounds, 8 ounces of bread flour
                     $(7 \times 16) + 8 = 120$ ounces

    Example: 3½ ounces of granulated sugar = $\frac{7}{2}$ ounces

Step 3: Multiply all ingredients by the working factor (¾).

    Example: bread flour (120 ounces $\times$ ¾ = 90 ounces)

    Example: granulated sugar ($\frac{7}{2}$ ounces $\times$ ¾ = $\frac{21}{8}$)

Step 4: Convert new amounts back to pounds and ounces.

    Example: bread flour (90 ounces divided by 16 = 5 pounds and 10 ounces)

    Example: granulated sugar ($\frac{21}{8}$ = $2\frac{5}{8}$ ounces)

Step 5: Continue converting all ingredients in 9 dozen rolls recipe.

Practice Problems 8–2   Converting Standard Recipes

The following recipe yields 50 portions of curried lamb. Convert it to yield 350 portions.

11. The working factor is ____7____.

Ingredients for 50 Portions	Amount Needed to Yield 350 Portions
18 lbs. lamb shoulder; boneless, cut into 1-inch cubes E.P.	12. ___126___
2½ gallons water	13. _____
2 lbs. butter or shortening	14. ___14___
1 lb. 8 oz. flour	15. ___12 6___
⅓ cup curry powder	16. ___2.33___
2 qt. tart apples, diced	17. ___14___
2 lbs. onions, diced	18. ___14___
½ tsp. ground cloves	19. ___3.5___
2 bay leaves	20. ___14___
1 tsp. marjoram	21. ___7___
salt and pepper to taste	22. _____

The following recipe yields 100 portions of Hungarian goulash. Convert it to yield 75 portions.

23. The working factor is _____3/4_____. 0.75

Ingredients for 100 Portions	Amount Needed to Yield 75 Portions
36 lbs. beef chuck or shoulder, diced 1-inch cubes E.P.	24. ___27___
1¼ oz. garlic, minced	25. ___0.93___
1 lb. 4 oz. flour	26. _____
1¼ oz. chili powder	27. ___0.93___
10 oz. paprika	28. ___7.5___
2 lbs. tomato puree	29. ___1.5___
2 gal. brown stock	30. ___1.5___
4 bay leaves	31. ___3___
¾ oz. caraway seeds	32. _____
3 lbs. 8 oz. onions, minced	33. _____
salt and pepper to taste	34. _____

The following recipe yields nine 8-inch lemon pies. Convert it to yield six 8-inch pies.

35. The working factor is _____.

Ingredients for 9 Pies	Amount Needed to Yield 6 Pies
4 lbs. flour	36. _____
3 lbs. 6 oz. granulated sugar	37. _____
½ oz. salt	38. _____
3 oz. lemon gratings	39. _____
1 lb. water	40. _____
8 oz. corn starch	41. _____
12 oz. egg yolks	42. _____
1 lb. 6 oz. lemon juice	43. _____
4 oz. butter, melted	44. _____
yellow color, as needed	45. _____

The following recipe yields 12 dozen hard rolls. Convert it to yield 48 dozen rolls.

46. The working factor is _____.

Ingredients for 12 Dozen Rolls	Amount Needed to Yield 48 Dozen Rolls
7 lbs. 8 oz. bread flour	47. _____
3 oz. salt	48. _____
3½ oz. granulated sugar	49. _____
3 oz. shortening	50. _____
3 oz. egg whites	51. _____
4 lbs. 8 oz. water (variable)	52. _____
4½ oz. yeast, compressed	53. _____

The following recipe yields 8 dozen soft dinner rolls. Convert it to yield 5 dozen rolls.

54. The working factor is _____.

Ingredients for 8 Dozen Rolls	Amount Needed to Yield 5 Dozen Rolls
10 oz. granulated sugar	55. _____
10 oz. hydrogenated shortening	56. _____
1 oz. salt	57. _____
3 oz. dry milk	58. _____
4 oz. whole eggs	59. _____
3 lbs. 12 oz. bread flour	60. _____
2 lbs. water	61. _____
5 oz. yeast, compressed	62. _____

Finding Approximate Recipe Yield

Yield is defined as the amount of portions, servings, or units that a particular recipe or formula will produce. It is one of the most important features of a recipe or formula. Yield is probably one of the first items that a cook will look at when selecting a certain recipe for preparation. Observing a recipe or formula yield provides the preparer with an approximate guide to the numbers that the recipe or formula will produce. The yield must also be known before conversion can take place.

Most recipes provide an approximate guide as to the number or amounts that the recipe will produce. However, occasions arise when you will want to determine your own yield because the suggested recipe or formula portion size is too large or small for your need.

You may also wish to work out your own recipe for a preparation—a recipe that you have used many times but for which you have never determined an approximate yield.

Suggested recipe or formula yields will fluctuate if you determine that a larger or smaller portion is required. To show how this situation could happen, let us assume that a yellow cake batter is prepared from a recipe that states the approximate yield is 20 cakes, with 14 ounces of batter used in each cake. You wish to use a smaller pan that will hold only 10 ounces. The yield will, of course, fluctuate and produce a larger amount of yellow cakes.

It is for these reasons that the student cook or baker must understand how a yield can be determined by applying some simple mathematics. The chef can approximate the serving size by determining a formula yield (see Figure 8–2).

The yield for some recipes or formulas is found by preparing a certain amount, determining a serving portion, and measuring it to see what it will produce. The yield for other recipes, such as cake or muffin batters, roll or sweet doughs, pie filling, and some cookie doughs, can be determined by taking the total weight of all ingredients used in the preparation and dividing that figure by the weight of an individual portion or unit. Let us take the formula of a white cake and of a roll dough to show how an approximate yield can be obtained by this method.

Figure 8–2
By determining a formula yield, the chef can approximate the serving size.
© Cengage Learning 2012

The formula is:

Total weight of preparation ÷ weight of portion = recipe yield

Example:
White Cake
Ingredients: The approximate yield _____.
2 lbs. 8 oz. cake flour (40 oz.)
1 lb., 12 oz. shortening (28 oz.)
3 lbs., 2 oz. granulated sugar (50 oz.)
1½ oz. salt (1.5 oz.)
2½ oz. baking powder (2.5 oz.)
14 oz. water (14 oz.)
2½ oz. dry milk (2.5 oz.)
10 oz. whole eggs (10 oz.)
1 lb. egg whites (16 oz.)
1 lb. water (16 oz.)
vanilla to taste (to taste)
total ounces = 180.5 oz.

The total weight of all ingredients is 11 pounds, 4½ ounces. Each cake is to contain 14 ounces of batter. The first step is to convert the weight of all ingredients to ounces because only like things can be divided: 11 pounds, 4½ ounces contains 180½ ounces. The second step is to divide the weight of one cake (14 ounces) into the total weight of all ingredients, as follows:

$$
\begin{array}{r}
12 \text{ cakes} \\
14\overline{)180.5} \\
\underline{14} \\
40 \\
\underline{28} \\
12
\end{array}
$$

When preparing a cake from scratch—that is, step-by-step preparation—the baker must first determine the size of each pan to be used and the amount of batter that each pan is to contain. He or she may determine that an 8-inch cake pan will be used and that each pan is to contain 14 ounces of batter to produce the size of cake desired. Many times, the cake recipe will state, in the method of preparation, the amount of batter to place in a certain size pan. Usually the type of cake prepared will have a bearing on the amount of batter placed in each pan. For example, light semi-sponge cake batters will not require as much batter as a pound cake.

There is no reason to carry the division any further because only figures on the left side of the decimal point are whole numbers. So 12 cakes, each containing 14 ounces of batter, can be made from this recipe.

When preparing a roll dough, the baker must determine how much each roll will weigh. Some bakers like a larger roll than others. The usual size is 1¼ to 2 ounces. Once the size is determined, an approximate yield is easy to find.

Example:

Soft Dinner Roll Dough

Ingredients: The approximate yield _____.

1 lb., 4 oz. granulated sugar (20 oz.)

1 lb., 4 oz. shortening (20 oz.)

2 oz. salt (2 oz.)

6 oz. dry milk (6 oz.)

6 oz. whole eggs (6 oz.)

7 lbs., 8 oz. bread flour (128 oz.)

4 lbs. water (64 oz.)

10 oz. compressed yeast (10 oz.)

The total weight of all ingredients is 15 pounds, 8 ounces. Each roll is to weigh 1½ ounces. The first step is to convert the weight of all ingredients to ounces because only like things can be divided; 15 pounds, 8 ounces contain

248 ounces. Now, dividing the total weight by the weight of one roll gives the recipe yield:

$$
\begin{array}{r}
165. \\
1.5\,\overline{)248.0.} \\
\underline{15} \\
98 \\
\underline{90} \\
80 \\
\underline{75} \\
5
\end{array}
$$

Thus, the yield is 165 rolls, or 13¾ dozen rolls, which is also equivalent to 13 dozen and 9 rolls, when yielding a 1.5-ounce roll.

Most recipes used in the commercial kitchen will be stated in weights, and an approximate yield is easier to determine when ingredients are listed in weights. Weights will also produce a more accurate preparation. There are occasions when recipes will be stated in measures. In this case, the formula used to determine a yield will be the same, but the measuring units in finding an approximate yield will differ.

Example:

Honey Cream Dressing

Ingredients: The approximate yield _____.

3 cups cream cheese

2 cups honey

½ cup pineapple juice (variable)

¼ tsp. salt

2½ qt. mayonnaise

In this example, total cups must be determined. There are 15½ cups in the preparation. A 2-ounce ladle is used to portion. A 2-ounce ladle contains ¼ cup, so following the formula given to determine an approximate yield, the math involved would be as follows:

15½ cups (total measure of preparation ÷ ¼ cup (portion measure)
= ³¹⁄₂ × ⁴⁄₁ = 62 portions (yield)

Practice Problems 8–3   Finding Approximate Recipe Yields

63. Determine the approximate yield of the following formula if **each** coffee cake is to contain a 12-ounce unit of sweet dough.

Coffee Cakes

1 lb. granulated sugar

1 lb. golden shortening

1 oz. salt

3 lbs. bread flour

1 lb., 8 oz. pastry flour

12 oz. whole eggs

4 oz. dry milk

2 lbs. water

8 oz. compressed yeast

mace to taste

vanilla to taste

The yield of coffee cakes is _____.

64. Determine the approximate yield of the following formula if *each* cookie is to contain 1½ ounces of dough.

Fruit Tea Cookies

1 lb., 6 oz. shortening

1 lb., 6 oz. powdered sugar

2 lbs., 8 oz. pastry flour

2 oz. liquid milk

6 oz. raisins, chopped

2 oz. pecans, chopped

3 oz. pineapple, chopped

2 oz. peaches, chopped

8 oz. whole eggs

¼ oz. baking soda

¼ oz. vanilla

½ oz. salt

The yield of fruit tea cookies is _____.

65. Determine the approximate yield of the following formula if each cake is to contain 11 ounces of batter.

Yellow Cakes

2 lbs. 8 oz. cake flour

1 lb., 6 oz. shortening

3 lbs., 2 oz. granulated sugar

1 oz. salt

1¾ oz. baking powder

4 oz. dry milk

1 lb., 4 oz. water

1 lb., 10 oz. whole eggs

12 oz. water

¼ oz. vanilla

The amount of yellow cakes is _____.

66. Determine the approximate yield of the following recipe if each gelatin mold is to hold ¾ cup of liquid gelatin mix.

Sunshine Salad

1 pt. lemon-flavored gelatin

1 qt. hot water

1 qt. cold water

¼ cup cider vinegar

1 qt. grated carrots

1 pt. pineapple, crushed

The yield of Sunshine Salad is _____.

67. Determine the approximate yield of the following recipe if a 6-ounce ladle (¾ cup) is used to portion.

Beef Stroganoff

2 gal. beef tenderloin, cut into thin strips E.P.

1 cup flour

½ cup shortening

3 qt. water

½ cup tomato puree

½ cup cider vinegar

1 lb. onions, minced

1 qt. mushrooms, sliced

1 qt. sour cream

1 tbsp. salt

3 bay leaves

The yield of beef stroganoff is _____.

Practical Use of Ratios and Proportions

Ratios and proportions were covered in Chapter 4. This chapter requires the student to use them in solving problems. The term *ratio* is used to express a comparison between two numbers. A **ratio** between two quantities is the number of times that one contains the other. For example, to prepare pie dough, the baker must use 1 quart of liquid to every 4 pounds of flour. Therefore, the ratio is 1 to 4.

Mathematical or word problems that include ratios may be solved by using proportions. A **proportion** is defined as a relation in size, number, amount, or degree of one thing compared to another. For example, when preparing the pie dough, the ratio is 1 to 4—that is, 1 quart of liquid to 4 pounds of flour. It is important to realize that the order in which the numbers are placed when expressing a ratio is crucial, as was explained in Chapter 4.

Using the ratio discussed previously, we will illustrate how to solve the following word problem using a proportion:

Your chef tells you to make 10 pounds of pie dough. You must find out how much liquid is required.

As a review from Chapter 4, this is the information about proportions that you must know:

> The unknown is represented by an *x* because that is the answer to be determined.
>
> "Is to" in a mathematical equation is represented by a full colon (:).
>
> The numbers on the outside of the equation are called *extremes*.
>
> The numbers on the inside of the equation are called *means*.

Step 1:　　Set up a proportion.
How much liquid is required to make 10 pounds of pie dough?
You know that when preparing pie dough, the ratio is 1 to 4—that is, 1 quart of liquid to 4 pounds of flour.

Step 2:　　Set up a mathematical equation.
How much liquid is required is represented by the *x*, which is the unknown factor?
The pie dough is represented by the 10, the pounds of pie dough that have to be made.
The 1 is equal to 1 quart of liquid.
The 4 is equal to 4 pounds of flour.
So, the equation reads: The unknown amount of liquid to 10 pounds of pie dough is equal to 1 quart of liquid to 4 pounds of flour.

$$x{:}10 = 1{:}4$$

Step 3:   Multiply the means (1 times 10), which is equal to 10.
Multiply the extremes (x times 4), which is equal to 4x.
The formula now reads:

$$4x = 10$$

Step 4:   Divide both sides of the equation by the number next to the x.

$$4x/4 = 10/4$$

(The fours on the left side of the = sign cancel each other out.)
You are left with x = 10 divided by (÷) 4 = 2.5.

Step 5:   The cook needs 2.5 quarts of liquid to make 10 pounds of pie dough.

Practice Problems 8–4   Practical Use of Ratios and Proportions

Use proportions to solve the following problems. Before setting up the proportion, convert all amounts to like amounts. For example, if the ratio is stated as a quart and the problem is stated as gallons, convert all gallons to quarts before attempting to solve the problem. Please note that the ratio information is given to solve the problems.

Determine the amounts of liquid required if a pie dough formula contains the following amounts of flour. The ratio is 1 part liquid to 4 parts flour.

68. 16 pounds   _____

69. 28 pounds   _____

70. 32 pounds   _____

71. 24 pounds   _____

Determine the amount of dry milk required to produce the following amounts of liquid milk. The ratio is 4 ounces of dry milk to 1 quart of water.

72. 1½ gallons liquid milk   _____

73. 3 gallons liquid milk   _____

74. 3½ quarts liquid milk   _____

75. 4¾ gallons liquid milk   _____

Determine the amount of unflavored gelatin required to jell the following amounts of aspic. The ratio is 6 ounces of unflavored gelatin to each gallon of water.

76. 8 quarts aspic   _____

77. 2¾ gallons aspic   _____

78. 4½ gallons aspic   _____

79. 3½ gallons aspic   _____

Determine the amount of liquid needed to prepare the following amounts of raw barley. The ratio calls for 4 parts of liquid to every 1 part of raw barley.

80. 1 pint raw barley _____

81. 3 pints raw barley _____

82. 3 quarts raw barley _____

83. 1 cup raw barley _____

Determine the amount of pudding powder needed to prepare the following amounts of pudding. The ratio is 3.25 ounces of pudding powder to every pint of milk.

84. 4 quarts pudding _____

85. 2½ quarts pudding _____

86. 6 quarts pudding _____

87. 3½ quarts pudding _____

Determine the amount of dry nondairy creamer required to produce the following amounts of liquid cream. To convert dry nondairy creamer to liquid, mix 1 pint of dry creamer with 1 quart of hot water.

88. 2 gallons liquid cream _____

89. 1½ gallons liquid cream _____

90. ½ gallon liquid cream _____

91. 3½ gallons liquid cream _____

Determine the amount of dry instant potato powder needed to prepare the following amounts of mashed potatoes. To prepare mashed potatoes using the dry instant potato powder, use 1 pound, 13 ounces of the powder to each gallon of water or milk.

92. 4 gallons mashed potatoes _____

93. 6 gallons mashed potatoes _____

94. 3½ gallons mashed potatoes _____

95. 4½ gallons mashed potatoes _____

When preparing pasta or egg noodles, you use 1 gallon of boiling water to every pound of pasta. Determine the amount of liquid required to cook the following amounts of pasta.

96. 3.5 pounds pasta _____

97. 5 pounds pasta _____

98. 6.5 pounds pasta _____

99. 7 pounds pasta _____

When preparing egg wash, how many eggs will be needed when preparing the following amounts?
To prepare a fairly rich egg wash, mix together 4 whole eggs to every quart of milk.

100. 3 cups milk   _____

101. 3 pints milk   _____

102. 5 quarts milk   _____

103. 3 quarts milk   _____

To prepare pan grease, thoroughly mix 8 ounces of flour with every pound of shortening.
Determine the amount of flour needed to prepare pan grease if the following amounts of
shortening are used.

104. 1½ pounds of shortening   _____

105. 8 ounces of shortening   _____

106. 12 ounces of shortening   _____

107. 2¾ pounds of shortening   _____

Baker's Percentage

In cooking, if a recipe or formula should become unbalanced or if a mistake should occur when adding ingredients, the situation might easily be corrected by making a few adjustments. This is not the case when working with baking formulas. Bakers use a simple yet versatile system designed to balance all formulas that feature flour as the main ingredient. Each minor ingredient is a percentage of the main (flour) ingredient. Industry standards determine the percentages of each ingredient in most of the popular formulas to ensure that the formula is balanced.

The ingredients in baking formulas must be balanced if the finished product is to possess all the qualities necessary to please the customer and to warrant return sales. Most formulas used in bake shops today have been developed in research laboratories operated by the companies that manufacture the products that bakers use. The formulas are used to test the manufacturer's products and are passed on to bakers in the hope that they will use the manufacturer's products.

Keeping in mind that flour is the main ingredient, **baker's percentages** designate the amount of each ingredient that would be required if 100 pounds of flour were used. Thus, flour is always 100 percent. If, for instance, two kinds of flour were used in a preparation, the total amounts of the two would represent 100 percent and any other ingredient that weighs the same as the flour is also listed at 100 percent. To find ingredient percentages, divide the total weight of the ingredient by the weight of the flour, and then multiply by 100 percent.

Example:
The following ingredients for a yellow pound cake illustrate how these percentages are found.

Yellow Pound Cake Recipe

Ingredients	Weights	Baker's percentage
Cake flour	2 lbs., 8 oz., or 40 ounces	100%
Vegetable shortening	1 lb., 12 oz., or 28 ounces	
Granulated sugar	2 lbs., 8 oz., or 40 ounces	
Salt	1.5 ounces	
Water	1 lb., 4 oz., or 20 ounces	
Dry milk	2.5 ounces	
Whole eggs	1 lb., 12 oz., or 28 ounces	
Vanilla to taste	——	
Total Weight	160 ounces	

In this chart, all ingredients have been converted to ounces so that we can calculate like amounts.

To determine the percentage of each item, take the weight of each ingredient and divide by the weight of the flour (because the flour represents 100 percent), and then multiply by 100 percent (%).

> Weight of each ingredient ÷ total weight of the flour times (×) 100%
>   = percentage of each item

Here is how we determine the percentage of vegetable shortening:

> Vegetable shortening (28 ounces) is divided by the flour (40 ounces)
>   = 0.7 × 100% = 70%

$$\begin{array}{r} 0.70 \\ 40\overline{)28.0} \\ 28.0 \end{array}$$

$$0.70 \times 100\% = 70\%$$

After doing the math, the chart looks as follows. Please check the figures in the chart to practice obtaining the baker's percentage.

Yellow Pound Cake Recipe

Ingredients	Weights	Baker's percentage
Cake flour	2 lbs., 8 oz., or 40 ounces	100%
Vegetable shortening	1 lb., 12 oz., or 28 ounces	70%
Granulated sugar	2 lbs., 8 oz., or 40 ounces	100%
Salt	1.5 ounces	3.75%
Water	1 lb., 4 oz., or 20 ounces	50%
Dry milk	2.5 ounces	6.25%
Whole eggs	1 lb., 12 oz., or 28 ounces	70%
Vanilla to taste	——	——
Total Weight	160 ounces	400%

The advantage of finding and using these percentages when flour is the main ingredient is that the formula can be changed easily to any yield and, if a single ingredient needs to be altered, it can be done without changing the complete formula.

Why Are Baker's Percentage Used?

One advantage occurs when new items are added to the recipe to enhance it. For example, the authors would like to add chocolate chips to the recipe to make it a yellow chocolate chip pound cake. If they add 8 ounces of chocolate chips, they figure out the baker's percentage of chocolate chips based upon the weight of the flour. They do not have to change all the ingredients and all the percentages. In this example, 8 (the ounces of chocolate chips) is divided by 40 (the ounces of the flour). The chocolate chip percentage is 20 percent. Notice that the sum of the total weight and the sum of the baker's percentage have also been increased.

Yellow Pound Cake Recipe Modified with Chocolate Chips

Ingredients	Weights	Baker's percentage
Cake flour	2 lbs., 8 oz., or 40 ounces	100%
Vegetable shortening	1 lb., 12 oz., or 28 ounces	70%
Granulated sugar	2 lbs., 8 oz., or 40 ounces	100%
Salt	1.5 ounces	3.75%
Water	1 lb., 4 oz., or 20 ounces	50%
Dry milk	2.5 ounces	6.25%
Chocolate chips	8 ounces	20%
Whole eggs	1 lb., 12 oz., or 28 ounces	70%
Vanilla to taste	——	——
Total Weight	168 ounces	420%

The second advantage occurs when the amount of flour is changed. If the baker has a 5-pound bag of flour left over and wants to use it, the baker can make up another batch of yellow chocolate chip pound cake by using the baker's percentage. The baker first changes the weight of the flour to 80 ounces. The remaining ingredients are calculated by multiplying the baker's percentage from the original recipe. The amount of the vegetable shortening is now increased to 56 ounces (70% × 80) or 3½ pounds (56 divided by 16 is equal to 3 pounds and 8 ounces). The baker continues to convert all ingredients using the baker's percentage method for each ingredient. This will keep the recipe in balance and assure consistency for each cake.

The third advantage occurs when the total formula weight for the recipe is known and your head baker tells you to make up a certain amount of dough. As an example, your head baker tells you to make up 50 pounds of batter for our yellow chocolate chip pound cake. You know that for one cake, you must use 168 ounces total weight for the recipe. How much of each ingredient will be used for 50 pounds (16 × 50 = 800 ounces)? This is how you solve the problem using the baker's percentage.

Step 1:   Add up the total baker's percentage formula. The answer comes to 420 percent.

Step 2:   Calculate the total flour weight using this formula:

$$\frac{\text{Total formula weight} = 800 \text{ ounces}}{\text{Total formula percentage} = 420\%}$$

or

$$\frac{800 \text{ ounces}}{4.20} = 190.47619 \text{ total ounces of flour}$$

Step 3:   The total flour weight is 190.47619 ounces of flour needed to make 50 pounds of batter. Mathematically, this is the correct answer. Realistically, we would increase this to 191 ounces.

Step 4:   Convert each ingredient using the flour as the base.

In the original recipe, our chocolate chips weighed 8 ounces, or 20 percent of the recipe.

Using the baker's percentage of 20 percent, multiply the 0.20 × 191, which equals 38 ounces.

The result is the recipe shown in the following chart, with a yield of 50 pounds of batter.

Yellow Pound Cake Recipe Modified with Chocolate Chips
(Yield: 50 Pounds of Batter)

Ingredients	Weights	Baker's percentage
Cake flour	11 lbs., 15 oz., or 191 ounces	100%
Vegetable shortening	8 lbs., 6 oz., or 134 ounces	70%
Granulated sugar	11 lbs., 15 oz., or 191 ounces	100%
Salt	7.16 ounces	3.75%
Water	5 lbs., 15 oz., or 95 ounces	50%
Dry milk	12 ounces	6.25%
Chocolate chips	2 lbs., 6 oz., or 38 ounces	20%
Whole eggs	8 lbs., 6 oz., or 134 ounces	70%
Vanilla to taste	——	——
Total Weight	50 lbs., 2.12 oz., or 802.16 ounces	420%

Notice that the total amount of the batter is not exactly 50 pounds. This allows for losses in preparing the batter. Rounding up using the baker's percentage does not affect the proportion of the recipe.

What if I want to increase the yield from 1 cake to 20 cakes; do I have to use the baker's percentage?

You may go through all the steps, but, realistically, it would be better to use the working factor method that was covered earlier in this chapter.

$$\frac{\text{New recipe}}{\text{Old recipe}} = \text{Working factor}$$
$$^{20}/_1 = 20$$

In this example, all the ingredients will be multiplied by the working factor of 20. As an example, the chocolate chips will be multiplied by 20. This results in 160 ounces of chocolate chips, or 10 pounds.

Practice Problems 8–5   Baker's Percentage

Find the percent of each ingredient used in the following formulas. Remember that flour is always 100 percent. Round your answers to the tenths place.

A. **Pie dough**

(a)

Ingredients	Weight	Percentage
Pastry flour	10 lbs.	108. _____
Shortening	7 lbs., 8 oz.	109. _____
Salt	5 oz.	110. _____
Sugar	3 oz.	111. _____
Cold water	2 lbs., 8 oz.	112. _____
Dry milk	3 oz.	113. _____

Using the percentage found for each ingredient, determine the amount of each ingredient if the flour amount is changed to 12 pounds. Round your answers to the tenths place.

(b)

Ingredients	Weight
Pastry flour	12 lbs.
Shortening	114. _____
Salt	115. _____
Sugar	116. _____
Cold water	117. _____
Dry milk	118. _____

B. **Golden dinner roll dough**

Find the percent of each ingredient used in the following formulas. Remember that flour is always 100 percent. Round your answers to the tenths place.

(a)

Ingredients	Weight	Percentage
Bread flour	9 lbs.	119. _____
Pastry flour	1 lb.	120. _____
Shortening	1 lb.	121. _____
Sugar	18 oz.	122. _____
Eggs	13 oz.	123. _____
Salt	5 oz.	124. _____
Dry milk	8 oz.	125. _____
Compressed yeast	10 oz	126. _____
Cold water	5 lbs.	127. _____

Using the percentage found for each ingredient, determine the amount of each ingredient if the flour amount is changed to: bread flour 10 lbs., pastry flour 2 lbs.

Round your answers to the tenths place.

(b)

Ingredients	Weight
Bread flour	128. _____
Pastry flour	129. _____
Shortening	130. _____
Sugar	131. _____
Eggs	132. _____
Salt	133. _____
Dry milk	134. _____
Compressed yeast	135. _____
Cold water	136. _____

C. Brown sugar cookies

Find the percent of each ingredient used in the following formulas. Remember that flour is always 100 percent. Round your answers to the tenths place.

(a)

Ingredients	Weight	Percentage
Pastry flour	4 lbs., 8 oz.	137. _____
Hydrogenated shortening	2 lbs., 4 oz.	138. _____
Whole eggs	1 lb.	139. _____
Brown sugar	3 lbs., 2 oz.	140. _____
Salt	1 oz.	141. _____
Baking soda	½ oz.	142. _____
Vanilla	to taste	143. _____

Using the percentage found for each ingredient, determine the amount of each ingredient if the flour amount is changed to 6 lbs., 10 oz. Round your answers to the tenths place.

(b)

Ingredients	Weight
Pastry flour	144. _____
Hydrogenated shortening	145. _____
Whole eggs	146. _____
Brown sugar	147. _____
Salt	148. _____
Baking soda	149. _____
Vanilla	150. _____

Discussion Question 8-1

What is the purpose of using the working factor? What happens if the formula is figured incorrectly?

Discussion Question 8-2

Give an example of when to use the baker's percentage and when to use a working factor in converting recipes.

"As a producer of fine wines from Napa Valley, Sonoma Coast, and Carneros, in California, I need math skills to be able to purchase the proper amount of grapes to produce my wines to meet the demand for our quality wines. Every day, math is used in decision making that will have an effect on the profitability of my company. I use my math skills to determine the price to charge for my wines to cover my costs and to obtain a return on my investment. Math is used to set a fair price for my wines, so wine establishments, hotels, and restaurants can afford to sell them profitably. Believe me, you will need to master math skills in order to be a successful owner, chef, manager, or professional because they are used daily in our profession!"

Joseph Carr
Fine Wine Producer
Joseph Carr Wines
www.josephcarrwine.com
Napa Valley, California

Joseph Carr produces fine wines in the tradition of Bordeaux and Burgundy varietal wines. As a *négociant*, he works with small estate growers, coopers, and winemakers to produce handcrafted boutique wines. Under his Joseph Carr label, he produces Sauvignon Blanc, Chardonnay, Pinot Noir, Merlot, and Cabernet Sauvignon wines made from grapes grown in Sonoma Coast, Napa Valley, and Carneros in California. He also produces some wines under the Josh Cellars brand. Mr. Carr began his career as a wine steward while a fine arts major in college. Later, he became a sommelier for Hyatt Regency Hotels, and eventually went on to be the wine director for the Sagamore Hotel in Bolton Landing, New York. He was president of Mildara Blass, North America, and has worked with legendary winemakers including Wolf Blass and Freemark Abbey's Ted Edwards. While at Mildara Bass, he created the Greg Norman Estates wine collection. He works closely with winemaker and estate grower Tom Larson of Larson Vineyards to make his Joseph Carr wines. He began Joseph Carr Wines in 2005 and has received many favorable comments by the media about his wines, among them the *New York Times*. He produces wines that are complex yet approachable and dare to proclaim "luxury value." Joseph Carr Wines are sold and served worldwide at wine shops and fine dining establishments.

nine

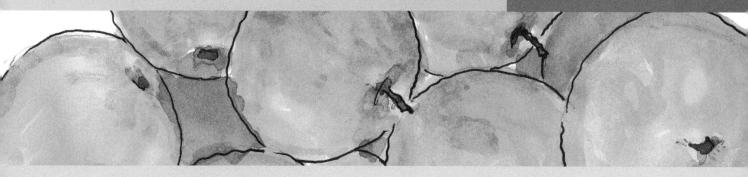

Food, Recipe, and Labor Costing

Objectives

At the completion of this chapter, the student should be able to:

1. Define food costs.
2. Define labor costs.
3. Calculate the unit costs of individual items.
4. Define a standard recipe.
5. Recognize the importance of A.P. (As Purchased) versus E.P. (Edible Portion) in determining cost per ounce.
6. Calculate recipe cost charts to determine the extension costs of recipes.
7. Calculate recipe costs charts to determine the yield costs of recipes.
8. Identify and calculate the costs of labor.
9. Calculate gross and overtime wages.
10. Calculate payroll.

Key Words

food costs	shrinkage	gross wages	salary
labor costs	standard recipe	payroll	overtime
wraparounds	yield	wages	
costed out	unit cost	hourly rate	

The price of food fluctuates, making it difficult for the food service operator to maintain a selling price for his or her food that will continue to show a profit. If a profit is not maintained, it means the owner is working for nothing and has no reason to stay in business. Ways must be found to keep up with changing prices. The answer to this problem could be to standardize and cost all recipes used in food service operations. This means staying current with the changing market prices so management will continually know the cost of the items to be sold. It is important in any business venture to *know your cost* before establishing a selling price.

In most food service operations, the two areas that incur the greatest costs are food and labor. **Food costs** are moneys spent to prepare any and all products used in an individual recipe or an entire meal. **Labor costs** are defined as the total moneys needed to pay all the employees who create recipes and make and serve food to the guests. The purpose of this chapter is to teach the food service professional how to recognize and calculate both food and labor costs. It is essential that the food service professional knows how to calculate the individual cost of every item that is served to guests. This is one of the most important steps to obtaining profitability in the food service business.

Andre Halston, the chief culinary officer of the 62-unit, French-themed La Madeleine restaurants, was quoted in an October 2003 interview in *Chef* magazine. Melanie Wolkoff wrote that Mr. Halston said, "You have to be great in math outside of measurements. You must be able to justify percentages, know cost, understand profit and loss, and basically all aspects of financial math" (p. 28). George Tice, writing in the June 2005 *Santé* magazine, stated that "All restaurateurs would agree that controlling food costs is a primary constituent of any winning operating formula" (p. 36). At his restaurants Toulouse and Portofino, in Atlanta, Georgia, Tice has developed a method of costing out each menu item that the restaurants serve. His key to his winning formula is that he knows the exact food cost of *every item* that is served in the restaurants. He further states that once a system is set in place to figure out food costs, menu prices can be set or adjusted.

Calculating the Individual or Unit Cost of Food

This is a simple mathematical operation, if two facts are known. First, the food service professional must know the size of the portion of food or beverage that will be served to the guest. Second, the cost that the establishment paid for all the raw ingredients that are used to create the menu item has to be known. As an example, our restaurant will serve our guests an 8-ounce glass of milk (this is the first known fact). Our restaurant buys milk in half-gallon containers that cost $1.49 each (this is the second known fact). By using division and multiplication, the cost of a glass of milk in our restaurant can be determined.

Step 1:   Divide the amount of ounces in the half-gallon (64) into the cost of the milk ($1.49).

$1.49 \div 0.64 = 0.023$ cents per ounce for the milk

Step 2:   Multiply the size of the portion (8 ounces) by the cost per ounce of milk (0.023 cents).

$$8 \times 0.023 = 0.184$$

Each 8-ounce glass of milk that is consumed (whether it is sold or given away) costs our restaurant $0.184 cents.

For our restaurant's breakfast menu, every menu item would be calculated in the same manner as previously described. If a guest ordered a bagel, not only the cost of the bagel would have to be included, but also the cost of butter and/or cream cheese that the guest may use must be included. These additional items are referred to as **wraparounds.** If a guest has a breakfast that consists of two eggs, three slices of bacon, an 8-ounce glass of milk, and the bagel, each item must be calculated (or, in the language of food service, **costed out**) individually, and then all items are added up to obtain the total raw food cost for the restaurant to serve this breakfast.

To Insure Perfect Solutions

Remember that, when calculating costs, all figures should represent the same quantity; that is, pounds multiplied or divided by price per pound, ounces multiplied or divided by price per ounce, and so on.

Practice Problems 9–1 Calculating the Individual or Unit Cost of Food

Find the food costs of each item. You may use knowledge learned from information in Chapters 1 to 8 to solve the problems. Round off each answer to the hundredths place (e.g., $1.984 becomes $1.98).

1. Two limes were purchased for $1.98. How much does one lime cost? _____

2. One dozen eggs were purchased for $0.89 cents. How much do three eggs cost? _____

3. Six baked potatoes were purchased for $4.15. How much does one potato cost? _____

4. Sour cream was purchased for $1.14 per pint. How much does 1 ounce cost? _____

5. Using the answers from questions 3 and 4, what is the cost of the baked potato if each guest is served a baked potato and 2 ounces of sour cream? _____

6. From your invoice, you have purchased 2.6 pounds of red grapes. The cost is $5.15. If each guest is served a garnish consisting of three grapes that weigh 2 ounces each, what is the cost of the garnish?

   _____

7. One loaf of bread was purchased for $3.98. There are 20 slices of bread in the package, but the 2 end pieces cannot be used. What is the cost of an order of toast that consists of 2 slices of bread?

   _____

8. Butter for toast is purchased at $2.99 per pound. If your restaurant serves 2 ounces of butter with the toast, what is the cost of the butter? _____

9. A package of sausage was purchased for $4.59. There are 10 links of sausage in each package. How much does 1 link of sausage cost? _____

10. Using the information from questions 2, 6, 7, 8, and 9, figure out the **total cost** of our gigantic breakfast if each guest receives three eggs, three pieces of sausage, four pieces of toast with 3 ounces of butter, and the plate is garnished with 8 ounces of grapes. How much is the total cost of the food for the breakfast that will be served to each guest? _____

....

Costing Meat and Fish Portions

Meat and fish items are popular on a food service menu. They are also the most expensive. In fact, many food service establishments estimate that 25 to 35 percent of their food dollar goes for these two items. Therefore, the portion cost of these items must be controlled and reviewed from time to time because of fluctuating prices.

To find the cost of a portion, the total cost of the amount purchased must be established first. This is accomplished by multiplying the price per pound by the number of pounds purchased.

Price per pound × A.P. (As Purchased) amount purchased = Total cost

The amount purchased is then converted into ounces by multiplying the number of pounds purchased by 16 (16 ounces to one pound).

$$\text{A.P. amount purchased} \times 16 = \text{Total ounces}$$

The amount lost through boning, trimming, or **shrinkage** is converted into ounces and subtracted from the original amount.

$$\text{Amount lost} \times 16 = \text{Total ounces lost}$$
$$\text{Total ounces purchased} - \text{total ounces lost} = \text{E.P. (Edible Portion) ounces}$$

The actual usable amount (the E.P.) is divided into the total cost (carrying the division three places to the right of the decimal). This gives the cost of 1 ounce of cooked meat.

$$\text{Total cost} \div \text{E.P. amount} = \text{Cost of 1 ounce}$$

The cost of 1 ounce is multiplied by the number of ounces contained in one portion.

$$\text{Cost of 1 ounce} \times \text{serving portion} = \text{cost of one portion}$$

Example: A 9-pound A.P. leg of lamb costs $4.85 per pound. A total of 15 ounces is lost in boning and trimming, and 1 pound, 8 ounces is lost through shrinkage during the roasting period. How much does a 3-ounce serving cost?

```
$ 4.85    Price per pound
  × 9     Pounds purchased (A.P.)
$43.65    Total cost

   16     Ounces in 1 pound
  × 9     Number of pounds purchased
 $144     Number of ounces purchased

  144     Number of ounces purchased
 − 39     Number of ounces lost
  105     Number of E.P. ounces

              0.415    Cost of 1 ounce of cooked meat
E.P. ounces 105)43.650  Total cost
              420
              165
              105
              600
              525

$0.415    Cost of 1 ounce
  × 3     Ounce serving portion
$1.245    Cost of each 3-ounce serving of roast lamb
$ 1.25    Cost of each 3-ounce serving of roast lamb
```

The following table shows another way to solve this problem using the butcher's yield chart/yield test from Chapter 8.

Item	Pounds	Ounces	Total Ounces	Percent of the Original Weight
Leg of lamb	9	0	144	100%
Boning and trimming	0	15	15	10.42%
Cooking and carving loss	1	8	24	16.67%
Total Production Loss	1	23	39	27.08%
E.P. Weight			105	72.92%

Here are the formulas from this table:

Percentage of weight = Ounces of item divided by the original weight
E.P. weight = Original weight − Total production loss

From this test, the result for the A.P. leg of lamb is a yield of 72.92 percent. Once this yield has been determined, the E.P. cost must be calculated. It is figured in the following manner:

A.P. price per pound/Product yield % = E.P. price per pound

Putting the numbers into the formula, we get this result:

A.P. Price per pound: $4.85
Product yield % = 72.92%
4.85/0.7292 = $6.65112 E.P. price per pound

After rounding, the answer comes to $6.65 per pound.

Now we want to find the cost of the lamb per ounce. This is done as follows:

6.65/16 = 0.415625 cents

Rounding off to the thousandths place, the final answer is 0.416 cents per ounce of lamb.

Our portion is 3 ounces, so figure out the cost per portion as follows:

3 × 0.416 = 1.248

Round to the hundredths place to get a cost of $1.25 per portion.

Once the actual cost of a serving is established, a selling price (called the menu price) can be determined. Pricing the menu will be explained in Chapter 10.

Using the correct mathematical procedures that have been explained previously concerning rounding sometimes does not make sense in a food service establishment. The restaurant owner should take every opportunity to maximize the amount of money that can be charged to a guest without exploiting the guest's pocketbook. Smart restaurant owners will disregard the rounding rule, even though it is mathematically correct, and automatically round up to the next cent no matter what. For example, one portion of meat costs $2.433. Rounded correctly, the restaurant owner would figure the cost at $2.43 for the portion. However, this means that each portion sold would result in a loss of 0.003 cents. If the restaurant owner disregards proper math and rounds up to $2.44, the restaurant will not lose the 0.003 cents. Instead, rounding up will result in a positive income flow for the restaurant and most likely will not have a negative impact on the price of the meal for the guest.

To Insure Perfect Solutions

It would be profitable for the chef or manager to round up when calculating food cost.

Practice Problems 9–2 Costing Meat and Fish Portions

When you figure out the cost per ounce, this number should be rounded to three digits to the right of the decimal place. For example, if the cost per ounce is 0.59168; the cost per ounce must be shown as 0.592. Then use this number (0.592, for example) to multiply by the amount of ounces served. After you have carried out all the steps, the last step must be to round to the hundredths place.

11. If a 23-pound (A.P.) leg of veal costs $8.50 per pound, and 5 pounds, 6 ounces are lost through trimming and boning, how much does a 5-ounce veal cutlet cost? _____

12. A 24-pound (A.P.) rib of beef costs $2.85 per pound. A total of 4 pounds are lost through trimming, and ¼ of the remaining weight is lost through shrinkage when it is roasted. How much does a 6-ounce serving cost? _____

13. A 50-pound (A.P.) round roast costs $149.50. A total of 5 pounds are lost through trimming, and 5 more pounds are lost through shrinkage when it is roasted. How much does 1 pound of cooked meat cost?

_____

14. A 6-pound 6-ounce (A.P.) beef tenderloin costs $90.00. A total of 1 pound, 5 ounces are lost through trimming. How much does an 8-ounce filet mignon cost? _____

15. If a 24-pound (E.P.) rib of beef costing $45.00 is purchased oven-ready, and ¼ of it is lost during roasting, how much does a 6-ounce serving cost? _____

16. A 9-pound (E.P.) leg of lamb costing $4.85 per pound is roasted. When the roast is removed from the oven, only ⅔ of the original amount is left. How much does a 3½-ounce serving cost?

_____

17. Roast sirloin of beef is served to a party. Each sirloin weighs 18 pounds (E.P.) and costs $5.90 per pound. If 17 portions are cut from each sirloin, what is the cost per serving? _____

18. A 10-pound (E.P.) box of halibut steaks is ordered costing $4.65 per pound. If each steak weighs 5 ounces, what is the cost of each steak? _____

19. A 12-pound pork loin costs $2.92 per pound. A 10-ounce tenderloin is removed from the loin, and 2 pounds, 2 ounces are lost through boning and trimming. How much does a 4-ounce chop cost? _____

20. A 9-pound (A.P.) saddle of lamb costs $5.62 per pound. A total of 12 ounces are lost through trimming. How much does a 4-ounce chop cost? _____

Discussion Question 9-1

Many food service professionals do not take the time to do a butcher test or a yield test to determine the amount of ounces that are lost to boning and shrinkage. Both of these tests take time and accuracy to complete and record the results. Those food service operations that conduct and record the results of the tests and then figure out the actual cost of the portion size will be able to price their menu items accurately and make money, instead of losing money because a step was skipped and E.P was not figured. The following example will illustrate this point.

A restaurant buys a 24-pound (A.P.) rib of beef. The price per pound of the beef is $9.50, so the total cost of this piece of meat is $228 (24 × 9.50). If our lazy food service professional figured out the cost of 1 ounce of beef, he would arrive at a cost of $0.59375. He determined, in this manner, that 24 pounds times 16 ounces results in 384 ounces of beef. The 384 ounces of beef are divided into the $228 cost of the rib of beef.

In reality, when the cook prepares the beef, 4 pounds (or 64 ounces) are lost through boning and trimming (as determined by a butcher test). This leaves the rib weighing 320 ounces. The cook seasons and puts the roast into the oven, and when it is done cooking, it is weighed. During the cooking process, the roast loses 25 percent of its weight (320 ounces minus 25 percent of 320), or another 80 ounces. Now the cooked rib weighs 240 ounces (320 − 80). The math is calculated by the food service professional, and it is determined that 1 ounce of beef costs $0.95.

Our lazy food service professional serves three hundred 8-ounce portions of beef each night. He thinks that it costs him $4.75 (8 × 0.59375). Actually, it costs him $7.60 (8 × 0.95). What may happen to the lazy food service professional's business?

The Standard Recipe

A **standard recipe** is one that will produce the same amount, quality, and taste of each menu item each time it is prepared. If consistency is a factor in the recipe, that too will be the same. The standard recipe provides assurance that the preparation will not fluctuate from one day to the next, regardless of who is preparing the food. If the recipe is followed correctly, quality is maintained. This type of recipe is ideal for food preparation in schools, hospitals, nursing homes, retirement villages, in-plant food service, and other similar institutions, as well as in restaurants.

Figuring the Cost of the Standard Recipe

When figuring the cost of a standard recipe, the cost of each ingredient that goes into the preparation is totaled and a per-unit cost is calculated. (See Figure 9–1.) In the food service industry, the term **yield** refers to the amount of product that is produced. For example, when preparing a recipe that yields 50 servings, the cost of all the ingredients used in making these 50 servings are added together to obtain the complete cost of the preparation. The total cost of the preparation is then divided by 50 (the yield) to find the unit cost. The **unit cost** represents what one serving of this particular item costs to prepare. With this knowledge, the manager or food and beverage controller can establish a menu price. The formula for finding the unit cost is:

$$\text{Total cost} \div \text{Yield} = \text{Unit cost}$$

Figure 9–1
Standardized recipe—costs included.
© Cengage Learning 2012

Hungarian Beef Goulash		Approximate Yield: Fifty 6-ounce servings	
Ingredients	**Amount**	**Market Price**	**Extension Cost**
Beef chuck E.P.	18 lbs.	$2.25 per lb.	$40.50
Garlic, minced	1 oz.	$2.52 per lb.	0.158
Flour	8 oz.	0.18 per lb.	0.09
Chili powder	¾ oz.	3.65 per lb.	0.171
Paprika	5 oz.	4.50 per lb.	1.406
Tomato puree	1 qt.	1.88 per gal.	0.47
Water	8 lbs.	—	—
Bay leaves	2	—	—
Caraway seeds	½ oz.	5.72 per lb.	0.179
Onions, minced	2 lbs.	0.75 per lb.	1.50
Salt	1 oz.	0.42 per lb.	0.026
Pepper	¼ oz.	5.18 per lb.	0.081
		Total cost	$44.581
		Cost per serving	$0.892

The form used to record the cost of a certain recipe may differ depending on the food service establishment. However, the forms all usually supply the same information: the exact cost to produce one serving. Of course, to obtain the proper yield and determine the correct unit cost, all servings must be uniform. (See Figure 9–2.)

A typical standardized recipe showing the market price of each ingredient, the extension cost, total cost, and unit cost per serving is provided in Figure 9–1. An explanation of the standardized recipe shown in this figure follows.

The first column in Figure 9–1 (Ingredients) lists all the ingredients used in the preparation of this dish—in this case, Hungarian beef goulash.

The second column lists the amount of each ingredient needed to prepare fifty 6-ounce servings.

The third column lists the current market price of each ingredient. These prices must be watched carefully because they fluctuate (go up and down) from time to time. The price is listed in quantities that are usually quoted by the vendor. For example, meat is always purchased by the pound, eggs by the dozen, milk by the gallon, and so forth.

The fourth column in Figure 9–1 is the extension cost of the quantity listed. This figure is found by multiplying the amount of the ingredient by the market price. Remember that when multiplying, both figures should represent the same quantity. That is, pounds multiplied by price per pound, ounces multiplied by price per ounce, and so on.

The following information explains how the cost was determined for one serving of Hungarian beef goulash.

The market price of beef chuck is $2.25 per pound E.P. The amount is also in pounds (18). Because both the amount and market price are represented by the same quantity (in this case, pounds), the extension cost of $40.50 was determined by multiplying the amount (18) by the market price ($2.25).

The next ingredient, minced garlic, shows the amount and market price represented by different quantities—the amount in ounces and the market price in pounds. To determine the extension cost, a series of small steps must be performed. First, convert the market price to a cost per ounce. The garlic costs $2.52 per pound. Divide $2.52 by 16 (the number of ounces in a pound), which equals $0.1575. This is the cost of 1 ounce of garlic. (Note: The answer has *not been* rounded off.) Because both the amount and market price are in like quantities (ounces), the extension cost can be determined. The next step is to multiply the $0.1575 (cost of 1 ounce) by 1 (amount of ounces that the recipe requires), which equals $0.1575. Because we round off to the mill, the extension cost of 1 ounce of garlic is $0.158.

Figure 9–2
Uniform size allows the food service employee to determine the proper yield and unit costs.
© Cengage Learning 2012

Flour, chili powder, paprika, tomato puree, caraway seeds, onions, salt, and pepper also have the amount and market price represented by different quantities. Before extension costs can be calculated for these ingredients, the amount and market price have to be converted to the same quantities (ounces). All the extension costs for these ingredients, except for the tomato puree, can be calculated by following the steps in the previous paragraph.

Tomato puree is slightly different. The amount is represented in quarts and the market price is represented in gallons; therefore, both must be converted into like amounts. There are three quantities that gallons and quarts can be converted into: quarts, gallons, or ounces.

For example, the market price can be converted into a price per quart. There are 4 quarts in a gallon. Therefore, the market price of $1.88 per gallon is divided by the amount of quarts in a gallon (4). This equals $0.47 per quart.

Alternatively, one quart is equal to a ¼ (0.25) of a gallon. To determine the cost of the tomato puree, 0.25 is multiplied by $1.88, which equals $0.47.

Finally, both the market price and the amount can be converted to ounces. There are 128 ounces in a gallon. The cost of a gallon, $1.88, is divided by 128 (amount of ounces in a gallon), which equals $0.0146875. This is the cost of 1 ounce of tomato puree. That cost of $0.0146875 is multiplied by the ounces in a quart (32). This results in a cost of $0.47.

In calculating costs, the authors have demonstrated that the three methods used just discussed all result in the same answer. We used different methods to determine the correct answer. The one constant was that the amount and market price were represented in like quantities.

Once all the extension costs have been calculated, the column is added to determine the total cost of the recipe.

To find the cost per serving, divide the total cost by the number of servings that the recipe will yield. In this case, the yield is 50, so 50 is divided into $44.581 to get $0.892, which is the cost of each serving. (Note: Prices have been carried to the mill, three places to the right of the decimal.)

In this type of standard recipe, where market price and extension cost are stated, the procedure or method of preparation is listed on the back of the card. This is done so that the card can be kept to a size that is easy to file. Other standard recipes that do not list market price and extension cost (the total cost of each ingredient used in the preparation) have the procedure or method of preparation listed on the face of the recipe. (See Figure 9–3.) In some kitchens, standardized recipes are stored and printed from software on a computer.

YIELD	Fruit Sauce (Hot)					
	Port	Oz.	Port	Oz.	Port	Oz.
Ingredients	25	2	100	2		**Method**
Orange juice	2 cups		2 qts.			1. Combine first eight ingredients. Bring to a boil.
Pineapple juice	2 cups		2 qts.			
Water	¾ cup		3 cups			2. Dissolve cornstarch in cold water.
Cloves, whole	2 ea.		4 ea.			
Lemon juice	1 tbsp.		¼ cup			3. Add to hot mixture, cook over low heat until thick and clear. Hold hot in bain-marie. Taste.
Salt	½ tsp.		2 tsp.			
Granulated sugar	12 oz.		3 lbs.			
Fruit cocktail (drained)	8 oz.		2 lbs.			*Note: Serve with baked ham, Canadian bacon, chicken*
Cold water	¾ Cup		3 cups			
Cornstarch	2½ oz.		10 oz.			
Yield:	1¾ qt.		1¾ gal.			

Cooking Equipment: Saucepan, stock pot **Service Equipment:** 2 oz. ladle **Garnish:**
Temperature: 160°F **Color:** Multicolor **Date:**

Figure 9–3
Standardized recipe—costs not included.
© Cengage Learning 2012

Practice Problems 9–3 Figuring the Cost of the Standard Recipe

Complete the following recipe cost charts to determine the extension costs. When calculating the cost per ounce, per pound, etc., do not round off at this point. Carry the price three places to the right of the decimal when calculating the extension cost, the total cost, and the cost per serving.

A. Braised Swiss Steak   **Yield 50 servings**

Ingredients	Amount	Price	Extension Cost
6 oz. round steak E.P.	50 ea.	2.35 per lb.	21. _____
Onions	12 oz.	0.75 per lb.	22. _____
Garlic	1 oz.	2.52 per lb.	23. _____
Tomato puree	1 pt.	2.88 per gal.	24. _____
Brown stock	6 qts.	4.25 per gal.	25. _____
Salad oil	3 cups	8.55 per gal.	26. _____
Bread flour	12 oz.	0.23 per lb.	27. _____
Salt	¾ oz.	0.42 per lb.	28. _____
		Total cost	29. _____
		Cost per serving	30. _____

B. Salisbury Steak   **Yield 50 servings**

Ingredients	Amount	Price	Extension Cost
Beef chuck E.P.	14 lbs.	$2.25 per lb.	31. _____
Onions	3 lbs.	0.75 per lb.	32. _____
Garlic	½ oz.	2.52 per lb.	33. _____
Salad oil	½ cup	6.57 per gal.	34. _____
Bread cubes	2 lbs.	0.65 per lb.	35. _____
Milk	1½ pt.	2.18 per gal.	36. _____
Whole eggs	8	0.89 per doz.	37. _____
Pepper	¼ oz.	5.18 per lb.	38. _____
Salt	1 oz.	0.42 per lb.	39. _____
		Total cost	40. _____
		Cost per serving	41. _____

C. Buttermilk Biscuits   **Yield 6 dozen = 72 biscuits**

Ingredients	Amount	Price	Extension Cost
Cake flour	1 lb., 8 oz.	0.25 per lb.	42. _____
Bread flour	1 lb., 8 oz.	0.18 per lb.	43. _____

Baking powder	3½ oz.	1.68 per lb.	44. _____
Salt	½ oz.	0.42 per lb.	45. _____
Sugar	4 oz.	0.36 per lb.	46. _____
Butter	12 oz.	2.25 per lb.	47. _____
Buttermilk	2 lbs., 4 oz.	1.59 per qt.	48. _____
		Total cost	49. _____
		Cost per dozen	50. _____
		Cost per biscuit	51. _____

D. Brown Sugar Cookie   **Yield 14 dozen = 168**

Ingredients	Amount	Price	Extension Cost
Brown sugar	3 lbs., 2 oz.	0.38 per lb.	52. _____
Shortening	2 lbs., 4 oz.	0.48 per lb.	53. _____
Salt	1 oz.	0.42 per lb.	54. _____
Baking soda	½ oz.	0.44 per lb.	55. _____
Pastry flour	4 lbs., 8 oz.	0.20 per lb.	56. _____
Whole eggs	9	0.89 per doz.	57. _____
Vanilla	¼ oz.	1.77 per qt.	58. _____
		Total cost	59. _____
		Cost per dozen	60. _____
		Cost per cookie	61. _____

E. Soft Dinner Rolls   **Yield 16 dozen = 192 rolls**

Ingredients	Amount	Price	Extension Cost
Sugar	1 lb.	$0.36 per lb.	62. _____
Shortening	1 lb., 4 oz.	0.48 per lb.	63. _____
Dry milk	8 oz.	1.93 per lb.	64. _____
Salt	2 oz.	0.42 per lb.	65. _____
Whole eggs	3	1.25 per doz.	66. _____
Yeast	6 oz.	3.27 per lb.	67. _____
Water	4 lbs.	—	68. _____
Bread flour	7 lbs.	0.18 per lb.	69. _____
		Total cost	70. _____
		Cost per dozen	71. _____
		Cost per roll	72. _____

The Cost of Labor and Types of Payment

It may go without saying, but food service establishments must pay employees for the work that they perform. The cost of labor has to be controlled, just as food costs are controlled. Management must have enough staff to meet the demands of the business, but not too much staff as to create a situation where money is being paid to employees when there is no work for them to do. Employees are paid in a variety of ways. One method is by paying them an hourly wage. Another method is to pay them a salary. Some establishments pay a salary plus a commission. Waitstaff are paid a wage, and often their income is supplemented with tips given to them by their customers. In most instances, tips are voluntarily determined by the amount of money that the customer wants to leave. In other instances, however, a flat service charge percentage is set by the establishment. The percentage is added to the bill automatically and is distributed to the employees of the establishment in a formula set by management. Some businesses pay employees (both culinary workers and waitstaff) a flat rate for a day or a party. So long as laws and union contracts are not broken, any method of paying employees is acceptable. In some food service establishments, overtime is paid at the rate of one and a half times the hourly rate. Other businesses pay a bonus for working holidays. Some establishments pay double the hourly rate for certain events. Whatever method is used, the **gross wages** (pay before any deductions are taken from the employee's wages) should be used to figure out the labor cost of the establishment. This labor cost is calculated in every pay period and recorded as payroll.

Payroll

A **payroll** is a record of earnings kept by the employer on all persons classified as employees. The employer is required by law to record and maintain complete, up-to-date, accurate records on all employees. How this information is recorded and maintained is up to the employer. In a small operation, records may be kept up to date by an individual bookkeeper, controller, or accountant using customary office machines; or the operation may hire a bank or company that offers a payroll service for a fee that is based on the number of employees on the payroll. Forms and methods used in compiling a payroll will vary from company to company and even from state to state. State laws and company policy differ in certain areas of the United States and the world. The authors recommend that you consult the government agencies that have jurisdiction over the geographical area you are operating in for specific regulations.

Wages refer to a payment made for a service rendered, usually referring to payment for total hours of work at a designated hourly rate. The amount of money per hour paid to an individual is the **hourly rate.** When a person accepts employment by a company, an agreement is made on wages. The wages will be based on a specific amount for each hour worked.

When the term **salary** is used, it usually refers to payment set for a week, month, or year. When payment is based on salary, the work may exceed 8 hours a day or 40 hours a week. Many food service establishments pay a salary plus a bonus for outstanding work, especially for management employees. Some examples of bonus payments are as follows: A chef may earn a bonus if the food cost percentage is kept in a designated range. Banquet and sales managers may get a bonus based upon sales. Managers may get a bonus if service ratings from an outside consulting firm meet the required criteria.

When an employee is paid on an hourly basis, a definite amount of money is paid for each hour worked. The total number of hours scheduled to work each day may be 8, or 40 for a week. These are called regular hours. Hours worked over these regular hours are called **overtime** hours. In accordance with federal wage and hour laws, companies that engage in interstate commerce or companies that have union contracts with an overtime clause must pay overtime at a rate of time and a half for work over 8 hours a day or 40 hours a week. Some union contracts specify that when an employee works on certain days, such as Sundays and holidays, he or she receive *double time.* That is, the employee is paid two times his or her regular rate of pay for each hour worked.

In some establishments, the hours that an employee works are still recorded on a *time card,* which is punched on a *time clock* when the employee reports to work and again when he or she leaves for the day. (See Figure 9–4.) When a time clock is used, the company will have a set policy on time limits for punching in and out before a penalty is imposed. More and more food service operations are using their point of sales computer to keep track of employees' hours. The employee punches a certain number assigned to him or her when arriving and leaving work, and the computer records the time.

Figure 9–4
Time card.
© Cengage Learning 2012

```
5 MALTSEV, SERGEY
TIMECARD # 2                    PAGE   1
- - - - - - - - - - - - - - - - - - - - - - - -
IN/OUT   TIME   #HRS DAY/PERIOD

1 IN  MON FEB21 10:26AM
       5/1 SERVER
1 OUT MON FEB21 02:32PM
       5               4.10/4.10
```

Calculating Gross Wages

To compute an employee's wage, the hourly rate of pay is multiplied by the number of hours worked.

Hourly rate × hours worked = Gross pay

For example:

Thomas Payne is paid $9.75 per hour. He works a regular 40-hour week. To calculate his gross pay for one week:

$$40 \times \$9.75 = \$390.00$$

$9.75	per hour worked
× 40	hours worked
$390.00	Gross pay

When overtime is involved, gross pay can be calculated in two ways but with the same results:

1. Multiply the number of hours over the regular work time of 40 hours by 1½ (for time and a half) or by 2 (for double time). Multiply this result by the hourly rate. Add the overtime pay to regular pay.

Overtime hours × 1½ = Total regular hours
Total regular hours × hourly rate = Overtime pay
Overtime pay + regular 40 hours pay = Gross wages

For example:

Tim Macke earns $9.00 per hour for a regular work week of 40 hours with overtime pay at time and a half. To calculate his gross wages for a week in which he worked 48 hours:

Overtime hours 8 × 1½ = 12 regular hours
12 × $9.00 hourly rate = $108 overtime pay

Overtime pay	$108.00
Regular pay (40 × $9.00)	+ 360.00
Gross wages	$468.00

or

2. Multiply the hourly rate by 1½ or 2 to get the correct overtime rate.

Then multiply the number of hours over 40 (regular time) by the overtime rate to get the overtime pay, and add the overtime pay to the regular pay to get the gross pay.

Hourly rate × 1.5 = Overtime rate
Overtime rate × overtime hours = Overtime pay
Overtime pay + regular pay = Gross pay

For example (using the same problem as example number 1):

$9.00 hours rate $\times$ 1.5 = $13.50 overtime rate
$13.50 $\times$ 8 overtime hours = $108.00 overtime pay

Overtime wages	$108.00
Regular pay (40 $\times$ $9)	+ 360.00
Gross wages	$468.00

In comparing the two methods of calculating overtime pay, you will notice that the results are the same; only the method differs.

Calculating the Daily and/or Weekly Payroll

To control the cost of labor, food service managers would be well advised to know exactly how much they are paying their employees on an hourly, daily, and weekly basis. Just as the food service manager calculates the cost of food, the labor cost is calculated with basic mathematical operations: multiplication, division, and addition.

If an employee is receiving $11.00 per hour, to find the total daily cost, the manager multiplies the amount of hours times the rate per hour. The hourly cost for this employee is $11.00. During the week, the employee worked 40 hours. The amount of money paid to the employee would be calculated as the number of hours worked (40) times the rate of pay ($11.00). This employee would cost the establishment $440 for the week.

Our chef receives a salary of $75,000 a year. To determine the cost of a salaried employee, the food service manager divides the salary by the number of weeks in the year. This problem is calculated in the following manner: $75,000 ÷ 52 = $1,442.3076 per week.

To determine the cost of our weekly payroll, the amount paid for all employees is added together. In this example, the $440 and the $1,442.3076 results in a total of $1,882.3076 that the establishment had to pay out in wages this week. Depending on the size of the staff, the food service manager would calculate the wages paid to all employees for the day and the week. This step is basic and must be done to control the cost of labor.

Practice Problems 9–4   The Cost of Labor and Types of Payment

Calculate the cost of labor in the following problems.

73. Bill Miller, a cook at the Blue Boar Restaurant, earns $9.75 per hour for a 40-hour week, with time and a half for all hours worked over 40 hours per week. This past week he worked a total of 46 hours. What was his gross wage for the week?

_____

74. Faiza Khan, a fry cook at the Conservatory Restaurant, works on a 40-hour-a-week basis, with time and a half for all overtime. Her regular hourly rate of pay is $8.75. Last week, she worked a total of 49 hours. What was her gross wage for the week?

_____

75. Gloria Luran, a salad person at Lang's Cafeteria, works on an eight-hour-per-day basis, plus time and a half for time worked over eight hours in any one day. Her regular hourly rate of pay is $7.50 per hour. This past week, her time card recorded the following hours:

S	M	T	W	TH	F	S
	12	9	8.5	8	10	

What was her gross wage for the week?

_____

76. Mario Astor, the sauce cook at the Metropole Hotel, worked a total of 49½ hours during a recent week. He is paid $12.25 per hour, plus time and a half for all hours over 40 hours per week. What was his gross wage for the week?

_____

77. Jacob Rowe, a salad person at the Gibson Hotel, worked seven consecutive days, eight hours a day, from Monday through Sunday. His regular pay rate is $7.75 per hour. The hotel pays time and a half for all hours worked on Saturday and double time for all hours worked on Sunday. What was his gross wage for this period of work?

_____

78. Chef Monique Estranza receives a salary of $90,000 annually. What is her weekly gross pay?

_____

79. The Chardonnay Café employs 12 waitstaff, each of whom earns $7.50 per hour. During the week, they each work five 6-hour shifts. What is the cost of labor for the waitstaff?

_____

80. The Chardonnay Café employs 6 culinary staff, each of whom earns $10.50 per hour. During the week, they each work five 8-hour shifts. What is the cost of labor for the culinary staff?

_____

81. The Chardonnay Café employs 4 dishwashers who each earn $7.25 per hour. During the week, they each work five 8-hour shifts. What is the cost of labor for the dishwashers?

_____

82. Using questions 73 to 81, determine the total payroll that was paid in all the establishments.

_____

References

Tice, George. (2005, June). Plate cost analysis. *Santé,* 9(4), 36.

Wolkoff, Melanie. (2003, October). Corporate calling. *Chef,* 13(10), 28.

four

p a r t

Math Essentials in Food Service Recordkeeping

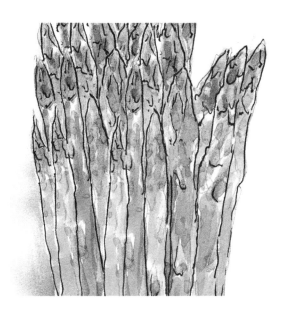

Chapters 10 through 13 will focus on controlling costs for the purpose of making a profit. Food service operations that are successful develop and use formulas and different types of reports to control food and liquor costs. The information and problems presented in all four chapters are essential for the food service professional to understand and know how to use to have a successful business.

Chapter 10 explains how a food service professional determines food cost percentages and what they mean. This chapter also gives strategies for pricing the menu. Chapter 11 explains the importance of keeping track of inventory; failure to do so can mean the loss of revenue and customers. In Chapter 12, the authors emphasize the importance of proper purchasing and receiving techniques. Chapter 13 highlights the ways that food service establishments determine how to produce the correct amount of food and track what food has been sold. This chapter also explains the financial challenges and rewards of alcoholic beverage operations.

Most of the information that will be learned in Part 4 is now entered and controlled using computer software programs. The material is presented in the simplest form to convey how this information is acquired and recorded. Once students master Part 4, they can transfer this knowledge of recordkeeping to computer software. This book does not teach the student how to use any computer software; the authors recommend that students learn about computer software after mastering these basic skills of food service recordkeeping.

The chapters in this part of the book explain how and why functions such as determining cost percentages, pricing the menu, taking inventory, purchasing, and keeping accurate records are vital to the success of a food service operation.

Part 5 of this text will consist of more managerial tasks for determining the profitability of a food service operation.

ten

Determining Cost Percentages and Pricing the Menu

Objectives

At the completion of this chapter, the student should be able to:

1. Define food cost.
2. Define labor cost.
3. Explain the purpose of food cost percentages.
4. Explain the purpose of labor cost percentages.
5. Calculate food cost percentages.
6. Calculate labor cost percentages.
7. Calculate the daily sales of an establishment.
8. Calculate the daily food cost of an establishment.
9. Calculate the daily labor cost of an establishment.
10. Identify the strategies to determine menu prices.
11. Find the menu price using the markup strategy.
12. Find the menu price using the food cost percent method.
13. Find the food cost, food cost percent, or sales price using the Chef's Magic Circle.

Key Words

food costs

labor costs

food cost
    percentage

labor cost
    percentages

daily food cost
    report

storeroom
    requisition

direct purchases

invoice

total sales

customer count

amount of average
    sales

menu

raw food cost

markup

menu or selling
    price

food cost percent

multiplier effect

Food and Labor Cost Percentages

Purpose of Food and Labor Cost Percentages

As was stated in the last chapter, the two areas that incur the most costs are food and labor in most food service establishments. **Food costs** are the moneys spent to prepare any and all products used in an individual recipe or an entire meal. **Labor costs** are defined as the total amount of money needed to pay all the required employees to create, make, and serve food to the guests. The purpose of this chapter is to teach the food service professional how to recognize and calculate both food and labor cost percentages. It is essential that the food service professional know how to calculate the food and labor cost percentages and know how to calculate the individual cost of every item that is served to guests.

Every food service operation should set a goal to determine how much money should be spent on buying food and providing labor for the food service establishment. Because of the great fluctuation in the volume of food sales, it is impractical to state this goal in a dollar amount, such as $6,000 each month. One month the sales could be $40,000, while another month they may be only $3,000. Therefore, it is impractical to use a dollar figure because food service professionals would have a hard time understanding whether $10,800, $9,000, or $910 is a reasonable amount to spend on buying food. Instead, food service professionals use percentages to help them control and understand food costs. For example, a pizza operation sets a monthly food cost percentage goal of 27 percent. Regardless of how many pizzas are sold in that month, the raw cost of the food to prepare all the pizzas sold should be 27 percent of the amount of money received in sales dollars. If the number is lower than 27 percent, it could be that the cost of cheese has gone down. If the number is higher than the goal, it could be that an employee is giving away free pizzas to friends. There can be many reasons for the fluctuation in the food cost percentage. A manager knows that if the cost does not equal the goal, then an investigation must take place to determine why the cost is different from the goal. The manager can use the same concept in determining the ideal labor cost percentage needed to provide staff to operate the business.

To explain and illustrate the value of the concept of food and labor cost percentages, the following example is given. The manager receives a monthly printout stating the amount of raw food and raw labor cost. The cost of food was $11,000 and the cost of labor was $14,000. Do these numbers mean anything to the food service professional? Yes, they are numbers, and yes, a lot of money was spent. The food service operation's goal is to have a raw food cost of 27 percent and a labor cost of 30 percent at the end of the month. Figure 10–1 illustrates the value of using food and labor cost percentages for the months of June and July.

	June	July
Total sales for the month	$40,000	$55,000
Raw cost of food for the month	$11,000	$11,000
Food cost percentage for the month	27.5%	20%
Raw cost of labor for the month	$14,000	$14,000
Labor cost percentage for the month	35%	25.5%

Figure 10–1

Illustration of food and labor cost percentages for the months of June and July.

© Cengage Learning 2012

From the chart, the food service professional can see that using percentages for food and labor costs gives meaningful figures. In June, the cost of food was 27.5 percent, or 27 and a half cents of each dollar earned in sales. In July, sales went up, and the costs of both food and labor were reduced. In other words, the food service manager observes that in July, only 45.5 cents were spent on food and labor, compared to 62.5 cents in June, making July a more profitable month.

Meaning of Food and Labor Cost Percentages

Food cost percentage is the cost of food as it relates to the amount of dollars received in sales. **Labor cost percentage** is the cost of labor as it relates to the amount of dollars received in sales. In the previous section, we stated that our goals for our pizza shop were to have a food cost percentage of 27 percent and a labor cost percentage of 30 percent. This means that for every $1.00 charged for a cheese pizza, it costs $0.27 for the food to make that cheese pizza. So if our pizza shop sells the pizza to the customer for $10.00, we should pay 27 percent of $10.00, or $2.70, for the food cost.

To explain this further, refer back to Figure 10–1. These percentage figures represent numbers that are now quickly understood by the food service professional. In the month of June, for every $1.00 that was collected in sales, $0.275 were paid for food and $0.35 were paid for labor, totaling $0.625. There will still be money left over to pay other bills and make a profit. In July, because sales were higher, our costs dropped and the business was more profitable.

Using and understanding percentages assists food service professionals in setting menu prices and managing their businesses. If the price of cheese rises and the pizza shop owner gives the staff a raise, the percentages of both food and labor will go up, leaving less money for profit.

Food and Labor Costing

As stated previously, in any food service operation, the two biggest expenditures are the cost of food and labor. If the operation is to have any chance for success, these two items must be controlled. It is not an easy task, because it seems that both are constantly rising. One of the tools that is used to control the cost and use of food is the

daily food cost report, the purpose of which is to show management the exact cost and amount of food used on any given day. This report is a guide that keeps the manager aware of costs, thus helping to control the cost of food being used in the establishment. The high cost of food, waste, and theft by employees make it essential that tight controls be maintained on the items that can lead a food service operation to bankruptcy. The same process should be used to keep track of the daily cost of labor. A **daily labor cost report** should be generated each day for the manager's review.

The daily food cost report also helps to provide a more accurate picture of the food service operation's monthly food cost pattern. That is, if the planned monthly food cost percentage is set at a certain rate to ensure a profitable operation, and each day this rate is exceeded, something is not right. It would therefore be apparent to management that all factors, such as portion size, waste, theft, and food production, must be investigated to find the cause.

There are several kinds of food cost reports in use. The simplified type is made up of the totals of storeroom requisitions and direct purchases for the day. (See Figure 10–2.)

A **storeroom requisition** is a list of food items issued from the storeroom upon the request of the production crew. These may be requests for certain meats, other groceries, canned foods, or frozen foods. The requisitions are priced and extended at the end of each day. The unit prices are usually marked on all storeroom items as they are received, or they may be stored on a computer. This way, the requisitioned foods can be priced immediately. **Direct purchases** are those foods that are usually purchased each day or every other day. They include produce, dairy products, fresh seafood, bread, rolls, and any other items that are considered perishable. The total for direct purchases can be obtained from the **invoice** (a list of goods sent to the purchaser with their prices and quantities listed), which is sent with each order.

Figure 10–2
Daily food cost report.
© Cengage Learning 2012

| Customer Count | 400 | Date | January 15, 20 |
| Average Sale | $18.20 | Day | Thursday |

Issues	Today	To Date	Last Month to Date
Storeroom			
Canned goods	$ 425.60	$ 1,600.50	$ 1,700.50
Other groceries	315.60	915.60	1,015.60
Meat	635.25	4,237.25	4,137.25
Frozen foods	410.60	1,210.60	1,375.25
Direct Purchases			
Poultry, fresh	420.15	1,620.15	1,205.75
Seafood, fresh	621.30	1,821.30	1,625.85
Produce	108.00	510.00	575.00
Dairy products	96.00	399.00	375.00
Bread and rolls	55.00	210.00	285.00
Miscellaneous	24.00	46.00	58.00
Total Cost	$3,111.50	$ 12,570.40	$ 12,353.20
Total Sales	$7,280.00	$ 31,320.00	$ 30,320.00
Food Cost Percentage	42.74%	40.14%	40.74%

A raw labor cost report is generated daily using the same method as the daily food cost report. The manager is given a report that shows how much is spent on wages each day for all employees. The report can be set up in categories of management, waitstaff, cooks, dishwashers, and so forth. Each operation should set up its own type of report, but the key fact that must be known is how much money was paid in wages daily. In Chapter 15, we will discuss labor costs more in detail.

Finding the Total Sales

In Figure 10–2, the total sales for the day is $7,280.00. This figure is found by totaling the point of sales (POS) or the cash register sales for the day (whichever is used at the establishment). **Total sales** is defined as the amount of money that has been recorded as sales during a specified time period. This figure can be checked by multiplying the average sales by the customer count.

Average Sales × Customer Count = Total Sales

Average Sales	$18.20
Customer Count	400
Total Sales	$7,280.00

$18.20 × 400 = $7,280.00

Finding the Amount of Average Sale

The **customer count** is obtained by checking the POS or cash register sales, which records the total number of customers for the meal period. The **amount of average sales** for the day is found by dividing the customer count into the total sales.

Total Sales ÷ Customer Count = Amount of Average Sales

$$\begin{array}{r} \$18.20 \\ 400\overline{)\$7280.00} \\ \underline{400} \\ 3280 \\ \underline{3200} \\ 800 \\ \underline{800} \end{array}$$

Customer Count $400)\$7280.00$ Average Sales / Total Sales

Finding the Food and Labor Cost Percentages

To find the food cost. The manager must add together the cost of all items issued for the day's food production (see Figure 10–2). If the total cost of food that was used to produce the food for sales for the day is $3,111.50 and the sales for the day is $7,280, the food cost percentage is 42.74 percent.

Cost of Food ÷ Total Sales = Food Cost Percent

$$\begin{array}{r} 0.42740 \text{ equals } 42.74\% \\ \$7,280\overline{)3111.50000} \\ \underline{2912\,0} \\ 199\,50 \\ \underline{145\,60} \\ 53\,900 \\ \underline{50\,960} \\ 2\,9400 \\ \underline{2\,9120} \\ 2800 \end{array}$$

Total Sales Food Cost Percentage / Cost of Food

To calculate the labor cost for a food service operation. The manager must add together the cost of all wages paid for the day. If the total wage cost is $2,221.75 and the sales for the day is $7,280.00, the labor cost percentage is 30.52 percent.

Cost of Labor ÷ Total Sales = Labor Cost Percent

$$
\begin{array}{r}
0.30518 \text{ equals } 30.52\% \\
\text{Total Sales} \quad \$7,280 \overline{)2221.7500} \\
-\,2184\ 0 \\ \hline
37\ 75 \\
-\,00\ 00 \\ \hline
37\ 750 \\
-\,36\ 400 \\ \hline
1\ 3500 \\
-\ \ \ 7280 \\ \hline
62200 \\
-\,58240 \\ \hline
3960 \quad \text{Remainder}
\end{array}
$$

Labor Cost Percentage
Daily Cost of Labor

In computing both the food cost and labor cost percentages, we recommend that the division be carried out to the hundred thousandths place (the fifth number to the right of the decimal point) and then rounded off to the ten thousandths place using the rounding rules that were taught in Chapter 2. The reason that we recommend that they are carried out to this degree is because it will give food service operators a more accurate accounting of their costs. For example, if the total sales for a business at the end of the year amounted to $2,000,000, using the food cost percentage of 42 percent instead of 42.74 percent would give a food cost of $840,000.00. Carrying the calculation out further would show that it actually is $854,800.00, which means that we actually spent an additional $14,800 on food. The benefit of carrying out the division to the hundred thousandths place is especially valuable when the business does a large volume of sales. The food service operator can use this information to determine how much money is being spent on food, labor, and beverages (or, for that matter, any expenses) and control the costs of the operation better. As the saying goes, knowledge is power, and that is never truer than in food and beverage controls.

To find the individual menu item's food cost percentage. The food service professional must know the exact cost of the food needed to produce the menu item and the price of the menu item. For example, The Simpson Restaurant at the Desmond Hotel in Albany, New York (see Figure 10–3) lists the price of New England clam chowder as $5.50. Suppose the following scenario: When the Desmond's executive chef calculated the exact cost of the recipe for the chowder, he determined the cost to be $0.069 for one portion. To calculate the individual clam chowder's food cost, he would divide the menu price by the cost of the food to prepare the clam chowder.

$$
\begin{array}{r}
0.12545 \text{ equals } 12.55\% \\
\text{Menu price} \quad \$5.50 \overline{)0.69.000000} \\
-\ 55\ 0 \\ \hline
14\ 00 \\
-\ 11\ 00 \\ \hline
3\ 000 \\
-\ 2\ 750 \\ \hline
2500 \\
-\ 2200 \\ \hline
3000 \\
-\ 2500 \\ \hline
400 \quad \text{Remainder}
\end{array}
$$

Food Cost Percentage
Cost of the Clam
Chowder Ingredients

It is recommended that all menu items be calculated to determine the individual food cost. This will greatly assist management to determine what items should be on the menu and what items should be removed, or if prices of the items should be increased or decreased.

In addition to the daily food and labor cost percents, some daily reports also show the increasing totals for the month and the totals of the previous month to date. By including this information, the owner or manager has a clearer picture of the food cost pattern.

Practice Problems 10–1   Calculating Sales, Food Costs, and Food Cost Percentages

For the following daily food cost reports, find:

- The total cost of food for today, to date, and last month to date.
- The total sales for today.
- The food cost percentage today, to date, and in the last month, to date.

When computing the food cost percentage, carry the division out to the hundred thousandths place (the fifth number to the right of the decimal point) and then round off to the ten thousandths place. If the initial answer you get is 0.394216, then the answer is 39.4216 percent, which should be rounded to 39.42 percent.

A.

Customer Count	390		Date	July 15, 20
Average Sales	$1.45		Day	Monday

Issues	Today	To Date	Last Month to Date
Storeroom			
Canned goods	$24.30	$ 106.55	$ 98.40
Other groceries	17.80	40.50	42.20
Meat	47.25	325.50	312.30
Frozen foods	9.50	25.22	23.60
Direct Purchases			
Poultry, fresh	18.15	75.45	72.53
Seafood, fresh	20.35	52.60	48.22
Produce	10.56	37.65	34.25
Dairy products	6.90	23.75	19.85
Bread and rolls	5.85	24.43	23.46
Miscellaneous	6.20	12.24	11.47
Total Cost	—	—	—
Total Sales	—	$1,650.00	$1,560.00
Food Cost Percentage	—	—	—

1. The total cost for Today is _____.

2. The total cost for To Date is _____.

3. The total cost for Last Month to Date is _____.

4. The total sales for Today is _____.

5. The food cost percentage for Today is _____.

6. The food cost percentage for To Date is _____.

7. The food cost percentage for Last Month to Date is _____.

B.

| Customer Count | 290 | | Date | August 3, 20____ |
| Average Sales | $1.50 | | Day | Tuesday |

Issues	Today	To Date	Last Month to Date
Storeroom			
Canned goods	$30.24	$ 110.50	$ 112.25
Other groceries	15.20	40.65	45.50
Meat	58.65	228.60	248.40
Frozen foods	10.90	30.75	25.95
Direct Purchases			
Poultry, fresh	17.55	68.30	75.35
Seafood, fresh	25.40	59.42	65.75
Produce	15.50	49.25	52.20
Dairy products	8.22	22.00	20.80
Bread and rolls	8.45	18.80	21.50
Miscellaneous	6.30	12.43	13.65
Total Cost	—	—	—
Total Sales	—	$1,600.00	$1,700.00
Food Cost Percentage	—	—	—

8. The total cost for Today is _____.

9. The total cost for To Date is _____.

10. The total cost for Last Month to Date is _____.

11. The total sales for Today is _____.

12. The food cost percentage for Today is _____.

13. The food cost percentage for To Date is _____.

14. The food cost percentage for Last Month to Date is _____.

C.

Customer Count	380		Date	September 8, 20
Average Sales	$1.35		Day	Wednesday

Issues	Today	To Date	Last Month to Date
Storeroom			
Canned goods	$36.75	$ 115.25	$ 116.35
Other groceries	16.26	42.75	43.85
Meat	68.40	245.30	240.75
Frozen foods	12.65	28.80	27.60
Direct Purchases			
Poultry, fresh	18.95	58.35	85.62
Seafood, fresh	24.15	46.12	58.14
Produce	18.85	39.25	48.20
Dairy products	9.95	20.90	21.76
Bread and rolls	10.22	18.80	22.87
Miscellaneous	7.50	9.20	13.70
Total Cost	—	—	—
Total Sales	—	$1,550.00	$1,590.00
Food Cost Percentage	—	—	—

15. The total cost for Today is _____.

16. The total cost for To Date is _____.

17. The total cost for Last Month to Date is _____.

18. The total sales for Today is _____.

19. The food cost percentage for Today is _____.

20. The food cost percentage for To Date is _____.

21. The food cost percentage for Last Month to Date is _____.

22. The menu price of a turkey sandwich is $5.95. The raw cost of food is $1.50. Find the food cost percentage.

_____

23. A chicken marsala dinner has a menu price of $18.95. The raw cost of food is $4.89. Find the food cost percentage. _____

24. A lazy man's lobster dinner has a menu price of $19.95. The raw cost of food is $6.89. Find the food cost percentage. _____

25. A fajita platter has a menu price of $15.95. The raw cost of food is $4.82. Find the food cost percentage.

_____

26. The total cost of all food purchased for the day is $1,020, and total sales for the day is $350. Find the daily food cost percentage. _____

27. The total cost of all food purchased for the day is $426, and total sales for the day is $989.50. Find the daily food cost percentage. _____

28. The total cost of all food purchased for the day is $20, and total sales for the day is $1,642.78. Find the daily food cost percentage. _____

29. Chef Monique Estranza receives a salary of $96,000 annually. What is her daily gross pay, figuring she works five days a week for 52 weeks of the year? _____

30. The Chardonnay Café employs 12 waitstaff, each of whom earns $6.50 per hour. They each work an eight-hour shift. What is the cost of labor for the waitstaff? _____

31. The Chardonnay Café employs six culinary staff, each of whom earns $10.50 per hour. They each work an eight-hour shift. What is the cost of labor for the culinary staff? _____

32. The Chardonnay Café employs four dishwashers, each of whom earns $6.50 per hour. They each work an eight-hour shift. What is the cost of labor for the dishwashers? _____

33. Using questions 29 to 32, determine the daily payroll. _____

Determine the daily labor cost percentage for questions 29 to 32 if the daily sales were $5,000. In computing the food cost percentage, carry the division out to the hundred thousandths place (the fifth number to the right of the decimal point) and then round off to the ten thousandths place. If the initial answer you get is 0.394216, then the final answer would be 39.42 percent.

34. Chef Monique   _____%

35. Waitstaff   _____%

36. Culinary staff   _____%

37. Dishwashers   _____%

38. Daily labor cost   _____%

....

Discussion Question 10-1

What reasons can be given to prove that your answers to questions 26 and 28 are correct?

....

The Restaurant Menu

The **menu** is a detailed list of the dishes being offered for sale in the food service establishment, most of the time with prices for these items. It should be organized in such a way that selections are appealing to the guests and can be made in a short period of time. For example, the Desmond Hotel in Albany, New York, offers its guests a choice of menus depending upon the time that they are dining and the restaurant that they choose to dine in. The three-course pre-theater menu at the Scrimshaw Restaurant is available from 5:30 to 7:00 p.m. and costs $39.95 per person (see Figure 10–4). The three-course prix fixe menu at Simpson's Restaurant is available from Monday through Friday from 4:30 to 6:30 p.m. and Sunday from 1:00 to 10:00 p.m. for $24.95 (see Figure 10–5). Because more guests like to eat after 6:30 p.m. from Monday through Friday, guests who choose this menu pay $29.95. Guests who want to order each course individually also have the option of ordering from the à la carte menu at Simpson's (Figure 10–3). In addition, Simpson's and the Scrimshaw restaurants offer additional specials each day depending on the seasonal foods availabile. Each item listed on a menu is priced for sale to customers, and in this chapter, we will show how prices are determined.

Traditional Fare

Prime Rib
Choose your portion of this succulent aged prime rib, cooked as you like it,
served with a tangy horseradish sauce on the side
12~ounce $20.95   16~ounce $24.95   24~ounce $29.95

Fresh Roast Turkey Breast $17.95
Tender sliced turkey, served with a rich brandied giblet gravy and cranberry relish

Chicken Marsala $19.95
Boneless breast of chicken sautéed with wild mushrooms and finished with a rich
marsala wine demi glace

New York Sirloin Steak $25.95
A thick 14~ounce tender aged New York sirloin char~grilled to your
liking, topped with crispy fried onions and a side of Sauce Béarnaise
add fresh Atlantic salmon for just $4.00 more

Filet Mignon $29.95
8~ounce center~cut, char~grilled Filet Mignon, topped with crispy
fried onions and a side of Sauce Béarnaise

Veal Piccata $19.95
Tender veal Scalloppine sauteed with portabella mushrooms in lemon caper butter

Roasted Half Chicken $18.95
Tender split chicken dry rubbed and slow roasted. Served with a savory glaze

Char ~grilled Ribeye Steak $23.95
14 ounce tender ribeye grilled to your liking

Each entrée includes your choice of Desmond salad or Caesar salad,
choice of potato (au gratin, baked, garlic mashed or french fries) or rice pilaf
and fresh vegetables of the day.

Health Conscious Lifestyle

Chicken Breast Tequila $17.95
Boneless breast of chicken rubbed with fresh herbs, sauteed and finished with a tequila lime glaze,
accompanied by blended wild rice

Mediterranean Pasta $17.95
A blend of Mediterranean vegetables, kalamata olives and cherry peppers sauteed and tossed with a sun
dried tomato pesto and penne pasta, garnished with feta cheese

Pasta Primavera $15.95
Roasted seasonal vegetables, tossed with herb olive oil and mini penne pasta.
Garnished with toasted focaccia points.

An automatic 18% gratuity will be added to the total check for parties of 6 people or more.

Figure 10–3
Simpson's à la carte menu. (*continued*)
Courtesy of The Desmond Hotel and Conference Center, Albany, New York.

Appetizers

Desmond Shrimp	$7.95		
Horseradish stuffed jumbo shrimp, wrapped in pancetta and broiled			
New England Clam Chowder	$5.50	Maryland Crab Cakes	$8.95
A rich and creamy Desmond specialty		Served with tarter & cocktail sauce	
French Onion Soup	$5.50	Clams or Oysters on the Half Shell	$9.95
You will love this traditional cheesy soup		Shrimp Cocktail	$9.95
Soup of the Day	$4.50	Spinach Salad	$4.95
Eggplant Panini	$6.95		

Medallions of eggplant lightly sautéed and layered with smoked
mozzarella, topped with herbed tomato concasse

Salads

Cobb Salad $12.95
Field greens tossed with Dijon vinaigrette topped with turkey breast, proscuitto, avocado, cheddar cheese,
hard boiled egg and crumbled bleu cheese. Garnished with grilled scallions.

Drunken Goat Cheese Salad $13.95
A char-grilled boneless breast of chicken served over mesclun greens, accompanied by
red wine soaked goat cheese, pecans, cranberry vinaigrette and garnished with strawberry halves

Selections From The Sea

Seafood Pasta Alfredo $18.95
A combination of Alaskan crabmeat, Jumbo Gulf shrimp and Georges Bank sea scallops,
served in a garlic cream sauce over mini penne,
topped with grated parmesan cheese

Glazed Swordfish $19.95
North Atlantic swordfish steak brushed with a honey mustard glaze and sauteed.

Citrus Grilled Shrimp $18.95
Marinated Jumbo Gulf shrimp, char-grilled and
accompanied by a tropical fruit salsa

Sole Francaise $16.95
Fresh fillet of Atlantic sole dredged in a parmesan egg batter, sauteed to a golden brown and
finished with a lemon chardonnay butter sauce.

Pesto Herb Crusted Sea Scallops $18.95
Georges Bank sea scallops encrusted with fresh herbs and pesto, broiled and
served with tomato vinaigrette

Grilled Salmon $18.95
Fresh Atlantic salmon fillet basted with dill butter,
char-grilled and served with dill hollandaise on the side

Southwestern Style Char-grilled Tuna Steak $19.95
Southwestern rubbed, center cut Tuna steak char-grilled medium rare, accompanied by a chilled black
bean and roasted corn relish

Figure 10–3
Simpson's à la carte menu. (*continued*)
Courtesy of The Desmond Hotel and Conference Center, Albany, New York.

Pre-Theatre Menu

Available
5:30PM – 7 PM

Dinner Menu

Appetizers

Baby Lamb Chops
Caesar Salad
Desmond Salad
Scrimshaw's Famous Clam Chowder

Soup du Jour
Desmond Shrimp
Caramelized Pear Phyllo Purse

Intermezzo

Entrées

Filet Mignon
An 8 ounce filet Char-grilled and finished to your liking, garnished with foie gras butter and tobacco onions.

Sole Bienville
Fresh Fillet of Atlantic sole sautéed and finished with a béchamel sauce, laced with shrimp, mushrooms and sherry.

Veal Boursin
Tender veal medallions, sautéed with a rich Boursin cream sauce and garnished with oven-roasted tomatoes.

Chicken Roulade
Boneless breast of chicken layered with black Mission fig, wild mushroom and brie compote, oven roasted and served with a bourbon cream sauce.

Shrimp & Scallop Mornay
Jumbo Gulf shrimp & a Georges Bank scallop sautéed in a rich Mornay sauce and served with cheese filled tortelloni.

Crabmeat Stuffed Salmon
Fresh Atlantic Fillet of salmon stuffed with Alaskan King Crabmeat, brushed with coriander butter, oven-roasted and topped with sauce choron.

Prime Rib
12 ounce, coated with our house blend of herbs and spices, then slow roasted to achieve optimum flavor.

Desserts

Desmond Signature "Bread Pudding"
Strawberry Napolean   Chocolate Lava Cake
Chocolate Polenta Cake   Berry Torte

$39.95
An automatic 18% gratuity will be added to the total check to parties of 6 people or more

Figure 10–4
Scrimshaw pre-theatre menu.
Courtesy of The Desmond Hotel and Conference Center, Albany, New York.

Simpson's Prix Fixe Menu
Complete Three-Course Dinner
*Additional $3 charge will apply for select items

Appetizers

Fresh Fruit Medley

The Desmond Salad
Chilled Strawberry Soup
Caesar Salad

Scrimshaw's Famous Clam Chowder
Soup du Jour
French Onion Soup

Entrées

Atlantic Salmon
Herb encrusted fresh fillet of salmon, broiled and finished with a lemon beurre blanc.

Pesto Herb Crusted Sea Scallops
Georges Bank sea scallops encrusted with fresh herbs and pesto, broiled and served with tomato vinaigrette.

Maryland Crab Cakes
Served with a selection of tartar and cocktail sauces.

Desmond Shrimp
Horseradish stuffed jumbo shrimp, wrapped in pancetta and broiled.

Sole Paupiettes
North Atlantic sole fillets rolled with seafood mousseline baked and served with a chardonnay cream sauce.

Roasted Half Chicken
Tender split chicken dry rubbed and slow roasted. Served with a savory glaze.

Chicken Florentine
Marinated boneless breast of chicken char-grilled and served over a bed of sauteed cream spinach.

*Prime Rib
Succulent aged prime rib, cooked as you like it, served with a tangy horseradish sauce on the side.

*Filet Mignon Au Poivre
Center cut tenderloin crusted with black pepper, sauteed and finished with a mushroom cognac cream sauce.

*New York Sirloin Steak
Center cut 12oz. sirloin steak, char-grilled to your liking and finished with maitre d' hotel butter.

Cheese Tortellini Casserole
Cheese filled tortellini sauteed with a tomato vodka sauce, baked with a Parmesan crust and accompanied by a garlic crustade.

Fresh Roast Turkey Breast
Tender sliced turkey served with a rich brandied giblet gravy and cranberry relish.

Each entrée includes your choice of potato (garlic mashed, au gratin, baked or french fries), and fresh vegetables of the day.

Desserts

Grand Marnier Frozen Torte
Old Fashioned Rice Pudding
Desmond Bread Pudding
Warm Apple Pie ala Mode

Warm Peach Cobbler ala Mode
Frozen Mocha Almond Mud Pie
Ice Creams and Sherbets
Key Lime Pie

Monday thru Friday 4:30pm to 6:30pm $24.95
6:30pm to 10pm $29.95
Sunday 1:00pm to 10:00pm $24.95

An automatic 18% gratuity will be added to the total check for parties of 6 people or more.

Figure 10–5
Simpson's prix fixe menu.
Courtesy of The Desmond Hotel and Conference Center, Albany, New York.

Pricing the Menu

In the past, pricing menus was often done in a random fashion. Arriving at a selling price per item was based on your competition rather than your cost. If your competition charged $24.95 for prime rib of beef au jus, you would charge the same or less. Although there is still no one standard method of pricing items on a menu, food service operators must now determine their cost before deciding how much should be charged to make a profit. Many elements must be considered before a menu price is determined. The cost of all items purchased, rent, labor costs, equipment, taxes, and so forth must be considered before establishing a price.

Large food service operations and chain operations doing a significant volume of business usually have accountants and computers to supply an accurate picture of the overall cost of maintaining a food service business. This makes pricing decisions easier for those involved. In smaller operations, however, the overall cost is more difficult to compute because controls are not always as tight as they should be and records are not always as accurate because of the time and cost involved.

Determining the menu price per item is one of the most challenging and difficult tasks that a food service professional will have to accomplish. As previously stated, large food service operations and chain operations have an easier time setting menu prices than smaller operations. One of the first questions asked by small operators, caterers, and students is, "How do I price my menu?"

Ideally, the food service professional should *figure out and know all the costs before* setting the menu price. Then the menu price can be determined based on costs, type of service, location, and other factors. The final question that has to be answered concerns the amount of profit that is desired. Small operators may not have this information available before the restaurant is opened.

However, there is one thing a restaurant owner *can* and *must* do before setting the menu price of an individual entree or sandwich. Taking Chef Fritz Sonnenschmidt's advice from Chapter 9 (see the "Chef Sez"), the price of the raw food cost for each menu item *must* be determined. In other words, each food service business should know *exactly* how much it costs to place one meal in front of one guest (called the **raw food cost**). Once that is determined, the menu price can be calculated. This food cost must include the entree, starch, vegetable, and whatever else is included. For example, if a restaurant is serving a lobster roll, the cost of the lobster meat, roll, and butter has to be included. A 3-ounce portion of lobster meat costs $2.50, the roll costs $0.10, and the butter costs $0.10. Therefore, it costs the restaurant $2.70 to serve one lobster roll to a guest.

The restaurant owner must also include all the costs involved in serving one lobster roll to one guest. The cost of people to prepare the food (labor cost), paper plates, garbage removal, snow plowing, and so on must be figured into the equation before establishing a price for the lobster roll. Then an amount of money (the profit) must be added to the costs, and a final menu determination can be made.

When pricing the menu, food service professionals use three methods that take into account all the factors listed here. They are *amount of markup using a percentage, food cost percentage, and multiplier effect.*

Markup

In menu pricing, the only standard is that cost must be established before a markup can be added to determine an item's selling price. **Markup** is the money added to raw food cost to obtain a menu price. The amount of markup usually varies depending on the type of establishment. A cafeteria might mark up all its items by one-half the cost to obtain a menu price; a gourmet restaurant might mark up all its items by two or three times the cost. The markup is not always figured using fractions, however. In many cases, percents are used because they are easier to work with and fewer mistakes are made.

Figuring the Amount of Markup Using a Fraction

If the price of a raw food is $1.95 and the markup rate is ⅔, markup is obtained by multiplying the cost by the markup rate. The formula for this is:

Step 1:   Raw food cost $\times$ markup rate = markup amount

Step 2:   Raw food cost + markup amount = menu or selling price

For example:

$$\$1.95/_1 \times \tfrac{2}{3} = \$3.90/_3 = \$1.30 \text{ markup amount}$$

$1.95 raw food cost + $1.30 markup amount = $3.25 menu or selling price

Amount of Markup Using a Percentage

If the markup is figured by using percentages, the **menu or selling price** of an item is determined by multiplying the raw food cost by the percent and adding the markup to the raw food cost. The formula for this is:

Step 1:   Raw food cost $\times$ percent = markup amount

Step 2:   Raw food cost + markup amount = menu or selling price

When multiplying or dividing with percentages, it is best to convert the percentage to its decimal equivalent. This is done by removing the percent sign (%) and moving the decimal point two places to the left. For instance:

$$60\% = 0.60$$
$$75\% = 0.75$$
$$25.5\% = 0.255$$
$$50.5\% = 0.505$$

For example: If the raw food cost is $1.95 and the markup rate is 45 percent, convert 45 percent to 0.45 and multiply.

$1.95	Raw food cost
$\times$0.45	Markup percent
975	
780	
$0.8775	= $0.88 markup amount

Then add the markup ($0.88) to the raw food cost to determine the selling cost or menu price.

$1.95   Raw food cost
+ 0.88   Markup amount
$2.83   Menu or selling price

Food Cost Percentage

Another method of menu pricing is to determine the monthly **food cost percent** and divide the food cost percent into the raw food cost. The formula for this is:

Raw food cost ÷ food cost percent = menu or selling price

For example: if the raw food cost is $2.90 and the monthly food cost percentage is 35 percent, the menu price is determined by dividing 35 percent (or 0.35) into $2.90.

```
                           8.285 = $8.29 menu or selling price
Food cost percentage  0.35)2.90000   Raw food cost
                           2 80
                           ____
                           100
                            70
                           ____
                           300
                           280
                           ____
                           200
                           175
                           ____
                            25
```

Many operators rely on the food cost percentage method of pricing the menu. In the example, our restaurant has set a goal of 25 percent for food cost for the lobster roll. That will leave 75 percent of the menu price to pay for all the expenses (plates, snow plowing, etc.) as well as make a profit.

$2.70 raw food cost ÷ 0.25 food cost percentage = $10.80 menu price

Our menu price of one lobster roll will be $10.80.

Multiplier Effect

Many restaurant owners do not take the time or effort to figure out their exact costs before they price the menu. An easier and quicker system has been developed to price the menu, called the **multiplier effect.** It works on the principle of food cost percentage, but instead of dividing, the restaurant owner multiplies the cost of the raw food by a number that corresponds to the food cost percentage goal. Therefore, to obtain a food cost percentage, the restaurant owner takes the cost of the raw food and multiplies that number by the multiplier. In our example with the lobster roll, if we desire a food cost percentage of 25 percent, we take the cost of the raw food ($2.70) and multiply by 4 (dividing the desired food cost percentage of 25 into 100 resulted in the multiplier number of 4).

$2.70   Cost of the lobster roll
× 4   Multiplier
$10.80   Menu price

This is the same menu price that was obtained by dividing the raw cost of food by the food cost percentage.

$$\$2.70 \text{ raw food cost} \div 0.25 \text{ food cost percent} = \$10.80 \text{ menu price}$$

This method of pricing is used to figure out desired food cost percentages quickly. If a chef desires a food cost percentage of 50 percent, the raw food cost will be multiplied by 2; 40 percent by 2.5; 33.3 percent by 3; 25 percent by 4; and 20 percent by 5, as illustrated in Figure 10–6. Using this method is quick and involves less figuring.

For example: If the raw food cost is $2.90 and the desired food cost is 40 percent (2½ times the raw food cost), the price is determined by multiplying 2½ × $2.90.

$$2\tfrac{1}{2} \times \$2.90 = \tfrac{5}{2} \times {}^{2.90}\!/_{1} = \$7.25 \text{ menu or selling price}$$

This problem can also be done by converting 2½ to the decimal 2.5 before multiplying.

$$
\begin{array}{r}
\$2.90 \\
\times\ 2.5 \\
\hline
1450 \\
580 \\
\hline
\$7.250
\end{array}
$$
$\$7.250 = \$7.25$ menu or selling price

In addition to using mathematical formulas to set prices, chefs and food service managers also take into account psychological factors. Look at the Desmond's menus in Figures 10–3 to 10–5. Notice how many of the menu items end with $0.95. Most likely, very few (if any) of the menu items, when costed out, resulted in the exact ending price of $0.95. As was stated previously, it is always a great idea to cost up. Examples of this idea are listed here.

Determined Price	Menu Price
$11.15	$11.95
$13.35	$13.95
$15.60	$15.95
$18.90	$18.95

Remember that prices are important in a customer's appraisal of a food service operation. It is essential that a price level be established that appeals to all types of potential customers. It must not only be a price that customers can afford, but one that they feel is closely related to the quality of food and service that they receive.

Remember, too, that the food service operator is in business to make a profit and that profits will usually result if an establishment is built on a solid foundation of quality food, attractive decor, fair prices, good service, and a commitment to hospitality.

"Food and labor costs can quickly erode your bottom line. Control what you can control. At the end of the day, you can't control attendance and how much the guest will spend."

Derek Swartz
Director of Operations
Citi Field, Queens, NY

Mr. Swartz opened up the new Citi Field, the home of the New York Mets professional baseball team. This open-air ballpark has many varied food outlets for the potential 41,800 fans at the ballpark. The food, beverage, and merchandise concessions are managed by ARAMARK. The fans can eat and drink at two sit-down restaurants, and they also can visit many concession stands throughout the park. The cuisine at the park consists of varied selections ranging from sushi to pizza to hot dogs (of course). In addition, there is a children's menu. Before opening up Citi Field, Mr. Swartz was the manager of seven restaurants at the Media Village in Beijing, China, for the 2008 Summer Olympics, three of which were open around the clock. Before this, he was the Warehouse Director for ARAMARK's food at the 2004 Summer Olympics in Athens, Greece.

In August 2010, Mr. Swartz was promoted to general manager of the ARAMARK account at Camden Yards, home field of the Baltimore Orioles.

Pricing the Menu

Every food service operation has to determine how much money to charge a guest for the food served, which is called the *menu price* or *selling price*. The three methods that can be used to price the menu—amount of markup using a percent, food cost percent, and multiplier effect—will all yield the same final menu price. Figure 10–6 illustrates how each method is to be used.

Raw Food Cost	Percent Using a Markup	Food Cost Percent	Multiplier Effect	Menu Price
$3.00	100%	50%	2	$ 6.00
$3.00	150%	40%	2.5	$ 7.50
$3.00	200%	33.3%	3	$ 9.00
$3.00	300%	25%	4	$12.00
$3.00	400%	20%	5	$15.00

Figure 10–6
Pricing the menu.
© Cengage Learning 2012

For example, the cost of the raw food is $3.00. To find the menu price of the item with a markup of 100 percent, the $3.00 is multiplied by 100 percent, which equals $3.00. This product of $3.00 is added to the original raw food cost to arrive at a menu cost of $6.00.

To find the menu price of the item using a 50 percent food cost, the 50 percent, or 0.50, is divided into the raw cost of food ($3.00). The menu price with a 50 percent food cost is $6.00.

The easiest way to obtain the answer to these questions is to use the multiplier. From the chart, the student can see that a markup of 100 percent or a food cost of 50 percent is arrived at by multiplying the raw food cost by 2. The menu price using 2 as a multiplier is $6.00.

Practice Problems 10–2   Pricing the Menu

Calculate the menu price for each item in the following circumstances. Round off your answers to the hundredths place.

39. The raw food cost is $5.45 and the markup rate is ⅔.

_____

40. The raw food cost is $6.60 and the markup rate is ⅝.

_____

41. The raw food cost is $4.23 and the markup rate is 43 percent.

_____

42. The raw food cost is $5.55 and the markup rate is 60.5 percent.

_____

43. The raw food cost is $5.40 and the markup rate is 38 percent.

_____

44. The raw food cost is $3.72 and a 25 percent food cost is desired.

_____

45. The raw food cost is $5.92 and a 59 percent food cost is desired.

_____

46. The raw food cost is $12.72 and a 100 percent food cost is desired.

_____

47. The raw food cost is $2.15 and a 43 percent food cost is desired.

_____

48. The raw food cost is $5.63 and a 17 percent food cost is desired.

_____

49. The raw food cost is $4.25 and a 41 percent food cost is desired.

_____

50. The raw food cost is $4.25 and a 20 percent food cost is desired.

_____

51. The raw food cost is $4.25 and a 30 percent food cost is desired.

_____

52. The raw food cost is $4.25 and a 50 percent food cost is desired.

_____

53. The raw food cost is $4.25 and a 23.3 percent food cost is desired.

_____

54. The raw food cost is $4.25 and a 200 percent markup is desired.

_____

55. What is the menu price using the multiplier of 4 if the raw food cost is $4.25?

_____

56. What is the menu price using the multiplier of 2.5 if the raw food cost is $4.25?

_____

57. What is the menu price using the multiplier of 3 if the raw food cost is $4.25?

_____

58. What is the menu price using the multiplier of 5 if the raw food cost is $4.25?

_____

The Method—Food Cost

The Chef's Magic Circle is a paper calculator that allows for the easy calculation of food cost, food cost percentage, and sales price. The method involves covering up what it is you want to find. Place your thumb over what you want to calculate on the circle, such as Food Cost, and see what is left. Notice that Food Cost Percentage and Sales Price remain, separated by a vertical line. When calculating Food Cost, multiply Food Cost Percentage by Sales Price, with Food Cost Percentage expressed as a decimal. The vertical line indicates multiplication. In algebraic terminology, this calculation would be expressed as $FC = SP*FC\%$, but who wants, or needs, to remember formulas when you have the Chef's Magic Circle? Just plug in the numbers and perform the calculation indicated.

To Insure Perfect Solutions

The Chef's Magic Circle

The Chef's Magic Circle (see Figure 10–7) was developed at the Community College of Southern Nevada by certified executive chef Thomas Rosenberger. He developed this technique to help students learn a method that is *easy to use* and *easy to remember.* This method was presented at a seminar at The American Culinary Federation's national convention. The material given in the text is reproduced from the handout given to participants at the convention.

To Insure Perfect Solutions

A vertical line goes up and down. A horizontal line goes from left to right or right to left.

The Method—Sales Price (or Menu Price)

To calculate Sales Price, cover Sales Price on the circle and notice that Food Cost and Food Cost Percentage are divided by the horizontal line. When calculating Sales Price, divide Food Cost by Food Cost Percentage, which is expressed as a decimal. The horizontal line indicates division. In algebraic terminology, this calculation would be expressed as SP = FC/FC%, but who wants, or needs, to remember formulas when you have the Chef's Magic Circle? Just plug in the numbers and perform the calculation indicated.

Figure 10–7
The Chef's Magic Circle.
© Cengage Learning 2012

The Method—Food Cost Percentage

To calculate Food Cost Percentage, cover Food Cost Percentage on the circle and notice that Food Cost and Sales Price are divided by the horizontal line. Again, the horizontal line indicates division. In algebraic terminology, this calculation would be expressed as FC% = FC/SP, but who wants, or needs, to remember formulas when you have the Chef's Magic Circle? Just plug in the numbers and perform the calculation indicated.

Practice Problems 10–3   The Chef's Magic Circle

Using the Chef's Magic Circle, complete the following chart.

Calculate the cost for each item. Round off your answers to the hundredths place for the food cost and sales price, and for the food cost percentage, carry the division out to the hundred thousandths place (the fifth number to the right of the decimal point) and then round off to the ten thousandths place. If the initial answer you get is 0.394216, then the answer is 39.4216 percent, and then you round it to 39.42 percent.

Question	Food Cost	Food Cost Percentage	Sales Price
59.	$ 2.79	31.40%	$——
60.	$ 3.97	39.80%	$——
61.	$——	24.90%	$ 7.35
62.	$——	19.40%	$24.95
63.	$ 2.48	——%	$11.95
64.	$ 6.93	——%	$19.95
65.	$11.99	——%	$49.95

66. In our restaurant, we used a total of $43,189 in food last month. We earned revenue of $99,687. What was our food cost percentage for the month? _____

67. In May, we spent $51,590 for food. Revenue for May was $109,213, and we projected a 32.85 percent food cost percentage for the month. What was our actual food cost percentage for the month?

_____

68. Next month, we have forecasted a revenue of $61,484 and want a food cost percentage of 33.30 percent. What should our total expenditure of food dollars be for the month to achieve the desired food cost percentage? _____

Use the Chef's Magic Circle to arrive at your answers to the following questions. Use the Desmond menus in Figures 10–3 to 10–5 for your calculations.

69. Find the sales price from Figure 10–3 for the glazed swordfish. If the food cost is $8.75, what is the food cost percentage? _____

70. Find the sales price from Figure 10–3 for the chicken Marsala. If the food cost was $9.75, what was the food cost percentage? _____

71. Find the sales price from Figure 10–3 for the char-grilled ribeye steak. If the food cost was $12.98, what was the food cost percentage? _____

72. Find the sales price from Figure 10–3 for the Cobb salad. If the food cost was $4.29, what was the food cost percentage? _____

73. Find the sales price from Figure 10–3 for the citrus grilled shrimp. If the food cost was $11.27, what was the food cost percentage? _____

74. If the food cost percentage was 29 percent for the Atlantic salmon on Simpson's prix fixe menu (Figure 10–5), what was the cost of food on Monday at 5 p.m.? _____

75. In the same circumstances as in question 74, what would it be on Monday at 8 p.m.?

_____

76. If the food cost percentage was 24 percent for the cheese tortellini casserole on Simpson's prix fixe menu (Figure 10–5), what was the cost of food on Sunday at 2 p.m.? _____

77. In the same circumstances as in question 74, what would it be on Tuesday at 8 p.m.?

_____

78. If the food cost percentage was 48 percent for the filet mignon au poivre on Simpson's prix fixe menu (Figure 10–5), what was the cost of food on Sunday? _____

79. In the same circumstances as in question 74, what would it be on Tuesday at 7 p.m.?

_____

80. If the food cost percentage was 29 percent for the Atlantic salmon on Simpson's prix fixe menu (Figure 10–5), what was the cost of food on Wednesday at 6 p.m.?

_____

81. In the same circumstances, what would it be on Wednesday at 8 p.m.?

_____

82. If the food cost percentage was 29 percent for the prime rib on Scrimshaw's pre-theatre menu (Figure 10–4), what was the cost of food? _____

83. If the food cost percentage was 42 percent for the filet mignon on Scrimshaw's pre-theatre menu (Figure 10–4), what was the cost of food? _____

Discussion Question 10-2

In question 67, if you were the chef, what would you look for to figure out why the food cost percentage was not 32.8 percent? What would make it higher than the ideal food cost?

eleven

Inventory Procedures and Controlling Costs

Objectives

At the completion of this chapter, the student should be able to:

1. Identify perpetual inventory.
2. Identify physical inventory.
3. Find the cost of food sold.
4. Find the monthly food cost percent (or monthly food cost percentage).
5. Identify computer applications for inventory procedures.
6. Explain the purpose of taking both a perpetual and a physical inventory.
7. Calculate physical inventory.
8. Identify and explain the concept of food in production.
9. Calculate how to determine variations in purchases using food cost percentages.

Key Words

inventory	final inventory	cost of food sold	beginning inventory
perpetual inventory	food in production	purchases	monthly food cost percent
physical inventory	transfer	recapitulation	

In the previous two chapters, the importance of determining food and labor costs was explained, along with how to determine food and labor cost percentages. The purpose of this chapter is to explain the importance of determining the amount of inventory in a food service operation and the role that inventory plays in determining food cost percentages. Both the actual taking of inventory and the costing out of inventory can be tedious and time-consuming jobs. However, for a food service operation to obtain an accurate monthly and yearly food cost percentages, they must be done.

Inventory is a well-known business term because it is an activity that takes place in many business operations at least once a year. In a food service operation, it can be a continuous activity. An **inventory** is a catalog or itemized list of stock and its estimated value. An inventory of food service equipment may be taken from time to time. The most important inventory concerns food and beverage products. There are two kinds of inventories pertaining to food and beverages that are of major importance: the perpetual inventory and the physical inventory.

Perpetual Inventory

A **perpetual inventory** is a continuous or endless inventory. It is a record that is taken in the storeroom to show the balance on hand for each storeroom item. (See Figure 11–1.) As a requisition from the production crew is received and the items are issued, the amounts are subtracted from the inventory balance. When new shipments of each item arrive and are placed on the shelves, they are added to the inventory balance.

If the food service operation does a large volume of business, a computer would probably be placed in the storeroom to handle these functions. If a computer is not available, the functions are done manually. At the end of each month, when the physical inventory of each item is taken, the physical inventory should match the perpetual inventory. If the two do not match, a problem exists. The problem may be poor bookkeeping, negligence in checking incoming orders, theft, or a similar situation. Keep in mind that, in a business operation, control is a key word. The more departments, functions, or activities that can be controlled by management, the more profits will show up on the profit and loss (P&L) sheet.

"Understanding inventory control is the difference between running a profitable operation or not. We cannot stress the importance of tracking and maintaining the product in your establishment."

Phelps Dieck, chef/owner
The Green Monkey, Portsmouth, NH
Brazo, Portsmouth, NH

"Inventory control is a key player in maintaining a profitable and successful business. Businesses without inventory control practices might as well not open their doors. If you do not track your product, how do you know where your bottom line ends?"

Deb Weeks, owner
The Green Monkey, Portsmouth, NH
Brazo, Portsmouth, NH

Deb Weeks and Phelps Dieck are the owners of two profitable and successful restaurants in Portsmouth, New Hampshire: The Green Monkey and Brazo. Brazo is a casually elegant Latin-American restaurant that showcases exciting Latin and South American cuisine, finely prepared. Chef Dieck uses locally grown produce, fresh fish, and the finest meats to create this festive, welcoming, vibrant, and robust restaurant. The Green Monkey features New American cuisine with a flair. The restaurant has won the Best of Taste of 2009 award from *Seacoast* magazine in three categories: Best Restaurant, Best Martini, and Best Dining. The Green Monkey was also mentioned as a "place to go" in *Gourmet* magazine's October 2009 issue. *New Hampshire* magazine cited The Green Monkey for serving the best martinis in New Hampshire, and it also has cited Dieck as "The Queen of Cuisine."

Figure 11–1
Formal storeroom operation.
© Cengage Learning 2012

Physical Inventory

The **physical inventory** may be taken at the end of each month, or as frequently as needed, to determine the accurate cost of food and beverage consumed during that period. When doing a **physical inventory,** an actual count is taken of all stock on hand. The physical inventory figures are most important when making out the P&L sheet.

The inventory sheet should be prepared in advance using a standard form. This form should contain the name of each item, the quantity, size or bulk, unit price, and total price of items on hand. Two people usually take the inventory, one calling out the items on hand and the other recording the items and quantities. (See Figure 11–2.) While this task can be done by one person, it would be time-consuming. Two people ensure accuracy and make it more difficult to steal inventory. Of course, if they work together, it will be easy for them to steal. That is why it is beneficial for the food service operator to have different individuals take the physical inventory from time to time. The unit price for each item listed can be obtained from invoices and purchase records. When setting up an inventory sheet, most establishments classify the food, beverages, and supply items into common groups such as:

- Canned foods
- Other groceries
- Butter, eggs, and cheese
- Coffee and tea
- Fruits and vegetables
- Meat, poultry, and fish

- Beer
- Liquor
- Wine
- Soda
- Supplies

Figure 11–2
Two employees conducting an inventory of the storeroom.
© Cengage Learning 2012

Once the inventory is counted and recorded on the inventory sheet, it must be extended by multiplying the amount of items on hand by the unit price. The inventory is then added up to arrive at a total cost called the **final inventory.** When the total inventory value is found, this figure represents the cost of food and beverages still on hand or in storage. It represents food and beverages that have not been sold during this inventory period. The inventory value is then used to find the monthly food cost percent. When computing the monthly food cost percent, this figure is referred to as the **final inventory.**

Food in Production and Transfers

To obtain an accurate food cost percentage, the amount of food that has been pre-pared, but not served, called **food in production,** must be included. This figure also includes the food that is in the refrigerators or freezers on the cooking and dessert lines. The amount of food can equal a large amount of dollars, and, if not calculated into the food cost percentage, the percentage will not be accurate. The authors know of a chef who thought his food costs were a bit too high. Then he realized that he should include food in production in his food cost percentage; once he did this, he achieved his desired food cost percentage.

A **transfer** is moving food or beverage ingredient costs from one depart-ment to another. For example, if all the fruits and vegetables that are used to garnish alcoholic beverages at the bar are not transferred to the bar costs, the food cost percentage will increase. Other transfers also affect food cost percent-age. A more detailed explanation of transfers will be included in Chapter 12, "Purchasing and Receiving." The reader should be aware that if transfers are used in the operation where he or she is employed, the transfers should be included when calculating costs.

Calculating the Monthly Food Cost Percentage

To find the monthly food cost percent, the **purchases** for the month are added to the inventory at the beginning of the month, and the final inventory plus the amount of food in production is subtracted to give the **cost of food sold** for the month. The food cost percentage is then found by dividing the total sales for the month into the cost of food sold. The division should be carried four places to the right of the decimal to give the percentage. (See Figure 11–3.)

Purchases + beginning inventory − (food in production + final inventory)
= (equals)
Cost of food sold

Cost of food sold ÷ total sales
= (equals)
Food cost percentage

The amount of sales is the total food sold during that particular month. It is the total of all sales made during that period. The **purchases** for the month represent the total of all the food purchased during that month. This is found by adding the totals of all invoices sent with each food purchase. The inventory at the beginning of the month is the **final inventory** from the previous month. A **recapitulation** is a totaling up of all items, in this instance the weekly or period inventory. (For an example of a physical inventory recapitulation, see Figure 11–4.)

Figure 11–3
How to find the cost of food sold and monthly food cost percent.
© Cengage Learning 2012

Sales for the Month	$ 2,550.00
Inventory at the Beginning of the Month	300.00
Purchases for the Month	895.00
Food in Production	150.00
Final Inventory	250.00

Step 1	**Step 1**
To find the **Cost of Food Sold,** first add the Inventory at the Beginning of the Month	$ 300.00
To the purchases for the month	+895.00
Sum of the Beginning Inventory and Purchases for the Month	**$ 1,195.00**

Step 2	**Step 2**
Add the Food in Production	$ 150.00
To the Final Inventory	+ 250.00
Sum of the Food in Production and the Final Inventory	**$ 400.00**

Step 3	**Step 3**
Take the Sum of the Beginning Inventory and Purchases for the Month	$ 1,195.00
And subtract the Sum of the Food in Production and the Final Inventory	−400.00
Cost of Food Sold is	**$ 795.00**

Step 4	**Step 4**
To find the Monthly Food Cost Percent Divide the Sales for the Month	$ 2,550.00
Into the Cost of Food Sold	$ 795.00

$$
\begin{array}{r}
0.31176 \\
2550\overline{)795.000000} \\
-765\ 0 \\
\hline
30\ 00 \\
-25\ 50 \\
\hline
4\ 500 \\
-2\ 550 \\
\hline
1\ 9500 \\
-1\ 7850 \\
\hline
16500
\end{array}
$$

Monthly Food Cost Percent is	**31.18%**

Example of a Physical Inventory
Weekly or Period Inventory Recapitulation

Week Ending   Period Ending
August 9, 20___   August 31, 20___

Item No.	Item	Amount
1.	Canned Goods	$ 628.59
2.	Other Groceries	779.48
3.	Butter, Eggs, and Cheese	42.44
4.	Coffee and Tea	45.69
5.	Fruits and Vegetables	294.12
6.	Meat, Poultry, and Fish	1,140.14
	TOTAL FOOD	$ 2,930.46
7.	Supplies	$ 590.77
	Total Inventory Value	$3,521.23

Called By_____   Extended By _____
                                  Manager _____

Figure 11–4
Example of a physical inventory recapitulation.
© Cengage Learning 2012

Practice Problems 11–1   Determining the Value of Inventory

Calculate the extension prices for items 1–7 on the following pages and total all categories.

Item No. 1. *Canned goods*

Quantity/Size	Item	Unit Price	Extension
8-#10	Apples	$3.52	1. $_____
6-#10	Apricots	5.29	2. _____
9-#10	Beans, green	2.61	3. _____
10-#10	Beans, kidney	1.84	4. _____
12-#10	Beans, wax	2.07	5. _____
14-#10	Bean sprouts	2.79	6. _____
4-#10	Beets, whole	3.03	7. _____
3-#10	Carrots, whole	3.44	8. _____
8-#10	Cherries	7.31	9. _____
2-#10	Fruit cocktail	4.10	10. _____
3-#10	Noodles (chow mein)	2.74	11. _____
6-#10	Peach halves	3.71	12. _____
5-#10	Peaches, pie	3.60	13. _____
5-#10	Pears	3.51	14. _____
4-#10	Pineapple tidbits	3.79	15. _____
10-#10	Pineapple slices	3.84	16. _____
4-#10	Plums	3.24	17. _____
6-#10	Pumpkin	3.85	18. _____
7-#10	Sweet potatoes	3.26	19. _____
9-#10	Tomato catsup	2.12	20. _____
8-#10	Tomato puree	3.67	21. _____
3-#10	Tomatoes	3.41	22. _____
6-#10	Asparagus spears	6.50	23. _____
8-#10	Cream-style corn	2.08	24. _____
12-#10	Whole-kernel corn	2.15	25. _____
24-#2	Salmon	2.30	26. _____
	Canned Goods Total		27. $_____

Item No. 2. *Groceries—Dry bulk goods*

Quantity/Size	Item	Unit Price	Extension
8 lbs.	Baking soda	$0.22	28. $_____
9 lbs.	Baking powder	8.40	29. _____
8 lbs.	Cocoa	5.90	30. _____
6 lbs.	Coconut shred	1.12	31. _____
10 lbs.	Cracker meal	0.18	32. _____
4 lbs.	Chicken base	1.12	33. _____
7 lbs.	Beef base	1.15	34. _____
6 lbs.	Raisins	1.19	35. _____
9 lbs.	Cornmeal	0.15	36. _____
12 lbs.	Cornstarch	0.46	37. _____
20 lbs.	Tapioca flour	0.22	38. _____
63 lbs.	Bread flour	0.20	39. _____
53 lbs.	Cake flour	0.25	40. _____
74 lbs.	Pastry flour	0.22	41. _____
15 lbs.	Elbow macaroni	0.49	42. _____
18 lbs.	Spaghetti	0.52	43. _____
6 lbs.	Rice	0.45	44. _____
12 lbs.	Noodles	1.13	45. _____
		Subtotal	46. $_____

Item No. 2. *Groceries—Oils and fats*

Quantity/Size	Item	Unit Price	Extension
12 cases	Margarine	$50.52	47. $_____
1½ tin	Shortening, 50-lb. tin	26.00	48. _____
2 cans	Salad oil, 5-gal. can	22.10	49. _____
		Subtotal	50. $_____

Item No. 2. *Groceries—Spices*

Quantity/Size	Item	Unit Price	Extension
1½ lbs.	Allspice, ground	$ 7.02	51. $_____
1¾ lbs.	Bay leaves	4.20	52. _____
2 lbs.	Chili powder	4.35	53. _____
3 lbs.	Cinnamon	6.20	54. _____
4 lbs.	Cloves, ground	6.95	55. _____
1¼ lbs.	Ginger, ground	4.50	56. _____
1½ lbs.	Cumin seed	3.82	57. _____
2½ lbs.	Celery seed	5.10	58. _____
2¼ lbs.	Caraway seed	2.90	59. _____
1¾ lbs.	Mace	12.50	60. _____
2¾ lbs.	Mustard, dry	2.80	61. _____
1½ lbs.	Marjoram, dry	3.50	62. _____
3 lbs.	Nutmeg	8.50	63. _____
4 lbs.	Oregano	4.25	64. _____
5 lbs.	Pepper, white	6.00	65. _____
3 lbs.	Pepper, black	5.00	66. _____
2 lbs.	Pickling spice	4.18	67. _____
1½ lbs.	Rosemary leaves	8.12	68. _____
1¼ lbs.	Sage	10.82	69. _____
1¾ lbs.	Thyme	5.89	70. _____
		Subtotal	71. $_____

Item No. 2. *Groceries—Dressing and condiments*

Quantity/Size	Item	Unit Price	Extension
3 gal.	Mayonnaise	$8.44	72. $_____
2 gal.	Dill pickles	3.22	73. _____
1½ gal.	Sweet relish	4.60	74. _____
4 gal.	Salad dressing	3.88	75. _____
6½ gal.	Vinegar	1.20	76. _____
1¼ gal.	Soy sauce	6.48	77. _____
4 gal.	Worcestershire sauce	3.73	78. _____
5 gal.	French dressing	4.54	79. _____
		Subtotal	80. $_____

Item No. 2. *Groceries—Coloring and extracts*

Quantity/Size	Item	Unit Price	Extension
1½ qt.	Caramel color	$5.95	81. $_____
1¼ pt.	Yellow	3.12	82. _____
1¾ pt.	Red	2.82	83. _____
2 pt.	Green	3.16	84. _____
1 pt.	Lemon extract	6.99	85. _____
3 pt.	Vanilla extract	11.89	86. _____
1½ pt.	Maple extract	4.09	87. _____
		Subtotal	88. $_____
		Other Groceries Total	89. $_____

Item No. 3. *Butter, eggs, and cheese*

Quantity/Size	Item	Unit Price	Extension
8 lbs.	American cheese	$1.70	90. $_____
15 lbs.	Chip butter	1.12	91. _____
14 doz.	Eggs	0.86	92. _____
	Butter, Eggs, and Cheese Total		93. $_____

Item No. 4. *Coffee and tea*

Quantity/Size	Item	Unit Price	Extension
16 lbs.	Coffee	$2.68	94. $_____
½ pkg.	Tea—indiv. (100)	2.50	95. _____
¼ pkg.	Tea—iced (48)	6.24	96. _____
	Coffee and Tea Total		97. $_____

Item No. 5. *Fruits and vegetables—fresh*

Quantity/Size	Item	Unit Price	Extension
4 bushel	Carrots	$0.89	98. $_____
3 lbs.	Endive	1.45	99. _____
7 head	Head lettuce	0.89	100. _____
8 lbs.	Leaf lettuce	1.25	101. _____
20 lbs.	Dry onions	0.46	102. _____
54 lbs.	Red potatoes	0.53	103. _____
44 lbs.	Idaho potatoes	0.51	104. _____
6 lbs.	Tomatoes	0.88	105. _____
3 bu.	Parsley	0.45	106. _____
5 lbs.	Green peppers	0.48	107. _____
8 lbs.	Apples	0.83	108. _____
7 lbs.	Bananas	0.35	109. _____
4 doz.	Lemons	2.25	110. _____
5 doz.	Oranges	2.25	111. _____
5 bu.	Radishes	0.35	112. _____
3 bu.	Celery	0.89	113. _____
		Subtotal	114. $_____

Item No. 5. *Fruits and vegetables—frozen*

Quantity/Size	Item	Unit Price	Extension
9 lbs.	Strawberries	$1.06	115. $_____
12 lbs.	Peaches	1.17	116. _____
16 lbs.	Blueberries	1.52	117. _____
34 lbs.	Lima beans	1.23	118. _____
25 lbs.	Corn	0.63	119. _____
18 lbs.	Broccoli	0.78	120. _____
12 lbs.	Brussels sprouts	0.87	121. _____
18 lbs.	Mixed vegetables	0.57	122. _____
22 lbs.	Peas	0.56	123. _____
16 lbs.	Cauliflower	0.90	124. _____
		Subtotal	125. $_____
		Fruits and Vegetables Total	126. $_____

Item No. 6. *Meat, poultry, and fish*

Quantity/Size	Item	Unit Price	Extension
15 lbs.	Beef ground	$1.72	127. $_____
21 lbs.	Beef round	2.25	128. _____
30 lbs.	Beef ribs	2.95	129. _____
22 lbs.	Beef rib eyes	3.20	130. _____
19 lbs.	Beef chuck	1.95	131. _____
15 lbs.	Club steak	3.58	132. _____
14 lbs.	Beef tenderloin	6.20	133. _____
28 lbs.	Pork loin	5.40	134. _____
22 lbs.	Boston butt	2.20	135. _____
36 lbs.	Veal leg	7.40	136. _____
12 lbs.	Veal shoulder	6.22	137. _____
14 lbs.	Veal loin	8.20	138. _____
32 lbs.	Ham	2.35	139. _____
		Meat, Poultry, and Fish Total	140. $_____

Item No. 7. *Supplies*

Quantity/Size	Item	Unit Price	Extension
4	Napkins	$41.00	141. $_____
8	Butter Chips	5.48	142. _____
22	Soufflé Cups	7.80	143. _____
15	Paper Bags	7.95	144. _____
12 gal.	Bleach	1.24	145. _____
13 gal.	Dish	3.89	146. _____
21 lbs.	Salute	0.58	147. _____
5 ea.	Pot Brushes	2.89	148. _____
		Supplies Total	149. $_____

Practice Problems 11-2   Determining Inventory Value

From Practice Problems 11–1, fill in the totals for all the categories and then calculate the weekly or period inventory recapitulation.

Example of a Physical Inventory
Weekly or Period Inventory Recapitulation

Week Ending   Period Ending
August 9, 20____   August 31, 20____

Item No.	Item	Amount
1.	Canned Goods	150. $_____
2.	Other Groceries	151. _____
3.	Butter, Eggs, and Cheese	152. _____
4.	Coffee and Tea	153. _____
5.	Fruits and Vegetables	154. _____
6.	Meat, Poultry, and Fish	155. _____
	TOTAL FOOD	156. $_____
7.	Supplies	157. $_____
	Total Inventory Value	158. $_____

Called By_____   Extended By _____

Manager _____

Practice Problems 11–3   Determining the Food Cost and Food Cost Percentage

Find the monthly food cost percent and the cost of food sold using the following information. Calculate the food cost to four places to the right of the decimal. For example, if the answer is 0.29748, go to the fifth number to the right of the decimal and use that number to round off to the fourth number to the right of the decimal. Now the answer is 0.2975. Next, convert 0.2975 to a percentage. Calculate the food cost percentage to two places to the right of the decimal. Therefore, the final answer would be 29.75 percent.

Sales for the Month	$54,000.00
Beginning Inventory	6,780.50
Purchases for the Month	15,890.00
Food in Production	2,005.10

Final Inventory will be the answer from Practice Problems 11–2.

159. The cost of food sold is _____.

160. The monthly food cost percentage is _____.

Identifying Beginning and Final Inventory

To explain the beginning inventory further and to clarify a point that can be confusing, let us use the months of October and November as examples. The final inventory for the month of October becomes the **beginning inventory** for the month of November. The final inventory, as stated before, is obtained from the physical inventory taken at the end of each month. To carry this point further, the final inventory for the month of November becomes the beginning inventory for the month of December.

The **monthly food cost percent** tells the food service operator what percentage of the total sales for that period was used to purchase food for the operation. This is a very important figure and one that must be controlled because the cost of food and labor are the highest costs in any food service operation.

Practice Problems 11–4 Determining the Monthly Food Cost and Food Cost Percentage

In problems A through E, find the cost of food sold and the monthly food cost percent. Calculate the monthly food cost percentage. For example, if the answer is 0.29748, go to the fifth number to the right of the decimal and use that number to round off to the fourth number to the right of the decimal. Now the answer is 0.2975. Next, convert 0.2975 to a percentage. Therefore, the final answer would be 29.75 percent.

A. Food in Production $5,025.00
   Sales   48,500.00
   Inventory at Beginning of Month   4,890.00
   Purchases for the Month   41,465.00
   Final Inventory   3,682.00
   161. Cost of Food Sold   _____
   162. Monthly Food Cost Percent   _____

B. Food in Production $2,017.25
   Sales   76,585.54
   Inventory at Beginning of Month   8,296.25
   Purchases for the Month   18,440.25
   Final Inventory   4,635.65
   163. Cost of Food Sold   _____
   164. Monthly Food Cost Percent   _____

C. Food in Production $1,025.00
   Sales   29,760.00
   Inventory at Beginning of Month   1,495.00
   Purchases for the Month   12,025.00
   Final Inventory   675.00
   165. Cost of Food Sold   _____
   166. Monthly Food Cost Percent   _____

D. Food in Production $895.00
   Sales   125,545.00
   Inventory at Beginning of Month   6,264.36
   Purchases for the Month   28,418.00
   Final Inventory   3,268.45
   167. Cost of Food Sold   _____
   168. Monthly Food Cost Percent   _____

E. Food in Production $1,395.00
   Sales   66,342.50
   Inventory at Beginning of Month   4,615.15
   Purchases for the Month   22,728.00
   Final Inventory   3,785.00
   169. Cost of Food Sold   _____
   170. Monthly Food Cost Percent   _____

Using Computer Applications

An important application of the computer involves the recording of the food service establishment's inventory. The calculations involved in completing an inventory sheet are very time-consuming. The computer inventory sheet will eliminate most of the mathematical calculations, saving the establishment both time and money.

There are many types of software available to complete this task. Some chefs and managers use "canned programs," while others set up their own spreadsheets using programs like Microsoft Excel.

The format of the computer inventory sheet varies from the form used when taking inventory by hand. (See Figure 11–5.) You will be responsible for entering the quantity. What is entered into the quantity column is determined by how much you have in stock, and by how the product is packaged. It is important that the quantity entered is in terms of the unit. For example, suppose you have 16 pounds of margarine in inventory, and the cost of the margarine is $16.64 for a 32-pound case. The amount that you enter into the quantity column is 0.5 because the 16 pounds you have in inventory is one-half of the 32 pounds that is in one case.

Example: The following has been found in inventory:

- 8 lbs. of margarine at $16.63 for a 32-lb. case
- 20 lbs. of shortening at $26.00 for a 50-lb. tin
- 3 lbs. of salad oil at $22.00 for a 5-gal. can

Figure 11–6 shows how the computer inventory sheet would look.

Groceries—Oils and Fats

Quantity	Item	Size	Unit Price	Extension
	Margarine	32-lb. case	$16.64	
	Shortening	50-lb. tin	26.00	
	Salad oil	5-gal. can	22.00	
			Subtotal	

Figure 11–5
Computer inventory sheet.
© Cengage Learning 2012

Groceries—Oils and Fats

Quantity	Item	Size	Unit Price	Extension
0.25	Margarine	32-lb. case	$16.64	$ 4.16
0.4	Shortening	50-lb. tin	26.00	10.40
0.075	Salad oil	5-gal. can	22.20	1.67
			Subtotal	$16.23

Figure 11–6
Computer inventory sheet, completed.
© Cengage Learning 2012

Practice Problems 11–5   Calculating Inventory

Calculate the extension prices for items 1–7 on the following pages and total all categories using either a computer or calculator.

Item No. 1. *Canned goods*

Quantity	Item	Size	Unit Price	Extension
6	Apples	#10	$3.52	171. $_____
7	Apricots	#10	5.29	172. _____
10	Beans, green	#10	2.61	173. _____
7	Beans, kidney	#10	1.84	174. _____
12	Beans, wax	#10	2.07	175. _____
13	Bean sprouts	#10	2.79	176. _____
5	Beets, whole	#10	3.03	177. _____
6	Carrots, whole	#10	3.44	178. _____
7	Cherries	#10	7.31	179. _____
2	Fruit cocktail	#10	4.10	180. _____
1	Noodles (chow mein)	#10	2.74	181. _____
4	Peach halves	#10	3.71	182. _____
6	Peaches, pie	#10	3.60	183. _____
5	Pears	#10	3.51	184. _____
3	Pineapple tidbits	#10	3.79	185. _____
8	Pineapple slices	#10	3.84	186. _____
3	Plums	#10	3.24	187. _____
5	Pumpkin	#10	3.85	188. _____
7	Sweet potatoes	#10	3.26	189. _____
8	Tomato catsup	#10	2.12	190. _____
7	Tomato puree	#10	3.67	191. _____
4	Tomatoes	#10	3.41	192. _____
6	Asparagus spears	#2	6.50	193. _____
10	Cream-style corn	#22	2.08	194. _____
8	Whole-kernel corn	#2	2.15	195. _____
16	Salmon	#2	2.30	196. _____
		Canned Goods Total		197. $_____

Item No. 2. *Groceries—Spices*

Quantity	Item	Size	Unit Price	Extension
1.25	Allspice, ground	lb.	$7.02	198. $_____
2.5	Bay leaves	lb.	7.20	199. _____
1	Chili powder	lb.	4.35	200. _____
3	Cinnamon	lb.	6.20	201. _____
2.5	Cloves, ground	lb.	6.95	202. _____
1.75	Ginger, ground	lb.	4.50	203. _____
2.25	Cumin seed	lb.	3.82	204. _____
1.5	Celery seed	lb.	5.10	205. _____
3.25	Caraway seed	lb.	2.90	206. _____
0.25	Mace	lb.	12.50	207. _____
1.25	Mustard, dry	lb.	2.80	208. _____
2.75	Marjoram, dry	lb.	3.50	209. _____
2	Nutmeg	lb.	8.50	210. _____
3.5	Oregano	lb.	4.25	211. _____
2	Pepper, white	lb.	6.00	212. _____
4	Pepper, black	lb.	5.00	213. _____
3	Pickling spice	lb.	4.18	214. _____
2	Rosemary leaves	lb.	8.12	215. _____
1.74	Sage	lb.	10.82	216. _____
2.25	Thyme	lb.	5.89	217. _____
			Subtotal	218. $_____

Item No. 2. *Groceries—Dressing and condiments*

Quantity	Item	Size	Unit Price	Extension
4	Mayonnaise	gal.	$8.44	219. $_____
2	Dill pickles	gal.	3.22	220. _____
3	Sweet relish	gal.	4.60	221. _____
3.5	Salad dressing	gal.	3.88	222. _____
7	Vinegar	gal.	1.20	223. _____
2.75	Soy sauce	gal.	6.48	224. _____
5	Worcestershire sauce	gal.	3.73	225. _____
6.25	French dressing	gal.	4.54	226. _____
			Subtotal	227. $_____

Item No. 2. *Groceries—Oils and fats*

Quantity	Item	Size	Unit Price	Extension
0.43	Margarine	3-lb. case	$7.28	228. $_____
1.5	Shortening	50-lb. tin	20.80	229. _____
0.8	Salad oil	5-gal. can	6.60	230. _____
			Subtotal	231. $_____

Item No. 2. *Groceries—Dry bulk goods*

Quantity	Item	Size	Unit Price	Extension
7	Baking soda	lb.	$0.22	232. $_____
1.6	Baking powder	5-lb. box	8.40	233. _____
1.6	Cocoa	5-lb. box	5.90	234. _____
5	Coconut shred	lb.	1.12	235. _____
9	Cracker meal	lb.	0.18	236. _____
3	Chicken base	lb.	1.12	237. _____
8	Beef base	lb.	1.15	238. _____
5	Raisins	lb.	1.19	239. _____
8	Cornmeal	lb.	0.15	240. _____
13	Cornstarch	lb.	0.46	241. _____
18	Tapioca flour	lb.	0.22	242. _____
0.58	Bread flour	100-lb. bag	20.00	243. _____
0.61	Cake flour	100-lb. bag	25.00	244. _____
0.75	Pastry flour	100-lb. bag	22.00	245. _____
13	Elbow macaroni	lb.	0.49	246. _____
16	Spaghetti	lb.	0.52	247. _____
7	Rice	lb.	0.45	248. _____
10	Noodles	lb.	1.13	249. _____
			Subtotal	250. $_____

Item No. 2. *Groceries—Coloring and extracts*

Quantity	Item	Size	Unit Price	Extension
2	Caramel color	qt.	$5.95	251. $_____
1.5	Yellow	pt.	3.12	252. _____
2.25	Red	pt.	2.82	253. _____
3	Green	pt.	3.16	254. _____
2	Lemon extract	pt.	6.99	255. _____
2	Vanilla extract	pt.	11.89	256. _____
2.5	Maple extract	pt.	4.09	257. _____
			Subtotal	258. $_____
			Other Groceries Total	259. $_____

Item No. 3. *Butter, eggs, and cheese*

Quantity	Item	Size	Unit Price	Extension
6	American cheese	lb.	$1.70	260. $_____
12	Chip butter	lb.	1.12	261. _____
18	Eggs	doz.	0.86	262. _____
			Butter, Eggs, and Cheese Total	263. $_____

Item No. 4. *Coffee and tea*

Quantity	Item	Size	Unit Price	Extension
18	Coffee	lb.	$2.68	264. $_____
	Tea—indiv. (100)	pkg.	2.50	265. _____
	Tea—iced (48)	pkg.	6.24	266. _____
			Coffee and Tea Total	267. $_____

Item No. 5. *Fruits and vegetables—fresh*

Quantity	Item	Size	Unit Price	Extension
3	Carrots	bu.	$0.89	268. $_____
2	Endive	lb.	1.45	269. _____
8	Head lettuce	head	0.89	270. _____
9	Leaf lettuce	lb.	1.25	271. _____
18	Dry onions	lb.	0.46	272. _____
50	Red potatoes	lb.	0.53	273. _____
46	Idaho potatoes	lb.	0.51	274. _____
4	Tomatoes	lb.	0.88	275. _____
2	Parsley	bu.	0.45	276. _____
6	Green peppers	lb.	0.48	277. _____
9	Apples	lb.	0.83	278. _____
8	Bananas	lb.	0.35	279. _____
6	Lemons	doz.	2.25	280. _____
4	Oranges	doz.	2.25	281. _____
6	Radishes	bu.	0.35	282. _____
4	Celery	bu.	0.89	283. _____
			Subtotal	284. $_____

Item No. 5. *Fruits and vegetables—frozen*

Quantity	Item	Size	Unit Price	Extension
8	Strawberries	lb.	$1.06	285. $_____
10	Peaches	lb.	1.17	286. _____
18	Blueberries	lb.	1.52	287. _____
27	Lima beans	lb.	1.23	288. _____
30	Corn	lb.	0.63	289. _____
17	Broccoli	lb.	0.78	290. _____
11	Brussels sprouts	lb.	0.87	291. _____
19	Mixed vegetables	lb.	0.57	292. _____
23	Peas	lb.	0.56	293. _____
18	Cauliflower	lb.	0.90	294. _____
			Subtotal	295. $_____
			Fruits and Vegetables Total	296. $_____

Item No. 6. *Meat, poultry, and fish*

Quantity	Item	Size	Unit Price	Extension
16	Beef ground	lb.	$1.72	297. $_____
20	Beef round	lb.	2.25	298. _____
25	Beef ribs	lb.	2.95	299. _____
23	Beef rib eyes	lb.	3.20	300. _____
20	Beef chuck	lb.	1.95	301. _____
16	Club steak	lb.	3.58	302. _____
15	Beef tenderloin	lb.	6.20	303. _____
27	Pork loin	lb.	5.40	304. _____
19	Boston butt	lb.	2.20	305. _____
33	Veal leg	lb.	7.40	306. _____
10	Veal shoulder	lb.	6.22	307. _____
13	Veal loin	lb.	8.20	308. _____
30	Ham	lb.	2.35	309. _____
	Meat, Poultry, and Fish Total			310. $_____

Item No. 7. *Supplies*

Quantity	Item	Size	Unit Price	Extension
6	Napkins		$41.00	311. $_____
9	Butter chips		5.48	312. _____
20	Soufflé cups		7.80	313. _____
17	Paper bags		7.95	314. _____
6	Bleach	gal.	1.24	315. _____
9	Dish	gal.	3.89	316. _____
20	Salute	lb.	0.58	317. _____
6	Pot brushes	ea.	2.89	318. _____
	Supplies Total			319. $_____

Practice Problems 11–6   Determining Inventory Value

From Practice Problems 11–5, fill in the totals for all the categories and then calculate the weekly or period inventory recapitulation.

Weekly or Period
Inventory Recapitulation

Week Ending   Period Ending
September 12, 20____   September 30, 20____

Item No.	Item	Amount
1.	Canned Goods	320. $_____
2.	Other Groceries	321. _____
3.	Butter, Eggs, and Cheese	322. _____
4.	Coffee and Tea	323. _____
5.	Fruits and Vegetables	324. _____
6.	Meat, Poultry, and Fish	325. _____
	TOTAL FOOD	326. $_____
7.	Supplies	327. $_____
	Total Inventory Value	328. $_____

Called By_____   Extended By _____

                                                          Manager _____

Practice Problems 11–7 Determining Monthly Food Cost and Food Cost Percentage

Calculate the monthly food cost percent using the final inventory from Practice Problems 11–6. The amount of food in production is $15,020.

Total Sales	$53,265.00
Inventory at the Beginning of the Month	6,525.35
Purchases for the Month	16,001.19
Final Inventory	329. _____
Cost of Food Sold	330. _____
Monthly Food Cost Percentage	331. _____

Discussion Question 11-1

Based upon your answer in Practice Problems 11–7, does this establishment have problems with its monthly food cost percent? What will happen to the food cost percentage if no one counts the amount of food in production?

Controlling Costs by Comparing Purchases

Food service managers need to control costs to make a profit. One of the techniques to use is a system that allows the manager to compare the costs of purchases versus the ideal cost percentages for the operation (see Figure 11–7). In our fictional restaurant, the manager has determined the ideal food costs to be 35 percent of sales and that the most popular menu items being sold are in the meat category. She has broken down her purchases into categories as follows: meat (which includes poultry), fish, produce, groceries, and dairy. Our manager uses only five categories, but the authors recommend that managers break down their menu into smaller categories (like adding a poultry category). More categories will give managers the benefit of additional information that may give a more accurate picture of the purchasing procedures and areas of concern.

On a regular basis (monthly, weekly, or daily), a document is compiled from the invoices of the purchases. This document places the purchases into the proper categories and totals them. For instance, for the month of January, our restaurant has purchased $29,679 from all our meat purveyors. Our accounting staff has identified all the meat and poultry that has been purchased during the month and put

Purchases by Category for the Month of January
Figures as of January 31

Total Sales	$247,325.00			
Category	**Amount Purchased**	**Percentage**	**Goal**	**Variance**
Meat	29,679.00	12%	12%	0.00%
Fish	19,786.00	8%	8%	0.00%
Produce	14,839.50	6%	6%	0.00%
Groceries	12,366.25	5%	5%	0.00%
Dairy	9,893.00	4%	4%	0.00%
Total	**86,563.75**	**35%**	**35%**	**0.00%**

Figure 11–7
Purchases and percent goals for the month of January.
© Cengage Learning 2012

this total into the meat category; and then they did the same with the purchases in the other four categories. Figure 11–7 illustrates the purchases for the month of January, along with the ideal food cost percentages that have been set forth to reach our desired 35 percent food cost percentage. The chart illustrates that all our costs are in line with our established goals by category for our costs and that there is no variance in any category.

But what would the manager do if the food costs for the month rose to 55 percent? Obviously, there would be a problem. There could be many reasons for this increase in food costs. We continued to buy food at the same volume as for the same month in the previous year. But the price of some items may have gone up, or our sales volume may have gone down. Maybe our employees are giving away food, or our delivery person knows that no one checks the order thoroughly, so, instead of leaving ten boxes of meat, he steals one box. If management initiates this type of control and checks it on a regular basis, once the food cost percentage numbers vary from the ideal food cost percentage, management can try to determine where and if a problem is occurring. The manager's next step would be to determine how to solve the problem.

The math that is needed to calculate the figures in the chart in Figure 11–7 is illustrated next. Each category is divided by the sales. For example, the meat purchases are shown here.

Meat purchases divided by total sales = food cost percentage
$29,679 divided by $247,325 = 0.12, or 12%

The authors have used this system to identify problems in a business that was losing money and then turn it into a profitable one. They were able to identify where the major abuses were occurring. Their next step was to solve the problems where the abuses occurred, and this resulted in getting food costs back in line. This system works!

Practice Problems 11–8   Controlling Costs by Comparing Purchases

Complete the chart figuring both the percentage and the variance for each category. Round off all answers to four places after the decimal point. For example, if the answer is 0.29748, go to the fifth number to the right of the decimal and use that number to round off to the fourth number to the right of the decimal. Now the answer is 0.2975. Next, convert 0.2975 to a percentage. Therefore, the final answer would be 29.75 percent.

Purchases by Category for the Month of January
Figures as of January 31

Total Sales	$328,291.75			
Category	**Amount Purchased**	**Percent**	**Goal**	**Variance**
Meat	$52,725.38		12%	
Fish	26,263.34		8%	
Produce	32,627.85		6%	
Groceries	16,212.78		5%	
Dairy	15,128.35		4%	
Total			35%	

332. What is the food cost percentage for meat? _____

333. What is the variance for meat? _____

334. What is the food cost percentage for fish? _____

335. What is the variance for fish? _____

336. What is the food cost percentage for produce? _____

337. What is the variance for produce? _____

338. What is the food cost percentage for groceries? _____

339. What is the variance for groceries? _____

340. What is the food cost percentage for dairy? _____

341. What is the variance for dairy? _____

342. What is the total amount of purchases for the month? _____

343. What is the total food cost percent for the month? _____

344. What is the total variance for the month? _____

Discussion Question 11-2

Based upon your answers from Practice Problems 11–8, are there any concerns that the manager should be aware of with the food cost percentages? If there are concerns, what categories would you recommend that management review to determine where the problems are occurring? What steps should management take to solve the problems?

Purchasing and Receiving

Objectives

At the completion of this chapter, the student should be able to:

1. Prepare requisitions.
2. Prepare invoice forms and find extension prices.
3. Prepare purchase specifications and purchase orders.
4. Identify the computer as a means of communication.

Key Words

requisition	purchase	purchase order	transfers
invoice	specifications	point of sales	convenience
	purveyors	(POS)	products

To run a successful food service operation, it is essential that the chef, manager, and food service professional keep accurate, up-to-date, and detailed records. Records must be kept of all business transactions that are carried on within an organization. In this chapter, we will discuss three vital business forms that are used in the food service industry. Invoices, requisitions, and purchase orders are familiar forms to managers who buy and sell products.

Vital Business Forms

Business forms used in food service operations vary depending on the accounting system. The accountant may be a full-time employee or hired on a part-time basis. He or she provides the operation with forms that must be kept up to date and that reflect the daily business operation. It is important to keep a daily record of such items as the cash register readings, cash on hand, bank deposits, cash paid out, checks issued, invoices, requisitions, and purchase orders.

It can be said, without hesitation, that behind every successful business is usually a good recordkeeper. In a food service operation, that person might be the manager, assistant manager, or someone designated for this specific duty, such as the food and beverage controller.

Requisitions

In a food service operation, all supplies (food, beverages, cleaning products, paper products, etc.) are kept in the storage area. The storage area may be located on the same floor as the kitchen for easy access, or on another floor or basement area, making it a little difficult to reach. A cook in the kitchen needs certain supplies from the storage area to carry out the day's production. To obtain these supplies, the cook fills out a storage area **requisition.** (See Figure 12–1.) A requisition is a demand, usually made in written form, for something that is needed. On the form, the cook states the quantity needed, the unit, and a description or name of each item. The requisition may be approved by a superior. The cook who is going to use the items must also sign the requisition. This requisition is then taken to the storage area and the supplies are issued. If the storage area is a distance from the cook's station, the requisition may be given to a runner who acquires the supplies for the cook. The person in charge of the storage area, usually referred to as the steward, marks the unit price and extension price on each item. The steward also finds the total price of the food items issued. The requisition is then filed and used for the following purposes:

1. Accounts for all items issued from the storage area each day
2. Controls theft and waste
3. Provides the figures necessary for the daily food cost report
4. Ensures that all items are issued only to the proper personnel
5. Assists in controlling purchasing and eliminating large inventories

To Insure Perfect Solutions

Multiply the quantity by the unit price to find the extension price.

Storeroom Requisition

Date: October 23, 20 ____   Charge to Kitchen

Quantity	Unit	Item	Unit Price	Extension Price
6	#10 cans	Sliced apples	$3.55	$21.30
4	#10 cans	Tomato juice	1.97	7.88
1	lb.	Fresh mushrooms	1.55	1.55
2	lb.	Beef base	5.21	10.42
4	lb.	Cornstarch	0.46	1.84
			TOTAL	$42.99

Approved By _____

Signed _____

Figure 12–1
Storeroom requisition form.
© Cengage Learning 2012

Practice Problems 12–1   Extending Storage Area Requisition Forms

Prepare four storage area requisition forms using the example shown in Figure 12–1.

Work the following problems by finding the extension price and the total using the information from questions A to D. Round off all answers to the hundredths place using the information from the mill, when necessary.

A. 8—#10 cans sliced peaches @ $3.71 per can   1. _____

    7—#10 cans whole tomatoes @ $2.83 per can   2. _____

    12 heads iceberg lettuce @ $1.29 per head   3. _____

    3 dozen eating apples @ $4.50 per dozen   4. _____

    5 pounds corn starch @ $0.56 per pound   5. _____

    4 pounds margarine @ 2.09 per pound   6. _____

    TOTAL   7. _____

B. 5—#10 cans sliced pineapple @ $3.50 per can

4—#10 cans cherries @ $7.21 per can

3 bunches celery @ $0.89 per bunch

6 pounds tomatoes @ $0.76 per pound

2 bunches carrots @ $0.59 per bunch

9 dozen eggs @ $0.92 per dozen

TOTAL

C. 8—13-ounce cans tuna fish @ $1.79 per can

5 dozen eggs @ $0.92 per dozen

9—1-pound cans salmon @ $3.10 per can

6—2½-pound boxes frozen peas @ $0.56 per pound

8—2½-pound boxes frozen corn @ $0.58 per pound

7 heads iceberg lettuce @ $1.29 per head

TOTAL

D. 3—#10 cans tomato puree @ $2.65 per can

4—1-pound boxes cornstarch @ $0.56 per pound

2½ pounds leaf lettuce @ $0.89 per pound

5—2½-pound boxes lima beans @ $1.23 per pound

2½ pounds fresh mushrooms @ $1.26 per pound

4 bunches green onions @ $0.95 per bunch

3 bunches parsley @ $0.49 per bunch

5 heads iceberg lettuce @ $0.79 per head

TOTAL

8. _____

9. _____

10. _____

11. _____

12. _____

13. _____

14. _____

15. _____

16. _____

17. _____

18. _____

19. _____

20. _____

21. _____

22. _____

23. _____

24. _____

25. _____

26. _____

27. _____

28. _____

29. _____

30. _____

Invoices

An **invoice** is a written document listing goods sent to a purchaser by a vendor with their prices, quantity, and charges. (See Figure 12–2.) Individual companies have their own types of invoices depending upon what they feel is necessary to list. Some invoices are simple, while others are more complex. Most invoices today, in our computerized world, are computer printouts. An invoice accompanies each shipment or delivery of food brought into a food service operation. Before signing for a shipment, the person receiving the delivery must check the items delivered with those listed on the invoice to ensure all items listed have been received. This person also checks for sanitation and quality of the purchased items.

Distributor:	Haines Foods, Inc.		Phone: _____
			Date: October 20, 20___
Address:	70 Greenbrier Ave.		
	Ft. Mitchell, KY 41017		

Distributors of Fine Food Products—Wholesale Only

No. of Items	Salesperson		Order No.	Invoice #
5	Joe Jones		2860	J2479

Packed by:	Sold To:	Mr. John Doe	
G.C.	Street:	120 Elm Ave.	
City/State:	Covington, KY		

Case	Pack	Size	Canned Foods	Price	Amount
4	6	#10 can	Sliced apples	$20.87	$83.48
3	6	#10 can	Pitted cherries	43.85	131.55
2	12	#5 can	Apple juice	11.97	23.94
1	24	1 lb.	Cornstarch	11.04	11.04
2	24	#2½ can	Asparagus	25.73	51.46
			Total Amount		$301.47

Figure 12–2
Invoice form.
© Cengage Learning 2012

The invoice is important to the food service operator or manager because it provides the figures for the food purchased. These figures are necessary when computing the food cost percentage. The invoice is also important when checking the charges listed on the bill or statement sent by the vendor. Some businesspeople opt to pay cash for the delivery, or they must pay cash on delivery because of a poor credit rating. Most wait for a bill or statement and check all charges against the invoices received with each delivery. This is a good business practice.

If an establishment has a policy of using purchase orders, then the invoice can be used by the bookkeeper to check against a copy of the purchase order before the bill is paid.

To Insure Perfect Solutions

To find the amount column, multiply the number of cases by the price.

Practice Problems 12-2 Preparing Invoice Forms

Prepare four invoice forms using the example from Figure 12–2. Work questions E, F, G, and H by finding the extension price and the total. Assume that you work for Curran Foods, Inc. Use today's date and your own name as salesperson.

E. Order No. 2861; Invoice No. J2480; packed by R.G.;
    sold to Manor Restaurant, 590 Walnut St.,
    Cincinnati, OH 45202.

    4 cases 6—#10 cans whole tomatoes @ $16.98 per case   31. _____

    6 cases 12—50-ounce cans tomato soup @ $16.40 per case   32. _____

    2 cases 20 pounds spaghetti @ $9.77 per case   33. _____

4½ cases 4—1-gallon jars mayonnaise @ $14.84 per case   34. _____

2 boxes—15 pounds sliced bacon @ $24.30 per box   35. _____

2 cases 24—1-pound cans coffee @ $68.17 per case   36. _____

TOTAL   37. _____

F. Order No. 2862; Invoice No. J2481; packed by R.H.;
sold to Sinton Hotel, 278 Vine St.,
Cincinnati, OH 45202.

3 cases 4—1-gallon whole dill pickles @ $16.10 per case   38. _____

6 cases 12—15-ounce chicken rice soup @ $27.37 per case   39. _____

4 cases 4—1-gallon sweet pickle relish @ $18.40 per case   40. _____

6 cases 6—#10 cans tomatoes diced @ $13.97 per case   41. _____

5 cases 6—#10 cans sliced pineapple @ $22.70 per case   42. _____

3 cases 4—5-pound American cheese, sliced @ $33.98 per case   43. _____

TOTAL   44. _____

G. Order No. 2863; Invoice No. J2482; packed by B.B.;
sold to Cincinnati Businessmen's Club, 529 Plum St.,
Cincinnati, OH 45202.

3 cases 6—#10 cans catsup @ $19.51 per case   45. _____

2 cases 6—#10 cans chili sauce @ $22.49 per case   46. _____

1 case 6—1-gallon cider vinegar @ $10.41 per case   47. _____

3 boxes 10 pounds lasagna @ $6.84 per box   48. _____

9 cases 6—#10 cans sliced peaches @ $22.26 per case   49. _____

2 pack 16-ounce cracked black pepper @ $5.30 per pack   50. _____

TOTAL   51. _____

H. Order No. 2864; Invoice No. J2482; packed by J.M.;
sold to Norwood High School Cafeteria,
2078 Elm Ave., Norwood, OH 45212.

7 cases 6—#10 cans sliced apples @ $20.87 per case   52. _____

6 boxes 10 pounds medium egg noodles @ $8.86 per box   53. _____

2 cases 6—#10 cans bean sprouts @ $16.72 per case   54. _____

3 bags 50 pounds granulated sugar @ $16.70 per bag   55. _____

2 cases 12—2-pound brown sugar @ $12.67 per case   56. _____

2 cases 30—1-pound margarine @ $10.77 per case   57. _____

TOTAL   58. _____

Discussion Question 12-1

What possible mistakes could occur in preparing invoice forms that will affect the cost of food?

Purchase Specifications

Purchase specifications are an important part of a successful food service operation. They provide a detailed description of the items being purchased. They should be written as exactly and precisely as possible to allow the food service operator to obtain bids from different **purveyors** (companies that supply provisions or food). This allows the food service operator to obtain the best product at the lowest price, and it allows the purveyor to submit a bid with exact knowledge of the specific needs of the food service business. These purchase specifications should be written based upon the menu needs and the availability of products.

Most restaurants use purchase specifications when purchasing meat, seafood, and produce (fruit and vegetables). For example, when purchasing ribs of beef, the specifications may be:

1. Grade—Choice.
2. Weight—20 to 22 pounds.
3. Short ribs removed after measuring 1½ inches from the "eye" of the rib.
4. The back should not have a heavy covering of fat.
5. Ribs should be aged 15 to 20 days.
6. Back bones should be separated from the seven rib bones.
7. Rib tied—oven-ready.

When purchasing fruit, the specifications usually list the size, weight, softness, brand, number desired, and, when appropriate, the color. A copy of purchase specifications is submitted to prospective vendors before the food service establishment begins purchasing the specific products. Purchase specifications may be used with food, beverages, and alcoholic beverages.

Discussion Question 12-2

Name and discuss three problems that may occur in your business if purchase specifications are not used.

Purchase Orders

Purchase orders may be used in the food service business. Large restaurant chains are more likely to use them than small or independent operators.

A **purchase order** is a written form that indicates to the vendor how many items are to be delivered to an establishment, and lists the prices for each item. (See Figure 12–3.) Two individual employees of the food service operation, such as the manager and purchasing agent, should sign the order. This step is necessary for control purposes. With two signatures, there is less chance for collusion between the purveyor and the person who buys the products. This form tells the vendor that if the items delivered compare favorably with the items and prices listed on the order, then payment will be made.

Figure 12–3
Purchase order form.
© Cengage Learning 2012

Hasenours Restaurant
Barret and Oak Streets
Louisville, KY 40222

Purchase Order No. 1492
Date: October 20, 20____

To: Jefferson Meat Co.
     2868 Baster Ave.
     Louisville, KY 40222

Ship To: Hasenours Restaurant
          Barrett and Oak Streets
          Louisville, KY 40222

Date of Delivery: January 10, 20____
Deliver the items listed below, which are being purchased in accordance with descriptions and prices stated.

Description	Unit	Quantity	Unit Price	Amount
Ribs of beef — choice 20 to 22 lbs. Aged 15 to 20 days Short ribs removed	lb.	132 lbs.	$2.95	$389.40
12 oz. sirloin steaks — choice 1½ -inch thick Packed for storage	lb.	288 lbs.	$3.75	$1,080.00
Beef chuck for stew Cut into 1-inch cubes Grade Choice	lb.	40 lbs.	$2.28	$91.20
			Total Cost	$1,560.60

Purchasing Agent

In most food service operations, one person is designated to do the purchasing. This person is usually called the *purchasing agent.* In small operations, this duty is often performed by the manager, assistant manager, or chef. In any case, the person doing the buying checks prices and quality with different vendors before the purchase order is sent to the one offering the best deal. Recently, the trend has been to compare vendor prices at the beginning of the year and purchase from one vendor throughout the year. This vendor is referred to as the primary vendor.

The purchase order is usually made out in triplicate (three copies). An original copy is sent to the vendor via mail or Internet or, if both have fax (facsimile) machines, it is faxed to them. Copies are kept by the receiving clerk (sometimes called the steward) and the bookkeeper. The receiving clerk uses a copy of the purchase order to check the merchandise when it is delivered by the vendor. A bookkeeper uses a copy to check what was ordered against invoices and statements. Purchase orders eliminate controversy over what was ordered, how much was ordered, who ordered it, and when it was ordered. Purchase orders are another tool used to exercise good business practices. The memory sometimes fails, which is why records are essential.

To Insure Perfect Solutions

To find the amount on the purchase order form, multiply the quantity by the unit price.

Discussion Question 12-3

What are the benefits of having written purchase specifications as they relate to the financial implications of running a food service establishment? Give at least three examples of why a business should have these specifications.

Practice Problems 12-3 Preparing and Calculating Purchase Orders

Prepare four purchase order forms as shown in this section. These purchase order forms were based upon the purchase specifications developed by our food service company. Work the following problems by finding the amount and total cost for all items. Assume that you are purchasing for Scarlet Oaks Vocational School, 3254 East Kemper Road, Cincinnati, OH. Use today's date, and show the date of delivery as one week from that date.

59. Purchase Order No. 1493; To: Hands Packing Co., 8567 Spring Grove Ave., Cincinnati, OH.

Description:	Ground Beef—Chuck 85% lean 15% suet Medium grind
Quantity:	165 pounds
Unit Price:	$2.05 per pound
Description:	10-ounce Sirloin Steaks—Choice 1½-inch tail Fresh
Quantity:	260 pounds
Unit Price:	$3.26 per pound
Description:	14 pounds pork loins—spine bones removed; rib and loin end are separated, leaving 2 ribs on loin end. Tenderloin left on loin end.
Quantity:	84 pounds
Unit Price:	$2.70 per pound

60. Purchase Order No. 1494; To: Ideal Bakers Supply, 458 Ross Ave.,
    Cincinnati, OH.

Description:	Cake Flour, 100 pounds
Quantity:	9
Unit Price:	$24.58 per 100 pounds
Description:	Pastry flour, 100 pounds
Quantity:	9
Unit Price:	$17.52 per 100 pounds
Description:	Powdered sugar, 10X, 25-pound bag
Quantity:	5
Unit Price:	$9.01 per bag
Description:	Meringue powder, 10-pound box
Quantity:	3
Unit Price:	$21.20 per box

61. Purchase Order No. 1495; To: Deluxe Foods,
    6870 High Street, Hamilton, OH.

Description:	Tuna fish, light meat, chunk, 24—13-ounce cans
Quantity:	12 cases
Unit Price:	$50.89 per case
Description:	Coffee, drip grind, 12—2-pound cans
Quantity:	5 cases
Unit Price:	$42.25.16 per case
Description:	Sliced pineapple, 50 count, 6—#10 cans
Quantity:	13 cases
Unit Price:	$32.70 per case
Description:	Pear halves, 50 count, 6—#10 cans
Quantity:	7 cases
Unit Price:	$28.75 per case

62. Purchase Order No. 1496; To: Surk's Meat Packing Co.,
    1520 Eastern Avenue, Covington, KY.

Description:	Boston Butt, average, 4 pounds, cottage butt and blade bone removed.
Quantity:	48 pounds
Unit Price:	$1.92 per pound
Description:	Ham, average, 12 pounds, shank bone removed
Quantity:	36 pounds
Unit Price:	$2.12 per pound
Description:	Sausage, 6 to 1 pound
Quantity:	26 pounds
Unit Price:	$1.79 per pound
Description:	Bacon, lean, 28 slices to 1 pound
Quantity:	28 pounds
Unit Price:	$1.82 per pound

Receiving

The person receiving food must check all invoices carefully to determine that all goods that were ordered were received. The receiving clerk should check for the quality of the goods and reject any items that do not meet the purchase specifications. All items that are delivered should be counted and weighed. If invoices are not checked correctly, delivery people may deliberately or accidentally omit the products that they are supposed to deliver. In addition, the receiving clerk should check to make sure that products have been handled correctly (that is, frozen foods arrive frozen, cold foods arrive at the proper temperature, dry ingredients arrive dry, and packages are not mutilated). The receiving clerk must also compare the prices on the invoice to the prices that were quoted on the purchase order. The receiving clerk must sign for all purchases after he or she verifies the quality, quantity, and price of the delivered products.

"During the economic downturn that started during 2008, our company had to take steps to control our costs while keeping our food and beverage quality up to the Starwood standards. We had to analyze every food and beverage facet of our operation to determine where we could cut our costs without any negative effect on our food and beverage quality. We know that controlling costs occurs in many areas of the purchasing and receiving cycle. One of the positive steps that we took to control our food costs was to make certain that all of our properties had a scale available at the receiving area. The receiving scale must be used to weigh food orders to verify that we received the correct weight of the food that we had purchased."

Michiel Bakker
Senior Director of Food and Beverage/Co-leader, North American Division
Starwood Hotels & Resorts Worldwide, Inc.

Starwood Hotels & Resorts Worldwide owns, leases, manages, and franchises 942 hotels with approximately 285,000 rooms in 100 countries. The company's brand names include St. Regis, The Luxury Collection, W, Westin, Le Meridien, Sheraton, Four Points, Aloft, and Element. The Food and Beverage division at Starwood represents approximately one-third of Starwood's total business and is a key driver of the guest experience. The food and beverage function is critical to the overall success and reputation of Starwood's individual hotels and its portfolio of hotels as a whole. Mr. Bakker is responsible for Starwood's third-party food and beverage operators strategy, relationships, and support for North America; food and beverage support for Starwood's new builds and transitions hotels in North America (owned, managed, and franchised); bar and beverage strategy, management, and programs; and overall support for Starwood's North American food and beverage activities for all owned, managed, and franchised hotels.

Point-of-Sale Computers

Computers have also revolutionized the dining experience. In many restaurants, the waitstaff enters the order of the guest into a computer called **point of sales (POS),** either via a touch screen or a handheld terminal. The order is then transmitted to printers in the kitchen. The culinary staff prepares the orders as they are printed in the kitchen. These computerized POS systems save time for food service professionals in many ways—in taking inventory, making reports, handling accounting, and so forth. The systems will calculate the total amount of meals served, the individual items ordered, and numerous other reports that enable a chef to manage the kitchen effectively. Some POS computers are integrated with inventory programs; when an item is ordered, the inventory is updated instantaneously. The computer has been programmed to list the ingredients in each item ordered. Every time an item is ordered, the computer program subtracts the amount from its inventory database. The chef must know math basics to eyeball the reports and determine if the computer is programmed incorrectly.

Purchasing Food Using the Computer

Most major food **purveyors** have a software program that enables a food service professional to place orders using a computer. This allows information to be transmitted directly.

Each purveyor has developed a software program that lists all the products that the purveyor for sale. The products are categorized (e.g., fish, meat, poultry), or they may be looked up alphabetically. Each product lists information concerning quality, pack, size, and pricing. Many programs also give the buyer nutritional information about the product. Once the purchaser decides how much food to order, the food order is entered into the computer and transmitted to the purveyor. The food company delivers the order at the next scheduled delivery. The food service professional can print the order, invoice, and the receiver's copy before it arrives at the establishment. The purveyor can also give the food service professional a list of products and amounts purchased during a specific time period.

Purchasing Ready-to-Cook or Convenience Foods

In today's business environment, food service operators have a variety of options to determine what types of menu items to offer to their guests. As more food service distributors and manufacturers produce items that can be cooked and served with minimum preparation time, the food service operator must decide whether to make a menu item from scratch or use a convenience item instead. There are many products that can be purchased either partially or fully prepared. For example, salad greens may be purchased already trimmed, cleaned, and packaged, so the food service operator can simply open up the package and serve the salad directly to guests. Other products, such as meat and poultry, can be purchased ready to be cooked. Such products are commonly referred to as ready-to-use or convenience foods.

There are many companies that make these products. For instance, Rich's Products Corporation offers a wide variety of items, from appetizers to pizza products to sweets. The food service operator that would like to add pizza on its menu can purchase dough balls to make pizza or wheat dough to make a healthy alternative style of pizza. A business may design an entire menu and use only convenience foods to serve the guests.

Before a business decides to use a convenience food, some judgments have to be made. First, is the quality of the product better than if it were prepared from scratch? The next question that must be considered is, will the guests care, or even be able to tell, that the staff did not prepare the menu item from scratch? The next consideration is to compare the cost of buying ingredients and preparing an item from scratch versus the cost of just buying the ready-to-use item. Another question that the food service operator must take into account is whether the operation has the type of equipment needed to make the particular menu item, or whether the equipment will have to be purchased. Other factors are the training of the culinary staff and the consistency of the finished product.

When the food service operator is trying to decide between making things from scratch versus using convenience foods, many companies are willing to share their knowledge and provide a cost comparison. For instance, when the authors worked with Rich's Products Corporation, they inquired about the cost of sheeted dough. This product is ready to use to make pizza; the food service operator simply thaws the dough, places the toppings on top, bakes it, and serves the pizza to the guest.

Upon request, Rich's Products Corporation will provide operators with a cost breakdown of the sheeted dough for the pizza, comparing the cost of its sheeted dough product with pizzas made from scratch. Factored into the cost comparison are the steps needed to prepare and cook the pizzas, the labor costs, and (if applicable) the price of equipment needed to mix, sheet, and press the dough. Rich's also reminds the operator to calculate any insurance costs. When providing this information for comparison purposes, Rich's must keep all circumstances the same, other than the ones affected by the choice to use the sheeted dough. For instance, Rich's needs to cite the same amount of toppings with both the sheeted dough product and pizza made from scratch, so that that cost is identical.

With all this information, the food service operator can determine whether to make the pizza dough from scratch or buy the dough already sheeted. In this text, the authors recommend that food service operators take all these factors into consideration when determining if and when convenience foods have a place in their operation.

Discussion Question 12-4

A salesperson offers to sell you boneless chicken breasts that are $2.99 per 8-ounce portion. Fresh chicken breasts cost $0.99 a pound. What considerations must you take into account to determine if you should buy the 8-ounce chicken breasts?

Transfers

When the food and beverage manager has to figure out percentage costs, he or she must consider transfers, which occur when products are bought by one department but used in (and hence charged to) another department. For example, at the bar, Bloody Mary ingredients are tomato juice, horseradish, salt, pepper, and celery, along with the alcohol. Other alcoholic beverages are sometimes garnished with fruits and vegetables, such as olives that go with martinis. When these items are purchased, they will be bought through the produce and grocery vendor, but they are used to make bar products, not food. When figuring out our food cost for groceries and produce, these costs will be calculated in the restaurant or food category. If the bar does a substantial amount of business, the food cost percentage for the restaurant will increase, while the bar cost percentage will decrease. Conversely, the culinary staff sometimes needs wines and other alcoholic beverages for recipes. The purchase of these wines and alcoholic beverages is made through the wine and liquor purveyors, but they are used to make food. As a result, if the kitchen uses a lot of alcoholic beverages, the food cost percentage will go down and the bar cost percentage will go up. In each of these cases, these percentages don't reflect what is actually going on in the restaurant.

To alleviate this problem, the food and beverage manager will calculate the ingredients that are moved from one department to another. Moving ingredients from one department to another is referred to as a **transfer.** When calculating percentage costs (either food or beverage), these steps must be taken to obtain accurate costs:

Step 1: Figure out the exact cost of all the ingredients that are being moved from one department to the other.

Step 2: Add the cost of the ingredients to the department that received the ingredients.

Step 3: Subtract the cost of the ingredients from the department that provided the ingredients.

For example, let's go back to our Bloody Mary scenario and pretend that the only item we sell is Bloody Marys. Our purchaser has to buy four cases of tomato juice, at $30 a case, and a half case of celery, costing $12, to make all the Bloody Marys we sell each day. So per day, the cost of the tomato juice is $120 and the cost of the celery is $12, for a total of $132. And the vodka used to make the

Bloody Marys sold in a day is $60. The number of Bloody Marys sold each day results in revenues of $528. Therefore, our cost percentage without transfers is in the following chart.

Bloody Mary Bar and Restaurant
Monday, January 12, 20—
Bar Costs

Item	Figures	Percentage
Sales	$528	100%
Cost of Vodka	$60	
Beverage Cost Percentage	60 is divided by 528	11.36% Beverage Cost Percentage

Now the transfer of the food items will be added into the bar costs. Observe what occurs.

Bloody Mary Bar and Restaurant
Monday, January 12, 20—
Bar Costs

Item	Figures	Percentage
Sales	$528	100%
Cost of Vodka	$60	
Add transfers from the produce department (1/2 case of celery)	$12	
Add transfers from the grocery department (4 cases of tomato juice	$120	
Total cost of ingredients to make the Bloody Marys	$192	
Beverage Cost Percentage	192 divided by 528	36.36% Beverage Cost Percentage

As these tables illustrate, it is important to use transfers if you want to calculate cost percentages effectively.

In computing and using transfers, you must take care to calculate the transfers accurately and to know when to add and when to subtract them. In our example, the $120 would be subtracted from the grocery department (because we transferred the ingredients to the bar) and the $12 would be subtracted from the produce department (because we transferred the ingredients to the bar).

Practice Problems 12–4 Calculating Transfers and Cost Percentages

Determine the answers from the following information and figure out the food and beverage cost percentages. Calculate the food cost to four places to the right of the decimal. For example, if the answer is 0.29748, go to the fifth number to the right of the decimal and use that number to round off to the fourth number to the right of the decimal. Now the answer is 0.2975. Next, convert 0.2975 to a percentage. Calculate the food cost percentage to two places to the right of the decimal. Therefore, the final answer would be 29.75 percent.

The sales for January 15 in the ZZZZ Restaurant were $5,125 for the food service and $12,265 in the bar. The food cost was $1,792, and the bar cost was $2,453.

The cost of the food that was sent from the kitchen to the bar was $425, and the cost of the alcoholic beverages that were sent from the bar to the kitchen was $63.50.

63. Without calculating transfers, what is the food cost percentage? _____

64. Without calculating transfers, what is the beverage cost percentage? _____

65. What is the food cost percentage, calculating transfers? _____

66. What is the beverage cost percentage, calculating transfers? _____

The sales for January 21 in the ZZZZ Restaurant were $8,125.00 for the food service and $8,265.00 in the bar. The food cost was $3,656.25, and the bar cost was $1,653.00.

The cost of the food that was sent from the kitchen to the bar was $725.00. The cost of the alcoholic beverages that were sent from the bar to the kitchen was $263.50.

67. Without calculating transfers, what is the food cost percentage? _____

68. Without calculating transfers, what is the beverage cost percentage? _____

69. What is the food cost percentage, calculating transfers? _____

70. What is the beverage cost percentage, calculating transfers? _____

Discussion Question 12-5

If you were the food and beverage manager of the ZZZZ Restaurant, what conclusions would you draw and what concerns would you have after completing questions 67 to 70?

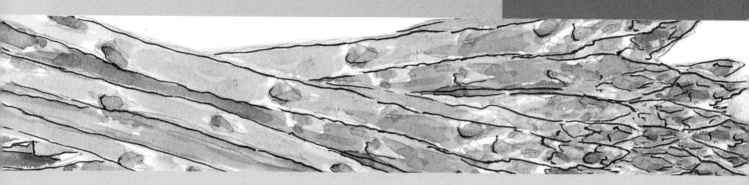

Daily Production Reports and Beverage Costs

Objectives

At the completion of this chapter, the student should be able to:

1. Complete the cook's production report.
2. Complete the baker's production report.
3. Complete the salad production report.
4. Complete the counter production report.
5. Calculate beverage percentages.
6. Identify the number of ounces in 750 ml and a liter of wine.
7. Identify the number of ounces in a barrel or keg of beer.
8. Recognize methods in which theft may occur in a beverage operation.
9. Calculate the sales from a barrel or a keg of beer using the cup method.

Key Words

food production report

forecasting

cook's production report

baker's production report

salad production report

counter production report

liter bottle

slippage

daily production report

Production Reports

There are a number of production departments in a commercial kitchen. The number and size depends on the size of the food service operation. Each department produces its own special kind of food to meet the needs required for serving breakfast, luncheon, and dinner menus. The production departments will include *cooking, salad, pastry, baking,* and *butchering.* The production that goes on in these departments must be *controlled.* The device used is called a **food production report.** These reports are probably more important in large operations because they help the chef or manager control production situations that can become out of control. In small operations, with a smaller production crew and work areas, it is easier to observe all that is taking place; however, production reports are still a necessity to control food cost.

"As the executive chef of the three Elephant Walk Restaurants (the only restaurants in the United States that serve authentic Cambodian cuisine), I must make certain that our culinary staff prepare our food as created by my mother when she was the executive chef. She still helps us develop recipes today and is clearly the best chef that I know. Since 1991, our unique restaurants have served Cambodian, French, vegetarian, and vegan menus. The knowledge and use of math plays a critical part in developing our recipes, keeping inventory, and ordering the specific ingredients critical to the execution of our authentic Cambodian cuisine, as well as our other cuisines. Additionally, we must use math to determine how much of our sales we can allocate to the charitable causes in the Boston area."

Nadsa de Monteiro
Executive Chef/Owner
The Elephant Walk Restaurant Group, Inc.
Boston, MA

Ms. De Monteiro took over as executive chef from her mother, Longteine De Monteiro, who is the founding chef (and continues to be the consulting chef) and owner of the Elephant Walk restaurants. The Elephant Walk Restaurant Group has three locations in the Boston area; one in Boston itself, the second in Cambridge, and the third in Waltham. Nadsa began to cook with her mother in mid-1992, and soon she and her mother began to experiment with other cuisines in addition to the authentic Cambodian food that they were already well known for. Nadsa has developed an informative website (elephantwalk.com) that specifically addresses many issues for independent restaurant operators and for aspiring food service professionals. From this site, the reader will learn about the many charitable organizations that the Elephant Walk Restaurant Group helps. In Nadsa's blogs, the reader will get a true understanding of the dedication and knowledge that it takes to be a successful restaurant operator. She illustrates why a chef must know how to do more than cook to be a success! The reader will also be able to understand the passion that the owners have brought to the restaurant business, which has resulted in the Elephant Walk winning many awards and accolades from the Boston restaurant community.

Uses of Daily Production Reports

Production reports help to control such essentials as:

- Over- or underproduction
- Leftovers
- Purchasing
- Labor cost
- Waste
- Theft

They will also inform the manager of popular preparations that are selling out, menu items that are not selling, and, to a degree, whether portion sizes should be adjusted. In addition, the report is used in predicting future sales, referred to as **forecasting.** Predicting future sales assists management in the purchasing of food and hiring of future food service employees. If a rotating menu is being used (for example, in retirement communities, assisted living communities, senior living centers, and cruise ships) on a monthly, biannual, or annual basis, these reports become even more valuable. Management can look back and see which items sold best and how many of each item was sold the last time the menu was used. If these reports are used properly, management can improve the food cost percentage.

Food Production Reports

The forms used in compiling the daily food production reports vary depending on the individual food service operation. Each establishment has its own ideas about control and the information it would like to have listed on the report. Most establishments do, however, request reports from cooks, pastry cooks, bakers, and the salad and counter service departments. The report forms are usually quite simple to fill out, so they do not take up too much of an employee's time to complete. Some forms, such as the one used in the counter report, show unit price, total price, and total sales.

Examples of four different daily food production reports are shown in Figures 13–1 through 13–4. These forms are typical of those used in the food service industry. Although these examples are easy to follow, a few comments on each can help you to become more competent when filling them out. The math involved in completing all these reports is counting and subtraction. The person who plans the size of the portion, the quantity required, and the amount of portions to prepare has to use additional math skills such as yield tests, proportions and ratios, and so forth. For the purpose of this chapter, the student should concentrate on learning how to complete the reports accurately because food cost and food cost percentages depend upon their accuracy.

Cook's Production Report (See Figure 13–1)

The **Cook's Production Report** assists the chef to establish amounts of food to prepare and to determine how much food was used or when all of the food were sold.

Recipe File Number.   This number is placed on the recipe for easy access when it is filed. Standard recipes are used in many food service establishments to control the cost, taste, texture, quality, and amount of food being prepared.

Size of Portion.   The manager or chef fills in this column to let the cook and the waitperson know the portion size he or she is serving or dishing up. In most establishments, the portion size is a set policy and is indicated on the portion charts on display in the production area.

Raw Quantity Required.   This is usually designated by the chef or cook. Sometimes the manager lists this figure, but it must be done by a person familiar with production and with the policy of the establishment. The chef, manager, or purchasing agent is responsible for ordering the raw quantity required from a vendor and seeing that it is on hand when needed.

Item	Recipe File Number	Size of Portion	Raw Quantity Required	Portions to Prepare	Portions Left or Time Out	Portions Served
Roast round of beef	15	3 oz.	25 lbs.	80	8:15	80
Roast loin of pork	20	4½ oz.	12 lbs.	30	8	22
Filet of sole	8	5 oz.	14 lbs.	42	2	40
Veal goulash	18	6 oz.	10 lbs.	24	9	15
Swiss steak	14	5 oz.	15 lbs.	48	12	36
Mashed potatoes	42	4 oz.	20 lbs.	60	5	55
Peas and carrots	51	3 oz.	9 lbs.	48	18	30
Succotash	52	3 oz.	5 lbs.	26	1	25

Unit: First National Bank   Day: Thursday   Meal: Luncheon   Date: June 23, 20___   Customers: 150

Figure 13–1
Cook's production report.
© Cengage Learning 2012

Portions to Prepare. This decision is made by the manager or chef and is based on previous production reports and sales history. It is important to know how much of a particular item was sold the last time it appeared on the menu. Also, consideration must be given to other external factors. For example, cold weather could have resulted in an increase of soup sales. This is called **forecasting.**

Portions Left or Time Out. This figure is recorded by the cook and is found by counting the number of portions left after the meal is over. Time out is recorded when the number of a certain item is completely sold out. The time an item sold out is important because it affects the number of items prepared the next time the item appears on the menu.

Portions Served. This is recorded by the cook and is found by subtracting the number left from the number prepared. It is an important figure because this number influences the number of portions prepared when the item appears again on the menu.

Practice Problems 13–1   Cook's Production Report

Complete the following cook's production reports to find the amount of portions served in these establishments. To complete the production report, use today's day and date. Please note that the questions are numbered on the left side.

A.   Unit: Mason Art Co.

Day: _____

Date: _____

Meal: Luncheon

Customers: 50

Item	Recipe Number	Size of Portion	Raw Quantity Required	Portions to Prepare	Portions Left or Time Out	Portions Served
1. Spanish steak	18	5 oz.	8 lbs.	25	7	_____
2. Salisbury steak	19	5 oz.	7 lbs.	22	9	_____
3. Beef pot roast	20	3 oz.	8 lbs.	32	13	_____
4. Au gratin potatoes	2	4 oz.	10 lbs.	35	6	_____
5. Succotash	10	3 oz.	5 lbs.	30	4	_____
6. Mashed potatoes	3	4 oz.	20 lbs.	60	13	_____
7. Lima beans	12	3 oz.	2½ lbs.	15	2	_____

B.   Unit: 2nd National Bank

Day: _____

Date: _____

Meal: Luncheon

Customers: 131

Item	Recipe Number	Size of Portion	Raw Quantity Required	Portions to Prepare	Portions Left or Time Out	Portions Served
8. Sautéed pork chop	32	4 oz.	6 lbs.	22	8	_____
9. Turkey steaks	45	4 oz.	12 lbs.	45	7	_____
10. Baked halibut	54	5 oz.	10 lbs.	32	12	_____
11. Roast veal	30	3 oz.	10 lbs.	38	13	_____
12. Parsley potatoes	4	4 oz.	15 lbs.	50	6	_____
13. Hash in cream potatoes	5	4 oz.	14 lbs.	45	11	_____
14. Peas and celery	13	3 oz.	7½ lbs.	44	9	_____
15. Cut green beans	16	3 oz.	5 lbs.	30	5	_____

C. Unit: Chase Machine Tool Co.

Day: _____

Date: _____

Meal: Luncheon

Customers: 155

	Item	Recipe Number	Size of Portion	Raw Quantity Required	Portions to Prepare	Portions Left or Time Out	Portions Served
16.	Sautéed veal steak	31	4 oz.	5 lbs.	26	3	_____
17.	Beef sauerbraten	21	3 oz.	8 lbs.	32	6	_____
18.	Beef goulash	26	6 oz.	15 lbs.	54	2	_____
19.	Swiss steak	22	5 oz.	20 lbs.	62	8	_____
20.	Rissel potatoes	1	4 oz.	12 lbs.	36	9	_____
21.	Escallop potatoes	6	4 oz.	8 lbs.	26	11	_____
22.	Stewed tomatoes	14	3 oz.	1 #10 can	22	5	_____
23.	Corn	15	3 oz.	7½ lbs.	44	12	_____

D. Unit: Norwood High School

Day: _____

Date: _____

Meal: Luncheon

Customers: 100

	Item	Recipe Number	Size of Portion	Raw Quantity Required	Portions to Prepare	Portions Left or Time Out	Portions Served
24.	Ham steak	34	4 oz.	7 lbs.	28	6	_____
25.	Roast turkey	37	3 oz.	15 lbs.	36	8	_____
26.	Hamburger steak	23	5 oz.	13 lbs.	42	7	_____
27.	Beef Stroganoff	25	6 oz.	7 lbs.	20	5	_____
28.	Macaroni au gratin	74	4 oz.	4 lbs.	45	11	_____
29.	Mashed potatoes	3	4 oz.	12 lbs.	40	9	_____
30.	Mixed greens	9	3 oz.	10 lbs.	58	13	_____
31.	Carrots Vichy	17	3 oz.	5 lbs.	29	16	_____

Baker's Production Report (See Figure 13–2)

The **Baker's Production Report** assists the chef or pastry chef to establish amounts of baked goods to prepare or order and to determine how much baked goods were used or when all of the baked goods were sold.

Order. The order is recorded by the manager, chef, or pastry chef, and this represents the amount of bakery and pastry items needed for service throughout the day in all departments of the food service operation. If the operation is a catering company, it represents the amount needed in all units served.

On Hand. This figure is recorded by the baker and represents the amount of each item that was left by the previous shift or from the previous day and is still in a usable condition. It may be raw or cooked, frozen or unfrozen.

Prepare. This figure is found by subtracting the amount on hand from the amount ordered. The remainder is the amount to prepare and is recorded by the baker or pastry chef.

Left. This figure is found by counting the number of pieces remaining after the day's service is over. This figure is recorded by the baker or pastry chef.

Sold. This figure is found by subtracting the number left from the number ordered. This figure is recorded by the cook or pastry chef.

Comments. This space is provided for any information that may be valuable to management. Examples: when a product is sold out, and the selling of the leftover baked products at a reduced cost or donating them to a charity.

Day: Monday		Date: June 27, 20___				Unit: Leo's Cafeteria
Item	**Order**	**On Hand**	**Prepare**	**Left**	**Sold**	**Comment**
Rolls						
Soft rye	20 doz.	3 doz.	17 doz.	2 doz.	18 doz.	
Soft white	35 doz.	4 doz.	31 doz.	6 doz.	29 doz.	
Hard white	26 doz.	5 doz.	21 doz.	4 doz.	22 doz.	
Cinnamon	18 doz.	2 doz.	16 doz.	1 doz.	17 doz.	
Rye sticks	15 doz.	6 doz.	9 doz.	0	15 doz.	Out 7 p.m.
Quick Breads						
Biscuits	12 doz.	1 doz.	11 doz.	3 doz.	9 doz.	Biscuits
Raisin muffins	24 doz.	5 doz.	19 doz.	5 doz.	19 doz.	left unbaked in freezer
Pies						
Cherry	22	6	16	0	22	Out 8 p.m.
Apple	25	4	21	2	23	
Chocolate	15	3	12	0	15	Out
Banana	12	1	11	8	4	7:30 p.m.
Cakes						
Bar	6	2	4	3	3	These left
899 White	10	4	6	6	4	in freezer
Mocha	8	1	7	0	8	Out 7 p.m.

Figure 13–2
Baker's production report.
© Cengage Learning 2012

Practice Problems 13–2 Baker's Production Report

Complete the following baker's production reports. Find the portions to prepare and how many items were sold at each establishment. To complete the production report, use today's day and date. Please note that the questions are numbered on the left side.

E.   Unit: Norwood High School

Day: _____

Date: _____

	Item	Order	On Hand	Prepare	Left	Sold
32.	Seed rolls	25 doz.	6 doz.	_____	4 doz.	_____
33.	Rye rolls	36 doz.	3 doz.	_____	5 doz.	_____
34.	Hard rolls	28 doz.	6 doz.	_____	2 doz.	_____
35.	Rye sticks	22 doz.	4 doz.	_____	3 doz.	_____
36.	Biscuits	12 doz.	0	_____	3 doz.	_____
37.	Banana muffins	10 doz.	0	_____	1½ doz.	_____
38.	Cherry pies	18	5	_____	2	_____
39.	Banana pies	16	2	_____	4	_____
40.	Boston cream pies	22	7	_____	6	_____
41.	Devil's food cake	13	5	_____	2	_____

F.   Unit: Deluxe Shoe Co.

Day: _____

Date: _____

	Item	Order	On Hand	Prepare	Left	Sold
42.	Soft rolls	30 doz.	4 doz.	_____	2 doz.	_____
43.	Hard rolls	28 doz.	6 doz.	_____	5 doz.	_____
44.	Rye sticks	22 doz.	4 doz.	_____	1 doz.	_____
45.	Pecan rolls	16 doz.	2 doz.	_____	½ doz.	_____
46.	Raisin muffins	9 doz.	1 doz.	_____	¾ doz.	_____
47.	Apple pies	18	3	_____	1	_____
48.	Peach pies	14	2	_____	2	_____
49.	Chocolate pies	22	4	_____	3	_____
50.	Lemon cake	9	2	_____	4	_____
51.	Chocolate bar cake	12	5	_____	3	_____
52.	Fudge cake	14	1	_____	5	_____

G. Unit: Joe's Cafeteria

Day: _____

Date: _____

Item	Order	On Hand	Prepare	Left	Sold
53. Cloverleaf rolls	40 doz.	7 doz.	_____	3 doz.	_____
54. Caramel rolls	26 doz.	3 doz.	_____	1 doz.	_____
55. Seed rolls	35 doz.	4 doz.	_____	2 doz.	_____
56. Biscuits	22 doz.	5 doz.	_____	½ doz.	_____
57. Corn muffins	18 doz.	2 doz.	_____	¾ doz.	_____
58. Pecan pie	12	3	_____	5	_____
59. Pumpkin pie	15	2	_____	4	_____
60. Custard pie	10	4	_____	3	_____
61. Éclairs	48	0	_____	8	_____
62. Cherry tarts	54	5	_____	7	_____

H. Unit: Wine & Dine Restaurant

Day: _____

Date: _____

Item	Order	On Hand	Prepare	Left	Sold
63. Soft rolls	68 doz.	9 doz.	_____	4¾ doz.	_____
64. Rye rolls	38 doz.	4 doz.	_____	5½ doz.	_____
65. Split rolls	26 doz.	7 doz.	_____	2¼ doz.	_____
66. Cinnamon rolls	32 doz.	6 doz.	_____	7¾ doz.	_____
67. Apple muffins	18 doz.	4 doz.	_____	4½ doz.	_____
68. Corn sticks	16 doz.	3 doz.	_____	2¼ doz.	_____
69. Blueberry pie	12	4	_____	2	_____
70. Coconut cream pie	14	3	_____	4	_____
71. White cake	9	2	_____	1	_____
72. Apple cake	8	1	_____	0	_____
73. Yellow cake	6	0	_____	3	_____

Salad Production Report (See Figure 13–3)

The **Salad Production Report** assists the chef to establish amounts of salads to prepare and to determine how many salads were sold.

Order. The order is recorded by the manager, chef, or head salad maker, and this represents the amount of each salad to be prepared. It is an estimate of the number or kind of salad needed for serving one meal or for the complete day. Cafeterias and buffet-style restaurants provide an array of assorted salads. The order is very helpful in this type of operation.

On Hand. This figure, recorded by the salad maker, represents the amount of each salad that was left by the previous shift or from the previous day and is still in a usable condition.

Figure 13–3
Salad production report.
© Cengage Learning 2012

Day: Tuesday		Date: June 29, 20___		Unit: First National Bank	
Item	**Order**	**On Hand**	**Prepare**	**Left**	**Sold**
Tossed	23	8	15	3	20
Italian	12	0	12	0	12
Garden	22	9	13	7	15
Waldorf	16	2	14	6	10
Potato	25	10	15	6	19
Cole slaw	32	8	24	1	31
Sliced tomato	26	0	26	3	23
Fruited gelatin	28	12	16	2	26
Sunshine	14	3	11	4	10
Green island	25	5	20	5	20
Mixed fruit	35	6	29	3	32
Chef	46	7	39	12	34
Cucumber	12	1	11	10	2

Prepare. This figure, recorded by the salad maker, is found by subtracting the amount on hand from the amount ordered.

Left. This figure, recorded by the salad maker, is found by counting the number of each kind of salad remaining after the meal or day's service is concluded.

Sold. This figure, recorded by the salad maker, is found by subtracting the number left from the number ordered.

Comments. This space is provided for information that may be valuable to the head salad maker or management. Examples: weather conditions that day, the time a certain salad is sold out, production information or mistakes, and the disposition of leftover salads.

Practice Problems 13–3 Salad Production Report

Complete the following salad production reports. Find the portions to prepare and how many items were sold at each establishment. To complete the production report, use today's day and date. Please note that the questions are numbered on the left side.

I. Unit: 1st Federal Bank

Day: _____

Date: _____

Item	Order	On Hand	Prepare	Left	Sold
74. Tossed	24	4	_____	4	_____
75. Chef	20	3	_____	2	_____
76. Garden	16	6	_____	6	_____
77. Slaw	12	2	_____	3	_____
78. Gelatin	9	1	_____	7	_____
79. Fruit	15	9	_____	5	_____
80. Sliced tomato	18	4	_____	1	_____
81. Waldorf	8	5	_____	0	_____

J. Unit: 2nd Federal Bank

Day: _____

Date: _____

Item	Order	On Hand	Prepare	Left	Sold
82. Italian	22	5	_____	1	_____
83. Cucumber	24	4	_____	4	_____
84. Jellied slaw	18	2	_____	5	_____
85. Green island	16	1	_____	2	_____
86. Macaroni	12	3	_____	6	_____
87. Carrots	15	6	_____	3	_____
88. Mixed greens	14	4	_____	0	_____
89. Sunshine	26	2	_____	1	_____

K.   Unit: Western Insurance Co.

    Day: _____

    Date: _____

Item	Order	On Hand	Prepare	Left	Sold
90. Chef	32	6	_____	7	_____
91. Waldorf	18	7	_____	6	_____
92. Fruited slaw	14	8	_____	5	_____
93. Fruited gelatin	16	4	_____	1	_____
94. Sliced tomato	25	3	_____	0	_____
95. Garden	28	2	_____	2	_____
96. Italian	35	0	_____	3	_____
97. Mixed green	40	1	_____	4	_____

L.   Unit: Garrison Greeting Card Co.

    Day: _____

    Date: _____

Item	Order	On Hand	Prepare	Left	Sold
98. Tossed	35	4	_____	0	_____
99. Mixed green	25	8	_____	2	_____
100. Garden	20	6	_____	4	_____
101. Spring	22	2	_____	7	_____
102. Cottage cheese	18	0	_____	6	_____
103. Waldorf	16	3	_____	3	_____
104. Sunshine	14	0	_____	2	_____
105. Hawaiian	12	1	_____	0	_____
106. Macaroni	10	7	_____	1	_____

Counter Production Report (See Figure 13–4)

The **Counter Production Report** allows the food service manager to know the amount and value of items that were sold.

Number of Portions for Sale. This figure may be recorded by management or the person working the counter. It represents the number of on-hand items that are for sale.

Number of Portions Not Sold. This figure is recorded by the person working the counter. It is found by counting the remaining pieces of each item left after the day's service is concluded.

Number of Portions Sold. This figure is found by subtracting the number of portions not sold from the number of portions for sale. It is recorded by the person working the counter.

Value Sold. This figure is found by multiplying the number of portions sold by the unit price. It is found and recorded by the person working the counter.

Total. This figure is found by adding the figures in the Value Sold column. It is found and recorded by the person working the counter.

Customer Count. This figure is recorded on the point-of-sale (POS) registers.

Figure 13–4
Counter production report.
© Cengage Learning 2012

| Unit: Latonia Racetrack | | | | Customer Count: 405 | |
| Day: Tuesday | | | | Date: June 28, 20___ | |
Item	Number of Portions for Sale	Number of Portions Not Sold	Number of Portions Sold	Unit Price	Value Sold
Hot dogs	135	26	109	$3.25	$354.25
Chicken patty	75	15	60	5.75	345.00
Hamburgers	150	23	127	5.75	730.25
Barbecue	50	5	45	5.75	258.75
Cube steaks	70	6	64	6.25	400.00
Milk	125	18	107	1.50	160.50
Shakes	80	7	73	3.50	255.50
Soda	225	28	197	2.00	394.00
Cake	15	2	13	4.75	61.75
Pie	35	8	27	4.75	128.25
Ice cream	65	9	56	2.25	126.00
Potato chips	85	13	72	1.50	108.00
Pretzels	45	11	34	1.50	51.00
Name: Bill Thompson				Total	$3,373.25

Practice Problems 13-4 Counter Production Report

Complete the following counter production reports. Find the number of portions not sold, the value of the amount that was sold, and the total value sold at each establishment. To complete the production report, use today's day and date. Please note that the questions are numbered on the left side.

M. Unit: Stevens Processing Co.

Customer Count: 305

Day: _____

Date: _____

Item	Number of Portions for Sale	Number of Portions Not Sold	Number of Portions Sold	Unit Price	Value Sold
107. Hot dogs	85	6		$3.25	
108. Hamburgers	95	7		5.75	
109. Chicken patty	65	19		5.75	
110. Barbecue	55	2		5.75	
111. Cube steak	40	5		6.25	
112. Soda	120	21		2.00	
113. Shakes	60	8		3.50	
114. Milk	110	7		1.50	
115. Pie	48	12		4.75	
116. Ice cream	60	5		2.25	
117. Total Value Sold					

N. Unit: Wall Manufacturing Plant

Customer Count: 435

Day: _____

Date: _____

Item	Number of Portions for Sale	Number of Portions Not Sold	Number of Portions Sold	Unit Price	Value Sold
118. Hot dogs	120	6		$3.25	
119. Hamburgers	115	7		5.75	
120. Chicken patty	651	19		5.75	
121. Barbecue	557	2		5.75	
122. Cube steak	408	5		6.25	
123. Soda	1,201	21		2.00	
124. Shakes	6,090	8		3.50	
125. Milk	1,101	7		1.50	
126. Pie	4,890	12		4.75	
127. Ice cream	6,090	5		2.25	
128. Total Value Sold					

O. Unit: Deluxe Playing Card Co.

    Customer Count: 308

    Day: _____

    Date: _____

Item	Number of Portions for Sale	Number of Portions Not Sold	Number of Portions Sold	Unit Price	Value Sold
129. Hot dogs	120	19		$3.25	
130. Hamburgers	115	24		5.75	
131. Chicken patty	651	38		5.75	
132. Barbecue	557	5		5.75	
133. Cube steak	408	17		6.25	
134. Soda	1,201	42		2.00	
135. Shakes	6,090	5		3.50	
136. Milk	1,101	23		1.50	
137. Pie	4,890	16		4.75	
138. Ice cream	6,090	125		2.25	
139. Total Value Sold					

P. Unit: United Shoe Co.

    Customer Count: 390

    Day: _____

    Date: _____

Item	Number of Portions for Sale	Number of Portions Not Sold	Number of Portions Sold	Unit Price	Value Sold
140. Hot dogs	175	19		$3.25	
141. Hamburgers	195	24		5.75	
142. Chicken patty	751	38		5.75	
143. Barbecue	587	5		5.75	
144. Cube steak	427	17		6.25	
145. Soda	1,238	42		2.00	
146. Shakes	6,290	5		3.50	
147. Milk	1,025	23		1.50	
148. Pie	4,792	16		4.75	
149. Ice cream	6,193	125		2.25	
150. Total Value Sold					

Discussion Question 13-1

With the availability of POS registers and computers, what is the value of the staff learning how to compute the production reports themselves? What is the value for managers?

Alcoholic Beverages and Controlling Costs

In the hospitality profession, selling alcoholic beverages is an area that can be quite profitable; however, it also lends itself to a tremendous opportunity for theft and loss of revenue. Therefore, the manager must be knowledgeable about and vigilant of all types of alcoholic beverage service. He or she must know the types of alcohol that can be sold. The manager must also know the size of the alcohol beverage containers so beverage costs can be calculated. Because most alcoholic beverages are sold in standard metric measurements, the manager must know how many U.S. fluid ounces are in the metric bottle. Because there is an enormous opportunity for theft and loss of money in an alcoholic beverage operation, the manager must know how to determine if an employee is stealing from the business. In addition to having to control costs, the manager has to be aware of the laws of the jurisdiction (country, state, and municipality) that allow the business to sell alcoholic beverages. This section will not discuss these laws. Readers are encouraged to consult their local jurisdictions for specific laws relating to the location of their business.

General Types of Alcoholic Beverages

The hospitality business generally sells three categories of alcoholic beverages: spirits, wine, and beer. Some establishments will sell all three types of alcoholic beverages, while others will sell only wine and beer.

Spirits can be thought of as alcoholic ingredients that are used to make mixed drinks. Some examples of these are scotch, rye, vodka, bourbon, and gin. At times, these alcoholic beverages are served by themselves, such as a shot of bourbon. At other times, spirits are mixed with other ingredients such as vermouth, soda water, and tonic. Most establishments that serve spirits use a bottle size of *750 milliliters or 750 ml. This size of bottle contains 25.4 U.S. fluid ounces.* Chefs create a recipe using portion size. When a beverage manager creates a drink recipe, he or she has to determine how many ounces of a spirit will be used. The amount could range from 1 to 4 ounces. The recipe will determine how many drinks can be obtained from a 750-ml bottle of spirits. Other alcoholic beverages are sold in a **liter bottle.** *This bottle has 33.8 U.S. fluid ounces.*

The consumption of wine in the world, and especially in the United States, continues to increase. Many establishments sell wine by the glass and the bottle to meet the increasing demands. Establishments use a half bottle *(which holds 375 ml or 12.7 U.S. fluid ounces)* or the 750-ml bottle. There are other restaurants that sell wine by the carafe, which contains either a half liter or a full liter. As with spirits, the beverage manager has to determine how much wine to pour when guests order wine by the glass. Complicating this decision is that glass sizes in most establishments are sold by the manufacturer to the establishment in a U.S. fluid ounce size. The bar manager has to determine the number of ounces that will be poured into the glass when the establishment uses a 12-ounce glass. The manager also has to be able to determine how many glasses of wine can be obtained from the 750-ml bottle. There are other sizes of wine bottles that wineries produce for different occasions. They range from the magnum, which is the size of two standard 750 ml bottles, to the Nebuchadnezzar, which is the size of twenty 750-ml bottles.

Beer sales pose a unique challenge for the beverage manager. Beer can be sold by the individual bottle, can, or by a glass or mug. The individual bottle is not difficult for a bar manager to control or figure out costs. Generally, bottled or canned beer is sold to the establishment by count; that is, 24 bottles to a case. Reports that have already been discussed in this chapter could be modified for the sale of bottled or canned beer. The challenge comes with selling beer by the glass. Glass sizes vary. There are pints, and some establishments use a glass called a yard, which literally is a yard in length. Beer served in this manner is usually obtained from a barrel or keg.

The beverage manager must know that a *barrel of beer contains 3,968 U.S. fluid ounces* and a half-barrel (commonly called a *keg*) *contains 1,984 ounces*. To control costs, bar managers determine the ounces of beer that they will serve in a glass or a mug, thereby having a good idea of how many servings they will get from a barrel or a keg. They also take into consideration how much waste they will allow for faulty pouring or spilling.

Once beverage managers determine the yield that they will obtain from the barrel or keg, they control their costs by various methods. One common method that is used at sporting events is to give employees a specific amount of cups. The employees, at the end of the shift, must return their remaining cups. The amount of beer sold should equal the amount of cups used for the shift. This type of control can be used for any beverage in which a beverage is served from a large container. A report can be devised that can be used by the managers of the company to verify the amount of sales of beer at the sporting event and to prevent theft.

Determining the Beverage Cost Percentage

This procedure is the same as determining food or labor costs. The mathematical operation is simple if two facts are known. First, the manager must know the size of the portion of beverage that will be served to the guest. Second, the manager must be aware of the cost that the establishment paid for all the raw ingredients that are used to create the menu item. For example, our restaurant will serve our guests an 8-ounce glass of wine (this is the first known fact). Our restaurant buys wine in a 750-ml bottle, and each bottle costs $5.49 (this is the second known fact). By using division and multiplication, the cost of a glass of wine in our restaurant can be determined.

Step 1:   Divide the number of ounces in 750 ml (25.4 U.S. fluid ounces) into the cost of the wine ($5.49).

$5.49 ÷ 25.4 = 0.216 cents per ounce for the wine

Step 2:   Multiply the size of the portion (8 ounces) by the cost per ounce of wine (0.216 cents).

$$8 \times 0.216 = \$1.728 \text{ or } \$1.73$$

Each 8-ounce glass of wine that is consumed (whether it is sold or given away) costs our restaurant $1.73 cents.

Step 3:   Divide the cost of the wine by the menu price of the wine. For example, our establishment sells our 8-ounce glass of wine for $7.50. To figure out our cost, we take the $1.73 and divide it by $7.50.

$$\$1.73 \div 7.50 = 0.2306 \text{ wine percentage cost} = 23.06\%$$

The bar manager should be responsible for determining the desired beverage costs for all spirits, wine, and beer. It is recommended that the bar manager determine the beverage cost for *each and every alcoholic beverage,* whether it is a martini, gin and tonic, liter of wine, glass of wine, or pitcher of beer. Once standards have been set for each item, the beverage manager can verify the beverage cost percentages. If there is a variation in the percentages or if the beverage costs are too high, the manager must take steps to determine where the problem is occurring. Once the manager identifies where the problem is occurring, steps must be taken to control the costs. The general formula for finding out the beverage cost percentage is as follows:

Cost of Alcoholic Beverages ÷ Total Sales = Beverage Cost Percentage

Potential Areas of Theft with Alcoholic Beverages

Once the beverage manager determines that the beverage costs do not match the desired cost percentages, an investigation must be undertaken to determine where the loss of alcoholic beverage revenue (called **slippage**) is occurring. There are many areas that can cause beverage costs to be out of line. Some reasons for this occurring are legitimate, while other slippage occurs because of theft. The authors will explain a few of the ways in which slippage of alcoholic beverages can occur, but be aware that there are others.

All beverage operations must have a control system in place to verify that the alcoholic beverages that are being sold are actually the property of the establishment. There have been instances where bartenders have brought their own liquor bottles in from home, sold drinks from their bottle, and put the sales revenue in their pocket. To control this situation, establishments have a policy that bottles are stamped with a unique code. When a new bottle of alcohol is requisitioned, the empty bottle with the proper stamp must be returned.

One of the common methods for theft is that bartenders simply do not charge the guest for the drink, or if they do, they do not ring up the drink in the POS system. If the manager observes that a bartender is making change from his or her "own bank," or if the POS drawer is left open, the bartender may be stealing. Most of the time, this problem is identified through the use of undercover agents or mystery shoppers. Another tipoff is that if the bartender has some sort of unique counting system, such as toothpicks next to the POS or a plate of fruit (where a cherry represents a spirit sale; an orange a wine sale, etc.). This problem can be solved by the manager taking the cash drawer from the register and taking a reading of how much money should be in it. Generally, with the fruit and toothpicks "system," there is more money in the register than the sales that have been rung up. The bartender waits until it gets quiet in the bar to take out the amount of money that he or she is stealing from the establishment. The mystery shopper can also report on whether the bartender is giving away free drinks or if he or she is overpouring or overportioning drinks. However, by no means are the above methods the only ways that beverage costs can go out of line. It is imperative for the bar manager to control beverage costs on a daily basis.

Practice Problems 13–5   Alcoholic Beverages and Controlling Costs

Answer the following questions.

151. How many ounces are in a 750-ml bottle? _____

152. How many ounces are in a liter? _____

153. How many ounces are in a barrel of beer? _____

154. How many ounces are in a keg of beer? _____

155. How many ounces are in a magnum of wine? _____

156. How many ounces are in a Nebuchadnezzar of wine? _____

For the following questions, calculate the beverage costs. Round off each answer to the hundredths place.

157. The menu price of a glass of wine is $5.95. The raw cost of the wine is $1.50. Find the wine cost percentage. _____

158. The menu price for a 750-ml bottle of wine is $130. The raw cost of the wine is $30.25. Find the wine cost percentage. _____

159. Ideally, how many 8-ounce cups of beer can be obtained from a keg if there is no waste?

   _____

160. How many glasses of wine can be obtained from a liter of wine if each guest receives a 7-ounce glass of wine? _____

161. Each cup of beer sells for $5.50. Our establishment gives an employee 240 cups, and she returns 25. How much money should be turned in as sales income from a full keg of beer? _____

162. The total cost of all beer purchased for the day is $1,520, and total sales for the day is $350. Find the daily beer cost percentage. _____

163. The total cost of all wine purchased for the day is $426, and total sales for the day is $989.50. Find the daily wine cost percentage. _____

164. The total cost of all alcoholic beverages purchased for the day is $20, and total sales for the day are $1,942.78. Find the daily alcohol cost percentage. _____

The following questions refer to the variance chart (Figure 11–7) that was presented in Chapter 11. This chart can also be used to control alcoholic beverage costs.

Complete the chart, figuring both the percent and the variance for each category. Round off all answers to the fourth place after the decimal point. For instance, if the answer is 0.29748, go to the fifth number to the right of the decimal and use that number to round off to the fourth number to the right of the decimal. Now the answer is 0.2975. Next, convert 0.2975 to a percentage. Therefore, the final answer would be 29.75 percent.

Purchases by Category for the Month of January
As of January 31

Total Sales	$228,291.75			
Category	**Amount Purchased**	**Percent**	**Goal**	**Variance**
Wine	52,725.38		14%	
Beer	26,263.34		4%	
Spirits	32,627.85		6%	
Total			24%	

165. What is the alcoholic beverage cost percentage for wine? _____

166. What is the variance for wine? _____

167. What is the alcoholic beverage cost percentage for beer? _____

168. What is the variance for beer? _____

169. What is the alcoholic beverage cost percentage for spirits? _____

170. What is the total amount of purchases for the month? _____

171. What is the alcoholic beverage cost percent for the month? _____

172. What is the total variance for the month? _____

Discussion Question 13-2

Based upon your answers from problems 165 through 172, are there any concerns that the bar manager should be aware of with the alcoholic cost percentages? If there are concerns, what categories would you recommend that management review to determine where the problem occurs? What steps should management take to solve the problems?

Essentials of Managerial Math

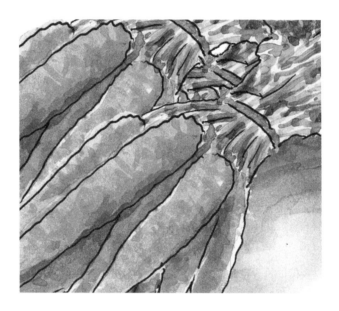

People are attracted to the idea of running or working in a food service establishment because they have heard that it offers excellent food; competent, friendly hospitality and a positive price-value relationship; and, perhaps, an attractive atmosphere. The customers may keep coming, but this does not necessarily ensure a successful operation. Behind these necessary elements must be skilled management—an individual or team that can direct people, provide efficient service, and control both money and material so that a profit can be made. In this section of the text, the emphasis is on the math functions that help management control money and material and at the same time provide the records necessary for a good accounting system. In addition, information will be presented concerning personal taxes, payroll, and financial reports.

Not all food service students have the desire or ability to manage a food service establishment. However, it is helpful to learn management procedures to better understand the functions of management and to know what makes a successful operation. With this knowledge, you can become a better food service employee, which may lead to a position of greater responsibility.

fourteen

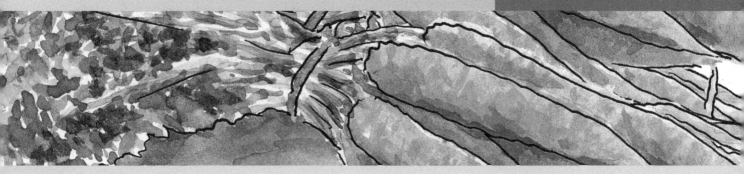

Front of the House and Managerial Mathematical Operations

Objectives

At the completion of this chapter, the student should be able to:

1. Identify how guest checks are controlled.
2. Compare and contrast old method versus new methods in guest check writing.
3. Calculate guest checks.
4. Calculate sales tax and gratuity.
5. Back out sales tax and gratuity.
6. Identify the terms *minimum* and *cover charge*.
7. Identify items on the daily cash report.
8. Complete and calculate a daily cash report.
9. Identify and fill out a deposit slip.
10. Write a check.
11. Identify the items on a bank statement.
12. Identify and balance a check register.

Key Words

point-of-sales (POS)	tipping	cash in drawer	deposit slip
guest check	gratuity	over or short	interest
receipts	cashier's daily report	all-inclusive	check
cover charge	gross receipts	expenditures	check register
minimum charge	bank	savings or checking	
sales tax	cash paid outs	account	

As creatively as the culinary staff prepares the food and as good as it tastes, someone has to serve the food, collect the guest check, and account for the amount of money paid for the superb culinary creations. There has to be a partnership among the culinary staff, the front of the house (waitstaff, counter people, cashiers, etc.), and managerial employees to collect and account for the revenue received from the guests. This is necessary to exceed the costs of doing business and to make a profit. There are many different types of operations in the food service business. The procedures discussed in this chapter are used in traditional, quick, or casual service restaurants; banquet facilities; city or country clubs; business and industry accounts; or hospital and sports venues. The list can be expanded to any operation that serves and charges guests for food and beverages. The purpose of this chapter is to explain the importance of mathematical skills to the front of the house and managerial employees. These skills will enable employees to calculate and account for money earned by the waitstaff, as well as the business.

Waitstaff Mathematical Operations

Most food service operations have **point-of-sales (POS)** computers, used by the waitstaff to calculate the amount of the guest checks. Some establishments still prefer the system of using handwritten checks. Regardless of the methods used to keep track of and calculate the guests' orders, the waitstaff may use all four basic mathematical operations (addition, subtraction, multiplication, and division) to perform their jobs effectively. In addition, the knowledge of percentage calculation is of utmost importance because most waitstaffs' pay depend on receiving a percentage of the guest or banquet check. Some individuals argue that knowledge of math is not needed because of modern technology (such as POS computers), but the authors believe that all waitstaff should know how to do these mathematical operations. This knowledge is required when the waitperson has to calculate guest checks in the event of a power failure or a computer crash. More important to the waitperson, however, is knowing how to determine how much money is owed to him or her when a gratuity is automatically added onto the check.

Guest Check

In the food service industry, the bill or bill of sale is called a **guest check.** It is a list of items ordered and the cost of those items tallied when dining in a food service establishment. (See Figure 14–1.) In addition, a guest check will have other information listed on it. This information will be pointed out when explaining the types of checks usually used in the industry. The appearance of a guest check will vary from simple to elaborate, depending on the type and kind of operation. From the roadside truck stop to the gourmet restaurant, guest checks are in use and presented at the conclusion of the meal. There are exceptions, however, such as quick and casual service restaurants and buffet-type restaurants, where the guest has to pay for the food and beverages before they are received.

Guest Check Responsibility

Regardless of whether the food service operation is using a POS computer or a guest check that is written and totaled by the waitperson, controls must be in place to eliminate theft by members of the waitstaff and cashiers.

Guest checks are the responsibility of the waitperson. Although other employees are guided by the information listed on the check during and after the dining period, the waitperson is held responsible for its safekeeping. If a guest walks out without paying or if a check is misplaced or lost, the waitperson may be required to pay the amount due.

If the food service establishment is using handwritten guest checks, the following procedure should be put in place to prevent theft: At the beginning of the dining period, the waitperson is issued a book or stack of blank checks with serial numbers on them. (See Figure 14–2.) Each individual check is numbered consecutively. The waitperson should sign for each book or stack of checks received. In this way, management can account for each check issued. If a check is missing, it will indicate which person is responsible. At the end of the day, or at the end of a service period, the checks are reviewed to determine whether any are missing or contain any errors. Numbering checks and being able to identify the person responsible for each check are also important in checking the daily **receipts** and assisting the accounting department or accountant in finding and correcting any errors.

With a POS system, each waitperson is assigned a personal number or code that identifies him or her, which makes the waitperson accountable for each electronic guest check. This code must be entered into the POS in order to process a guest check. The waitperson must enter all vital information, such as the table number and the guests' order. Figure 14–1 shows that Devin (server number 1283) was the waitperson, and the check was numbered 9834. The POS will keep track of the status of the guest checks, whether they are closed or open. In simple terms, a closed check means that the bill has been paid; an open check means that the guest has not yet paid the bill. It is easy for managers to see which waitpersons have not turned in their (still opened) guest checks. Regardless of the system being used, a waitperson should never destroy or discard a check without receiving permission from the supervisor. The authors emphasize that controls are necessary in any business operation. Accounting for guest checks, whether written or computer-generated, is essential to have a successful business.

```
              Pavilion
            The Sagamore

    1283 DEVIN
    ---------------------------------
    TBL 4/1     CHK 9834 GST 2
          JUL12   12:44PM
    ---------------------------------

      1 CHARD PRIVATE        7.00
      1 HONIG SAUV BLANC     7.50
      1 COCONUT SHRIMP       8.25
      2 TURK/BACON  WRAP    16.50

      Food                 24.75
      Wine                 14.50
      18% Service Chg       7.07
      7% Tax                2.75
      Total Due    $49.07

       Automatic 18% gratuity
       is included. Additional
       tip is at your discretion.

     Add'l Tip:  $_____

      Room Number: _____

     Print Name: _____

     Signature : _____
```

Figure 14–1
Point-of-sales guest check.
© Cengage Learning 2012

Figure 14–2
Blank check.
© Cengage Learning 2012

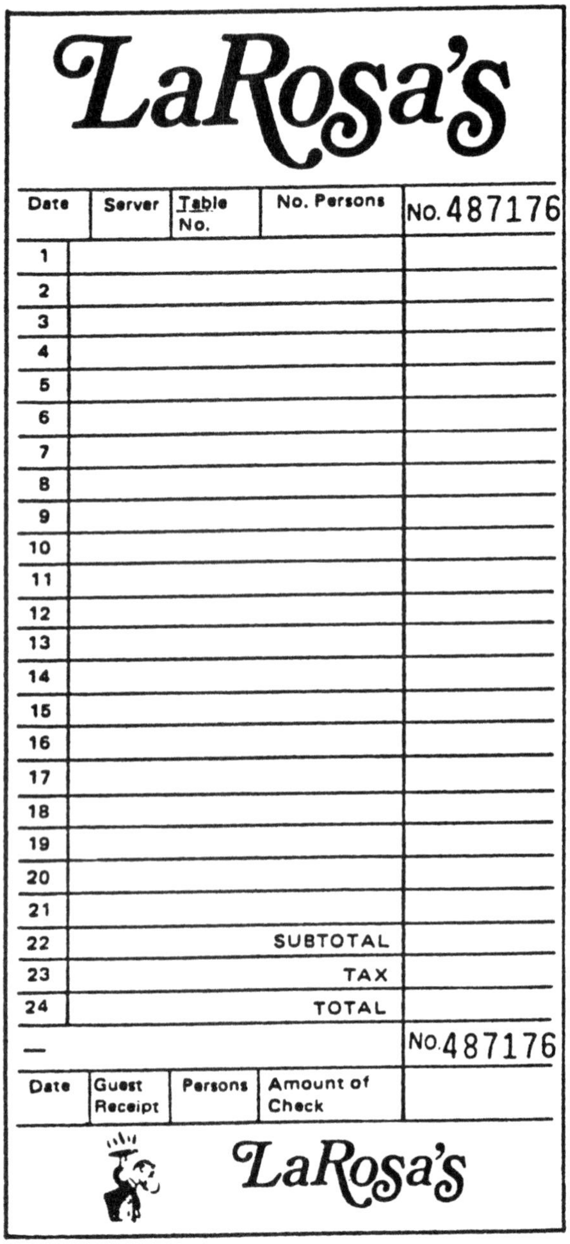

Minimum or Cover Charge

Establishments featuring live music, a floor show, or some special type of entertainment usually add a **cover charge** to the check. The cover charge is a form of admission fee charged to each person to help pay for the cost of the entertainment. Another method of collecting for entertainment or service is by having a **minimum charge.** This means that a guest is required to spend a certain amount of money, once seated, even if the total check amounts to less. For example, if the minimum charge is $15.00, but the check amounts to only $4.25, the guest is still required to pay the $15.00 minimum charge.

Calculating Guest Checks

In calculating guest checks, two mathematical operations are normally used: multiplication and addition. Figure 14–3 illustrates a bill that shows the operations of multiplication and addition. The first ordered item on the guest check is for

"3 Clos Du Bois Merlot" that cost $103.50. The POS is programmed to multiply the quantity by the cost of the individual bottle of wine. The cost of each item has been put into the POS (programmed) by management. In our example, the cost of one bottle was $34.50, so the total was calculated by multiplying $34.50 by 3. As each new item was added to the guest bill, the total amount of that item or items was multiplied to arrive at the subtotal. When the guests had completed their meal, the bill was added to obtain a subtotal. In Figure 14–3, the tax was added to the guest check, and a final total was printed.

There are times when a waitperson will also have to use the mathematical operation of subtraction. Subtraction will occur when an establishment offers a discount, coupon, or some type of reduction on the guest check. In this instance, the discount amount has to be subtracted from the original total.

```
        TRELLIS  RESTAURANT
            MERCHANT'S SQUARE

   0383     Table 42   #Party 8
   BRYAN S     SvrCk: 19 18:58 12/30


   3 CLOS DU BOIS MERLOT        103.50
   3 LENTIL APPETIZER            23.85
   1 CHOWDER                      4.95
   2 SAUSAGE APPETIZER           17.50
   1 SHRIMP APPETIZER             9.50
   1 TROUT APPETIZER              8.95
   6 PORK ENTREE                112.50
   1 DUCK ENTREE, med well       24.50
   1 WINTER SUPPER               20.00
   2 ICE CREAM                    7.90
   1 BALLOON                      4.95
   1 PASTRY 5.95                  5.95
   4 DEATH BY CHOCOLATE          22.00
   5 COFFEE                       9.75
   1 hot tea                      1.95
   1 GL/SUDUIRAUT                11.50
   1 GALLIANO, rocks              5.00

                    Sub Total:  394.25
                         TX1:    37.45
   12/30 20:29  TOTAL:  431.70

   DESSERTS TO GO
   DAZZLING CAKES BY THE SLICE
   COLOSSAL COOKIES, ONE OR A DOZEN
   ICE CREAM AND SORBETS BY THE CUP OR PINT

   CHECK  NUMBER:    383
```

Figure 14–3
Printed check used for computerized cash register.
© Cengage Learning 2012

Practice Problems 14–1 Calculating Guest Checks

Calculate the food and beverage totals on the following guest checks.

1. Three guests had lunch at the Lake Resort. They each had one order of coconut shrimp @ $8.25 as an appetizer; two glasses of Sauvignon Blanc @ $7.50 each; and three glasses of Chardonnay @ $7.00 each. For their main courses, they each had a turkey bacon wrap @ $8.75, a club sandwich @ $10.95, and a chicken wrap @ $8.50. _____

2. Two guests ordered a ½ bottle of Chianti at $21.00; a bruschetta @ $6.95; an entrée portion of sausage con verde @ $11.95, and a lunch portion of sausage con verde @ $8.95.
   _____

3. Four guests dined at a golf club for lunch. They had three pints of Saranac Pale Ale, which cost $4.50 each; one iced tea @ $2.00; two Birdies @ $9.95 each; and two Bunkers @ $10.50 each.
   _____

4. Two guests had dinner, and they had an entertainment card that qualified them for a $14.00 discount. The guests had three glasses of Camelot Pinot Noir @ $6.25 each; a veal artichoke entrée @ $16.95; and a pork tenderloin entrée @ $18.95.
   _____

5. Four guests went to a buffet show at a casino. The cost of the buffet was $22.95 each. The minimum charge was $30.00 for each person.
   _____

Calculating Sales Tax

Most states and many municipalities have passed laws that mandate that the food service establishment collect a percentage of the guest bill in the form of **sales taxes.** The percentage amount is not the same in each municipality; even the items that have to be taxed are different. The food service professional must know what is taxed and what is exempt from tax in the municipality in which his or her business is being conducted. Knowing how to multiply using percentages is essential in determining the amount of tax that must be added to the subtotal of the guest check. For example, consider the following scenario:

Bob and Dolores received a dinner check at the Blue Star Restaurant for $30.75. The sales tax for that particular state is 6 percent. How much tax did they pay? What was the total bill?

$30.75 Cost of two dinners
× 0.06 6% sales tax
$1.8450 = $1.85 amount of tax

$30.75 Cost of two dinners
+ 1.85 Amount of tax
$32.60 Total bill

Amount purchased + Amount of tax = Total bill

Practice Problems 14–2 Calculating Sales Tax

Calculate the sales tax and compute the total amount of the guest check for each problem in Practice Problems 14–1. Round off each answer to the hundredths place.

6. Sales tax of 6.5 percent of the total from problem 1.
   Sales tax amount _____ Guest check total _____

7. Sales tax of 8.25 percent of the total from problem 2.
   Sales tax amount _____ Guest check total _____

8. Sales tax of 5.5 percent of the total from problem 3.
   Sales tax amount _____ Guest check total _____

9. Sales tax of 7.125 percent of the total from problem 4.
   Sales tax amount _____ Guest check total _____

10. Sales tax of 6.75 percent of the total from problem 5.
    Sales tax amount _____ Guest check total _____

Tipping, Gratuity, Service Charge, and Administrative Fees

Tipping, also referred to as a **gratuity,** is the giving of a fee for a service rendered. By law, it is defined as an amount of money given voluntarily by the customers to the waitperson for waiting on them. Many à la carte restaurants add the gratuity onto the guest check automatically for larger parties. In many restaurants, a statement like the following is printed on the menu: "A gratuity of 18 percent will be automatically added to your check for parties of six guests or more."

However, a gratuity or service charge of a specified amount or percentage is never mandatory unless it is spelled out in advance in a written, signed contract, as is common with banquets. Merely printing a statement on the menu that an automatic gratuity will apply is not a legally enforceable contract. There are specific cases in New York and Pennsylvania where patrons refused to pay the automatic gratuity added onto the check because of perceived poor service. Subsequently, the patrons were arrested for theft of services.

For example, the *Albany Times Union* on November 20, 2008, reported a case in Lake George, New York. In 2003, a patron of Soprano's Italian and American Grill was arrested for misdemeanor theft of services after he argued that requiring an 18 percent tip for large parties was not legal. The Warren County district attorney dropped the charges after determining the patron could not be forced to pay a gratuity.

To Insure Perfect Solutions

To figure out a 15 percent tip quickly:

1. Use the cost of the food and beverage on the guest check (such as $240.00).
2. Take a look at the first two numbers, which equal 24.
3. Divide by 2, which equals 12.
4. Add the 12 to the 24; hence, the 15 percent tip is $36.00.
5. If you get great service and want to leave a 20 percent tip, just take the first two numbers and multiply them by 2.

Figure 14–4

Computerized register receipt with suggested tips.

© Cengage Learning 2012

Most patrons of a restaurant tip based on a percentage of the total check. The accepted practice used to be 15 percent, but in recent years, inflation has even found its way into this old custom. Now the accepted practice is 15 to 20 percent. Some establishments automatically add 15 to 20 percent of the check amount to the bill. If this is done, guests should be made aware of this policy before they are served. Often, when the tip is added to the check, the guest is unaware of this policy and still leaves a tip at the table. If the gratuity is added automatically to the check, the gratuity can be calculated only on the amount of food and beverage, not including the tax.

For the guest who wishes to tip 15 or 20 percent of the amount of the check, or for the waitperson who is asked to figure the amount, there is an easy way to do this without a calculator. First, find 10 percent of the bill by moving the decimal point in the total bill one place to the left. Next, take half of the figure just found, and add the two figures together if the tip is to be 15 percent. If the tip is to be 20 percent, just double the 10 percent amount.

For example: The total bill is $18.00. To find 10 percent, move the decimal one place to the left, yielding $1.80. Half of $1.80 is $0.90. Add the two together, $1.80 + 0.90 = $2.70, the amount of the 15 percent tip. If tipping 20 percent, take the amount found for 10 percent, $1.80, and double it. $1.80 × $1.80 = $3.60, the amount of the 20 percent tip.

Computerized registers may be programmed to print out suggested amounts of tips at the bottom of the receipt. (See Figure 14–4.)

```
SERVICE AMERICA CORP

BEL AQU SAR RACTRACK 34

300 UNION AVE

SARATOGA SPRINGS, NY 12866

AMOUNT: $47.88

TIP TABLE PROVIDED FOR YOUR

CONVENIENCE

15%=$7.18      20%=$9.58      25%=$11.97
```

In banquet service, a service charge is almost always added automatically onto the bill. This practice has become common and is legal because the patrons sign a contract in advance agreeing to the extra charge. However, a controversy has arisen about the distribution of the amount and percentage of the service charge to the individual members of the staff, especially in New York State.

The legal consul for the New York State Restaurant Association (NYSRA), Labor & Monitoring Consultants, LLC, recommends the use of the term *administrative fee* instead of *service charge* on all banquet contracts. Recent enforcement actions and determinations made by the New York State Department of Labor are treating service charges the same as gratuities, indicating that they must be distributed only to the waitstaff and "similar employees" serving the banquet or special function. The reason for the proposed change is that for banquets, the service charge or administrative fee was split among the banquet manager, the chef, and the waitstaff instead of all of the money being paid to the waitstaff. The authors recommend that food service professionals consult their lawyers to comply with the language and the laws in their municipality.

Practice Problems 14–3 Calculating Tips

Find the amount of tip for each of the following bills if the tip equals 15 percent of the bill. Round off each answer to the hundredths place.

11. $12.00 _____   16. $52.85 _____

12. $20.00 _____   17. $70.65 _____

13. $24.25 _____   18. $82.60 _____

14. $30.25 _____   19. $105.40 _____

15. $32.50 _____   20. $125.50 _____

Tipping

Guests, for the most part, generally tip 15 to 20 percent regardless of the service that they receive. Some guests will tip more for exceptional service, some less for poor service. If a waitstaff's gratuity depends on the amount of the guest check, then they should be encouraged to sell more items in order to increase their income (which will also increase the establishment's income)! This is another reason for the food service professional to understand and use math. It can serve as a motivational tool. For example, if one additional $30.00 bottle of wine is sold and the guest leaves an 18 percent tip, the waitperson will make an additional $5.40. To understand this concept, complete Practice Problems 14–4.

Practice Problems 14–4 Tipping and Income

Calculate the additional tip for each server, using logic and multiplication to solve the problems. Question 4 also requires addition. Round off each answer to the hundredths place.

21. Marisa works three shifts a week. If she sells nine additional $35.00 bottles of wine a night and the gratuity is 18 percent, what is her additional income?

 Each shift _____ Weekly total _____

22. Joe works five shifts a week. He sells 10 additional $7.00 desserts each shift. If the gratuity is 15 percent, what is his additional income?

 Each shift _____ Weekly total _____

23. Valerie works four shifts a week. She sells 20 additional $7.95 appetizers each shift. If the gratuity is 16 percent, what is her additional income?

 Each shift _____ Weekly total _____

24. Antonio works seven shifts a week. He sells 20 additional $45.00 bottles of wine during the week. He also sells 12 additional $8.50 desserts each shift and 15 additional $9.50 appetizers each shift. If the gratuity is 20 percent, what is his additional income?

 Wine_____ Desserts _____ Appetizers _____Weekly income _____

Checking the Amount of the Gratuity

If your income depends upon receiving gratuities and the gratuity is automatically added to the check, you should know how to calculate the gratuity and determine if you have been paid the correct amount by the establishment. When waitstaff receive their total gratuity at the end of the pay period, they should check to make certain they've received all the gratuities coming to them. Using a percentage to find the total amount of the checks, when only the tip is known, is one way for the waitperson to check that the gratuity is correct.

This is the formula that you will use when you know the percent and the amount of the gratuity:

Amount of tip ÷ Percent = Amount of check

For example:

A gratuity of 15 percent is automatically added onto all guest checks. The amount of the tip was $2.00. How much was the check?

Solution:

Change 15 percent to 0.15. Divide 0.15 into the amount of the tip, which was $2.00.

$$
\begin{array}{r}
\$13.333 \\
0.15\overline{)\ 2.000} \\
-1\ 5 \\
\hline
50 \\
-45 \\
\hline
50 \\
-45 \\
\hline
\end{array}
$$

This procedure will result in the quotient, which is the total amount of the check: $13.33.

Practice Problems 14–5   Determining the Total Amount of the Check

Find the total amount of each check. Round off each answer to the hundredths place.

25. The amount of gratuity received was $18.25. How much was the check if the gratuity was 15 percent?

    _____

26. The amount of gratuity received was $16.50. How much was the check if the gratuity was 18 percent?

    _____

27. The amount of gratuity received was $12.26. How much was the check if the gratuity was 20 percent?

    _____

28. The amount of gratuity received was $29.17. How much was the check if the gratuity was 18 percent?

    _____

29. The amount of gratuity received was $218.25. How much was the check if the gratuity was 18 percent?

    _____

Discussion Question 14-1

You are a waitperson at a restaurant with a check average of $60.00 per person. A gratuity of 18 percent is automatically added onto each check. You worked five shifts and served a total of 168 guests during the week. Your paycheck summary states that the gratuity is $814.40. What would you do?

Cashier's Mathematical Operations

At the end of each day or each service period, the cashier is required to fill out a **cashier's daily report.** The report is a tool used by management to keep track of cash and charge sales. Its purpose is to determine whether the actual amount of cash in the register drawer equals the total amount of cash sales made during a specific time period, as well as whether all sales (cash and charges) show the same total that the register prints out. In the past, the largest percentage of sales was cash. Today, credit card sales may exceed cash sales.

The cashier's daily report may show a very small amount of cash over or under what should be in the cash register. With the constant exchange of cash between the guests and the cashier, small mistakes may occur. Management should become concerned when amounts exceed a couple of dollars. The report is designed not only to protect the business operator from theft, but also to protect the cashier from being suspected of stealing. If the cashier makes a costly mistake, the error can usually be found by checking the daily report. The cashier's daily report shows information that will assist the accountant or accounting department when filling out financial statements at the end of a financial period.

"Math is at the core of all successful businesses. We make decisions based on financial performance, which is predicated ultimately on daily cash sales reports. We add, subtract, multiply, and divide to obtain food, labor, and controllable percentages. These percentages are the basis of decisions that will affect the bottom line of your operation. It makes sense—we must do the math and do it correctly.

All the hard work in both the front and the back of the house would be for naught without current, accurate, and verified bank deposits from the daily cash register tapes. If you are the owner, manager, or the chef manager, insist on accurate daily cash reports. Anything less, and the integrity of your operation will be compromised. As managers, we are paid to make decisions. Without accurate, daily verified bank deposits, these decisions are jeopardized.

In this age of ultimate technological devices, it remains imperative for us to utilize these tools to our advantage. Whether it is a POS system or an Excel spreadsheet, we need to ensure that the fundamental business math rule that our revenues exceed our expenses' is constantly monitored. Invest the time . . . it may be your employment career that is in the balance."

James V. Bigley
Vice President
HMB Consultants
Voorheesville, NY

HMB Consultants assists self-operated school districts (college and K–12) in assessing and fine-tuning their food service operations. This company analyzes and makes recommendations to the school districts, both for financial and operational success. HMB Consultants assists school districts from Washington, D.C., to the Canadian border.

The Daily Cash Report

There are many different types of cashier's daily reports in use, since each establishment creates its own form that is best suited for its particular operation. For example, some operations may keep charge sales separate from the cash sales so that the actual cash in the register drawer can be determined more easily. In general, however, all forms will contain the same information. An example of a typical report is given in Figure 14–5. Students should be knowledgeable about accounting for credit card sales. Credit card receipts represent money taken in by the establishment in place of cash. On the daily cash report, there should be a place to enter both gift certificates that are sold and those that are redeemed. All credit card receipts have to be recorded. They should be broken down by companies—for example, American Express, MasterCard, and so forth. The total of each company's receipts should be listed on a separate line on the daily cash receipt form. When the food service establishment pays out tips in cash to the waitstaff, the cash amount should be recorded as cash paid outs.

Figure 14–5
Cashier's daily report.
© Cengage Learning 2012

Today's date _____	
POS Register Readings or Total of Guest Check Sales	
Food Sales	$2,035.78
Beverage Sales	3,015.95
Gift Certificate Sales	257.00
Total Sales	5,308.73
Add the Amount of Sales Tax	451.24
Gross Receipts	5,759.97
Add Start of Shift Money (Bank)	200.00
Total of Gross Receipts and Money Started With (Bank)	5,959.97
Cash Collected from Guest Checks During the Shift	689.25
Less Total Cash Paid Out	157.00
Total Cash in Drawer	532.25
Credit Card Receipts	
American Express	2,270.72
Discover	450.00
MasterCard	25.00
Visa	1,750.00
Gift Certificates (Redeemed)	732.00
Total Charge and Gift Certificate Receipts	5,227.72
Add Cash in Drawer	532.25
Total Cash and Charges (Should Equal the Amount of Gross Receipts)	5,759.97
Over or (Short)	0.00
Record of Cash Paid Out	
City Ice Company	25.00
Tips	132.00
Arkay Florist	0.00
Other	0.00
Total Cash Paid Out	157.00
Signed by: Thomas Kearney	

Items on the Daily Cash Report

The items listed on the daily cash report example are those most important to the food service operator. (See Figure 14–5.) These items will appear on most reports. An explanation of each is given.

Explanation of Items on Report

POS Register Readings or Total of Guest Check Sales.   Receipts are taken from the register. With the versatile and sometimes computerized registers in use today, items can be categorized, rung up, and totaled separately or together. For operations that do not have a computerized register, the guest checks have to be totaled.

Gross Receipts.   Gross receipts are a total of all separate register readings. The gross is the total before any deductions are made. In our example, **gross receipts** are a total of the amounts collected for food, beverages, gift certificates, and sales taxes. (See Figure 14–5.) Some operations may have a separate accounting line for items like clothing or books, or a category called Miscellaneous (this category is not included in Figure 14–5).

Add—Start of Shift Money (Bank).   An amount of money is placed into the POS register before any sales are made. It consists of both paper currency and coins. The purpose of the **bank** is to enable the cashier to make change during the dining period. The amount of money of the bank is the same amount at the beginning of the day and at the end of the day after all transactions have been calculated.

Cash Collected During the Shift.   This amount represents the cash that should be in the cash register drawer after adding the amount of cash received from guests before any paid outs are made.

Less—Cash Paid Outs.   The **cash paid outs** figure is acquired by totaling the amounts of money paid out of the register during the day. When a paid out occurs, a record must be made of the transaction by recording it on a report in the section headed "Record of Cash Paid Outs." For each cash paid out, the cashier should have a receipted bill, invoice, or cash payment voucher. Most registers have a key for recording paid outs. The total amount of paid outs on the report should equal the total amount of paid outs recorded by the register. Paid outs are subtracted from the total cash because this money was taken out of the register drawer.

Total Cash in Drawer.   The total **cash in drawer** figure, less paid outs, gives the amount of cash that should be in the register at the end of the day or whenever the totals are taken.

Gift Certificates.   The total amount of money that has been collected through direct sales of gift certificates which have been purchased.

Total Charge and Gift Certificates.   The total amount of money that has been collected in credit card charges from American Express, Visa, and other credit cards, as well as redeemed gift certificates.

Total Cash and Charges.   The total amount of money collected by adding the cash and charge receipts together.

Over/Short.   If the amount in the Total Cash and Charges line is not equal to the Gross Receipts line, the cashier is either **over or short** of money. If the amount shown in the Gross Receipts line is more than the Total Cash and Charges line, there is not enough money collected (a shortage). If the cashier has more money and credit card receipts than guest charges, there is an overage. In either case, the cashier must determine where the error has occurred before turning in the daily cashier report.

Record of Cash Paid Outs.   All money paid out of the register drawer is recorded here with the name of the person or company to whom it was paid. Items paid out of the cash register are usually small items that are needed in a hurry and picked up, such as flowers, ice, candy, candles, tips paid to the waitperson, and so forth.

Signed.   The cashier checks all the figures and is then required to sign the report.

Practice Problems 14–6   The Daily Cash Report

Complete the following cashier's daily reports, using Figure 14–5 as an example.

A.   Today's date

POS Register Readings or Total of Guest Check Sales

Food Sales	$2,856.63
Beverage Sales	1,474.68
Gift Certificate Sales	300.00

30. Total Sales

Add the Amount of Sales Tax	370.50

31. Gross Receipts _____

Add—Start of Shift Money (Bank)	150.00

32. Total of Gross Receipts and Money Started With (Bank) _____

Cash Collected from Guest Checks During the Shift	625.75

33. Less Total Cash Paid Out _____

34. Total Cash in Drawer _____

Credit Card Receipts

American Express	2,013.27
Discover	315.45
MasterCard	900.37
Visa	975.25
Gift Certificates (Redeemed)	528.82

35. Total Charge and Gift Certificates _____

Add Cash in Drawer

36. Total Cash and Charges (Should Equal the Amount
of Gross Receipts)   _____

37. Over or (Short) _____

Record of Cash Paid Out

City Ice Company	21.50
Tips	316.85
Arkay Florist	18.75
Other	0.00

38. Total Cash Paid Out _____

Signed by:

B. Today's date

POS Register Readings or Total of Guest Check Sales

Food Sales	$1,275.65
Beverage Sales	824.30
Gift Certificate Sales	116.45

39. Total Sales _____

Add the Amount of Sales Tax   155.15

40. Gross Receipts _____

Add—Start of Shift Money (Bank)   225.00

41. Total of Gross Receipts and Money Started With (Bank) _____

Cash Collected from Guest Checks During the Shift   625.75

42. Less Total Cash Paid Out _____

43. Total Cash in Drawer _____

Credit Card Receipts

American Express	550.56
Discover	260.00
MasterCard	450.37
Visa	9.50
Gift Certificates (Redeemed)	528.82

44. Total Charge and Gift Certificate Receipts _____

45. Add Cash in Drawer _____

46. Total Cash and Charges (Should Equal the Amount of
Gross Receipts) _____

47. Over or (Short) _____

Record of Cash Paid Out

City Ice Company	13.92
Tips	15.73
Arkay Florist	8.76
Other	12.95

48. Total Cash Paid Out _____

Signed by:

C. Today's date

POS Register Readings or Total of Guest Check Sales

Food Sales	$3,675.00
Beverage Sales	785.90
Gift Certificate Sales	96.48

49. Total Sales _____

Add the Amount of Sales Tax	319.02

50. Gross Receipts _____

Add—Start of Shift Money (Bank)	250.00

51. Total of Gross Receipts and Money Started With (Bank) _____

Cash Collected from Guest Checks During the Shift	625.75

52. Less Total Cash Paid Out _____

53. Total Cash in Drawer _____

Credit Card Receipts

American Express	2,500.92
Discover	260.00
MasterCard	450.37
Visa	89.50
Gift Certificates (Redeemed)	1,028.00

54. Total Charge and Gift Certificate Receipts _____

55. Add Cash in Drawer _____

56. Total Cash and Charges (Should Equal the Amount of
    Gross Receipts) _____

57. Over or (Short) _____

Record of Cash Paid Out

City Ice Company	20.50
Tips	25.80
Arkay Florist	10.40
Other	22.95

58. Total Cash Paid Out _____

Signed by:

D. Today's date

POS Register Readings or Total of Guest Check Sales

Food Sales	$6,296.50
Beverage Sales	1,457.95
Gift Certificate Sales	117.86

59. Total Sales _____

Add the Amount of Sales Tax   551.06

60. Gross Receipts _____

Add—Start of Shift Money (Bank)   125.00

61. Total of Gross Receipts and Money Started With (Bank) _____

Cash Collected from Guest Checks During the Shift   930.85

62. Less Total Cash Paid Out _____

63. Total Cash in Drawer _____

Credit Card Receipts

American Express	3,750.25
Discover	260.00
MasterCard	450.37
Visa	2,085.25
Gift Certificates (Redeemed)	1,028.00

64. Total Charge and Gift Certificates _____

65. Add Cash in Drawer _____

66. Total Cash and Charges (Should Equal the Amount of
Gross Receipts) _____

67. Over or (Short) _____

Record of Cash Paid Out

City Ice Company	20.65
Tips	15.75
Arkay Florist	11.75
Other	32.95

68. Total Cash Paid Out _____

Signed by:

E. Today's date

POS Register Readings or Total of Guest Check Sales

Food Sales	$10,650.00
Beverage Sales	2,460.55
Gift Certificate Sales	127.25

69. Total Sales _____

Add the Amount of Sales Tax	926.65

70. Gross Receipts _____

Add—Start of Shift Money (Bank)	75.00

71. Total of Gross Receipts and Money Started With (Bank) _____

Cash Collected from Guest Checks During the Shift	930.85

72. Less Total Cash Paid Out _____

73. Total Cash in Drawer _____

Credit Card Receipts

American Express	5,750.75
Discover	625.50
MasterCard	1,430.25
Visa	3,175.95
Gift Certificates (Redeemed)	2,408.60

74. Total Charge and Gift Certificates _____

75. Add Cash in Drawer _____

76. Total Cash and Charges (Should Equal the Amount of Gross Receipts) _____

77. Over or (Short) _____

Record of Cash Paid Out

City Ice Company	15.40
Tips	220.35
Arkay Florist	9.70
Other	12.00

78. Total Cash Paid Out _____

Signed by:

To Insure Perfect Solutions

Don't ask guests if they need change—assume that they do! You do not want to seem like you are taking shortcuts with your job.

Discussion Question 14-2

After completing Practice Problems 14–6, letter E, what might have happened to cause the report to be short? As a manager, would you have any concerns?

Returning Change to the Guest

Cashiers and waitstaff should know to verbally state and count the amount of change that a guest receives after that guest pays the bill with cash. Figure 14–6 illustrates how to count up change. For example, the guest check is for the amount of $12.90. The guest gives a $20.00 bill to whoever (waitperson or cashier) collects the money. Start by handing the guest a dime and say "$13.00." Next, hand her a dollar bill and say "$14," and then another dollar bill and say "$15." Finally, hand her a $5 dollar bill and say "$20.00." (Remember to thank her for her business, too.)

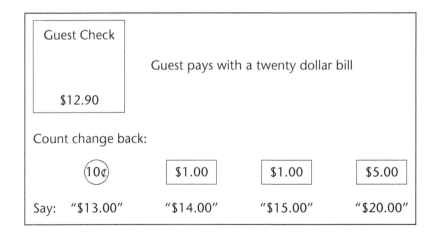

Figure 14–6
Diagram of change back.
© Cengage Learning 2012

Managerial Mathematical Functions

A manager of a food service operation has to be aware of the amount of money that is being received and the amount of money that has to be paid out in order to make a profit. Simply put, the manager must use math and common sense to control the profitability of a food service operation.

....

Discussion Question 14-3

You are the manager of a food service operation. As you are checking over the POS register tapes and the cashier's report for the previous day, you discover that a check for $97.20 is missing. What may have happened to the check, and what would you do?

All-Inclusive Pricing

Some food service operators find it advantageous to set their prices in a manner that is called **all-inclusive** pricing. This means that all charges (cost of food, beverages, tax, gratuity, etc.) are stated as one price, usually on a per-person basis. The guest will know the exact amount of money that he or she will spend for the meal or event. In order to compute and set the price, food service operators must know:

1. The raw cost of the meal and beverages
2. The goods and services that are subject to taxes in the municipality in which they conduct their food service business
3. The percentage amount of taxes that they must charge by law
4. The percentage of gratuity that they are charging the guest

Backing Out the Sales Tax and Gratuity

The business owner who utilizes all-inclusive pricing will need to determine how much money will be credited for each item included in the price. This is necessary for accounting purposes to make proper allocation to food and beverage costs, gratuity, and taxes. How will the owner figure out these amounts? He or she will have to use a mathematical process called backing out the sales tax and gratuity from the all-inclusive price.

It is a common practice for operators that serve alcoholic and nonalcoholic beverages to guests at a stand-up bar to include the sales tax in the cost of the beverage. In this instance, only the sales tax will be backed out because the gratuity is an additional amount that will be added voluntarily by the guest. For example, if a guest orders two glasses of wine at a bar, the price is $7.50 per glass and the tax is included. The guest then leaves a separate gratuity on the bar for the bartender.

How to Back Out the Sales Tax

Our guest has spent $15.00 on two glasses of wine. Included in the $15.00 price for both glasses of wine is the sales tax of 7.5 percent. It must first be determined how much money is collected for sales tax. It can then be determined how much money is left for the price of the wine, minus the sales tax. The procedure to back out the sales tax is done in the following way:

Step 1: Convert 7.5 percent to a decimal.

$$7.5\% = 0.075$$

Step 2: Add 100 percent, or 1, to the decimal of 0.075.

$$1 + 0.075 = 1.075 \text{ (divisor) sales tax rate}$$

Step 3: Divide the wine price by the (divisor) sales tax rate.

$15.00 divided by 1.075 = $13.95 (which equals the price without the tax)

Step 4: Subtract the results from the original wine price, which equals the sales tax owed.

$$\$15.00 - \$13.95 = \$1.05 \text{ (sales tax owed)}$$

To prove the formula:

Step 1: Multiply the price obtained, $13.95, by the sales tax rate of 7.5 percent.

```
  $13.95    Price
 × 0.75     Sales tax rate
   6975
 + 9765
 104625 = 1.04625 = $1.05
```

Step 2: Add the sales tax amount to the price of the food.

```
 $ 1.05    Sales tax
 +$13.95   Price
 $15.00    Original price for 2 glasses
             of wine
```

Backing Out Gratuity

Another example of backing out the amount of money from all-inclusive pricing occurs when the owner or manager includes the price of the gratuity with the meal. For example, a guest states that her tax-exempt group (they have obtained a form from the government stating that they do not have to pay taxes) would like to have an end-of-the year banquet. They tell the manager that their budget allows them to pay only $25.00 per person. The manager agrees to the $25.00 price, which includes the meal and the gratuity. In this instance, the percentage rate of the gratuity is backed out in the exact manner that the sales tax was backed out in the previous section. In addition to managers and cashiers knowing how to do this mathematical problem, waitstaff should also know how to back out the gratuity so they will be able to calculate the amount of gratuity owed to them. In our example, the cost of a meal is $25.00, which includes the 15 percent gratuity. The problem is solved as follows:

Step 1:   Convert 15 percent to a decimal.

$$15\% = 0.15$$

Step 2:   Add 100 percent, or 1, to the decimal of 0.15.

$$1 + 0.15 = 1.15 \text{ (divisor) gratuity rate}$$

Step 3:   Divide the menu price by the (divisor) gratuity rate.

$25.00 divided by 1.15 = 21.74 (which equals the price without the tax)

Step 4:   Subtract the results from the original menu price, which equals the gratuity owed.

$$\$25.00 - 21.74 = \$3.26 \text{ (gratuity owed)}$$

To prove the formula:

Step 1:   Multiply the menu price obtained, $21.74, by the gratuity rate of 15 percent.

$21.74   Price of meal
× 0.15   Gratuity percentage
10870
+2174
32610 = $3.26   Amount of gratuity

Step 2:   Add the gratuity to the price of the food to obtain the original menu price.

$ 3.26   Amount of gratuity
+ 21.74   Price of meal
$25.00   Original all-inclusive price

Practice Problems 14–7 Backing Out the Sales Tax and Gratuity

Back out the sales tax or gratuity from the following problems. Show the sales tax owed and the amount of money that the business or waitperson will receive. Round off each answer to the hundredths place.

79. John Curry purchased a new combination oven for $12,500, tax included. The sales tax was 7.25 percent.

     Sales tax owed _____ Amount of money for the oven _____

80. The Paridiso Restaurant charges $125.00 for its chef's seven-course meal, inclusive. The gratuity of 20 percent is included in the price. There is no sales tax.

     Gratuity owed _____ Amount of money for the restaurant _____

81. For a banquet, each guest pays $95.00, inclusive. A gratuity of 19 percent will have to be backed out.

     Gratuity owed _____ Amount of money for the restaurant _____

82. For a tax-exempt banquet, each guest pays $75.00, inclusive. A gratuity of 18 percent will have to be backed out.

     Gratuity owed _____ Amount of money for the restaurant _____

83. Judy Brown's wedding cost her $35,500, with the sales tax of 8 percent included.

     Sales tax owed _____ Amount of money for the restaurant _____

Backing Out Both the Sales Tax and Gratuity with All-Inclusive Pricing

Whenever the owner or a manager decides to engage in all-inclusive pricing, the backing out process has to be exact for accounting and recordkeeping purposes. In the following example, our restaurant charged each guest a price of $75.00, all-inclusive. This price was for the food, gratuity of 15 percent, and sales tax of 7 percent. It must be determined how much of the $75.00 will be allocated for food, how much for the gratuity, and how much for the sales tax.

   In the following example, the authors show how to back out both gratuity and sales tax in states where the gratuity is not taxed.

Step 1:   Back out the gratuity.

Convert 15 percent to a decimal

$$15\% = 0.15$$

Step 2:   Add 100 percent, or 1, to the decimal of 0.15.

$$1 + 0.15 = 1.15 \text{ (divisor) gratuity}$$

Step 3:   Divide the all-inclusive price by the (divisor) gratuity.

$75.00 divided by 1.15 = $65.22 (which equals food and sales tax)

Step 4:   Subtract the results from the original all-inclusive price, which equals the gratuity owed on each all-inclusive price.

$$\$75.00 - \$65.22 = \$9.78 \text{ (gratuity owed)}$$

Step 5:   Back out the 7 percent sales tax from the remaining all-inclusive price of food and sales tax.

$65.22 is the amount of money left after the gratuity has been removed.

Step 6:   Convert 7 percent to a decimal.

$$7\% = 0.07$$

Step 7:   Add 100 percent, or 1, to the decimal of 0.07.

$$1 + 0.07 = 1.07 \text{ (divisor) sales tax rate}$$

Step 8:   Divide the remaining all-inclusive price by the (divisor) sales tax rate.

$65.22 divided by 1.07 = $60.95 (which equals the food amount)

Step 9:   Subtract the results from the all-inclusive price (without the gratuity), which equals the sales tax owed.

$$\$65.22 - \$60.95 = \$4.27 \text{ (sales tax owed)}$$

To prove the formula:

Add the food, tax, and gratuity to obtain the all-inclusive price.

$$\$60.95 + \$4.27 + \$9.78 = \$75.00$$

If the readers of this textbook are in states where the service charge is taxed, the results would be as follows: The income for the food would be $60.95, the gratuity would be $9.14, and the sales tax would be $4.91, equaling a total of $75.00. In this example, the government gets $0.64 cents more and the service staff receives $0.38 cents less.

To Insure Perfect Solutions

It is essential that the food service executive consults with his or her accountant and lawyer to make certain that the service charge or gratuity is taxed. In some states it is, while in others it is not. For instance, when the authors dined at the Otesago Resort in Cooperstown, New York, the following message was on the guest check:

"A service charge of 18 percent is added to all food and beverage charges not included in a meal plan. The service charge is distributed to waitstaff, buspersons, bartenders, barbacks (people who assist bartenders), and cocktail servers. New York State Law requires service charges be subject to state tax."

Practice Problems 14–8   Backing Out Both the Sales Tax and Gratuity with All-Inclusive Pricing

Back out the sales tax and gratuity from the following problems. Show the sales tax owed, the gratuity owed, and the amount of money that the business will receive. Round off each answer to the hundredths place.

F.   An all-inclusive banquet was held that cost $52,100. The sales tax was 6.25 percent and the gratuity was 18 percent.

84. Sales tax owed _____

85. Amount of money for the restaurant _____

86. Gratuity owed _____

G.   Mr. Toby's restaurant charges $20.00 for an all-inclusive, complete meal. The sales tax is 8.25 percent and the gratuity is 15 percent.

87. Sales tax owed _____

88. Amount of money for the restaurant _____

89. Gratuity amount _____

H.   A guest has to pay $20.00 for a meal. Both the gratuity of 15 percent and the sales tax of 5 percent have to be backed out.

90. Sales tax owed _____

91. Amount of money for the restaurant _____

92. Gratuity amount _____

I.   An all-inclusive banquet was held that cost $72,100. The sales tax was 8.25 percent and the gratuity was 18 percent.

93. Sales tax owed _____

94. Amount of money for the restaurant _____

95. Gratuity owed _____

J.   An all-inclusive banquet was held that cost $152,100. The sales tax was 7.25 percent and the gratuity was 20 percent.

96. Sales tax owed _____

97. Amount of money for the restaurant _____

98. Gratuity owed _____

Bank Deposits

Bank deposits are a system used to entrust accumulated money for safekeeping in a bank. It is a system used by both individuals and businesses. It is unwise to store money at home or on the premise of a business. This can be an invitation to theft, or loss by a disaster. After opening an account, a deposit can be transacted in person—by taking a completed deposit slip and money to the bank—or the deposit can be made automatically. These two methods will be discussed further in this section. Depositing money in an account is a way of holding money in reserve for future **expenditures.**

When a bank deposit is made, the money deposited is placed in a **savings or checking account.** If the deposit is made in person at a bank, the money being deposited is accompanied by a **deposit slip,** which provides the depositor and the bank with a record of the transaction. (See below for more about the deposit slip.) If the deposit is made electronically, the transfer of funds is made through special communication lines set up between the depositor and the banking institution.

If the money deposited is placed in a savings account, it is held by the banking institution until the depositor wishes to withdraw some or all of the funds. While the money is in the savings account, the bank uses the money to make loans to customers for home or business improvements, the purchasing of new or existing homes, and so forth. At the same time, the bank pays you **interest** (the sum paid for the use of money) at a certain percent annually. This means that while your money is in the banking institution, it is earning money. This money can be withdrawn at any time without a penalty.

If the money is deposited in a checking account, it is held in reserve to cover any check amount written by the depositor. A **check** is a written order directing the bank to make a payment for the depositor. The bank honors the check and makes the payment, providing the depositor has enough money in the checking account. A checking account is more active than a savings account because the money is usually on the move. That is, deposits are made, checks are written, and money is withdrawn. Bills are sometimes paid by check whether they are for business or for personal and household expenses. Bills can also be paid by using debit cards or by authorizing the purveyor to allow the financial institution to transfer funds from your account to your purveyor's account electronically. Everyone should know how a checking account works. There are four important steps involved in using a checking account:

1. Filling out the deposit slip or having your money deposited electronically
2. Balancing the **check register**
3. Writing a check
4. Checking and balancing your bank statement

If these steps are not completed properly, problems result for both the depositor and the banking institution. These problems can sometimes result in a fine for the depositor, especially if the account is *overdrawn* (which means withdrawing money from an account for a larger sum of money than is in the account).

The Deposit Slip

The deposit slip provides the depositor and the banking institution with a record of the transaction when money is deposited in the checking account. (See Figure 14–7.) When filling out the deposit slip, cash and checks are listed separately. After this is done, they are added to find a *subtotal*. ("Sub" means under; therefore, this is a part of the total.) If cash is received when the deposit is made, the amount is subtracted from the subtotal, giving the net deposit, or the amount that you wish to place in the checking account. When receiving cash, some institutions require your signature on the deposit slips. In the upper-left corner of the slip, your name and address usually appear, and in the bottom-left corner, two groups of numbers appear. The first group is a routing number for the purpose of routing automatic deposits and checks to the correct institution. The second group is the customer's checking account number. (These numbers are not shown in Figure 14–7.) When deposits are made electronically, a deposit slip is not required, but the depositor is required to know the proper route number. All deposit slips are not the same. Each institution has its own idea of arrangement and information desired. However, you will find that most are very similar. The banking institution supplies the deposit slips to the customer.

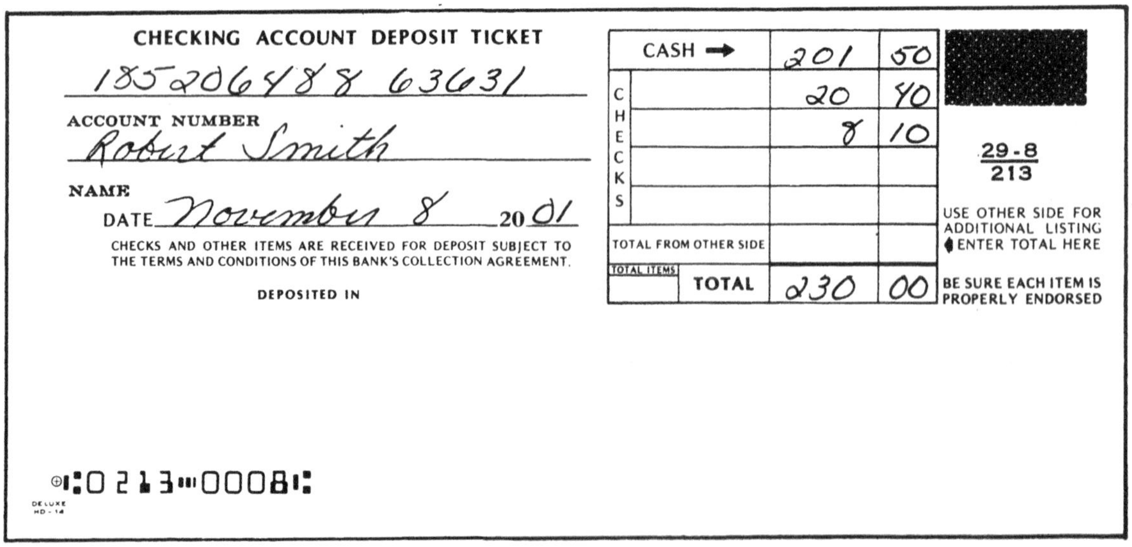

Figure 14–7
Deposit slip.
© Cengage Learning 2012

The Check Register

The check register is given to the depositor by the banking institution, so the depositor can record deposits and checks and know the balance of money on hand. (See Figure 14–8.) In this way, the depositor always knows the largest amount for which a check can be written and is less likely to overdraw the account.

CHECK NO.	CHECKS DRAWN IN FAVOR OF		DATE	BAL. BRT. FRD.	√	$ 283	00
111	TO	*Cinti Bell*	8/10	AMOUNT OF CHECK OR DEPOSIT		18	00
	FOR	*Telephone Service*		BALANCE		265	00
112	TO	*Allstate Insurance*	8/13	AMOUNT OF CHECK OR DEPOSIT		175	00
	FOR	*Car Insurance*		BALANCE		90	00
	TO	*Deposit*	8/16	AMOUNT OF CHECK OR DEPOSIT		250	00
	FOR			BALANCE		340	00
113	TO	*Shillito Dept. Store*	8/18	AMOUNT OF CHECK OR DEPOSIT		75	00
	FOR	*Charge Account*		BALANCE		265	00
114	TO	*Norwood Building & Loan*	8/20	AMOUNT OF CHECK OR DEPOSIT		135	00
	FOR	*House Payment*		BALANCE		130	00
	TO			AMOUNT OF CHECK OR DEPOSIT			
	FOR			BALANCE			
	TO			AMOUNT OF CHECK OR DEPOSIT			
	FOR			BALANCE			
	TO			AMOUNT OF CHECK OR DEPOSIT			
	FOR			BALANCE			
	TO			AMOUNT OF CHECK OR DEPOSIT			
	FOR			BALANCE			
	TO			AMOUNT OF CHECK OR DEPOSIT			
	FOR			BALANCE			
	TO			AMOUNT OF CHECK OR DEPOSIT			
	FOR			BALANCE			

Figure 14–8
Check register.
© Cengage Learning 2012

The balance brought forward (shown at the top in Figure 14–8) is the balance from the previous page in the register. It shows a total of $283.00. On August 10, a check was drawn for $18.00, leaving a balance of $265.00. On August 13, another check was drawn for $175.00, leaving a balance of $90.00. On August 16, a deposit of $250.00 was made. This amount was added to the previous balance, creating a new balance of $340.00. On August 18, a check for $75.00 was drawn, leaving a balance of $265.00, and on August 20, another check for $135.00 was drawn. The remaining balance, $130.00, is the net amount against which future checks may be drawn. When an amount of money is paid electronically, it is recommended that a written paper copy be sent to the person paying the bill so that the checkbook can be balanced and to control any opportunity for theft.

Writing a Check

The check, as pointed out previously in Chapter 2, is a written order directing the bank to make a payment for the depositor out of the money the depositor has in his or her checking account. The banking institution issues checks to the depositor. The depositor may be required to pay for the checks or the bank may deduct the cost from the balance in the checking account. Sometimes the checks are free if the depositor has a savings account or certificate of deposit (CD) at the same banking institution.

When writing a check, always write neatly and clearly in ink. (See Figure 14–9.) Be sure that all the information listed on the check is complete and correct, such as amount, date, check number, account number, and so forth. Do not forget to sign the check. Without your signature, the payment will not be made.

ROBERT OR JEANNE SMITH

No. _____21_____ $\frac{56\text{-}95}{42}$

HAMILTON, OHIO _____Feb. 4_____ 20 __

PAY TO THE ORDER OF _____Swift & Co._____ $ 12.50

_____Twelve and 50/100_____ DOLLARS

_____Robert Smith_____

⑈951084 7 7⑆   5

Figure 14–9
Writing a check.
© Cengage Learning 2012

To Insure Perfect Solutions

When writing a check, never use a pen with erasable ink. Otherwise, anyone can change the information that you write on the check.

The Bank Statement

At the end of a certain period of time (for example, one month, three months, etc.—each banking institution has its own regulations), the bank provides the depositor with a statement showing the activity of the account during that time period. In Figure 14–10 (showing a time period of three months), the statement lists the checks drawn and deposits made during that period of time. The bank may also return checks (canceled checks) or send a photocopy of the checks issued during that period. The canceled checks are the depositor's receipts if proof is needed that payment was made. The financial institution will also show the amount of money paid electronically from the checking account. This information will state the date of the transfer, the amount of money transferred, and to whom the money was transferred. For electronic transfers, the statement itself is the customer's receipt. The bank statement is used to check and balance the bank's figures against those recorded in the depositor's check register. In this way, mistakes can be detected before a problem arises or a fine is imposed.

486-174-8
Account Number

John or Jane Doe
9464 Stone Hill Dr.
Westchester, Ohio 45070

BALANCE FORWARD	DEPOSITS & CREDITS		CHECKS & DEBITS			CURRENT BALANCE
AS OF 05/20	NO.	AMOUNT	NO.	AMOUNT	SER. CHG.	AS OF 07/15
$0.00	8	$1,710.32	25	$1,435.25		$275.07

DATE	CHECK NO. OR CODE	AMOUNT	DATE	CHECK NO. OR CODE	AMOUNT	DATE	CHECK NO. OR CODE	AMOUNT
05 20	DP	200 00	07 05		50 00			
06 03	DP	200 00	07 05		139 88			
06 05		100 00	07 08		14 47			
06 07		132 00	07 09		10 50			
06 10	DP	500 00	07 10		14 44			
06 13		105 00	07 10		16 56			
06 13		110 35	07 10		18 40			
06 17	DP	200 00	07 11		50 00			
06 18		20 00	07 11		50 00			
06 19		255 92	07 15	DP	200 00			
06 24		10 00						
06 24		30 00						
06 24		50 00						
06 24		97 00						
06 27	DP	200 00						
06 28		25 16						
07 01	DP	200 00						
07 01		4 13						
07 01		7 00						
07 01		13 25						
07 01		100 00						
07 03	DP	10 32						
07 05		11 19						

Figure 14–10
Bank statement.
© Cengage Learning 2012

The upper-left corner of Figure 14–10 shows the depositor's account number. In the center, the depositor's name and address are given. The balance brought forward shows that, as of May 20, there was no money in this account. This was probably when the account was opened at the bank. Deposits and credits show that during this period (May 20 to July 15), eight deposits were made totalling $1,710.32. This figure can be checked by finding the sum of all the amounts listed with a DP (deposit) before them. Checks and debits (a charge against the account) show that 25 checks were drawn on the account, and the amount of those checks totaled $1,435.25. There is no service charge indicated by the bank during this period, which shows that the depositor received this service free of charge or paid for the checks when they were received. The current balance shows that as of July 15, $275.07 remained in the account. Other figures shown on this statement include the complete checking activity during this period of time, and the dates and amounts of all checks written. The bank statement shown in Figure 14–10 is a simplified one so that you can follow it without becoming confused. Many statements issued by financial institutions today combine statements for both the checking and savings accounts and show a service charge for regular account maintenance.

Practice Problems 14–9 Preparing Deposit Slips and Check Registers

K. Prepare deposit slips for problems 99 through 101. Follow the example given in Figure 14–7. If deposit slips are not available, make some by listing the necessary information on blank paper.

99. On August 18, Duane Johnstone deposited the following in his checking account:

2 twenty-dollar bills

4 ten-dollar bills

6 five-dollar bills

5 one-dollar bills

2 checks for $12.75 and $22.25

2 half dollars

8 quarters

6 dimes

7 nickels

100. On October 6, Carmen Santi-Roberts deposited the following in her checking account:

4 twenty-dollar bills

8 ten-dollar bills

7 five-dollar bills

4 two-dollar bills

9 one-dollar bills

1 check for $53.40

6 half dollars

3 quarters

7 dimes

9 nickels

101. On November 10, Sonna Kozlowski, treasurer of the Cuisine Club, deposited in the club's checking account the following checks and money collected for dues:

2 twenty-dollar bills

2 ten-dollar bills

8 five-dollar bills

6 one-dollar bills

3 checks for $10.40, $8.50, and $6.75

5 half dollars

5 quarters

4 dimes

L. Prepare check registers for problems 102 through 104. Follow the example given in Figure 14–8. If a check register is not available, make one by listing the necessary information on a sheet of paper.

102. Balance brought forward $520.65

October 2	Check No. 6 $43.50 Gas and Electric Co.
October 5	Check No. 7 $25.80 Best State Insurance Co.
October 10	Deposit $165.50
October 15	Check No. 8 $35.80 Albers Meat Market
October 20	Check No. 9 $265.00 Billís Service Station

103. Balance brought forward $680.48

December 3	Check No. 15 $63.45 Swallenís Dept. Store
December 5	Deposit $183.20
December 8	Check No. 16 $158.00
	Evanston Building and Loan Co.
December 9	Check No. 17 $178.25
	Bay State Insurance Co.
December 12	Deposit $98.75
December 15	Check No. 18 $62.78 G.M.A.C.

104. Balance brought forward $728.60

January 4	Check No. 19 $15.34 Webster Insurance Co.	
January 6	Check No. 20 $187.00	
	Home Savings and Loan Co.	
January 9	Deposit $223.50	
January 12	Check No. 21 $208.60 Joe's Service Station	
January 14	Deposit $197.60	
January 17	Check No. 22 $179.79	
	McMillians Dept. Store	
January 20	Deposit $368.75	
January 25	Check No. 23 $76.45 Metropolitan Hospital	

Balancing Bank or Financial Institutions Statements

As soon as a statement from the bank or financial institution (from now on referred to as the *bank*) arrives at your business, it should be checked and balanced to make certain that all monies received and disbursed in the specific account are accurate. The following procedure describes how to balance a checking account.

Preliminary Steps

Step 1: Compare your check register entries against the bank statement.

Step 2: Check to verify that the amount that was entered into the check register matches the amount on the bank statement. If you discover a legitimate mistake (a wrong figure recorded, etc.), correct the register.

Step 3: Add all electronic deposits or subtract all electronic withdrawals that had not been placed into the check register. This may include adding interest and deducting the service charge from the bank.

Step 4: Determine and total the amount of deposits that you have entered into the check register that have not appeared on the bank statement.

Step 5: Determine and total the amount of checks that have been entered into the check register that have not appeared on the bank statement.

This is a normal occurrence because deposits may be made and checks written after the statement is printed. There may be a few days between when the statement was printed and when the business receives the statement.

Actually Balancing the Statement

Step 6: List your statement ending balance.

Step 7: Add any outstanding deposits (from step 4).

Step 8: Add the results of steps 6 and 7 to get the subtotal.

Step 9: Subtract the outstanding checks from the subtotal.

Step 10: The total should balance with your checkbook register.

If you cannot balance the statement after checking and rechecking, or if there is an obvious problem with the account, your financial institution should be contacted immediately.

Practice Problems 14–10   Balancing the Bank Account

Using the bank statement from Figure 14–10, balance the bank account against Jane and John Doe's check register. First, you must complete the check register and then balance the check register against the bank statement.

Check Register for Jane and John Doe ending 7-22

Problem Number	Date	Check #	Add Amount	Subtract Amount	Balance
105.	May 20	Deposit	200.00		
106.	June 3	Deposit	300.00		
107.	June 5	1225		100.00	
108.	June 7	1226		132.00	
109.	June 10	Deposit	500.00		
110.	June 13	1227		105.00	
111.	June 13	1228		110.36	
112.	June 17	Deposit	200.00		
113.	June 18	1229		20.00	
114.	June 19	1230		255.92	
115.	June 24	1231		10.00	
116.	June 24	1232		30.00	
117.	June 24	1233		50.00	
118.	June 24	1234		79.00	
119.	June 27	Deposit	200.00		
120.	June 28	1235		25.16	
121.	July 1	Deposit	200.00		
122.	July 1	1236		4.13	
123.	July 1	1237		7.00	
124.	July 1	1238		13.25	
125.	July 1	1239		100.00	
126	July 3	Deposit	10.32		
127.	July 5	1240		11.19	
128.	July 5	1241		50.00	
129.	July 5	1242		139.88	
130.	July 8	1243		14.47	
131.	July 9	1244		10.50	
132.	July 10	1245		14.44	
133.	July 10	1246		15.66	
134.	July 10	1247		18.40	
135.	July 11	1248		50.00	
136.	July 11	1249		50.00	
137.	July 15	Deposit	200.00		
138.	July 16	1250		25.25	
139.	July 16	1251	100.00		
140.	July 17	Deposit	1250.00		
141.	July 19	1252		225.79	
142.	July 20	1253		82.46	
143.	July 21	1254		33.68	
144.	July 22	1255		25.72	

Discussion Question 14-4

Referring to Practice Problems 14–10, what mistakes did you discover, and where were the mistakes made?

Discussion Question 14-5

The bank statement for the checking account does not balance with your checkbook. The bank statement shows that your restaurant has $10,500. Your checkbook shows that you have $11,462. Give five possible reasons why the checkbook is out of balance with the bank statement.

Personal Taxes, Payroll, and Financial Statements

Objectives

At the completion of this chapter, the student should be able to:

1. Identify and understand the concept of employee's withholding tax (federal, state, local).
2. Identify and understand the concept of employee's income tax (federal, state, local).
3. Identify and understand the concept of FICA (Social Security) tax.
4. Calculate gross wages.
5. Calculate net pay.
6. Calculate salary plus commission.
7. Identify listings on the profit and loss statement.
8. Find the cost of food sold, gross margin, total operating expenses, net profit, and the percent of sales.
9. Identify listings on the balance sheet.
10. Find total assets, total liabilities, net worth and total liabilities, and net worth–proprietorship.
11. Identify and calculate the break-even point for a business using contribution rate and contribution rate percentages.
12. Identify items that are budgeted.
13. Find the amount or percent of items budgeted.

Key Words

federal taxes
withholding tax
income tax
FICA
wages
commission
state taxes
gross wages
net pay
overtime
financial
   statements

profit and loss
   statement
net profit
food in production
cost of food sold
gross margin
Social Security tax
depreciation
straight line
   method
balance sheet
assets

liabilities
net worth
proprietorship
capital
fiscal year
certificates of
   deposit
break-even analysis
break-even point
sales revenue
variable cost
cost of goods sold

serving expenses
gross profit
fixed cost
menu price
total variable profit
contribution rate
contribution rate
   percentage
budgeting
expenditures
income

There is a lot of truth to the old saying, "The only sure things in this life are death and taxes." People pay taxes to operate our federal, state, and local governments, as well as to administer our school districts and other services necessary to our daily lives.

In general, we are faced with the obligation of paying taxes to the three levels of government mentioned above: federal, state, and local (city and county). The following is a list of the taxes that food service operators and their employees are required to pay or the employer is required to collect by deductions (the amount of money subtracted) from the employee's paycheck:

Federal Taxes

Employee's Withholding Tax (a deduction from a person's paycheck for the purpose of paying yearly income taxes)

Income Tax

FICA (Social Security)

State Taxes

Employee's Withholding Tax

Income Tax

Sales Tax

Various Licenses

Local Taxes

Employee's Withholding Tax

Income Tax

Personal Property Tax

Occupational Tax

Various Licenses

Real Estate Tax

Because these taxes affect employers and employees, as they show up in the form of deductions on paychecks, it is important to learn as much as possible about them. Many people do not understand why all this money is taken out of their paychecks. Our goal is to acquaint you with these taxes and provide enough information to help you understand their importance.

Federal Taxes

Federal taxes are taxes collected by the federal government. They are established and enforced by federal law so that each individual citizen pays what he or she properly owes to support the functions financed by the federal government.

Employee's Withholding Tax

Employee's **withholding tax** is money withheld from each employee's paycheck during the year to pay for the income tax that he or she owes the federal government at the end of the year. The money withheld is sent to the government by the employer and is credited to the employee's account. Paying the tax as the money is earned, called "pay as you go," is a system devised by the federal government to ensure that your tax money is available when your taxes are due. At the end of the calendar year (December 31) and before January 31 of the following year, the employer sends each employee a W-2 form (wage and tax statement) indicating the total amount of money earned during the year, as well as how much money was withheld for taxes, Social Security payments, and any other money withheld, such as state and city income taxes. (See Figure 15–1.)

Sometimes the employer deducts too little or too much money from the employee's paychecks during the year. If too little money was deducted and money is owed the government, a check for the amount owed must be sent to the Internal Revenue Service (IRS) with the employee's federal tax return. If the amount owed is less than the amount deducted from the paychecks, the government sends the individual a check for the amount overpaid after the return is processed.

Figure 15–1
Form W-2 wage and tax statement.
© Cengage Learning 2012

The W-2 form annually received from the employer usually comes in four parts. One copy is to be filed with the employee's federal return, one with the state return, one for local use, and one for the individual's personal files.

Income Tax

The main source of income for operating the federal government is obtained from taxes levied on the income of individuals and corporations. **Income tax** returns must be filed by all people who earn over a specified amount of money. These individuals are required by law to file a federal income tax return with the Internal Revenue Service on or before each April 15th. If an employee does not earn enough money to pay taxes, he or she must file an income tax return to get the money back that was withheld by his or her employer for taxes.

Depending upon the income earned, tax forms can be submitted electronically, by using the telephone, or by sending the forms through the mail. Many individuals with limited income file simple forms, which are fairly easy to prepare and submit. For individuals with a high amount of income and deductions, tax forms can be confusing and difficult to complete. For those individuals, the authors recommend that an accountant or qualified person be hired to prepare the taxes.

A major concern for food service employees is that income tax must be paid on all tips received. The employee must give to the employer a written statement declaring how much money was received in tips during the pay period. The employer deducts from the employee's paycheck the proper amount of withholding tax for these tips, or the employee pays the employer the amount of tax due out of the tips collected.

The cost of meals furnished to the employee by the employer is also considered part of the employee's income. It is, therefore, subject to income tax unless it can be shown that the employee was given the meals for the convenience of the employer.

The authors advise all employees to consult the current tax code concerning tips, as well as any other questions that they may have, in order to be in compliance with the tax laws. This is because the law may (and usually does) change from year to year.

FICA (Social Security) Tax

The letters **FICA** stand for the Federal Insurance Contributions Act, which became law in 1935. This act established the Social Security system and tax. The Social Security system provides for the payment of retirement, survivor, and disability insurance benefits. It also provides hospital insurance benefits for persons age 65 and over who meet its eligibility requirements. This insurance, commonly known as Medicare, provides coverage for both hospital and doctor visits. Funds for payment of these benefits are provided by taxes levied on employees and their employers as well as self-employed persons.

Under the terms of the Social Security Act, the employer is required by law to deduct a certain percentage of the employee's wages each payday and remit the amount deducted to the federal government. For a self-employed person, the percentage is doubled. Each self-employed person has to pay the FICA rate as both the employer and the employee.

The term **wages** means "that which is paid or received for services" and includes salaries, **commissions** (pay based on the amount of business done), fees, bonuses, tips, and so forth. For example:

Bill Clark, manager of the Red Gate Restaurant, is paid a salary of $550 per week, plus a 2 percent commission on the private party business in excess of $6,000 per week. During the first week of June, the restaurant's private party business was $10,500. Assume that the Social Security tax rate is 7.65 percent. How much FICA tax was deducted from Bill's earnings for that week?

Salary	$550.00	
Commission	90.00	(2% of 4,500)
Total Earnings	$640.00	
7.65% of $640.00 =	$ 48.96	FICA tax

The amount of Social Security tax deducted from Bill's earnings that week was $48.96.

Besides the money deducted each payday from the employee's paycheck, a tax equal to that amount is levied on the employer. The tax is computed at the same rate as the employee's tax and is based on the total taxable wages paid by the employer. For example:

During the month of June, the Red Gate Restaurant paid out $10,650 in taxable wages. If the Social Security rate is 7.65 percent, the owner must pay the federal government $814.73.

$$\$10,650 \times 0.0765 = \$814.73$$

Self-employed persons must also pay Social Security taxes on income, but, as pointed out previously, at double the rate.

In the food service industry, once the knowledge of food preparation and managing is acquired, it is a fairly easy step to go from employee to employer. However, with tax obligations such as these, much thought must go into taking that big step.

Practice Problems 15–1 FICA (Social Security) Tax

Calculate the following problems concerning Social Security tax. Round answers to the hundredths place.

1. The cook at the Sea Shore Restaurant is paid a salary of $495 per week, plus 2 percent commission on all food sales for the week in excess of $20,000. During the second week of March, the food sales amounted to $25,000. If the Social Security tax rate is 7.30 percent, how much Social Security tax was deducted from his earnings for that week? _____

2. Bill Walters, a waiter at the Red Gate Restaurant, is paid a salary of $150 per week, plus tips. During the first week of July, his tips amounted to $220. Assuming that the Social Security tax rate is 7.30 percent, how much FICA tax was deducted from Bill's earnings for that week? _____

3. Jean Curran, a hostess at the Red Gate Restaurant, is paid a salary of $150 per week, plus tips. During the first week of May, her tips amounted to $145. Assuming that the Social Security tax rate is 7.30 percent, how much tax was deducted from Jean's earnings for that week? _____

4. Fred Hartzel, manager of the Kentucky Inn, is paid a salary of $525 per week, plus 2.5 percent commission on the food and beverage business in excess of $12,500 per week. During the second week of November, the business amounted to $24,600. Assuming that the Social Security tax rate is 7.30 percent, how much tax was deducted from Fred's earnings for that week? _____

5. The catering manager of the Gourmet Catering Company works on a 3 percent commission of total sales for each week. During the first week in June, total sales were $22,000. What were her total earnings? _____

6. Referring to question 5, how much Social Security tax did she pay if the rate is 7.30 percent?_____

···

State Taxes

State taxes are taxes collected by the state government. The taxes collected are for the purpose of operating all the state functions and agencies. Each agency submits a budget outlining how its money will be spent. Each state government operates independently from the others. The state governing body (generally the governor and state legislature) determines the amount of tax revenue required to operate and the way that those taxes will be imposed upon its citizens.

Employee's Withholding Tax

Employee's withholding tax is money withheld from each employee's paycheck by the employer during the year for the purpose of paying the employee's state income tax at the end of the calendar year. It is done for the same purpose as the employee's federal withholding tax. The amount of money withheld from each individual's paycheck is determined by the amount of income earned and the percentage set by the state. The tax is always lower than the amount withheld for federal tax.

Income Tax

Most states, and some municipalities as well, have an income tax. It is advisable to check with your state and/or municipality for specific tax requirements. The income tax laws in most states are patterned after the federal income tax laws. The percentage of tax collected on each individual's adjusted gross income varies from state to state, but it is usually a percentage that graduates with the increase of income and it is always less than the amount paid to the federal government. Your state income tax is paid to the state in which you live, even though you may actually have earned the money in another state.

Practice Problems 15–2   State Taxes

For the following problems, compute the state income tax due on net income. Round answers to the hundredths place. Use statements (a) through (e) as a guide in solving these problems.

(a)   Net income is $3,000 or less; your tax is 2 percent.

(b)   Net income is over $3,000, but not over $4,000; your tax is $60, plus 3 percent of any amount over $3,000.

(c)   Net income is over $4,000, but not over $5,000; your tax is $90, plus 4 percent of any amount over $4,000.

(d)   Net income is over $5,000, but not over $8,000; your tax is $130, plus 5 percent of any amount over $5,000.

(e)   Net income is over $8,000; your tax is $280, plus 6 percent of the any amount over $8,000.

State Taxes Due

7. Net income $12,990 _____

8. Net income $7,950 _____

9. Net income $19,589 _____

10. Net income $7,460 _____

11. Net income $45,980 _____

Calculating Net Pay

Gross wages are the amount of money that you earn before any deductions (the amount taken away) are made. After deductions are made, the result is called **net pay** (with the term *net* meaning "free of all deductions"). An employer is required by law, or in some cases by clauses in a union contract, to make certain required deductions. Any deductions beyond those required must be authorized by the employee. Some of the required deductions are FICA (Social Security) taxes, federal withholding taxes (income tax), state income tax, city income tax, health insurance, and retirement fund. Some of the deductions that you may authorize include union dues; contributions to charitable organizations, credit unions, and retirement plans; and company stock purchases.

To calculate net pay, all deductions are subtracted from gross wages. Net pay is the figure that will appear on your weekly, semimonthly, or monthly paycheck. The formula for calculating net pay is as follows:

Gross wages − Deductions = Net pay

For example:

Jerry Roth, an employee of the Terrace Plaza Hotel, receives $7.45 an hour for a regular 40-hour workweek, with time and a half for **overtime** (time worked beyond the 40-hour week). Last week Jerry worked 52 hours. Deducted from his gross wages were the following: $31.54 FICA (Social Security) taxes, $64.81 federal withholding taxes, $21.65 health insurance, and $25.93 state income tax.

To determine Jerry's gross wage and net pay, follow these steps.

Step 1: Add together the total hours that Jerry worked.

52	Total hours worked
− 40	Regular hours
12	Jerry has worked this many overtime hours.

Step 2: Convert Jerry's overtime hours to a number of regular hours.

12	Overtime hours
× 1.5	Time and a half
60	
+ 12	
18.0	Overtime hours converted to regular hours

18	Overtime hours converted to regular hours
+ 40	Regular hours
58	Total regular hours to be paid for working

$7.45	Per hour
× 58	Total regular hours
5960	
+ 3725	
$432.10	Gross wages

Step 3: Figure out Jerry's net pay.

$ 31.54	FICA tax
$ 64.81	Federal withholding tax
$ 21.65	Health insurance
+ $ 25.93	State income tax
$143.93	Total deductions

$ 432.10	Gross wages
− 143.93	Total deductions
$ 288.17	Net pay (take-home pay)

As you can see by comparing the steps to solving this problem, there is a great deal of difference between gross wages and net or take-home pay.

Sometimes the payroll department may not have all the proper schedules, tax guides, and tables put out by the various tax agencies of the federal and state governments. In such cases, they may be required to calculate deductible dollar amounts using percentages.

For example:

Jerry Roth, an employee of the Terrace Plaza Hotel, receives $7.45 an hour for a regular 40-hour workweek, with time and a half for overtime. Last week, Jerry worked 52 hours. Deducted from his gross wages were the following: 7.30 percent for FICA (Social Security) taxes, 15 percent for federal withholding taxes, 5 percent for state income tax, and 1.5 percent for city income tax.

To determine Jerry's gross wage and net pay, follow Step 1 and Step 2.

Step 1:

52	Total hours worked
− 40	Regular hours
12	Overtime hours

Step 2:

12	Overtime hours
× 1.5	Time and a half
60	
+ 12	
18	Overtime hours converted to regular hours
18	Overtime hours converted to regular hours
+ 40	Regular hours
58	Total regular hours to be paid for working
$7.45	Per hour
× 58	Total regular hours
5960	
3725	
$432.10	Gross wages

Up to this point, the calculations are the same as in the previous example. The difference lies in calculating the deductions because dollar amounts must be found when deductions are given in percentages.

Step 3:

FICA 7.30% × 432.10 gross wages	$ 31.54
Federal withholding tax 15% × 432.10	$ 64.82
State income tax 5% × 432.10	$ 21.61
City income tax 1.5% × 432.10	+ $ 6.48
Sum of deductions	= $ 124.45

$432.10	Gross wages
− 124.45	Sum of deductions
$ 307.65	Net pay (take-home pay)

Practice Problems 15–3 Determining Gross and Net Take-Home Pay

Find the answers to these questions based on the following scenario. Round answers to the hundredths place.

The chef at the Metropole Hotel is paid a salary of $4,500 per month and receives a paycheck twice a month. On a recent paycheck, the deductions from his total earnings were as follows: $127.75 FICA tax, $450.00 federal withholding tax, $87.50 state income tax, and $26.25 city income tax.

12. What was his gross wage for this pay period?　　　　　　_____

13. What was his net pay?　　　　　　　　　　　　　　　_____

A. For each of the following, find gross wages and amount of net pay based on a 40-hour workweek, with time and a half for all hours worked over 40.

Name	Total Hours Worked	Hourly Rate	Gross Wages	Total Deductions	Net Pay
Tisha Adams	46	$ 5.95	$	$ 79.95	$

14. Gross Wages for Tisha Adams are _____

15. Net Pay for Tisha Adams is _____

Rafael Romero	56	$ 7.50	$	$ 120.10	$

16. Gross Wages for Rafael Romero are _____

17. Net Pay for Rafael Romero is _____

Rose Fahery	45.5	$ 9.25	$	$ 126.90	$

18. Gross Wages for Rose Fahery are _____

19. Net Pay for Rose Fahery is _____

Paul Brown	49.5	$10.75	$	$ 137.50	$

20. Gross Wages for Paul Brown are _____

21. Net Pay for Paul Brown is _____

Kim Lee	57	$12.25	$	$ 142.60	$

22. Gross Wages for Kim Lee are _____

23. Net Pay for Kim Lee is _____

B. The head salad person at the Kemper Lane Hotel is employed for eight hours per day, with time and a half for all overtime hours she puts in. Her regular hourly pay rate is $10.50. In a recent week, she worked the following hours:

S	M	T	W	TH	F	S
—	9.5	9	10.5	8	12	—

Deducted from her gross wages were: FICA tax $21.00, federal withholding tax $76.70, state income tax $10.95, and health insurance $16.90.

24. What was her gross wage? _____

25. What was her net pay? _____

C. John Linsdale, a waiter at the Sands Hotel, receives a base salary of $125.00 per week, plus tips. Last week, his tips amounted to $260.00. From his gross wages, the following deductions were made: FICA tax 7.30 percent, federal withholding tax 15 percent, state income tax 4 percent, and $20.45 for health insurance.

26. What was his gross wage? _____

27. What was his net pay? _____

D. Elsa Suarez, a baker at the Chesapeake Hotel, works on a 40-hour-per-week basis, with time and a half for all overtime. During this past week, she worked 49 hours. Her regular pay rate is $13.95 per hour. The following deductions were taken from her gross pay: federal withholding tax $85.70, FICA $27.14, health insurance $12.95, and union dues $7.00.

28. What was her gross wage? _____

29. What was her net pay? _____

Calculating Salary Plus Commission

There are situations in the food service industry where an employee is paid a salary plus a commission (generally a percentage of sales for a given period). These situations usually occur to motivate supervisors and managers to increase production and sales. Commissions are calculated by the financial officers usually referred to as controllers in the hospitality industry.

To calculate a gross wage when a commission is involved, the amount of the commission is added to the basic salary. To find the amount of the commission, sales are multiplied by the percent of commission. The formula for calculating gross wages involving commission is as follows:

Amount of sales × Percent of commission = Amount of commission

Amount of commission + Salary = Gross wages

For example:

The banquet manager at the Alms Hotel is paid a salary of $590 per week, plus a 1.5 percent commission on the private party business in excess of $5,000 per week.

In a recent week, the party business amounted to $12,000. To determine the gross pay, refer to the following example:

$12,000	Total sales
− 5,000	Amount deducted
$7,000	Amount on which commission is paid
× .015	Percent of commission
35,000	
+ 7,000	
$ 105	Amount of commission
$ 590	Weekly salary
+ 105	Amount of commission
$ 695	Gross pay

Practice Problems 15–4   Calculating Salary Plus Commission

Solve the following problems. Round answers to the hundredths place.

30. The catering manager at Elegant Fare Catering Company receives a basic salary of $850 per month, plus a 2 percent commission on all the catered business. Last month, the catered business amounted to $235,000. What was her gross wage? _____

31. The manager of a local fast-food restaurant receives a monthly salary of $1,600, plus a commission of $0.12 for every sandwich sold during the month. Last month, 1,200 sandwiches were sold. What was his gross wage for the month? _____

32. The manager of the food concession at the local swimming club receives a small weekly salary of $125, plus a commission of 5 percent on all food sales for the week. Last week, the food sales amounted to $9,575. What was her gross wage for the week? _____

The preparation cook at Bob's Catering Company receives a salary of $350 per week, plus a commission of 1.5 percent on all the catered party business. In a recent week, the catered party business amounted to $15,000. Deducted from her gross wages were the following: FICA tax $41.98, federal withholding tax $126.50, and city income tax $8.63.

33. What was her gross wage? _____

34. What was her net pay?_____

35. The food and beverage manager at the Fountain Square Hotel receives a salary of $2,800 per month, plus a commission of 0.5 percent on all food and beverage business for the month. Last month, the food business amounted to $48,400. The beverage business was $8,600. What was her gross wage for the month?

_____

Financial Statements

Financial statements are the instrument used in a business operation to let management know its exact financial position. The figures tell a story of success or failure. There are two major financial statements that must be prepared and are essential to the operation of a business: the profit and loss (income) statement, sometimes referred to as the P&L sheet, and the balance sheet. These financial statements are especially important to the food service operation because of high labor cost and food prices that fluctuate quite rapidly.

The Profit and Loss Statement

The **profit and loss statement** is a summary or report of the business operation for a given period of time. The purpose of the statement is to determine how much money the business is making or losing. In the profit and loss statement, all income from sales is set off against expenses to determine the profit or loss. The following formula summarizes the profit and loss statement of a food service operation:

$$\text{Sales} - \text{Cost of food sold} = \text{Gross margin}$$

$$\text{Gross margin} - \text{Total operating expenses} = \text{Net profit or loss}$$

The **net profit** (the figure found by subtracting total operating expenses from the gross margin) or loss is the figure that is of greater concern to the food service operator because it determines the success or failure of the business.

Most of the figures used to compile a profit and loss statement are taken from the daily records that are recorded and made available by the bookkeeper. The daily records of the food service operation are kept in a book or a computer file that contains a record of all income and expenses. It is a means of keeping track of every sales dollar. The file or book is also important for securing the figures needed for tax purposes and other financial obligations. The availability of a computer simplifies the task of recordkeeping. It can produce the most complicated figures immediately.

A profit and loss statement can be made up whenever the food service operator wants to know the business's financial situation or feels it necessary to review the financial situation. It can be done every month, every three months, every six months, or even once a year. However, for control purposes, it is recommended that the profit and loss statement be completed each month. When the statement is completed, the food service operator analyzes all the figures and compares the dollar amounts in each category with those of previous months or years, looking for ways to cut costs for a more efficient operation. The operator may also wish to make a percent comparison of all figures with total sales, which represents 100 percent. The example of a profit and loss statement shows dollar amounts and percentages of the total sales. (See Figure 15–2.) As explained previously, percentages are usually the language spoken by the food service operator. Percentages, rather than dollar amounts, give a clearer picture of the overall operation. It is suggested within the food service industry that a successful operation must hold its food and labor cost below 70 percent.

Figure 15–2 shows that the cost of food sold is 42.3 percent and the labor cost is 32 percent, totaling 74.3 percent. This suggests that this business may be in trouble. The food service professional will have to increase the volume of sales and/or cut costs. The Crossgates Restaurant is still showing a profit of 6 percent, but a higher profit would be desired. As you review the profit and loss statement in Figure 15–2, notice that the cost of food sold (42.3 percent) and the gross margin (57.7 percent) add up to 100 percent. The total operating expenses add up to 51.7 percent. When the total operating expenses are subtracted from the gross margin, the results show a net profit of 6 percent.

"The locals keep us in business, and the tourists make us money. Financial statements allow us to budget for the slow and high seasons. Since we are always up and down in terms of business, we have to be nimble in our changes. We need to respond to an increase in sales immediately, with heavier staffing and ordering so that we don't run out of product or deliver subpar service due to staff being overtaxed. On the other hand, we need to respond quickly to a decrease in sales by cutting staff and ordering to keep labor costs under control and prevent food spoilage and loss. Constant monitoring of financial statements, especially year-to-year sales reports and profit and loss statements, is what makes this adaptibility possible and allows us to remain profitable by controlling our variable costs in a variable market."

Scott and Nora Behrens
Owners, Tomaato's Restaurant
Incline Village, Nevada

Tomaato's business focus is on producing consistently high-quality pizza, pastas, and salads at their 40-seat dining room, increased by an additional 30 seats on their patio in the summer. They do a significant carry-out and delivery business. Tomaato's is highly seasonal, being located in Incline Village, a small town near Lake Tahoe, directly across the street from the Hyatt Hotel. Scott and Nora have to be lean and mean in the off-season and fast and efficient in busy times. They feel that they have found their niche in their little town, and they harness the tourist trade effectively.

Crossgates Restaurant
Profit and Loss Statement
for the month of September, 20___

Category	Dollars	Summary	% of Sales
Total Sales	$96,000	$96,000	100.0%
Food Cost			
Inventory, beginning of month	$9,680		
Purchases for the month	$37,600		
Subtotal	$47,280		
Less Food in Production	$650		
Less Final Inventory	$6,000		
Cost of Food Sold		$40,630	42.3%
Gross Margin		$55,370	57.7%
Expenses			
Payroll/Labor Cost	$30,720		32%
Social Security Taxes	$1,920		2%
Rent	$4,800		5%
Laundry and Linens	$672		0.7%
Repairs and Maintenance	$2,688		2.8%
Advertising	$480		0.5%
Taxes and Insurance	$1,440		1.5%
Supplies	$672		0.7%
Depreciation	$1,920		2%
Utilities	$2,880		3%
Miscellaneous Expenses	$1,440		1.5%
Total Operating Expenses		$49,632	51.7%
Net Profit		$ 5,738	6%

Figure 15–2
Profit and loss statement.
© Cengage Learning 2012

Listings on the Profit and Loss Statement

Each item listed and explained in this section is an indispensable part of most food service profit and loss statements. Each item must be thoroughly understood, whether it represents income or expense. Knowledge of these items will give you a better understanding of the importance of a profit and loss statement.

Total Sales

Total sales are the income for that particular month. After business is completed each day, a total is taken of all sales. These totals are kept on file in the computer, on a disk or a flash drive, or in the income book.

Inventory at the Beginning of the Month

Inventory at the beginning of the month is acquired from the final inventory from the previous month. For example, the **final inventory** for the month of August is the beginning inventory for the month of September.

Purchases for the Month

The total of all food purchased during the month is the purchases for the month. Total all invoices sent with each order.

Cost of Food in Production

This is the amount of food that has been cooked, is being cooked, or is in refrigerators waiting to be served. For example, a food service operation may be having a banquet, and 10 prime ribs have been cooked or are being cooked. The prime ribs would not be counted as inventory in the meat cooler, so they must be considered **food in production** to achieve an accurate financial picture.

Total

The sum of the inventory at the beginning of the month and the purchases of the month is the total. It is a total of all food that was available during that month.

Final Inventory

Final inventory is acquired from the physical inventory taken at the end of each month's operation. It represents the cost of food that is still in stock and was not sold. Since it represents food that was not sold, it is subtracted from the total cost of food available during the month.

Cost of Food Sold

When the final inventory is subtracted from the cost of food on hand, the result is the **cost of food sold** that month.

Gross Margin

The **gross margin** or gross profit is found by subtracting the cost of food sold from the total sales. Gross means the total value before deductions are made. Margin is the difference between the cost and the selling price, so sales minus cost of food gives gross margin.

Payroll/Labor Cost

Payroll or labor cost consists of all wages paid to all employees, including the owner's salary. You will notice it is the largest figure listed under expenses. Except for the cost of food, this is the most important item to control.

Social Security Taxes

Social Security taxes are paid to the federal government for the purpose of retirement benefits. The employer must deduct a certain percent of the employee's salary for Social Security taxes and, at the same time, must match the amount the employee pays. The amount shown on the profit and loss statement represents only the amount the employer must pay.

Rent

Rent is a fixed amount paid at a certain time of each month to the owner of a property for the use of that property. If a food service operator owns the building in which the operation is located, this particular expense is not incurred. However, there may be a similar expense if the building is not paid for (for example, paying off the mortgage to a financial institution).

Laundry and Linens

These items include the cost of cleaning or renting all uniforms, napkins, tablecloths, towels, and so forth.

Repairs and Maintenance

These are expenses that result from equipment failure or building repairs. If the property is rented, the owner may assume the responsibility for all repairs. This item is an essential part of any food service operation because equipment must be kept in good working condition at all times for an efficient operation.

Advertising

Advertising is an expense that is incurred when notifying the public about a place of business. The advertising may be done through the newspaper, television, radio, entertainment book, billboards, periodicals, Internet, or other media.

Taxes and Insurance

These may be paid on an annual basis. If these are listed on the monthly statement, as shown in Figure 15–2, the monthly cost is found by taking one-twelfth of the yearly payment.

Supplies

Supplies are the cost of those items used other than food. These include janitorial supplies, paper products, and similar expenses.

Depreciation

Depreciation is the act of lessening the value of an item as it wears out. For example, if a new slicing machine is bought for $2,700.00, and is used constantly for one year, at the end of that year, it is worth less than $2,700.00. It has been worn out slightly through use, and therefore has less value. There are several methods used for figuring depreciation, but the simplest and most practical is the straight line method.

In the **straight line method,** estimate the length of time that a piece of equipment is expected to last, and the trade-in value that it should possess at the end of its estimated life. The difference between the original cost of the equipment and its estimated trade-in value gives the total amount of allowable depreciation. For example: A slicing machine that was purchased for $2,700.00 is expected to last 15 years, at which time it will probably have a trade-in value of $600.00.

Original cost	$2,700.00
Estimate trade-in	− 600.00
Allowable depreciation	$2,100.00

The allowable depreciation, $2,100, is divided by the number of years the item is expected to last (15).

$$
\begin{array}{r}
140.00 \\
15\overline{)2100.00} \\
-\underline{15} \\
60 \\
-\underline{60} \\
0
\end{array}
$$

Amount that can be deducted every year for 15 years

Some food service operators estimate that all their major pieces of equipment must be replaced every 10 or 12 years; instead of figuring depreciation on individual pieces of equipment, they figure it on the group. Thus, each year they charge off one-tenth or one-twelfth of the allowable depreciation. If a depreciation figure for a month is needed, find the depreciation figure for one year and take one-twelfth of that amount.

Utilities

Utilities include the cost incurred through the supply of gas, sewer, electricity, and water. These bills are usually based on monthly use and are presented to the customer on a monthly basis.

Miscellaneous Expenses

These are usually smaller amounts than the others listed. They include licenses, organization dues, charitable contributions, and so forth. These amounts vary with the size and policy of the operation.

Total Operating Expenses

Total operating expenses are the sum of all the expenses incurred during the period or month that the P&L statement covered.

To Insure Perfect Solutions

The percentage of the cost of food sold added to the gross margin percentage will always equal 100 percent.

Net Profit

The most important figure on the profit and loss statement, and probably the one first observed by the owner or manager, is the net profit. This figure is found by subtracting total operating expenses from gross margin. In Figure 15–2, the profit is not a large one, but at least it shows that the business is heading in the right direction. Concern occurs when that figure shows a net loss.

Practice Problems 15–5 The Profit and Loss Statement

Prepare profit and loss statements using the amounts given in problems 36–38. Use the same form as shown in the example in Figure 15–2. Find the cost of food sold, gross margin, total operating expenses, net profit, and the percent of sales for each problem listed. Round off all answers in this manner: If the answer is 0.29748, go to the fifth number to the right of the decimal and use that number to round off to the fourth number to the right of the decimal. Now the answer is 0.2975. Next, convert 0.2975 to a percentage. Therefore, the final answer would be 29.75 percent.

36. The Manor Restaurant had total sales for the month of November of $15,500. Its inventory at the beginning of the month was $5,280. During the month, it made purchases that totaled $8,200. Food in production equaled $225. The final inventory at the end of the month was $4,690.

    The Manor Restaurant had the following expenses during the month: salaries $3,220, Social Security taxes $115, rent $460, laundry $95, repairs and maintenance $421, advertising $75, taxes and insurance $195, supplies $120, depreciation $540, utilities $380, and miscellaneous expenses $210.

37. Connie's Cafeteria had total sales for the month of March of $25,830. Its inventory at the beginning of the month was $7,275. During the month, it made purchases that totaled $10,900. Food in production equaled $975. The final inventory at the end of the month was $6,870.

    Connie's Cafeteria had the following expenses during the month: salaries $5,225, Social Security taxes $313.50, rent $540, laundry and linens $98, repairs and maintenance $268, advertising $78, taxes and insurance $218, supplies $120, depreciation $395, utilities $270, and miscellaneous expenses $168.

38. The Golden Goose Restaurant had total sales for the month of April of $75,300. Its inventory at the beginning of the month was $8,880. During the month, it made purchases that totaled $25,500. Food in production equaled $1,250. The final inventory at the end of the month was $8,440.

    The Golden Goose Restaurant had the following expenses during the month: salaries $14,350, Social Security taxes $875, rent $650, laundry $225, repairs and maintenance $563, advertising $156, taxes and insurance $419, supplies $280, depreciation $690, utilities $345, and miscellaneous expenses $242.

The Balance Sheet

The **balance sheet** is a necessary part of any business operation, almost as important as the profit and loss statement. It is a statement listing all the company's **assets** (what it owns) and **liabilities** (what it owes) to determine **net worth, proprietorship** (ownership), or **capital** (money). It is a dollar-and-cents picture of a company's financial status at a given time. The given time is usually December 31 if based on the calendar year, or another date if based on the fiscal year. A **fiscal year** is defined as the time between one yearly settlement of financial accounts and another.

A balance sheet can be prepared by a company at any time that it wishes to know its net worth. The balance sheet is not restricted for use in the business community; it can also be used by individuals. It serves many purposes: to provide necessary information in reporting financial matters to the state and federal governments for income taxes, to secure loans from financial institutions, and, in the case of many business operations, to provide the information stockholders and partners want to see or hear in the annual report.

The balance sheet is another financial report that can be simplified by using a computer and storing the information on a disk. Since every food service operation does not have a computer, it is to your advantage to learn how to perform the functions manually.

The formula for preparing a balance sheet can be expressed by the following equation:

$$\textbf{Assets} - \textbf{Liabilities} = \textbf{Net worth or Proprietorship}$$

As the equation points out, a company totals all the money it owes and subtracts that amount from the total value of all it owns to find out its total worth.

To prove that the balance sheet has been prepared correctly, the liabilities are added to the net worth. The sum should equal the total assets. The relationship may be expressed by this equation:

$$\textbf{Assets} = \textbf{Liabilities} + \textbf{Proprietorship}$$

Two examples of balance sheets are shown in Figure 15–3. Example A is for an individual, and Example B is for a food service operation.

Listings on the Balance Sheet

The amounts shown on Example A, the William Jones balance sheet of Figure 15–3, come from various sources, as indicated in the following sections. (See Figure 15–3, Example A.)

Home

What a home is worth on the current market can be determined by a real estate appraisal.

Home Furnishings

This amount is more difficult to figure. The best method may be to list the original cost and deduct a certain percentage for age and wear.

Certificates of Deposit

Certificates of deposit are easy to total since the amounts are stated on each certificate. If the amount is difficult to find, just call your bank.

Cash in Savings Account

This figure is listed in the passbook or on your monthly statement received from the bank.

Automobile, Boat

The current worth of an automobile or boat may be found by checking with the company from which they were purchased. There is a book available that will list the value of an automobile, called the blue book.

Liabilities

Liabilities are available by checking with the institution that made the loan.

Charge Accounts

Statements of money owed are sent each month. If still in doubt, check with the company that issued the card.

The figures shown on the balance sheet for the Charcoal King Restaurant come from many sources, but they can be obtained from records kept on file by the food service establishment in the computer, on a disk, or in the income book. (See Figure 15–3, Example B.) The bookkeeper will keep these figures, discussed in the following sections, current.

Example A

William Jones
Balance Sheet, December 31, 20___

Assets		Liabilities	
Home	$165,000	Home mortgage	$ 66,000
Home furnishings	19,470	Houseboat loan	13,500
Certificates of deposit	30,000	Auto loan	4,500
Cash in savings account	13,500	Charge accounts (retail)	2,070
Cash in checking account	885	Total Liabilities	$ 86,070
Automobile	13,950	Net Worth-	
Houseboat	26,325	Proprietorship	183,060
Total Assets	$269,130	Total Liabilities and	
		Net Worth-Proprietorship	$269,130

Example B

Charcoal King Restaurant
Balance Sheet, June 30, 20___

Assets (Current)		Liabilities (Current)	
Cash in bank and		Accounts payable	$ 14,716
on hand	$ 21,800	Installment accounts	
Accounts receivable	6,700	or bank notes	
Food and beverage		payable	48,624
inventory	10,340	Payroll and	
Supplies	1,680	taxes payable	3,956
Total Current Assets	$ 40,520	Total Current Liabilities	67,296
Assets (Fixed)		Net Worth-	
Stationary kitchen		Proprietorship	49,024
equipment	$ 41,288	Total Liabilities and	
Hand kitchen		Net Worth-	
equipment	9,824	Proprietorship	$116,320
Dining room furniture			
and fixtures	13,548		
China glassware,			
silver, and linen	11,140		
Total Fixed Assets	$ 75,800		
Total Assets			
(Current and Fixed)	$116,320		

Figure 15–3
(A) Balance sheet for an individual. (B) Balance sheet for a company.
© Cengage Learning 2012

Cash

The cash amount is found in the income book, in the computer, or on a disk. This figure is kept up to date by the bookkeeper.

Accounts Receivable

Accounts receivable refers to money that is owed to the company by various people or companies for various reasons.

Food and Beverage Inventory

This figure is taken from the profit and loss statement.

Assets (Fixed)

The value of the fixed assets listed (which, in this case, are for various kinds of equipment) can be acquired by referring to purchase contracts or equipment records.

Accounts Payable

Accounts payable refers to money that the food service operation owes for purchases made (in other words, bills that have not been paid). The amounts may be found by referring to the unpaid bill or invoice file.

Installment Accounts or Bank Notes Payable

These figures are found by referring to sales contracts or equipment records. Another possible source is the bank or company to whom the money is owed.

Payroll and Taxes Payable

These figures are found by checking with the bookkeeper or accountant who keeps these figures up to date.

Practice Problems 15–6 The Balance Sheet

Prepare balance sheets for problems 39–43, using the figures listed. Find total assets, total liabilities, net worth and total liabilities, and net worth–proprietorship.

39. Tim Wu had the following assets as of May 15 this year: home $238,000, home furnishings $26,085, automobile $12,750, speedboat $6,450, cash in savings accounts $38,670, cash in checking account $5,034, and stocks $4,825. His liabilities were as follows: home mortgage $85,500, auto loan $7,200, boat loan $2,900, note payable to loan company $4,500, and charge accounts $2,682.

_____

40. Joe and Mary Hernandez had the following assets as of July 15 this year: home $157,500, house trailer $11,100, home furnishings $23,325, automobile $11,580, cash in savings account $18,795, cash in checking account $759, U.S. savings bonds $2,500, and certificates of deposit $15,000. Their liabilities were as follows: home mortgage $85,500, loan on house trailer $6,600, automobile loan $6,900, and charge accounts $2,691. _____

41. Robert and Dolores O'Shaunessey had the following assets as of December 31 this year: local home $216,250, vacation home $90,480, motorboat $8,400, automobile $19,650, home furnishings $17,970, certificates of deposit $20,000, cash in savings account $3,500, cash in checking account $1,695, and U.S. savings bonds $1,275. Their liabilities were as follows: local home mortgage $66,700, vacation home mortgage $31,650, motorboat loan $3,900, automobile loan $10,350, loan on home furnishings $5,400, and charge accounts $2,700. _____

42. Jim's Hamburger Palace had the following assets as of December 31 this year: cash $5,956, food and beverage inventory $4,800, supplies $392, equipment (stationary, hand, and serving equipment) $14,140, and furniture and fixtures $5,000. The restaurant's liabilities were as follows: accounts payable $344.80, notes payable to First National Bank $3,900, note payable to Mike Bryce $1,120, sales tax payable $278, and taxes payable $1,040.

43. Bill's Oyster House had the following assets as of December 31 this year: cash $18,770, accounts receivable $2,186.32, food and beverage inventory $5,982, supplies $1,559.60, stationary kitchen equipment $21,797.40, hand equipment $1,714.20, dining room furniture and fixtures $14,453, and serving equipment and dishes $11,507. The liabilities were as follows: accounts payable $25,191.20, installment accounts payable $10,682, bank notes payable to First National Bank $30,100, sales tax payable $1,061.60, payroll tax payable $1,112, and taxes payable $243.80.

Break-Even Analysis

Break-even analysis is a mathematical method for finding the dollar amount needed for a food service operation to break even.

Break-even analysis calculates the level of economic activity where the operation neither makes a profit nor incurs a loss. It is based on a certain amount that must be achieved through total sales before a profit can be realized and below which a loss is incurred. This method is beneficial to the food service operator for planning profits. Planning profits is extremely important to any business operation when financial planning decisions must be made. In the food service industry, where bankruptcy may occur, the break-even figure could be a key to survival.

Every business has peaks and valleys. These terms relate to the amount of sales for a business. The peaks represent the great business days when there is an abundance of sales. The valleys are the bad days when hardly anyone comes into the business and the owner loses money. Each food service operator must know how to determine the amount of sales dollars that equal the operating expenses. This is referred to as the **break-even point.**

The food service operator must know how to calculate and understand the meaning of the break-even point. Simply put, the **break-even point** occurs when sales volume covers all of the costs related to doing business. The operator should know the amount of sales that has to be generated in order to pay all of the bills. Once that point has been reached, the additional sales will create a profit. Another term for the break-even point is "cracking the nut."

In order to calculate the break-even point and understand the concept of break-even analysis, the food service operator must know and understand the meaning of some specific terms that are used in this mathematical process.

Mathematical problems are expressed by formulas. If the formula is followed, a solution can be found. It is important to be able to identify, understand, and be familiar with each part of the break-even formula.

Sales revenue is the money received from the sale of all products, food, beverages, and so forth. It represents all of the money received over a certain period of time through sales.

Variable cost is the changeable cost or expenses that will increase or decrease with the level of sales volume. The greater the number of people served and meals produced, the greater the variable cost. Variable cost may be divided into two categories: cost of goods sold and serving expenses.

Cost of goods sold is the amount it costs the operator to provide food, beverages, and so forth, to serve customers. It is the operator's cost of goods to be sold.

Serving expenses are additional expenses incurred as a result of serving customers. These include:

- Laundry—tablecloths, napkins, kitchen towels, uniforms
- Paper supplies—guest checks, report forms, register tapes
- Payroll—labor cost
- Tableware replacement—glassware, china, silverware

Gross profit is the sales revenue minus variable costs. This is the total value before deducting fixed cost.

Fixed cost is the expenses that remain constant regardless of the level of sales volume. They may be divided into two categories: occupational expenses and primary expenses.

Occupational expenses, also called the cost of ownership, are those that continue whether or not the restaurant is operating. They include such expenses as property tax, insurance, interest on the mortgage, and depreciation of equipment, furniture, and building. There may be others, depending on the local situation.

Primary expenses are those that result from being open for business. These expenses are constant, whether serving a few customers or many. They include such expenses as utilities, basic staff (preparation, service, etc.), telephone service, repairs and maintenance, licenses, and exterminating costs.

The authors will explain this concept by using the following example. This example, although not logical, will help to illustrate the concept of the break-even point.

Janet Downs has developed a great-tasting vegetable onion burger. Janet is a sharp businesswoman and has figured out that each burger that she serves will cost her $0.75 to produce. This price takes into account all the ingredients needed to make one 6-ounce burger. The price also includes the cost of the roll, salt and pepper, condiments, a napkin, and a paper plate on which to serve the burger. Janet has been offered a location to sell her burgers that will cost her $250 a week in rent. This cost of rent includes all refrigeration and cooking equipment, as well as the energy needed to produce the product. This rent will be her only other expense, in addition to the cost to produce the burger. Before Janet decides to open up her business, she has to determine how many vegetable onion burgers she must sell each week to "crack the nut," or reach the break-even point. Since Janet will do all the work herself, she will have no labor cost and will get paid only when she makes a profit.

Before this problem can be solved, the following terms must be defined and explained. In the food service profession, the vegetable onion burger is referred to as **cost of goods sold.** This is the amount of money it costs the operator to provide food, beverages, condiments, and so forth to customers.

Janet has also included in her price for the vegetable onion burger the serving expenses of the napkin and paper plate. **Serving expenses** are the costs incurred as a result of serving customers. Other examples of serving expenses are replacement costs for china, laundry, paper supplies, and payroll or labor costs.

Because Janet may sell 1 burger or 100 burgers a day, the cost of goods sold for the onion vegetable burgers will increase or decrease depending on the number of burgers she makes. The amount of burgers sold will also reflect the cost of the serving expenses. Adding together the **cost of goods sold** and the **serving expenses** results in the **variable cost.**

$$\text{Variable cost} = \text{Cost of goods sold} + \text{Serving expenses}$$

As stated previously, Janet has calculated her variable cost (of one burger and serving expenses) to be $0.75. Obviously, the amount of burgers made will cause her costs to vary; if she has to make more burgers, her variable cost will increase, and if she has a bad business day, her variable costs will decrease. If she must make 100 burgers, her cost will be $75.00 (0.75 × 100). If she makes only 25 burgers, the cost will be $18.75 (0.75 × 25).

Janet has determined that she wants to have a 25 percent food cost. As you have learned previously, to obtain a 25 percent food cost, you must multiply the variable cost by four. Thus, she multiplies the variable cost of $0.75 by four. This results in a menu price of $3.00 for each burger.

She now wants to determine how many burgers she must sell each week to reach her break-even point. But before she can make this calculation, she must determine exactly how much of the $3.00 (the menu price) that she receives in payment for her vegetable onion burger she will actually keep. This is calculated by subtracting the **variable cost** from her **menu price**, resulting in her **total variable profit.**

$$\text{Menu price} - \text{Variable cost} = \text{Total variable profit}$$

$$\$3.00 - \$0.75 = \$2.25$$

Her variable cost is $0.75 cents, and her menu price for one burger is $3.00. She receives a total variable profit of $2.25 for each burger sold.

The rent charged to Janet is called **fixed cost.** This is the expense that remains constant, regardless of the amount of burgers that are sold. Janet has to pay $250 in rent each week whether she sells 1, 25, or 100 burgers. Janet can now determine how many burgers she needs to sell each week to "crack the nut" by using the following formula:

$$\text{Break-even point} = \text{Fixed cost} \div (\text{total variable profit})$$

$$\text{Break-even point} = \$250 \div 2.25$$

$$\text{Break-even point} = 111.111 \text{ burgers}$$

Using this formula, Janet's fixed costs are $250 a week. Her total variable profit is $2.25 for each burger sold.

Because it is unrealistic to expect someone to buy 0.111 of a burger, Janet has to round up to reach her break-even point. She has to sell 112 vegetable onion burgers a week to break even.

To verify this formula, multiply 112 by $3.00, which results in total sales or income of $336. Because each burger costs Janet $0.75, multiply the cost (0.75) by the amount of burgers sold (112). Janet's variable cost to make the burgers is

(112 × 0.75) $84. The fixed rent of $250 is added to the $84, which equals $334. Once Janet sells 112 burgers, she will have covered all her costs and reached the break-even point. There is an additional $2.00 leftover because Janet had to sell an additional burger; she could not have sold 0.111 of a burger.

Contribution Rate and Contribution Rate Percentage

The previous example of Janet's burger business illustrated how to determine the break-even point for a business that sells only one item, has no employees, and has only one fixed cost. All food service operations are more complicated than the previous example. Most of them don't have the time to break down each item, as was done in the first example. Instead, they use a method called the contribution rate and contribution rate percentage to determine the break-even point. The authors will continue illustrating the break-even point by using Janet's business. This next section will illustrate how the monthly break-even point is determined using the contribution rate.

The **contribution rate** is the amount of money that is left after the variable costs are subtracted from the sales.

$$\text{Contribution rate} = \text{Sales} - \text{Variable costs}$$

The **contribution rate percentage** is calculated by dividing the contribution rate by the sales.

$$\text{Contribution rate} = \frac{\text{Contribution rate}}{\text{Sales}}$$

Janet's business is doing well. She has added more items onto the menu, increased her sales, and, as a result, increased her staff to meet the demand of the business. Her landlord has kept her rent at $250 a week, or $1,000 a month, but she now has to pay $2,000 in additional fixed costs. At the end of the month, Janet's profit and loss statement has been condensed into a document that will allow her to figure out her break-even point using the contribution rate percentage. She has determined which of her expenses are variable costs and which are fixed costs. Her April condensed profit and loss statement is shown in Figure 15–4.

Figure 15–4
Janet's Famous Vegetable Onion Burgers.
© Cengage Learning 2012

Janet's Famous Vegetable Onion Burgers
Condensed Profit and Loss Statement for the Month of April

Categories	Amount of Money	Percentage
Sales	$25,000	100%
− Variable Costs	$10,000	40%
Contribution rate	$15,000	60%
− Fixed Costs	$3,000	
Profit before taxes	$12,000	

Janet may now determine how many sales must be generated each month to reach her break-even point by using the contribution rate percentage. The formula to determine her break-even point is to take her fixed costs and divide them by her contribution rate percentage.

$$\text{Break-even point} = \frac{\text{Fixed costs}}{\text{Contribution rate percentage}}$$

Using all the information from Janet's condensed profit and loss statement, the authors will illustrate how Janet determines her break-even point in sales.

Step 1:   Determine the amount of the contribution rate.

Contribution rate = Sales − Variable costs

	Sales	**$25,000**
Minus	**Variable Costs**	**$10,000**
Equals	**Contribution Rate**	**$15,000**

The contribution rate is $15,000.

Step 2:   Determine the contribution rate percentage.

$$\text{Contribution rate percentage} = \frac{\text{Contribution rate}}{\text{Sales}}$$

	Contribution Rate	**15,000**
Divided by	**Sales**	**$25,000**
Equals	**Contribution Rate %**	**0.6, or 60%**

The contribution rate percentage is 60 percent.

Step 3:   Determine Janet's Famous Vegetable Onion Burgers break-even point.

$$\text{Break-even point} = \frac{\text{Fixed costs}}{\text{Contribution rate percentage}}$$

	Fixed Costs	**$3,000**
Divided by	**Contribution Rate %**	**60%**
Equals	**Break-Even Point**	**$5,000**

Janet's Famous Vegetable Onion Burgers has to generate $5,000 a month in sales to break even.

Janet, being the sharp businesswoman that she is, keeps meticulous records. She knows that the check average (how much a guest spends at each transaction) is $5.25. She would now like to determine how many guests she needs to purchase food and beverages each day to "crack the nut." Janet is open for 20 days each month. Her first step is to divide the break-even sales amount of $5,000 by the check average of $5.25. This equals 952.38095 transactions a month that must occur. Janet then takes her 20 days and divides that into the 953 (she rounds up from 952.38095) transactions, and determines that she must have 47.65 customers a day to break even. Janet has used mathematics for the food service industry to determine her break-even point and analyze her business. Janet determines that this is a great business and starts looking for new sites to expand her famous Vegetable Onion Burger Empire!

To Insure Perfect Solutions

When a profit occurs, the accounting profession writes the number in black ink . . . thus, the business is "in the black." If a loss occurs, the number is written in red ink . . . Thus, the business is "in the red." With computer-generated profit and loss statements, when a loss occurs, the dollar amount is written inside parentheses.

Practice Problems 15–7   Contribution Rate and Contribution Rate Percentage

For each problem, determine the contribution rate, contribution rate percentage, and break-even point. Identify whether the business made or lost money. If the business lost money, what possible steps could be taken to put the business "in the black"?

Round off all answers in this manner: If the answer is 0.29748, go to the fifth number to the right of the decimal and use that number to round off to the fourth number to the right of the decimal. Now the answer is 0.2975. Next, convert 0.2975 to a percentage. Therefore, the final answer would be 29.75 percent.

44. The Blue Bird Cafeteria did $80,000 in sales. Its variable cost was 40 percent of the total sales, and the fixed costs were $24,000. _____

45. The Castle Restaurant did $120,000 in sales. Its variable cost was 36 percent of the total sales, and the fixed costs were $32,000. _____

46. The Blue Angel Restaurant did $32,000 in sales. Its variable cost was 40 percent of the total sales, and the fixed costs were $24,000. _____

47. The Red Gate Cafeteria did $96,000 in sales. Its variable cost was 43 percent of the total sales, and the fixed costs were $63,600. _____

48. The Old Mill Restaurant did $72,500 in sales. Its variable cost was 44 percent of the total sales, and the fixed costs were $28,112. _____

Budgeting

Budgeting is a plan for adjusting **expenditures (amount of money that is spent)** to probable income for a calendar or fiscal year. It is a plan that works equally well for individuals, small businesses, and large corporations, for maintaining a fairly equal balance between income and expenses. Businesses use the budget not only to gauge expenses and income for the year, but also to keep all departments within the company on the proper financial track. Some companies even require department heads to submit a written report showing why they have exceeded their budget. The budget is just a plan, and, like most plans, if followed, good results often happen. If one goes astray, problems will probably develop.

In a budget, the areas listed under the two major components, **income** and **expenditures** will vary, depending on the size of the overall operation. Generally included under income are the total of register receipts and income from sales that would not pass through the register, such as payment for a catered affair. These figures can be obtained from income records of the previous year.

Expenditures might include:

- labor cost
- total supplies (food, paper goods, cleaning supplies, etc.)
- telephone service
- new equipment
- service calls on equipment
- worker's compensation
- utilities (gas and electric)
- printing service for menus
- fringe benefits (dental plan, hospitalization, etc.)

Many of the estimated figures required for these items can again be obtained from the records of the previous year. If, after checking the figures from the previous year, you are aware of or believe that an increase or decrease of funds will be required for the coming year, then adjustments are in order. Remember that the purpose of a budget is to give a general idea of what will happen. The budget is very seldom exact.

Using hypothetical figures, let us set up a budget as if it were a pie. The whole pie would be the food service operation's total income for a year. Two examples will be given.

Example 1: A food service budget (break-even budget) is shown in Figure 15–5. The yearly income from register and supplemental sales is $300,000. The total dollar amounts budgeted for each item are listed.

Food and Supplies (30%)	= $90,000
Labor (25%)	= $75,000
Worker's Compensation (3%)	= $ 9,000
Fringe Benefits (8%)	= $24,000
Utilities (9%)	= $27,000
Printing Service (5%)	= $15,000
New Equipment (10%)	= $30,000
Equipment Service (6%)	= $18,000
Telephone (4%)	= $12,000

Figure 15–5
Sample food service budget, example 1.
© Cengage Learning 2012

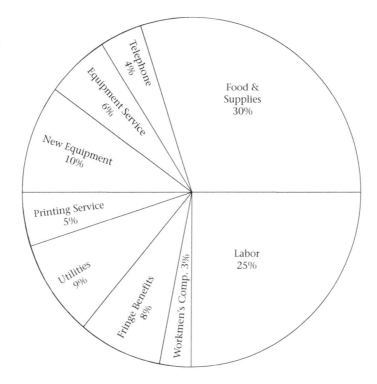

When taking a percent of a whole number, in this case $300,000, we must multiply. For example:

$$
\begin{array}{ll}
\$\ 300{,}000 & \text{Yearly income} \\
\underline{\times\ 0.30} & \text{Food \& supplies} \\
\$\ \ \ 90{,}000 & \text{Amount budgeted for food \& supplies} \\[6pt]
\$\ 300{,}000 & \text{Yearly income} \\
\underline{\times\ .25} & \text{Labor} \\
1{,}500{,}000 & \\
\underline{600{,}000} & \\
\$\ \ \ 75{,}000 & \text{Amount budgeted for labor}
\end{array}
$$

The other amounts shown in the budget are found by the same procedure.

Example 2: Another sample food service budget (break-even budget) is shown in Figure 15–6. The yearly income from register and supplemental sales is $300,000. The percentage of the total income that was budgeted for each item is listed. The sum of the completed percentages should equal 100 percent.

Food and Supplies ($75,000)	= 25%
Labor ($69,000)	= 23%
Worker's Compensation ($24,000)	= 8%
Fringe Benefits ($27,000)	= 9%
Utilities ($33,000)	= 11%
Printing Service ($9,000)	= 3%
New Equipment ($45,000)	= 15%
Equipment Service ($12,000)	= 4%
Telephone ($6,000)	= 2%

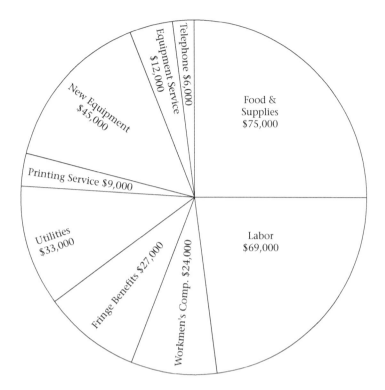

Figure 15–6
Sample food service budget, example 2.
© Cengage Learning 2012

To find what percent one number is of another number, divide the number that represents the part by the number that represents the whole. For example:

$$
\begin{array}{r}
0.25 \;=\; 25\% \\
\text{Represents the whole } \$300{,}000 \overline{\smash{\big)}\$75{,}000.00} \qquad \text{Food and supplies} \\
\underline{60{,}000.00} \qquad \text{represent the part} \\
15{,}000.00 \\
\underline{15{,}000.00}
\end{array}
$$

Thus, 25 percent is the percentage of the $300,000 yearly income set aside for the cost of food and supplies. The other percentages shown in the budget are found by the same procedure.

Budgeting is also an important step in the proper management of personal affairs. The family income certainly should be budgeted so that money will be on hand when the bills are due. The family budget may be set up on a monthly or yearly basis, with a percentage of income or a dollar amount set aside for each important family expense.

Example: For a monthly income of $2,000, the budget might be as follows:

Item	Percent	Dollar Amount
Food	25%	$ 500
Clothing	15%	$ 300
Mortgage Payment	35%	$ 700
Recreation	9%	$ 180
Benevolences	5%	$ 100
Savings	11%	$ 220
	100%	$ 2,000

Practice Problems 15–8 Budgeting

E. For a food service budget, the yearly income from register and supplemental sales is $550,000. Find the dollar amount that was budgeted for each item listed. Round answers to the hundredths place.

49. Food and Supplies   26% $_____

50. Labor   24% $_____

51. Worker's Compensation   4% $_____

52. Fringe Benefits   8% $_____

53. Utilities   11% $_____

54. Printing Service   2% $_____

55. New Equipment   10% $_____

56. Equipment Service   5% $_____

57. Telephone   3% $_____

58. Profit   7% $_____

F. For a food service budget, the yearly income from register and supplemental sales is $725,000. Find the percentage of total income that was budgeted for each item listed. If necessary, round your answers to the hundredths place.

59. Food and Supplies $188,500   _____%

60. Labor $166,750   _____%

61. Worker's Compensation $ 21,750   _____%

62. Fringe Benefits $ 65,250   _____%

63. Utilities $ 72,500   _____%

64. Printing Service $ 29,000   _____%

65. New Equipment $ 79,750   _____%

66. Equipment Service $ 43,500   _____%

67. Telephone $ 14,500   _____%

68. Profit $ 43,500   _____%

G. The Piazza family has a monthly income of $2,400. What percentage of the monthly income was budgeted for each item? Prove that your percentages are correct by adding the results. The sum should be 100 percent. If necessary, round your answers to the hundredths place.

Their monthly budget is as follows:

69. Food $ 600.00   _____ %

70. Clothing $ 432.00   _____ %

71. Charities $ 144.00   _____ %

72. Savings $ 192.00   _____ %

73. Mortgage Payment $ 648.00   _____ %

74. Recreation $ 216.00   _____ %

75. Utilities $ 168.00   _____ %

H. The Fahy family has a yearly income of $28,975. Find the dollar amount that was budgeted for each item listed. Round your answers to the hundredths place. The sum of the completed budget should equal their yearly income of $28,975. Their budget for the year is as follows:

76. Food   23% $_____

77. Mortgage Payment   27% $_____

78. Utilities   8% $_____

79. Clothing   13% $_____

80. Recreation   7% $_____

81. Family Welfare   6% $_____

82. Benevolences   3% $_____

83. Savings   9% $_____

84. Other Items   4% $_____

I. The Curran family has a monthly income of $2,260. What percentage of the monthly income was budgeted for each item? Prove that your percentages are correct by adding the results. The sum should be 100 percent. If necessary, round your answers to the hundredths place.

Their monthly budget is as follows:

85. Rent $ 565.00   _____ %

86. Food $ 519.80   _____ %

87. Clothing $ 429.40   _____ %

88. Utilities $ 180.80   _____ %

89. Entertainment $ 248.60   _____ %

90. Insurance $ 67.80   _____ %

91. Doctors' Fees $ 90.40   _____ %

92. Savings $ 158.20   _____ %

References

Case Western Reserve University Weatherhead School of Management. (2001). *The break-even calculator*. Retrieved November 2, 2005, from Case Western Reserve University Web site at http://connection.cwru.edu/mbac424/breakeven/breakeven.html.

Miller, J. E., Hayes, D. K., & Dopson, L. R. (2002). *Food and beverage cost control* (2nd ed.). New York: John Wiley & Sons, Inc.

Appendix A

Formulas

addition—Addend plus (+) addend = Sum.

amount of commission—Amount of sales times (×) percent of commission.

assets—Liabilities plus (+) proprietorship.

baker's percentage—Weight of individual ingredient divided by (÷) total weight of the flour times (×) 100%.

beverage cost—Sales (or menu) price times (×) beverage cost percentage.

beverage cost percentage—Beverage cost divided by (÷) sales or menu price.

break-even analysis—Sales revenue minus (−) variable costs = Gross profit; gross profit minus (−) fixed costs = Break-even point.

butcher's yield percentage—Edible Portion (E.P.) divided by (÷) As Purchased (A.P.).

check amount based on tip—Money amount of tip divided by (÷) percent of tip.

containers needed—Ounces needed divided by (÷) ounces in one container.

contribution rate—Sales minus (−) variable cost.

contribution rate percentage—Contribution rate divided by (÷) sales.

converting Celsius temperature to degrees Fahrenheit—Multiply (×) the Celsius temperature by $\frac{9}{5}$ and add (+) 32 to the result.

converting Fahrenheit temperature to degrees Celsius—Subtract (−) 32 from the given Fahrenheit temperature and multiply (×) the result by $\frac{5}{9}$.

converting standard recipes—Multiply (×) each ingredient in the original recipe by the working factor to find the new desired quantity.

cost of food sold—Beginning inventory plus (+) purchases minus (−) final inventory.

cost, ounce—Total cost divided by (÷) total ounces.

cost per serving—Cost of 1 ounce times (×) number of ounces served.

cost, total (per pound)—Number of pounds times (×) cost per pound.

division—Dividend divided by (÷) divisor = Quotient.

drained weight—Weight of original can minus (−) weight of liquid in the can.

edible portion (E.P.)—Weight of product after trimming or processing.

edible portion price per pound—A.P. price per pound divided by (÷) product yield percentage.

food cost—Sales (or menu) price times (×) food cost percentage.

food cost percentage—Food cost divided by (÷) sales or menu price.

gross margin—Sales minus (−) cost of food sold.

gross pay—Hourly rate times (×) hours worked.

gross profit percent—Sales minus (−) variable cost.

gross wages—Amount of commission plus (+) salary.

interest—Principal times (×) rate times (×) time.

interest paid—Interest per day times (×) number of days of loan.

interest per day—Amount of interest for one year divided by (÷) ordinary or exact days per year.

liquor cost—Sales (or menu) price times (×) liquor cost percentage.

liquor cost percentage—Liquor cost divided by (÷) sales or menu price.

menu pricing using the food cost percent method—Raw food cost divided by (÷) food cost percentage.

menu pricing using the markup amount method—Raw food cost times (×) markup rate. To obtain menu price, add (+) the markup amount to the raw food cost.

Multiplication—Multiplier times (×) multiplicand = Product.

net pay—Gross pay or wages minus (−) deductions.

net profit or loss—Gross margin minus (−) total operating expenses.

net worth or proprietorship—Assets minus (−) liabilities.

number of ounces required—Amount of portion times (×) number of people served.

number of servings—Total weight of all ingredients used divided by (÷) serving portion size.

number to order—Number of ounces required divided by (÷) ounces in container.

ounces in one container—Pounds in container times (×) 16.

ounces needed—Number of people to be served times (×) portion size.

ounces, total—Total weight times (×) 16.

percent of ingredient—Weight of ingredient divided by (÷) weight of flour.

pounds needed—Number of ounces needed divided by (÷) 16.

price, extension—Quantity of items times (×) the unit price.

recipe yield—Total weight of preparation divided by (÷) weight of portion.

salary plus commission—Amount of sales times (×) percent of commission = Amount of commission. Salary plus (+) amount of commission = Gross wages.

sales, average—Total sales divided by (÷) customer count.

sales price or menu price—Food cost divided by (÷) food cost percentage.

sales, total—Average sales times (×) customer count.

subtraction—Minuend minus (−) subtrahend = Difference.

total variable profit—Menu price minus (−) variable cost.

unit cost—Total cost divided by (÷) yield.

working factor—New yield divided by (÷) old yield.

yield percentage—Edible Portion (E.P.) divided by (÷) As Purchased (A.P.).

Glossary

A

abbreviation The shortened form of a word or phrase.

AC If it is included on the keyboard, this key clears the calculator of all functions, including the memory function.

account, checking or savings A record in which an individual's or a business's money is deposited or withdrawn, usually in a financial institution.

accountant A person skilled in keeping, examining, and adjusting financial records.

accounts payable Money owed by the business operator for purchases made.

accounts receivable Money owed to the business operator by customers.

addition The act of putting things together, or combining things or units that are alike, to obtain a total quantity.

addressing In data communication, the process of selecting another computer to send data via modem.

adhere To stick fast; to become attached or cling to.

à la carte Foods ordered and paid for separately; usually prepared to order.

all-inclusive A pricing system where all charges (cost of food, beverages, tax, gratuity, etc.) are stated as one price, usually on a per-person basis.

amount of average sale A business calculation found by dividing the customer count into the total sales.

analysis The division or separation of a thing into the parts that compose it.

annual Pertaining to a year; happening once in twelve months.

A.P. weight As Purchased weight; the weight of an item before processing.

approximate To come near to; nearly correct.

aspic A clear meat, fish, or poultry jelly.

assess To fix or determine the amount of a tax, fine, or damage; to rate or set a certain charge upon, as for taxation.

assessor A person appointed to estimate the value of property for the purpose of taxation.

assets Things of value; all the property of a person, company, or estate that may be used to pay debts.

automation The automatic control of production processes by electronic apparatus.

avoirdupois ounces A unit of measurement used to measure the weight of cooking ingredients.

B

backup A spare copy of data or a program.

baker's balance scale An instrument to weigh ingredients used in baking.

baker's percentage The weight of individual ingredients divided by the total weight of the flour times 100 percent.

baker's production report A report that assists the chef or pastry chef to establish amounts of baked goods to prepare or order and to determine how much baked goods were used or when all of the baked goods were sold.

balance Difference between the debit and credit sides of an account; an amount left over.

balance sheet A written statement made to show the true financial condition for a person or business by exhibiting assets, liabilities or debts, profit and loss, and net worth.

bank In a business, an amount of money that is placed into the POS register before any sales are made, so that a cashier can make change.

bank note A note issued by a bank that must be paid to the bearer upon demand. Bank notes are used as money.

beginning inventory The items that a business has in stock at the start of a month.

breading A process of passing an item through flour, egg wash (egg and milk), and bread crumbs before it is fried or otherwise cooked.

bottle (750-ml bottle of alcoholic beverages) A container that holds 25.4 U.S. fluid ounces.

break-even analysis A mathematical method used to find the dollar amount needed for a food service operation to break even.

break-even point The point at which the amount of sales dollars equals operating expenses.

budget A plan of systematic spending; to plan one's expenditures of money, time, and so forth.

C

C On a calculator, the key that, when pressed, clears the calculator of all functions except the memory function.

calculate To reach a conclusion or answer by a reasoning process.

calculator One who computes; a machine that does automatic computations.

calendar year A period that begins on January 1 and ends on December 31; consists of 365 days—366 days if it's a leap year.

capacity Power of holding or grasping; room; volume; power of mind; character; ability to hold cubic content.

capital Amount of money or property that a person or company uses in carrying on a business.

captain A service individual in charge of a station or stations.

carryover Products left over to be used at a later date.

cashbook A book containing records of all income and expenses of a business operation.

cashier's daily report A tool used by management to keep track of cash and charge sales.

cash in drawer In a business, the amount of cash (minus paid outs) that should be in the register at the end of the day or whenever the totals are taken.

cash paid outs In a business, the amounts of money paid out of the register during the day.

CE On a calculator, the key that clears an incorrect keyboard entry that has not been entered into the function, without clearing the memory function.

Celsius A term used to measure temperature in the metric system of measuring; graduated or divided into 100 equal parts called degrees; previously called centigrade.

cent A term used to represent the value of one-hundredth part of a dollar.

centigrade A term used to measure temperature in the metric system of measuring; graduated or divided into 100 equal parts called degrees. The term now used is *Celsius*.

centimeter The one-hundredth part of a meter.

certificate of deposit A document issued by a bank to a depositor indicating that a specific amount of money is set aside and not subject to withdrawal except on surrender of the certificate, usually with an interest penalty.

chain calculations Computations done in sequence, involving a series of numbers and a variety of math operations.

charge accounts Statements of money owed.

check A written order directing a financial institution to make a payment for the depositor.

check register A form given to the depositor by the financial institution so that the depositor can record deposits and check withdrawals and know the balance of money on hand.

cipher Zero.

CM or MC On a calculator, the Clear Memory or Memory Clear key, which displays memory figures and clears the memory.

commission Pay based on the amount of business done.

compensation Something given in return for a service or a value.

competency The state of being fit or capable.

complex Not simple; involved; intricate.

compound interest Money that is added to the principal (with interest then paid on a new principal).

compressed Made smaller by applying pressure.

computer Any of various mechanical, electrical, or electronic devices for computing; specifically one for solving complex, mathematical problems in a very short time.

computerized To use, perform, operate, etc., by means of a computer or computers.

concept A mental idea of a class of objects.

configuration A group or series of machines and programs that make up a complete data processing system.

constant function A calculator key used to multiply or divide repeatedly by the same number.

contribution rate The amount of money that is left over after the variable costs are subtracted from the sales.

contribution rate percentage The percentage that is obtained by dividing the contribution rate by the sales.

convenience foods Foods that are purchased ready-to-cook and for absolute portion control.

convenience products Food items that require little or no preparation.

convert Change; to turn the other way around.

cook's production report A report that assists the chef to establish amounts of food to prepare and to determine how much food was used or when all of the food was sold.

corporation A group of persons who obtain a charter giving them (as a group) certain legal rights and privileges distinct from those of the individual members of the group.

cost of food sold The monetary value of food on hand at beginning of the month, plus the purchases for the month, minus the monetary value of food in the final inventory.

cost of goods sold The amount it costs the operator to provide food, beverages, and so forth, to serve customers.

cost per serving The cost of a given number of avoirdupois or fluid ounces of a given item.

costed out The practice of calculating the cost of individual items sold.

counter production report A report that allows the food service manager to know the amount and value of items that were sold.

cover charge An admission fee charged in a nightclub or other establishment for entertainment.

cubic centimeter A measure of volume in the metric system with sides that are 1 centimeter long.

cubic meter A measure of volume in the metric system with sides that are 1 meter long.

currency Money in actual use in a country. In the United States, this term usually applies to paper money, although technically it means both coins and paper money.

cursor A short, blinking line on a computer screen that appears underneath the space where the next character is to be typed or deleted. The cursor indicates that the computer is ready for the input of the command.

customer count A calculation obtained by checking the POS or cash register sales, which records the total number of customers for the meal period.

D

daily food cost report A tool designed to show management the exact cost and amount of food used on any given day.

daily production report A report that helps a food service operator control aspects of the daily operation such as over- or underproduction, leftovers, purchasing, labor costs, waste, and theft.

data A collection of information, facts, statistics, or instructions arranged in definite terms, suitable for processing by manual or automatic means.

database management The sorting and categorizing of information or data.

debit The entry of an item in a business account showing something owed or due.

decimal A system of counting by tens and powers of 10. Each digit has a place value 10 times that of the next digit to the right.

decimal fractions Fractions that are expressed with denominators of 10 or powers of 10.

decimal point A point (.) used to indicate a decimal fraction.

decimeter A metric measure of length equal to one-tenth of a meter.

deduction The process of taking away; the amount of money subtracted.

default Failure to pay when due.

dekameter A metric measure of length equal to 10 meters.

denominator The bottom number of a fraction.

deposit To put in a place for safekeeping; money put in a bank is a deposit.

deposit slip A form that provides the depositor and the financial institution with a record of the transaction when money is deposited in a checking account.

depreciation A lessening or reduction in value.

designate Point out; indicate definitely.

diameter The length of a straight line through the center of a circle.

difference The answer in a subtraction problem.

digit Any one of the numerals 0 through 9.

direct purchases Those foods that are usually purchased each day or every other day.

disk A flat, circular plate used in computers for the purpose of magnetically recording information on one or both sides.

diskette A thin, flexible magnetic disk, sometimes called a floppy disk. Information can be recorded onto and played back from a diskette.

dividend (1) Money to be shared by those to whom it belongs. If a company shows a profit at the end of a certain period, it declares a dividend to the owners of the company. (2) The number that is to be divided by the divisor.

division Act of giving some to each. The process of dividing one number by another.

divisor A number by which another (the dividend) is divided.

drained weight (test) The amount of food product minus the weight of the drained liquid.

E

economic Pertaining to the earning, distributing, and using of wealth and income, public or private.

entree The main dish of a meal.

E.P. weight Edible Portion weight; the usable portion after processing.

equation A statement that two mathematical expressions are equal.

equivalent Equal in value or power.

estimate A judgment or opinion in determining the size, value, and other characteristics of an item.

evaluate Find the value or amount of; fix the value.

expenditure Amount of money that is spent.

extension To stretch out, lengthen, or widen.

F

fabricated Made up; in food service, creating a standardized portion.

facsimile To make an exact copy of. A rapid way of communicating, allowing one to send and receive any type of text or graphic information over telephone lines.

factor One of the two or more quantities which, when multiplied together, yield a given product. Example: 2 and 4 are factors of 8.

Fahrenheit A term used to measure temperature in the standard system of measuring; graduated or divided into 212 equal parts called degrees.

federal taxes Taxes collected by the federal government.

FICA The acronym referring to the Federal Insurance Contributions Act, which set up the Social Security system.

file To put away and keep in any easy-to-find order.

final inventory The total value of all goods on hand (e.g., in the storeroom). It is the food that has not been sold during the inventory period.

finances Money; funds; revenues; financial conditions.

financial Having to do with money matters.

financial statements Instruments used in a business operation to let management know its exact financial position.

fiscal year The time between one yearly settlement of financial accounts and another. In the United States, a fiscal year usually starts July 1 and ends June 30 of the following calendar year.

fixed assets Those assets (things of value) that stay stable and will not change.

fixed costs Those costs (moneys paid) that stay stable and will not change.

fluctuate Change continually.

fluid ounce A unit of measurement that measures the volume of a liquid.

food cost The money spent to prepare any and all products used in an individual recipe or entire meal.

food cost percentage The cost of food as it relates to the amount of dollars received in sales.

food in production The amount of food that has been prepared but not served.

food production report A form used to find how much product is made and sold.

forecast A prophecy or prediction.

format Size, shape, and general arrangement of a book, magazine, or other printed materials.

formula A rule for doing something; a recipe or prescription.

fraction One or more of the equal parts of a whole; a small part or amount.

function A quantity, the value of which varies with that of another quantity.

G

garnish To decorate, such as food.

gelatin An odorless, tasteless substance obtained by boiling animal tissues. It dissolves easily in hot water and is used in making jellied desserts and salads.

gourmet A lover of fine foods.

graduated Arranged in regular steps, stages, or degrees.

gram Metric system unit of weight (mass); 28 grams equal 1 ounce.

gratuity A present or money given in return for a service; also called a *tip*.

gross A term meaning that nothing has been removed or taken out. Gross receipts are all the money taken in before costs are deducted.

gross margin Sales minus the cost of food gives the gross margin. It is the margin before other deductions are taken.

gross pay Money earned before any deductions are removed or subtracted.

gross profit Sales revenue minus variable costs.

gross receipts The total of the amounts collected for food, beverages, gift certificates, sales taxes, and other transactions in a business.

gross wages Money paid to an employee for services before deductions.

guest check The bill or bill of sale used in a restaurant.

H

hectometer A measure of length in the metric system equal to 100 meters.

horizontally Parallel to the horizon; at right angles to a vertical line.

host/hostess An individual who receives guests at a private or public function.

hourly rate The amount of money paid to an individual employee per hour.

hypothetical Assumed or supposed.

I

improper fraction A fraction whose numerator is larger than its denominator and whose value is greater than a whole unit.

income All payments received for services provided.

income tax A tax paid to government by individuals who earn over a specified amount of income.

indicator Something or someone that points out something else.

ingredient One part of a mixture.

installment Part of a sum of money or debt to be paid at certain regular times.

interest Money that is paid for the use of borrowed money.

inventory A detailed list of items with their values.

inventory, beginning A detailed list of items with their values, which was the previous month's final inventory.

inventory, final A detailed list of items with their values at the end of a reporting period, such as a month or a year.

invert To turn upside down.

invoice A list of goods sent to a purchaser showing prices and amounts.

itemize To state by items, as to itemize a bill.

K

keyboard A bank of numeric, alphabetic, and function keys of a typewriter or computer. On the computer, the keyboard is used to enter information into the computer terminal.

kilogram A metric measure of weight equal to 1,000 grams.

kilometer A measure of length in the metric system equal to 1,000 meters.

L

labor cost percentage The cost of labor as it relates to the amount of dollars received in sales.

labor costs The total amount of money needed to pay all the employees required to create, make, and serve food to the guests.

ladles Utensils of various sizes used to pour liquids and control portions. A ladle is a cuplike bowl with a long handle.

lease A written contract whereby one party grants to another party the use of land, buildings, or personal property, for a definite consideration known as *rent*, for a specified term.

least common denominator The smallest number that is a multiple of the denominators of two or more fractions.

legumes Vegetables; also refers to dried vegetables such as beans, lentils, and split peas.

liability A state of being under obligation; responsible for a loss, debt, penalty, or the like.

licenses A form of taxation that individuals or businesses are required to obtain in order to conduct business.

like fractions Fractions that have the same denominator.

liter A measure of volume in the metric system. One liter equals 33.8 U.S. fluid ounces in customary liquid measure, or 0.908 quarts in dry measure.

M

M+ On a calculator, the Memory plus key, which adds a display number to the memory.

MRC On a calculator, the Memory Recall and Clear key, which recalls the memory and also clears the memory.

maitre d' The person in charge of dining room service.

manual Pertaining to the hand, or performed by hand.

margin The difference between the cost and the selling price of an article; also known as a *profit margin*.

markup The money that is added to the raw food cost to obtain a menu or selling price.

Medicare A federal health insurance program for people 65 or older and certain disabled people.

memory function A calculator key used to retain figures.

menu A list of the various dishes served at a meal.

menu price The cost of various food items served at a meal.

meringue Egg whites and sugar beaten together to form a white, frothy mass; used to top pies and cakes.

meter A unit of length in the metric system equal to 39.37 inches.

metric system The system of measurements based on the meter.

mill The third place to the right of the decimal when dealing with monetary numbers. It represents the thousandth part of a dollar, or one-tenth of one cent.

milligram Pertaining to the metric system of measure. It is the thousandth part of a gram.

milliliter Pertaining to the metric system of measure. It is the thousandth part of a liter.

millimeter Pertaining to the metric system of measure. It is a lineal measure equal to the thousandth part of a meter.

minimum charge A fee charged to the guest who is required to spend a certain amount of money even if the total check amounts to less.

minuend The original number in a subtraction problem.

mixed decimal fraction A number that is made up of a whole number and a decimal fraction.

mixed number A whole number mixed with a fractional part.

modem An electronic device that makes possible the transmission of digitized data from one location to another over telephone lines.

monetary Pertaining to money or coinage.

monitor A computer output device. Various information is shown on the monitor.

monthly food cost percentage The cost of food for the month as it relates to the amount of dollars obtained from sales of food for the month.

mortgage A claim on property given to a person who has lent money in case the money is not repaid when due.

mouse A computer device that will fit in the palm of your hand. When rolled on a flat surface, it relays signals that move the cursor on the computer screen.

multiple A number that contains another number a certain amount of times, without a remainder; for example, 16 is a multiple of 4.

multiplicand In multiplication, the number or quantity to be multiplied by another number called the multiplier.

multiplication An operation in which a whole number is added to itself a specified number of times.

multiplier The number by which another number, the multiplicand, is to be multiplied.

multiplier effect A method used to obtain a menu price.

N

net The amount remaining after deducting all necessary expenses.

net pay Money paid to an employee for services after deductions.

net profit The figure that is found by subtracting the total operating expenses from the gross margin.

net worth Excess value of resources over liabilities; also called *net assets*.

numeral The symbol for a number.

numerator The top number of a fraction.

O

occupational expenses The fees that continue to have to be paid whether or not the restaurant is operating.

occupational tax A fee that must be paid in order to operate any business within a certain city.

operating system Directs the flow of information to and from various parts of a computer and is needed by the computer to run programs.

over or short A situation when the Total Cash and Charges line is not equal to the Gross Receipts line, either more (over) or less (short).

overdrawn To draw from a bank account an amount that is larger than one actually has.

overtime Time worked beyond the regular 40-hour workweek.

P

P & L sheet Another name for a profit and loss statement.

pasta A dried flour paste product, such as spaghetti, vermicelli, and lasagna.

payroll List of persons to be paid and the amounts that each one is to receive; also, the total amounts to be paid to them.

percent Rate or proportion of each hundred; part of each hundred.

period A group of three digits set off by commas in a large number.

periodical A magazine that is published regularly.

perpetual inventory A continuous or endless record to show the balance on hand for each storeroom item.

physical inventory A count taken of all stock on hand.

plus/minus key On a calculator, this key converts a positive number to a negative one, and vice versa.

point of sale (POS) computer A computer that is used by the employees of a food service operation to calculate the amount of guest checks, as well as other computerized accounting functions.

portion A part or share.

portion control A term used to ensure that a specific or designated amount of an item is served to a guest.

portion scale A tool used for measuring food servings.

portion size The amount or quantity of prepared food that are served to an individual guest.

prefix A letter, syllable, or group of syllables placed at the beginning of a word to modify or qualify its meaning; for example, *deci* in front of *meter* indicates one-tenth of a meter.

primal cut One of the primary divisions for cutting meat carcasses into smaller cuts.

primary First in time; first in order; first in importance.

primary expenses The fees that result from an establishment being open for business.

principal The sum of money on which interest is paid in a loan.

printer An output device for the computer that produces hard copy of required information.

procedure A way of proceeding; a method of doing a task.

product The result obtained by multiplying two or more numbers.

production formula A standardized formula used to prepare foods in quantity.

profile An outline or contour.

profit The gain earned from a business venture; what is left when the cost of goods and carrying on the business is subtracted from the amount of money taken in.

profit and loss statement A summary or report of the food service operation's profitability or loss over a given period of time.

program Pertaining to the computer, a plan of related instructions or statements that is brought together as a task.

proper fraction A fraction whose numerator is smaller than its denominator.

property tax An amount of money collected from individuals or businesses based on the present value of the property.

proportion The relation in size, number, amount, or degree of one thing compared to another.

proprietorship Ownership.

purchases The inventory in a food business that is bought during a month.

purchase order A written form that indicates to the vendor how many items are to be delivered to an establishment and lists the prices for each item.

purchase specifications A detailed description of requirements for items being purchased.

purveyor One who supplies provisions or food.

Q

quantity Amount; a statement of how much there is of something.

quotient The number obtained by dividing one number by another; the final answer of a division problem.

R

ratio Relative magnitude; the ratio between two quantities is the number of times that one contains the other.

raw food cost The moneys spent for any and all products used to prepare an individual recipe or entire meal.

real estate tax See *property tax*.

recapitulation Totaling up of all items; a term most often used in accounting.

receipt A written statement that money, a package, a letter, and other items have been received.

recipe A set of directions for preparing something to eat.

recipe file number The number placed on a recipe for easy access when it is filed.

reconstitute To rebuild the way it was originally, to put back into original form. For example, to reconstitute dried milk, the water is put back.

recourse A person or thing appealed to or turned to for help or protection.

reduce To make less in value, quantity, size, or the like.

remainder The number less than the divisor that remains after the division process is completed.

report An account officially expressed, generally in writing.

requisition A demand made, usually in written form, for something that is required.

revenue Money coming in; income.

RM or MR On a calculator, the Recall Memory or Memory Recall key, which displays content of the memory, but does not clear the memory.

rotating menu A list of food offerings that alternates by turn in a series. The series is usually set up on a yearly basis.

roux A thickening agent consisting of equal parts of flour and shortening.

royalty The share of the receipts or profits paid to an owner of a patent or copyright; payment for use of any of various rights.

S

salad production report A report that assists the chef to establish the amounts of salads to prepare and to determine how many salads were sold.

salary A regular, periodical payment for official or professional services rendered.

sales revenue Money coming in from the sale of certain items.

sales tax Money collected on purchases of goods from consumers or businesses by governments.

sauté To cook in shallow grease.

savings or checking account Types of bank accounts that allow the depositor to either save money or access money to pay their bills.

scaling The weighing of ingredients in the baking profession.

scoops or dippers Utensils of various sizes used to serve foods and control portions.

serving expenses Additional expenses incurred as a result of providing table service to guests, such as laundry and paper supplies.

shrinkage The weight of food product that is lost through cooking.

simple interest Money paid only on the principal of a loan.

simplification A method used to express a fraction in lower terms without changing the value of the fraction.

simplify To reduce from the complex to the simple; to make plainer to understand.

slippage The loss of alcoholic beverage revenue by waste or theft.

Social Security tax The tax that funds the Social Security system, which provides for the payment of retirement, survivor, disability, and medical insurance benefits.

software A general term for programs that direct a computer operation. A set of instructions given the computer to perform a given task.

solar Working by means of the sun's light or heat.

specification A detailed statement of particulars.

spreadsheet A printout similar to an accountant's ledger that contains rows and columns of important calculations and financial information.

standard recipe A recipe that will produce the same quality and quantity every time.

standardize To make the same size, shape, weight, quality, quantity, and so forth.

state taxes Taxes collected by the state government to fund state functions and agencies.

stations Serving sections in a restaurant.

status Condition, state, or position.

stockholder Owner of stocks or shares in a company.

storeroom requisition A list of food items issued from the storeroom upon the request of the production crew.

straight-line method The simplest method to use when figuring depreciation on an item, such as a piece of equipment.

subproduct *Sub* means "under," "below," or "before." *Product* is the result of multiplying. Subproducts occur whenever the multiplier consists of two or more digits (see example in Chapter 3).

subtraction An operation that tells the difference between two numbers.

subtrahend The number removed from the minuend in a subtraction problem.

sum The total of two or more numbers or things taken together; the whole amount.

summarize Express briefly; give only the main points.

symbol Something that stands for or represents something else.

symbols of operations Symbols of the four mathematical operations: addition, subtraction, multiplication, and division.

T

table d'hôte A meal of several courses at a set price.

taxes Money collected from individuals or businesses by governments to pay for public services.

technology The application of science and technical advances in industry, the arts, and so forth.

terminology The special words or terms used in a science, art, business, and so forth.

tipping The voluntary giving of an additional fee to a server for a service rendered.

total cost The entire cost involved in preparing a recipe.

total sales The amount of money that has been recorded as sales during a specified time period.

total variable profit An amount calculated by subtracting the variable cost from the menu price.

trading (borrowing) To make a group of 10 from one of the next highest place value, or one from 10 of the lowest place value in a mathematical problem.

transfer To move food or beverages and their costs from one department to another department.

triplicate To make threefold; three identical copies.

U

unit A standard quantity or amount.

unit cost The amount that one serving of a particular food costs to prepare.

unlike fractions Fractions that have different denominators.

utilities Companies that perform a public service, such as railroads, gas and electric companies, and telephone companies.

V

variable costs Costs that are changeable.

variation The extent to which a thing changes.

vendor One who sells a product.

verbally Stated or expressed in words.

versatile Turning easily from one action, style, or subject to another; able to do many tasks well.

vertical Straight up and down.

volume Space occupied.

voucher A written evidence of payment; receipt.

W

wages Money paid or received for services.

whole numbers Numbers such as 0, 1, 2, and so forth that are used to represent whole units rather than fractional units.

withholding tax A deduction from a person's paycheck for the purpose of paying yearly income taxes.

word processing The system of recording, storing, and retrieving typewritten information.

working factor The number that will be used to multiply the amount of the original ingredients in a recipe to either increase or decrease a recipe.

wraparounds The additional items served with a food product or menu item; for example, jelly served with toast, or potato chips with a sandwich.

Y

yield The amount produced.

yield percentage An amount calculated by Edible Portion (E.P.) divided by As Purchased (A.P.).

yield test The actual yield obtained from meat that is purchased. Also known as "butcher's yield."

Index

Note: Page numbers in italics refer to figures